LOVING, HATING AND SURVIVAL

It may be a kind of loving but often it has to look like a kind of hating, and the key word is not treatment or cure but rather it is survival. If you survive then the child has a chance to grow and become something like the person he or she would have been if the untoward environmental breakdown had not brought disaster.

Donald Winnicott *The David Wills Lecture in Deprivation and Delinquency*, 1970.

This book is dedicated to the memory of
Michael Jinks
and to the work of the Caldecott
Foundation

Caldecott

This book has been commissioned and sponsored by the Caldecott Foundation which was founded by Leila Rendel in 1911 as the Caldecott Community, a nursery school for the children of working mothers in St. Pancras. Since then it has grown and developed into one of the country's foremost residential centres providing 52 week education and care for children and young people aged between 5 and 18 years. When they leave Caldecott there is a specialist Throughcare Service to support them.

Training and development is provided at Caldecott College for field and residential social workers, teachers, and foster carers. The training programmes at the College are a blend of the academic and vocational – university validated courses to degree level are linked to the practical assessments of the NVQ system.

For more information about the work of the Foundation – the Community, the Throughcare Service and the College – the following routes are available:

Caldecott Community and Throughcare Service

Telephone 01233 503954
Fax   01233 502650

Caldecott College

Telephone 01303 814232
Fax   01303 814621

e-mail–*info@caldecottcollege.org*
web site–*www.caldecottcollege.org*

LOVING, HATING AND SURVIVAL

A Handbook for all who work with Troubled Children and Young People

Edited by
Andrew Hardwick
and
Judith Woodhead

Ashgate
ARENA

Aldershot • Brookfield USA • Singapore • Sydney

© Andrew Hardwick and Judith Woodhead 1999

Published by
Ashgate Publishing Limited
Gower House
Croft Road
Aldershot
Hants GU11 3HR
England

Ashgate Publishing Company
Old Post Road
Brookfield
Vermont 05036
USA

Ashgate website: http://www.ashgate.com

British Library Cataloguing in Publication Data
Loving, hating and survival : a handbook for all who work
   with troubled children and young people
   1. Social work with children – Great Britain 2. Social work
   with youth – Great Britain
   I. Hardwick, Andrew II. Woodhead, Judith
   362.7'0941

Library of Congress Cataloging-in-Publication Data
Loving, hating, and survival : a handbook for all who work with
   troubled children and young people / edited by Andrew Hardwick and
   Judith Woodhead.
      p.   cm.
   Includes bibliographical references and index.
   ISBN 1–85742–424–7
   1. Problem children—Counseling of—Handbooks, manuals, etc.
   2. Child psychotherapy—Handbooks, manuals, etc. 3. Therapeutics—
   Handbooks, manuals, etc. 4. Helping behavior—Handbooks, manuals,
   etc. I. Hardwick, Andrew, 1947–   . II. Woodhead, Judith, 1950–   .

RJ499.3.L68   1999
618.92'8914—dc21
                                                                    98–40536
                                                                        CIP

ISBN 1 85742 424 7   06 JAN 2000

Printed in Great Britain

Contents

Acknowledgements

The late Michael Jinks, former Director of the Caldecott Community, to whom this book is dedicated, when discussing theory would simply say: 'Ask yourself, does it help?' That is not a bad test for this book and its mix of theory and practice.

We are responding to a challenge. In 1990 when Michael Jinks and James King, the Directors of the Caldecott Community, and their Trustees invited the Dartington Social Research Unit to spend four years looking in detail at the Caldecott Community, they could not have imagined some of the outcomes from the research. One was the recommendation that Caldecott should set up a college for the dissemination of theory and practice in a form and language accessible to those who work with troubled children and young people, a vision articulated with clarity by Michael Jinks. This book is part of our response to that challenge.

The College, founded in 1993, delivers its training at venues throughout the United Kingdom. This book is its first textbook which we hope will also be a useful handbook for those who work with troubled children and young people. It is not a study of outcomes but an attempt to explain how we can achieve the best possible outcomes for both staff and young people. We have incorporated both research and clinical experience into the chapters and we are hoping that *Loving, Hating and Survival* will be read together with Michael Little's study of the Caldecott, *A Life Without Problems?* (Arena, 1994).

We owe a debt of gratitude to a number of people who have supported the idea of the book from its inception: first, to The Caldecott Foundation, chaired by Simon Rodway who initially chaired the College Management Committee; to the Committee of Caldecott College now chaired by Mary Moser; to James Gunning, then Treasurer; John Shipton, and Caldecott's

Director, Derek Marshall. In the early years Lucy Faithfull was a passionate advocate for the College and she is much missed.

The Gatsby Foundation provided pump-priming funds as did a number of trusts who were approached by the Caldecott's Hope Appeal Committee chaired by Sir Evelyn de Rothschild. To them we owe a special thank you.

At the College, our Registrar, Marilyn White and College Secretary, Claudia Tijou-Smith, moved mountains of typing, collating and correcting. Thanks go to Peter Roycroft, Gill Saxton, Noela Punnet, Angela Cane, Ray Lloyd and Lisa Smith.

Most of the chapters in the book have been 'road-tested' on our students and their frank feedback has been of enormous value. Spencer Millham who chairs the College's Academic Board has been an ardent, often challenging, supporter and we recognise here the inspiration of his former Dartington colleagues, Roger Bullock and Michael Little. We have been fortunate to have the advice and support of Graham Fisher and Francia Kinchington at the University of Greenwich and Bill Forsyth and Gordon Jack at the University of Exeter. Other academic assistance has been generously provided by Gillian Miles, Maggie Calder, Elspeth Earle, Jean Packman and Eric Broekart. The Kent Post Qualifying Consortium has provided advice and support from the outset.

A special word of thanks to the staff and managers of the Caldecott Community who have made a huge contribution to the development of the College and the genesis of this book. Jo Gooderham, Kate Trew and Ann Newell at Ashgate Publishing have been most patient supporters.

Mary Moser and Margaret Stirling generously read draft after draft without complaint and made many useful suggestions.

A personal note of thanks to our two families for their support and good-humoured tolerance: to Prue Hardwick and George, Clare, Ruth and Ralph; to Martin Woodhead and Luke, Miriam, Daniel and Joseph.

Preface

Working with troubled children is one of the most important, daunting and uplifting tasks that face staff in residential settings, whether those of health, education, social care or the penal system. The peculiar importance of working with young people stems simply from their being young: what we do with, for and to them today reverberates through the whole of the rest of their lives. It affects the lives of all the people they relate to, partner and parent. The work is daunting for staff (and even potentially damaging) as they experience in therapeutic work the impact that emotional harm has upon children and the different effects it produces as they move rapidly through the stages of childhood and adolescence. It is uplifting when the resilience and stamina of youth can be engaged to build on what the supporting individuals and agencies offer, and the prospect of satisfying adult lives is achieved.

Our present systems for helping troubled children contain a strong element of chance in distributing them between children's homes, residential schools, psychiatric units and young offender institutions. This random allocation places them in the hands of staff who at one extreme are skilled practitioners operating in a professional culture and, at the other, are poorly trained, inexperienced workers in patently non-therapeutic settings. A strategy is required which allocates young people more discriminatingly within, as well as between, each of these sectors. Children with manifest needs for emotional growth and healing should be placed in settings which include a therapeutic purpose among their objectives, where staff are trained, skilled and experienced in therapeutic methods.

Such apparently obvious requirements are not always easily delivered. The context of policy towards young people, which is influenced (if not determined) both by public opinion and by conflicting priorities, is only intermittently favourable. The problems at the technical level of practice are no less formidable. This book, however, charts an intellectual and emotional journey towards proficiency in therapeutic work with children in residential settings. It sets out goals, maps the pathways to them and describes methods of tackling the demons and monsters that lie in wait. In doing so, it confirms incidentally the testing nature of the work but – more significantly – demonstrates how it can be done well.

Loving, Hating and Survival illuminates the residential task in ways which are valuable to all who have responsibilities towards children with special personal and social needs who live away from home. It discloses the essential nature of the healing task to those who commission and manage residential services, and it reveals much about the problems of young people that is commonly denied or overlooked. It will prove valuable professionally to all engaged in social work with abused children and in meeting the educational needs of behaviourally disturbed children. Above all, it sets out a carefully annotated agenda for the training and supervision of staff in therapeutic settings. This book marks an important stage in creating the capable and confident profession which is fundamental to the improvement of residential care. I congratulate Caldecott College on the initiative it has taken and on its achievement in producing such a valuable text.

Sir William Utting CB
April 1999

Foreword

It has been exciting to witness the creation of the Caldecott College over the last five years. Those of us who have been involved with the care and education of looked-after children over a period of time have become aware of the crucial importance but dire lack of training. The College has helped to fill this gap.

There have been few books written to help workers with children understand the theory that are so clearly linked to practice as this one is. Andrew Hardwick and Judith Woodhead have collected a group of people who have considerable individual experience and talents and who can do just that. This is a book by practitioners for practitioners. It will be of real practical use to those working with children and brings a strong message of hope and of confidence.

A key theme running through the book is one based on a psychodynamic approach to helping children, but the book is eclectic and not heavily analytically slanted. The pioneers of our work – Wills, Lyward, Shaw, Balbernie, Drysdale, Lenhoff and Rendel (the founder of the Caldecott Foundation) all had different approaches to working with damaged children. There is, however, a pattern that weaves in and out of the work linking those different approaches. The leaders were all charismatic, if unscientific at times, and had a therapeutic approach. This pattern, this basic philosophy, weaves in and out of the chapters of this book. The bibliographies at the end of most chapters contain Winnicott. Rightly so. For Donald Winnicott was one who wove theory into practice in a brilliant but caring and practical way. Those of us who knew him remember the therapeutic personality of this small and intensely compassionate man. One can feel his influence throughout this book.

What new workers with children seek is understanding and awareness of why children and young people act as they do, as well as an understanding of the reasons for their own responses. As an enthusiastic young housemaster at Caldecott 48 years ago, I acted intuitively with children, usually appropriately, but sometimes wrongly. I did not, however, realise why the young people acted as they did or why I reacted as I did. I did not appreciate what caused the stealing and the aggression, only how I should treat it. Training links the cause of emotional damage to treatment and can give the adults the awareness they need. I believe that this book will do a great deal to help in this process.

This is an important book by people of commitment and courage. Crucial issues are faced in a sensitive way, as in the chapter on touch. Practical ways of helping staff cope with violent children are discussed. The crucial issues of supervision and consultancy are looked at practically. Those workers in residential and day care settings and, indeed, foster carers will find it enormously helpful.

I am delighted to be associated with a book that can bring help to so many people. Such a book is long overdue. Let us hope that many working with young people will benefit from reading it. Most importantly, I hope that our looked-after children and young people will benefit as a result of the insights gained.

Simon Rodway OBE
Chair of Council, Caldecott Foundation
April 1999

Introduction

It may be a kind of loving but often it has to look like a kind of hating, and the key word is not treatment or cure but rather it is survival. If you survive then the child has a chance to grow and.become something like the person he or she would have been if the untoward environmental breakdown had not brought disaster. (Donald Winnicott, *The David Wills Lecture in Deprivation and Delinquency*, 1970)

Shortly before his death Donald Winnicott gave the David Wills Lecture. He ended with the words that are quoted above. They are some of his last words, that in the work of substitute caring it is not just the loving that is important for our children and young people, but 'often it has to look like a kind of hating.' The most important experience is that their anger and hate are survived by their carers. He finished his lecture with the following words: 'If you survive then the child has a chance to grow and become something like the person he or she would have been if the untoward environmental breakdown had not brought disaster.'

We have put this book together because we believe that children and young people who have experienced environmental breakdown in the shape of the worst of traumas need adults who can allow them to express and process their rage and who can survive their angry attacks. This includes being able to respond to their self-attacking suicidal feelings and despair. If no one provides this opportunity for them they will express their destructive feelings in other ways – in psychiatric illness, or criminal activity. All children and young people who enter substitute care, whether adoptive, foster, or residential, home or school, require the most sensitive understanding of the difficulties they have experienced in their development. The Warner Report (Warner 1992) described the population in the country's children's homes as 'violent, abused, abusing and self-mutilating children, rather than the orphans and truants of a bye-gone era and popular perception.' How can such children and young people gain the kinds of experiences they need to repair as much as possible of their damaged inner world and self-esteem?

Much substitute care has started out from a sentimental notion of giving such children a better experience than they had before and that with love they will thrive. But as Bettelheim (Bettelheim 1950) said and titled one of his books, 'Love is not Enough'; no amount of love alone will effect change in the children, nor can love alone withstand the intensity of the pressures of living or working day to day with disturbed children and young people. If they are to have the opportunity to choose to change they have to be able to express and work with their destructive, hateful feelings, for they have much to feel enraged about. Ideally no child or young person should have to experience the worst forms of terror of abandonment, or deprivation, or physical, emotional, or sexual abuse. Their development is likely to have been so affected by those experiences that mental pain is constant and their preoccupation is finding ways of getting rid of it through acts of aggression towards themselves or others. The pain they cannot accept gets expressed in difficult behaviour which disturbs others and which they in their turn cannot accept. And so they are caught in a vicious cycle. They are not simply 'difficult' or 'deprived'. No wonder that they are often omnipotent, manipulative, malevolent, and distrustful of adults, or apathetic, distant, withdrawn and on referral unable to relate to them. The roots of their disturbance, the intensity of their pain and the powerful effects they have on others need to be understood by their substitute carers and teachers. It is time to stem the rising tide of school exclusions which threatens to deny a significant number of young people of their access to education. The system must learn to survive them.

How can the most destructive feelings of rage and hate be both provided for, be allowed to be expressed, and be survived by the adults these children and young people need? The Utting Report (Utting 1991) indicates that children in care are characterised by 'a complex of personal and social difficulties' which indicate a need for sophisticated and expert treatment. If we are to provide this expert treatment for those children and young people who have a legitimate need for it, where do we start? For the pain to be relieved, for stuck points in development to be freed, they need to experience an approach which is sensitive to the thoughts and feelings that exist within their inner world. This approach we call 'therapeutic'. But it is really what all good substitute care should be about – foster care, residential care, special schooling, children and family centres. Substitute care which is not therapeutic is neglect.

We have produced this book to clarify what a therapeutic approach is. The impetus arose out of providing training in therapeutic care at Caldecott College, when we found that such a book was lacking. Through the training we realised that there is no coherent model which attempts to draw together the threads from different theories and form a usable whole. That is what we have set out to do – to bring together the different elements that we think comprise the core of therapeutic substitute care. Our aim is that all who work with disturbed and disturbing children and young people, in whatever context, will find that this book assists their understanding, expands their thinking and enhances their practice. We must minimise the possibility of burnout and maximise the probability of survival. This in turn will improve the care of very deprived and deserving young people.

Most of the chapters have been written through a process of initial discussion and several meetings with individual authors. Through this process we have tried to elicit writing and thinking that is both alive and current, a useful mix of the theoretical and the practical. We have had to make some assumptions about the context in which practice takes place and we wish to make these explicit at the outset.

First, there is now a body of research with which practitioners must become familiar and on which they must base their planning and their policies. Some research has already become part of practice – the Department of Health's *Looking After Children* assessment programme is a good example. The Dartington studies in Child Protection and Residential Care have provided a yardstick for monitoring practice (*Messages from the Research*, HMSO 1995). We have a special affection for *A Life Without Problems?* (Little 1994) which introduced the concept of children's career patterns in care and on which service planning can be based. Michael Little in Chapter 6 has written a short summary of recent important research in this area.

Secondly, the book seeks to develop practice which tackles discrimination in all its forms. Our focus is on developing the reader's understanding of the nature and needs of troubled young people which will deliver improved care and treatment plans. We offer models of thinking about individuals which reject stereotyping and institutional answers in favour of listening, exploring, communication and partnership. Our young people have developed an inner world conditioned from the early years by their contact with both their close family and the wider community. In helping them to come to terms with their intense, often overwhelming inner feelings we must not ignore issues on the outside which impinge upon them, undermining their progress and limiting their potential.

Thirdly, we are concerned that planning for young people in the care system only goes as far as the next placement. We have included a chapter which describes a model for an outreach, post-care, service but the effectiveness of such a service is enhanced if we think about leaving care from the moment the young person enters it. There needs to be a link between the two services, which should be seen as one – a 'throughcare' service.

Finally, and arguably most importantly, we make the risky assumption that all practitioners who read this book are receiving excellent and supportive, not just policing, supervision. Sadly we know that many receive none at all, just as many receive it sporadically and for many it is simply an unsatisfactory experience. There is no excuse for inadequate or non-existent supervision. It is absolutely essential, a sacrosanct, regular space in the schedule and yet so often abandoned for something 'more important'. We would ask all managers who read this to conduct an immediate audit of their supervision – its regularity, content, quality and value for both supervisor and supervisee, its purpose and general effectiveness and contribution to individual and team morale. We assume that everyone in management wishes to drive out the scourge of abuse from children's facilities especially in the wake of the obscene revelations at the inquiry conducted by Sir Ronald Waterhouse in North Wales. A haphazard system of supervision can only give paedophiles and other abusers encouragement. Unsupervised practice is private practice and that is totally unacceptable.

Contents of the book

In Part One we address therapeutic themes. Part Two goes on to explore through case material the practical implementation of therapeutic concepts. In Part Three we apply the principles to the carer, the family, the group and the management of the whole.

We feel there is also a need for people caring for disturbed children and young people to have easy access to some of the best writing and resources on therapeutic care. To this end we provide at the end of many chapters a useful list of reading and resources, indicating what we consider from our teaching to be primary texts. We hope that these will find their way more readily into facilities for children and young people, to inform practice and give ideas and support.

Part One: Therapeutic Themes

Part One explores some of the most basic aspects of therapeutic work. Fundamental to this part and to the rest of the book is the commitment to the idea that every aspect of care communicates an unconscious message to the child, so that all aspects of daily life must be regarded as part of the therapeutic process – not just times designated as therapy.

We begin Part One with Judith Woodhead's chapter, 'Containing care', in which she explores some of the practical challenges of life with troubled young people and offers models for thinking about them and working them out in practice. While recognising the power of the trauma of historical situations in the child's life, we must focus on giving care in the present which symbolises inwardly for the child the care that was missing. We do this by attempting to provide in the present a secure enough base within which the young person's most primitive feelings can be expressed. The key words are *containment* (Bion 1962) and *holding* (Winnicott 1964). In this way repair and reconstruction of the damage in the child's internal world can be initiated.

Young survivors of abuse experience emotional pain which is just too difficult to communicate in words. Christine Bradley describes in Chapter 2 how children express their pain symbolically, and also need to be understood and responded to symbolically. Adults often mistakenly expect young people to be willing partners in a verbal therapeutic partnership. That is an ideal. It will be realised sooner if we are prepared to take a non-verbal, often symbolic route which promotes trust and avoids feelings of persecution. Central to Christine's approach is the belief mentioned earlier that all aspects of a troubled young person's life can contribute to rehabilitation. Regular hour-long slots of therapy are very helpful but we must also be concerned with the other 23 hours.

One of the most important psychodynamic concepts in this work is *projective identification*. Through this mechanism troubled children can make adults feel the feelings they themselves cannot bear. Robin Shohet describes this in Chapter 3. For the adult it can feel unbearable to be made to feel hopeless or useless or cruel – the very feelings that a young person has and cannot own or bear to experience because they threaten to overwhelm him or her.

Andrew Collie in Chapter 4 provides vignettes to show the meaning of useful therapeutic concepts. He shows through small examples how they can be used in daily situations. Andrew bases his chapter on examples derived from his work as a practitioner and manager working with troubled adolescents.

Supervision and support are absolutely essential for any person working therapeutically. Without them the work cannot effectively take place. David Challender addresses this in Chapter 5. We believe that supervision is crucial for the safety and well-being of both worker and child and should never be cancelled. Yet cancelled or changed it often is – perhaps because it can feel challenging or threatening to sit with another person reflecting on practice.

Happen it must, regularly, at an agreed time, clearly on the rota, to give support and also protection to the worker and indirectly to the child. Ways need to be found of creating supervision sessions in which the worker feels valued and held in the mind of the supervisor. Otherwise the feelings evoked by the intense nature of the work may become overwhelming, affecting adversely child and worker; the adult may respond punitively or despair and leave. Supervision needs to minimise the consideration of administrative matters which may become a defensive way of dealing with painful issues and feelings that everyone understandably wishes to avoid. Thus we stress in this book that good training and support are mandatory. And this must be available to foster and adoptive parents too.

In Chapter 6, Michael Little reviews recent research on which all sound practice must be based.

Part Two: Direct Work

In Part Two, we explore direct work with individual children and adolescents.

How can the therapeutic needs of such children be assessed so that an individual treatment programme can be designed for each child and young person? The Department of Health assessment system *Looking After Children* should be used by all who provide children with substitute care, to ensure continuity in all aspects of the child's life as they move through and out of the care system. To go further and assess in depth the child's emotional state the Caldecott College Assessment Programme can be used. With support from colleagues and students Christine Bradley and Andrew Hardwick have put this together to enable practitioners in a variety of settings to assess the child or young person's emotional state and needs and then develop a programme of care and therapeutic management. This programme is discussed in Chapter 7.

In addition to a therapeutic setting in which repair and reconstruction processes can take place, some children may need and have the all-too-rare opportunity to have direct therapeutic treatment with a trained person external to their everyday care. Anna Maher undertakes this work with children and describes this in her chapter 'The development of a therapeutic response to troubled children'. She explores the role of the therapist in relation to the child and the adults who care for the child. Anna exemplifies what is meant by a therapeutic response through which she attends to the child's feelings which underlie behaviour.

Donald Winnicott would probably have agreed that play is one of the most potent tools for effective intervention with troubled young people. Linnet McMahon's chapter 'Healing play' looks at the nature of play, what it is and the developmental stages of play in the child. Linnet makes suggestions for play provision in the play-room and within daily living.

All substitute caring means working with emotions in the raw. Working with violent children in residential and foster care places enormous and complex demands on carers. To look after a small child in a rage is difficult enough. To be confronted with the rage of a young person, who may have suddenly become bigger than oneself, adolescently powerful, can feel terrifying and also humiliating. It evokes startling feelings in young person and carers alike, and also touches on the adult's own adolescent experiences of difficult issues. Sexuality is an especially fraught area in child care. Work with young children includes working with the child's expressions, often explicit, of sexual feelings. When the child reaches puberty the work intensifies. Coping with strong sexual feelings is hard for young people, and evokes all kinds of difficult feelings in their carers.

Kevin Healy in 'Adolescence: a time of transition' thinks about the nature of adolescence and describes his work in a hospital unit for adolescents. Yet to be adolescent, and looked after, often having suffered forms of abuse usually means to be very angry at an infantile and probably pre-verbal level. Andrew Collie explores working with violence in his chapter 'The difficulties of working with violence in young people'. He focuses on the problem of managing the young person's aggression and violence in a residential community. He looks at how a subculture of violence and delinquency can take hold, and explores ways of managing this.

Chapter 12 turns to the sexually abused child who may need treatment which includes family members. Annie Bousfield's chapter describes an NCH Action for Children model for treating the effects of sexual abuse through varied forms of direct work with children, adolescents and their families. The child's external world is included while working with their internal world. Their past experiences are worked with within the context of current family relationships.

To move out of residential care can be as traumatic as first being looked after. How that will occur should be thought about and broadly planned for at the outset. Otherwise it will be an even greater shock when the moving-on does finally occur. Young people find themselves suddenly in, for example, a hostel, or independent accommodation, after living in a structured care setting, often totally provided for. To cope with this is often more than so-called normal young persons can manage. The odds are stacked against emotional survival. Mick McCarthy is committed to providing practical help and support for such people in the period after they leave the Caldecott Community. With Prue Hardwick he describes supportive outreach work.

Part Three: The Carer, the Family, the Group and the Organisation

In Part Three the authors describe how unconscious dynamics play into all aspects of child care, within each individual participant in the care system, within the family, the foster family, the residential group and the management system. The unconscious processes at work are revealed in the strength of feelings evoked by the work, leading to much confusion, anxiety and conflict.

Ros Fanshawe carried out a piece of action research to find out about feelings of carers. Her findings are presented in her chapter entitled 'Working in substitute care settings with sexually abused children: issues for carers'.

Physical contact has become taboo because of fear of children alleging that contact has been either sexual or aggressive. Adrian Ward looks at this issue in his chapter '"Residential staff should not touch children": can we really look after children in this way?' Adrian draws attention to the fact that anxieties about physical contact between carers and children have often led to a prohibition on contact altogether. When children have suffered trauma in early infancy it is likely they will have experienced little or only distorted physical contact. Hence the development of their bodily self will have been affected. Adrian shows how in normal development different kinds of touch are needed and enjoyed and looks at how these forms of physical contact can be provided for safely, non-abusively, therapeutically.

Physical issues accompany emotional turbulence in the adolescent. Judith Woodhead explores further the nature of adolescence, focusing on 'The task for those who work with adolescents'.

Babs Seymour and David Reeves in 'The re-enactment of family dynamics in child care' show how the child's experience of the family can be worked with in another way, in residential and foster care. They reflect on how the family experience is brought unconsciously into the care system in such a way that everyone concerned with the child, such as the child's social worker, foster parent or residential worker, becomes drawn into the same pattern of dynamics.

Unconscious dynamics also exist within groups and organisations. David Challender in 'Working with unconscious dynamics in groups' describes how these dynamics need to be understood to reduce negative effects, and how they can be put to creative use. He shows how the defence mechanisms we use as individuals are also used by groups, and presents the ideas of Wilfred Bion, relating them to practice.

The kinds of work represented in the above chapters can only be carried out within a clear structure. Therapeutic work demands great sensitivity, skill and responsibility. It is extremely complex work that requires maximum clarity of organisation and can only effectively exist and develop within a setting that has a clearly defined system of management. Andrew Hardwick's chapter shows how to design a management structure for a team to use to implement the primary task for which it exists – to provide therapeutic care for a specific group of children and young people. Andrew addresses the need to design a structure in which vital authority and responsibilities are clearly delegated. Our attention is directed to the fact that making changes to an accustomed way of functioning evokes anxiety and resistance in whole staff groups. The unconscious processes at work need to be acknowledged, with a constant attempt to try and understand what may be going on in the unconscious of the whole establishment, the staff group, and the group of children and young people. It is a very complex task indeed.

And so we come full circle to the reasons for collecting together the chapters for this book. Therapeutic work is full of so many different dimensions that we wished to represent the experience of many practitioners. We believe that therapeutic work, based on a recognition of the existence and power of unconscious processes within the individual and the group, can make a real difference to the lives of children and young people who have suffered – deep within – damage, disturbance and distress beyond words. We are committed to therapeutic work not being for the few in specialised communities alone, but for the majority of troubled children, through the integration of therapeutic work into all substitute care provision. We believe the theoretical framework helps practitioners to survive longer, with great sensitivity and personal and professional satisfaction. The impact of their work may not be as effective as they would like – there are limitations to substitute care – but by staying with young people, stabilising and seeing them through life-threatening situations they can break the cycle of rejection and despair; opening up the possibilities for future planning and creative living.

References

Bettelheim, B. (1950) *Love is not Enough*, New York: The Free Press.
Bion, W. (1962) *Learning from Experience*, London: Heinemann.
Little, M. (1994) *A Life Without Problems*, Aldershot: Arena.
Utting, W. (1991) *The Utting Report: Children in the Public Care*, London: HMSO.
Warner, N. et al. (1992) *Choosing with Care*, London: HMSO.
Winnicott D.W. (1970) 'Residential Care as Therapy' in Winnicott, C., Shepherd, R. and Davis, M. (eds) *Deprivation and Delinquency*, London: Routledge.
Winnicott, D.W. (1964) *The Maturational Processes and the Facilitating Environment*, London: Karnac.

Contributors' notes

Annie Bousfield trained as a social worker in America and then as a Family Therapist. She subsequently worked in social work education and in adolescent psychiatry, before setting up a specialist child sexual abuse treatment project in 1991 under the auspices of NCH Action for Children. In 1997 she became manager of a fostering project for the same organisation. She is involved with East Kent Rape Line both as a supervisor and a trainer.

Christine Bradley is a child care consultant, trainer and psychotherapist. She has been an associate of Caldecott College since its inception. In her work with emotionally damaged children she has a particular interest and expertise in the therapeutic value of play and in the understanding and use of symbolic communication. Her clients include local authorities, the University of East Anglia and NCH Action for Children.

David Challender has worked for thirty years in child care in various settings including residential psychiatric units and therapeutic communities. For fifteen years he has been a consultant to the Caldecott Community. He also lectures in counselling and therapy at the University of Kent. He practises privately in psychotherapy with adults and young people. His academic interests include research in the field of child and adolescent psychology and for many years he has been Assistant Editor of the *Journal of Adolescence*.

Andrew Collie graduated in Social Sciences from York University in 1970. He trained as a residential social worker in 1973, and through this became interested in the therapeutic possibilities of residential care. He lectured in social work at a College of Further Education between 1974 and 1978, during which time he qualified as a teacher. Whilst working for MIND in London, he trained in consultation and supervision at the Tavistock Clinic. He worked at Peper Harow Therapeutic Community between 1984 and 1991. After a five year period as a Social Services manager he now writes, teaches and works as an organisational consultant.

Ros Fanshawe is the Senior Lecturer at the Caldecott College. She has substantial residential experience of working with abused and deprived children. Ros is committed to training residential carers as part of the process of improving the care of looked-after children.

Andrew Hardwick was a teacher at the Cotswold Community from 1974–79 and Principal of Caldecott College from its inception in 1993 until 1998. He was responsible for the design and academic and professional accreditation of the College's programmes and initiated the College's outreach strategy of training delivery. He is a Senior Teaching Fellow at Warwick Business School's Centre for Small and Medium Sized Enterprises.

Prue Hardwick was a residential social worker at the Cotswold Community from 1975–79 where she pioneered decentralised catering for therapeutic units. She is a consultant in the voluntary sector specialising in strategic planning, grant assessment and evaluation for charitable trusts, foundations and philanthropists. She is also a trustee of a charity providing care for the elderly in nine centres in the United Kingdom.

Kevin Healy is a Consultant Psychotherapist at, and Director of, the Cassel Hospital in Richmond, Surrey. Over the past 12 years at the Cassel Hospital he has developed and led inpatient psychotherapeutic services for personality disordered adults and severely disturbed adolescents. He is committed to evidence-based practice particularly where the evidence is in itself practice based.

Michael Little is a researcher at the Dartington Social Research Unit. Dartington is the Department of Health's designated centre for the study of children in need. The Unit has published many books on the care careers of vulnerable children including those placed in residential settings. The recently published *Caring for Children Away from Home* attempts to draw together the key evidence in this area.

Mick McCarthy joined the Caldecott Community in 1997 as Throughcare Manager. His previous posts include managing an adolescent resource centre, field work management in North West Kent and setting up a leaving care project for Kent Social Services Department in 1990. After qualifying with CQSW in 1985, Mick joined the Royal Philanthropic Society in 1988 where he worked with young people leaving care. His social work career began in 1979 as a residential and then field social worker in Greenwich.

Linnet McMahon is a lecturer in social work at the University of Reading, where she teaches courses on 'Infant and Child Observation and Attachment'. She is a tutor on the MA in Therapeutic Child Care course, and with Adrian Ward has edited *Intuition Is Not Enough: Learning for Therapeutic Practice in Child Care*. Previously she led a therapeutic play group for families with a young child with learning disabilities. She provides play therapy and supervision, and has written *The Handbook of Play Therapy*. She is currently writing about therapeutic work in family centres.

Anna Maher works as a child therapist and as a consultant at two children's homes, with a particular interest in staff development and training. Prior to this she worked for Kent Social Services Department, holding posts in child care, mental health and training. During this time she developed her interest in direct work with children, and undertook courses at the Tavistock Clinic and the Lincoln Centre.

David Reeves is currently working half time in a NHS out-patient psychotherapy department offering individual, couple and group therapy plus various staff support groups and the remaining half time he is in private psychotherapy practice. Formerly David managed the Family Day Unit at Marlborough Hospital, and was Deputy Manager of a Family Centre for Hammersmith and Fulham Social Services and Consultant to the Adolescent Unit of the Caldecott Community.

Babs Seymour was Assistant Director (Therapeutic Child Care) at the Caldecott Community for nine years. An infant teacher, she moved into residential social work with adolescents, Family Therapy Training with the Institute of Family Therapy and then became a Family Centre worker, before moving into managing a Family Day Unit for nine years working with David Reeves. Babs has worked as Family Therapist, Staff Group Consultant and Child Care Consultant.

Robin Shohet is a psychotherapist, supervisor, trainer and management consultant. He is co-author, with Peter Hawkins, of *Supervision in the Helping Professions* (OUP 1989). His most recent work is in the field of forgiveness, applying it to individuals, couples and organisations.

Adrian Ward is Senior Lecturer in Social Work at the University of Reading, where he is Course Leader of the MA in Therapeutic Child Care. He has extensive experience in residential child care, and he is the author of *Working in Group Care* (Venture 1993) and co-editor of *Matching Learning with Practice in Therapeutic Child Care* (Routledge 1998).

Judith Woodhead is interested in the emotional experience of children and adults. After teaching she worked in residential child care, and gained an MA in psychodynamic approaches. She is a freelance consultant/trainer and has done much work for Caldecott College. She has gained much experience of psychotherapy in NHS and student counselling settings. She is training as an analytical psychologist with the Society of Analytical Psychology.

Part One

Therapeutic Themes

To protect the anonymity of young people referred to in case material a single, unrelated capital letter has been used for names and important details have been changed.

1 Containing care

Judith Woodhead

Out again into the night where the dulled light obscures the decisive lines of reality and casts over the immediate world a kindly vagueness. Now, it is not a matter of all black and white. It is not a matter of 'this is it' because there is no light of unequivocal evidence in which one sees a thing and knows the answers. The darkened sky gives growing room for softened judgements, for suspended indictments, for emotional hospitality. (Axline 1964)

1 Containing care

Judith Woodhead

Introduction

Fundamental to this chapter is the affirmation that relationship, which is built up through attachments, is at the core of our human experience. Whatever our ancestral and cultural origin we begin life in relationship with care-givers. Otherwise we would die. We are conceived through sexual connection between male and female. We enter life through an other, our mother. Our existence forms a pattern of moving towards and away from others, of being together with others, or of being alone and separate. We move between dependence and independence, connectedness and solitariness. Connecting with others, separating from others and losing others forms a central thread in our lives. But when abandonment is experienced early in life there may feel to be an absence of that continuous thread.

In this chapter I explore the relationship between the child who experiences abandonment and the kinds of restorative experiences a substitute care setting can go *some* way to providing.

The abandoned child

L., aged 13, is very thin, and looks frozen through and through. He has a brittle manner. He rarely smiles, and when he does his eyes remain expressionless. He wears only black or grey. When newborn and an infant, he is said by the agencies to have experienced gross neglect in a house with glass in few windows and an empty larder, to have witnessed much violence, to have been left alone for long periods of time. When older, he has provided care for his younger siblings, and he cannot bear the fact that in entering the care system he has left them without his care. It is thought that until recently he has shared his mother's bed. He appears to love her, is fiercely protective of her. The reality is that he is one stage from going to a secure unit, because of his stealing and absconding. Having run away from previous residential establishments, he is placed far from home, to discourage him from running there. But he is attracted home as if by a strong magnet, risking harm to get there. Part of him longs to be 'put away', because then he will be kept safe and will be punished for whatever crime he feels inwardly he has committed. He avoids the pain of his reality by keeping the unreality in his mind of an ideal, wished-for-past, or an ideal hoped-for future. Within L. there lives the image of an ideal family he might have had, but did not have – and a part of him hopes that everything will one day change and his family will become a good one. Reality enrages him. He defends himself from his acute pain by appearing tough, streetwise and totally able to look after himself, restless and on the move, needing 'no help from no one'.

Children like L. experience traumatic abandonment as central to their destiny. For many, this originates from when they were very young and preverbal. As an unconscious level it is likely to shape the way they experience their world, how they perceive, respond and relate to others throughout life. Coming into care is a further kind of abandonment that re-evokes earlier traumatic experience. L. and thousands like him have an especially difficult developmental task. There have been such fragmenting discontinuities in their life development. Many experience physical, sexual, and emotional abuse. They are unable to integrate their different experiences and feelings to form a cohesive personality. Their inner world is structured around anxieties about their survival and they are unable to draw on the nourishment and energy of their deeper innermost self. Raw primitive feelings become acute, experienced by others as the child's intentional hostility or withdrawal; envious destructive rage exists against adults, with the fear also that this may destroy the very adults by whom they need to be looked after. Their inner worlds become as unsafe as their experience of their external worlds.

Unloved, unlovable and very afraid

The message within abandoned children is that they are unloved, unlovable, bad and somehow guilty of causing the situation that led to being in care. The very experience of being taken into care confirms that they have lacked care. Abandoned children have a deep wound in their core self. They most acutely lack an internal image of arms that can safely hold, of a mind and a face that responds to pain and joy – of a mother that can soothe terrors, of a father that can keep the monsters at bay. Sudden catastrophic loss feels a constant threat.

Winnicott spells out these 'unthinkable anxieties, primitive agonies' as:

- feelings of going to pieces
- falling forever
- having no relation to the body
- having no orientation
- complete isolation because of there being no means of communication. (collated in Davis and Wallbridge 1981)

Every subsequent separation may evoke such inner chaos – manifested in feelings of terror, rage, destructiveness, delinquency or withdrawal to a distant safe place inside, cut off and very quiet. To survive psychic trauma, these children have had to develop brittle defences against the feeling of terror within. For when feelings are so acute, and threaten to overwhelm, then for many children it becomes better to try not to feel.

Enraged, guilty, disillusioned and sad

When responsive parental care is rarely experienced, the infant receives little help to make sense of feelings. So feelings are too easily all mixed up. Sadness and rage become interfused. Truth and lies are indistinguishable. Humour may be empty of meaning. The good becomes bad. Nurturing feels like persecution. Interest feels like invasion. There may be a strong feeling of responsibility for everything – for the family failure, the mother's state, their own state – as well as a sense of guilt, a feeling of having no right to exist and no place to be.

For children who are sexually abused, and others too, different parts of the body may also feel mixed up, with bodily functions confused. Physical contact may be experienced not as reassuring, but as attacking, or overly sexually exciting. They may feel homeless in their own bodies. In other words the feeling of being a whole self, bodily, emotionally, mentally, may be damaged and the child's sense of reality may be threatened, undermined, distorted. This distortion in perception of reality may be an aspect of later mental illness requiring specialist help.

Abandonment is a catastrophic experience, different from the experience of separation in which grief is experienced, and may result in 'abandonment depression' (Schwartz-Salant 1990). Here the abandoned one suffers a consummate betrayal: the loss of a loved and needed person. On the other hand, persecution by that same person is experienced. As a result, one's sense of reality is totally threatened: the good becomes bad, the nurturing has become persecutory. From a seeming state of well-being a chaotic state of panic becomes imminent because the entire fabric of one's perception of reality has come into question. We see this with L.

At first, L. attempts daily to destroy the care he is given, especially around transitions, by being explosively aggressive in one instant, or silent and withdrawn in another. His emotions seem to be all or nothing. On one occasion in fury he tears his few family photographs to shreds; care workers trying to cope with his outburst are left feeling the sadness and despair beneath his rage, as images of his family lie in irreparable bits on his bedroom floor. He is unable to differentiate between feelings of rage and sadness. He sometimes goes off, finds a piece of broken glass he has kept hidden, and cuts his arm or leg. He is so unable to seek or accept care that on one occasion he cuts himself before going to bed, and when adults are alerted by an older boy, he is found in bed, blood seeping through the yarn he has crudely tied around a piece of dirty cloth over the wound. He fights away the adults, who have to hold him until he will allow the wound to be bathed and dressed. L. cannot feel safe enough to expect and allow anyone to give him care. He has to give himself a kind of self-care, which more resembles neglect and abuse than real care. It is empty independence.

L. is in the grip, which feels merciless, of frightening primitive feelings which flood him. The associated behaviours evoke very stark feelings and responses in carers too. Some are deeply committed to working with these states while others see him as beyond help and wish he would leave. In other words he communicates to adults his own conflict between wanting to be accepted and provided for, and wanting to be rejected.

Disoriented and dispossessed

Entering the care system is for many children a further disaster which reinforces trauma. Children like L. will have experienced insecure, unreliable attachments; the very fact of being in substitute care means that they must cope with further separation and the loss of whatever experiences were their own unique, familiar ones. These children become dispossessed of roles they are used to, along with the familiar things of everyday life like smells and sounds. Gross deprivation, even privation, of good enough care in infancy leads to impaired relationship capacities. Relocation means further dislocation and disruption of relationships. Dispossession, dislocation and disruption are in themselves unbearably tough, and make it even more difficult for each individual child to develop a cohesive, integrated self.

Protective behaviours

To deflect from experiencing emptiness, formless terror, nameless dread, children in care may use a range of behaviours, as exemplified above, as a form of protection, a defence. Rage may be mobilised against those attempting to provide care. They may denigrate and destroy what is good, or they may withdraw to a safer but bleak space within. By dissociating from terror that cannot be endured, the child splits off from feelings and thoughts that are too disturbing to acknowledge. Some children may become very compliant, eager to please, over-adapted, too independent (Winnicott's false and caretaker self). Other children may be too intellectual, cut off from feelings about themselves or others, and may live in a lonely place feeling omnipotently that they are 'king of the castle'. All these ways of functioning are characteristic abandonment behaviours (Asper 1987), which need to be understood as protective rather than as naughty or anti-social.

Providing restorative care

Dibs had his dark moments and had lived for a while in the shadows of life. But he had had the opportunity to move out of those dark moments and discover for himself that he could cope with the shadows and sunshine in his life.

Perhaps there is more understanding and beauty in life when the glaring sunlight is softened by the patterns of shadows. Perhaps there is more depth in a relationship that has weathered some storms. Experience that never disappoints or saddens or stirs up feelings is a bland experience with little challenge or variation in colour. Perhaps when we experience confidence and faith and hope that we see materialise before our eyes this builds up within us a feeling of inner strength, courage and security. (Axline 1964)

How can substitute carers use and extend their own skills to provide a quality of daily experience that can offer children, the opportunity and resources to heal pain? The child who has sustained damage requires adults who believe that the child does have forces within for healing and growth. S/he needs a setting in which inner forces of repair can be activated and supported; not a sentimental provision, but an environment in which his/her feelings can be transferred onto/projected into adults and worked with: 'Social work always has as its aim not a directing of the individual's life or development but an enabling of the tendencies that are at work within the individual, leading to a natural evolution based on growth' (Winnicott 1965).

The child ravaged by rage and despair requires space in which these most acute feelings can be voiced, experienced, contained and survived. Otherwise they are likely to destroy any feelings of goodness within and outside the child. The defensive structures that hinder the child's developmental process can slowly give way to more adaptive, less rigid ones.

For these developments to occur firm containment is required. Care-workers, foster carers and adoptive parents need to serve as the container for the child's feelings. Deprivation of responsive enough care in infancy and the present means the child's feelings are likely to be raw and persecutory.

Winnicott (1965) thus argues cogently for the care environment to be an environment which provides a 'facilitation of the maturational processes'. How can these concepts help children like L. get the kind of care that can symbolise the holding and containment they lacked in infancy? It cannot be given for real; the child and adolescent cannot return to infancy, be treated as a baby. But the processes can be symbolised in such a way as to repair damaged inner processes. Each aspect of the care process needs to symbolise for the child the 'holding' they may have been unable to experience in infancy. It begins with moving into a care setting.

Moving in, moving through, moving out

Moving into a residential or foster care setting, is often fraught. Real reflection may be rare as carers are caught up in complex dynamics. These may re-enact family dynamics (see Chapter 17 by Babs Seymour and David Reeves). This process itself conveys important messages to children about how they are viewed and treated. Preparation for their arrival is required.

Activity 1.1: Beginnings

How did a particular child you have in mind come to your establishment?

Reflect on all the details of meetings held, reports given, conversations had, etc. Think about what kind of messages the child was receiving/building up about the move.

If the move was done as an emergency, how was the speed of the change handled for and by the child? It is important in looking at the hows and whys to see where certain things done or not done were to relieve the discomfort and anxieties of all concerned.

What about the child's anxieties – how were these addressed before and after the transition?

Were there opportunities to think about what was being left behind, to say any goodbyes, to go on mourning what had been lost?

Also think carefully about how the other children in the establishment were told about the child, prepared for their arrival, how the others were introduced to the child, room preparation, etc.

Many children in care are all too frequently moved-on, which is likely to add to anxiety, anger and the use of defensive attitudes such as 'I don't care'. Carers, too, protect themselves by all kinds of defensive manoeuvres, such as denial of pain, blame of others in the system, hurried procedures that mask the pain of separation.

Moves can be used as an opportunity to allow the child to recognise and express a whole range of complex feelings, especially sadness and loss. Past separations may be re-evoked and worked with in the present. It is important that the child experiences carers who recognise, name and contain their feelings. Thus in leavings and arrivals, feelings, often unconscious, can be brought to light and worked with within the context of current relationships. The child needs help to be able to gain insight gradually into their troubling emotional world.

Activity 1.2: Endings

Think of a particular child you have worked with, who then moved on, in terms of the following:

- How was the child's move thought about by professionals, family, the child?
- In what ways was the child included in thinking about their future?
- How were feelings thought about and communicated?
- Did you use particular ways of preparing the child for their move?
- What was the nature of the good-bye rituals, and were feelings included?

Once in a care setting, every transition may evoke acute abandonment anxiety.

Transition time

Transitions mean moving between two different spaces, leaving behind what was and moving on to what becomes the new present. It means momentarily giving up one experience to take up a different one. Countless children and young people in residential and foster placements of all kinds find transitions very difficult to make. Perhaps this is because every transition feels like a frightening separation. The daily transition between home and school can be especially difficult. It is not helpful to regard the children as simply being difficult or kicking up a fuss about going to school. Inwardly, great anxiety is stirred. Children with a history of emotional disturbance cannot necessarily feel that the people and the place they are leaving behind at the beginning of the day will continue to exist and be there when they return at the end of the day. The same can happen in reverse, that the teacher and school may cease to exist when the child has gone. Teenagers too may need help in making those transitions. The kind of help required will differ from individual to individual. For one it may be enough to have the same ritual of leaving home each morning. For another it may help to have something to take from home to school and back again, which represents something good from what has been left behind, something that symbolises a feeling of being cared for (see Chapter 2). Another child or young person may need to be taken to school and into the classroom and be handed over to the teacher and vice versa at the end of the day.

Activity 1.3: Transitions

Put yourself into the place of a child you work with:

- Visualise the different transitions they make, the particular behaviours, and imagine what feelings they are expressing.
- Does the child have a favourite toy/object that helps the child feel less anxious, and is this encouraged and respected?
- Can you change anything that would make the child's feelings more conscious and help them slowly develop new ways of handling separations and returns?

Structuring space and time

Everyday routines form the matrix for these children to experience themselves and develop their own potentialities. To feel contained, every aspect of everyday experience must be looked at to see whether it helps or hinders developmental processes. For black children this is especially so, given the negative messages they receive about their identity and place in our racist society. The implicit messages buried in routines may deeply affect those children for whom this or other similar places is the only home they are likely to know for many years. Their daily experience of interactions with others will become models in their mind for how to experience their relationships as they go through life. This means taking a critical look at how the daily living experiences of the children are structured.

A creative approach must be generated that evaluates/imagines how each individual child can develop their own unique individual self. The sheer hard work, long hours, the number and combination of children together, the disturbed and disturbing behaviour of the children all combine to destroy creativity. Carers have their own understandable defences against creative work which feels threatening, due to the closeness of work which feels dangerous and their own primitive raw emotions. These defences, like those of the children, have to be respected – slowly recognised, worked with and allowed to change. Supervision can help this process.

How can time be used creatively? Real time or rota time?

The staff rota is ubiquitous. In my experience it is readily personified and becomes a kind of forbidding authoritarian figure, preventing rather than facilitating creative activity: 'We can't because of the rota.' It forms a potent defence against creativity and against relating directly with children. It can be used as a way of avoiding doing things, especially spontaneous things. For example, at the weekends the shift system may well hinder outings. It is not a normal kind of experience for Saturday shopping trips to have to end in time for the children to be back for lunch but it happens all too often to tie in with shift changeovers. Older residents can feel their weekends are geared to institutional constraints rather than to their own requirements and wishes. Though the rota may need to be changed to create more flexible weekends shifts, there seems to be resistance to changing the rota structure and altering shift patterns. An institutional force can subtly grow that prevents something as simple as youngsters being able to go out for a whole day on a weekend. Thus such children become discriminated against, having to be different from children who are not in care. Their disadvantage is reinforced.

Activity 1.4: Time use

In your work place how is the rota formed; could this be changed to promote more flexibility?

Note immediately any negative feelings you have about the rota, for these may reflect how children also feel.

Do you feel you have sufficient time to spend directly with a certain child you have in mind? If not, is there any way this could be altered? And when you do get this time, how do you feel about it?

Sleeping and waking time

When L. goes to bed at night he wants to keep his clothes on, ready to run, and puts his black anorak over him. It seems to serve as a comforter, a very concrete one, rather than a more symbolic transitional object. When he erupts in a violent rage he cuts or tears his coat – but he does not allow it to be repaired for a long time. It becomes as battle-scarred as he is himself.

Bedtimes can be very difficult, full of conflicting feelings. Bedrooms may feel like shut-away or frightening places and may connect with disturbing memories. Sensitivity is needed to feelings about going to bed, and bedroom space. For example, it may feel very intrusive for a certain member of staff, or for an unknown relief worker, to enter the bedroom. Some children however may react to past abusive experience by being over-familiar about their bedroom being entered. Individual children are likely to have very differing feelings which must be respected, responded to appropriately and worked with. Anxieties are easily evoked in adults about being alone in a bedroom with a child while reading a story or talking or settling a child. Safety needs to be built in, through effective teamwork and clear communication, so that opportunities for emotional closeness are not deleted through fear of possible accusation. Supervision is essential.

Bedtimes and morning waking times are opportunities for children to have something special of their own. It may be a chosen story, a song, or a special drink or supper. It does not really matter what it is as long as it is something that symbolises to the child the experience of being specially cared for and cared about. The chosen special thing/experience may change, and may often be rejected with hostility, scorn or sullen silence. The child needs to feel this attack can be survived, and that the provision continues.

The quality of handovers between day and night staff is important, so the child feels there is a continuity of care and concern. The rota should not dictate sleeping and waking times. To allow for flexible freedom of choice is difficult in a group care setting – but to be strived for.

Activity 1.5: Sleeping and waking

Think about how the child you work with wakes up/gets up in a morning. Perhaps there is a pattern to any upsets or difficult behaviour.

Who usually wakes that child? Is there as much continuity as possible, or could something be changed to make continuity more possible?

If there is little continuity could this be because no one actually wants to deal with that child in the morning? If so, why and what does it tell you about how the child may be *feeling*?

Bath time

'Children should have access to the normal range of toiletries, cosmetics and sanitary protection and should be entitled to exercise their own preference.' (Children Act Vol. 4: 27)

In residential settings, it is hard to allow for real personal choice and privacy, to ensure that the procedures allow for far more than lip-service to a child's cultural preferences, and to provide for privacy while at the same time managing other children. Emotional and behavioural disturbance make it all the harder. For abused children, bathroom times may evoke anxiety. Yet it is all the more important that individual children learn the skills of caring for/about their own bodies, and develop positive feelings. They may need much help to learn appropriate boundaries.

Whether toiletries are bought centrally and provided for everyone raises the question of individual choice. Yet children and young people often use the communally provided shampoos and sanitary towels. Being disturbed or learning disabled is no excuse for not promoting individual choice. Ways must be found of enabling children to keep their own supplies safely.

More shopping outings may be required. This may raise anxieties about how to shop with children with disturbing behaviour. If these anxieties come out into the open then they can be dealt with, rather than being kept hidden, thus preventing outings from happening.

Activity 1.6: Body time

Reflect on children/young people you work with. Think about their most personal care. Imagine you are giving a presentation to others about that child and describe how you think that child experiences their own body and most intimate care.

What are the messages in the ways the child acquires everyday products such as toothpaste, shampoo, sanitary towels, etc. How are these kept and looked after, and are they experienced as the child's own?

Describe any anxieties you feel in relation to their intimate care. Have you taken your concerns/anxieties/conflicts to supervision?

If you supervise others, is this an area of work that is discussed? Be aware of whether you feel concerned about boundaries between a care-worker and this part of caring for children; why you may feel reluctant to raise questions.

Eating time

> Meal times are a chance for social contact, as is the shared preparation of food, although care should be taken not to limit this to a fixed ritual ... There should be some flexibility over mealtimes and patterns. (Children Act Vol. 4: 25)

Food and eating can arouse great anxiety in many children due to past disturbing experience. To manage to sit through a meal, and also eat, and get to the end of it without a behavioural outburst can be more than many children can manage. L.'s eating habits reflect his 'all or nothing' pattern. At breakfast times he can only eat a lot of one food – many Weetabix to begin with – but feels completely unable to eat toast as well. At meal-times he often sits and looks at the plate of food and refuses to touch it, looking very pale, with jaw clenched, desperate to go ahead and have it and yet internally prevented from doing so. Gentle approaches are rebutted. He fights back tears. He may suddenly push back his chair, throwing it over, and run from the dining room.

What can be done? L. needs the practical support of the same person always sitting with him – chaos breaks out on the special carer's days off. He is likely to abscond and be brought back by police. He needs to develop trust that he is not going to be punished, that the food is not going to be taken away, that it is not poisonous. It requires sensitivity and patience on the part of the carer, other adults and children.

It is difficult to get the balance right between set meal times and the freedom allowed in many homes. Kitchens in many residential homes are out of bounds to children. Meal-times often have to be at set times because of other constraints. Snacks may be available only at certain set times because of the difficulty of regulating them. And food supplies may be locked away because of behavioural difficulties. It may be impossible to have a fruit bowl on the table. It is very important to find ways round these difficulties, so that most of the children and young people can have some sense of autonomy regarding what they eat and whether and when they can make themselves a drink. What is important is what the provision of food symbolises. L. begins to join in making things, helps lay tables, which seems to help him. The more he becomes a part of shared activity, the more he seems able to sit and eat.

What about what is to be eaten? Does it link in with the child's own past cultural family experience, or is it totally different? This does not call for token action of including e.g. occasional ethnic meals. It requires that children have some power; and play as much part as they are able in choosing and planning meals. It is too easy for a cook to do all the planning in advance, independent of the children. Especially where there are older children much can be gained from this being a shared activity. Meal planning is about making connections too; between being involved in some planning and then experiencing the results – on the plate. As for involvement in cooking, too often there is no possibility for children to be involved. One way round this is to equip a separate small area as a kitchen for residents to make snacks or cook a meal. The main difficulty is allowing for children to be messy and to explore and to have fun with different foods.

Then there is the buying of food. In residential establishments this is often done in an institutional way, with foodstuffs delivered through the county sources. But this denies children and young people the real-world experience of sometimes being able to join in shopping and choosing foods spontaneously. It deprives them of normal experience and can reinforce passivity. Children in foster families are hopefully much more likely to have opportunities for joining in with cooking and shopping activities. But this can also be fraught with difficulty. A. is 15 and B. 14, both fostered by experienced, very able foster parents. But meal-times can be hell. They push their foster parents to the limit by denigrating whatever food is cooked for them, by refusing to eat what everyone else is having. Yet if given freedom everyday to cook what they please they abuse the freedom by making the maximum mess, cooking anything randomly, poorly and making incompatible foods. They are big, and strong, and they are wielding power which frightens their foster parents and themselves too. They are close to wrecking their placement which they seem to want yet do not want. They cannot tolerate experiencing the goodwill of their foster parents and seek every opportunity at the moment to attack them, spoil the benefits of their placement and possibly destroy it. Much creativity and understanding is required. Yet carers own anxieties may make this difficult.

Activity 1.7: Food time

Think about the way children you work with experience meal-times.

Check on their experience of the physical lay-out of the dining room, for example, can undue noise, including phones ringing and disruption, be reduced?

Check that others are not using the dining room as a passageway to elsewhere during meal-times, or disturbing meal-times with administrative talk.

Do they participate to their maximum in planning, purchasing, preparing food? Are appropriate choices given and individual tastes allowed for?

What might be changed to create more enjoyable meal-times?

Leisure time

Leisure activities are important too. Yet institutional inertia, the rota, and fear of negative behaviour often prevent a range of activities being provided. Perhaps also adults fear creativity and are reluctant to engage creatively with children. Children of whatever age, adolescents especially, need to feel there is plenty going on, and need to experience enthusiastic adults with whom to build relationships; and they need new, good experiences that help raise esteem and confidence. Consciously planned activities need to be on offer, other than shopping and leisure centre trips. Ways need to be found, even within city provision, to offer activities such as sailing, canoeing, wind-surfing, horse-riding, shelter/camp-building, bike-riding, roller-blading, night adventures, which all have immense value. In particular, they allow for new exploration, and build up good experiences in the children's minds, which can slowly become a new part of them. Difficulties to be overcome are all part of it. To begin with, L. refuses to join in with anything. As he slowly thaws, so be begins to participate in adventures, but at the slightest set-back or failure he becomes angry, destroys the opportunity and has to disrupt or withdraw, depriving himself of further pleasure, which in itself is a form of sado-masochistic pleasure.

Safety standards are paramount, but equally, they must not cocoon children so they do not have the opportunities they need to grow on. Ways have to be found to ensure they can safely do such activities, for it is through such real-life experiences that a new sense of self grows. Activities need to be ongoing, and may need to be adult-inspired. In fact, an enthusiastic adult, leading a hobby or interest of their own, is the best possible role model for a child or adolescent. Games and puzzles need to be got out and used, kept in order and repaired or replaced when damaged. Facilities for creative play need to developed, including the messiest of play, using all kinds of materials. A sand-box is good to have. It is best, in addition to all the usual kinds of things on offer, for an area or a room to be set aside for special play-times, with, if needed, undivided adult attention for a time. Chapter 9, on play, by Linnet McMahon explores this further.

Activity 1.8: Activity time

Think about the leisure and play resources you provide.

Think of a particular child and reflect on how and when they play and also join in leisure activities. Do they tend to be solitary in these activities? Could you offer other activities that involve more participation with others?

Do you draw on interests the child already has – also draw on your own enthusiasms to initiate play activity?

Are adults in your establishment encouraged to use their own skills and enthusiasms?

Identify what seems to stop creative activity taking place, and what could be changed to allow for more possibilities.

Talking time

Setting aside time for talking and sharing information and feelings is crucial. As much opportunity as possible is needed to facilitate a feeling of continuity of experience, and to mitigate against confusion and the impersonal character of institutional life. The introduction of daily group meetings for the whole of a residential unit can be crucial. These meetings can be named, for example, 'talking times' and should be timetabled in, to happen without fail, and if possible at the same time each day. All kinds of issues, concerns, complaints, feelings can be brought and expressed. It is important that this is not used as a time to criticise/humiliate/scapegoat, but is used to explore what is happening and how each person feels about it.

For children and young people whose sense of self is weak, who feel powerless to affect the course of their lives, such opportunity for expression and contribution to the whole can feel deeply valuable. To be listened to and really heard may be quite a new experience. To feel that others value what they say may also be very different from past experience.

Activity 1.9: Talking time

Examine closely how events and experiences are communicated among adults and also between adults and children/young people.

Look at the opportunities for children to express how they feel about aspects of their day/placement/relationships with others: what they did at school or on a visit home; opportunities to show something important to others.

Is there as much opportunity as possible for the naming and exploring of emotions?

Be specially vigilant about dynamics in the organisational system that prevents or minimises effective communication, especially of feelings. Why does the establishment try to avoid communication?

Conclusion

In this chapter I have sought to show that children in care experience feelings of abandonment expressed in characteristic behaviours. I have explored their need for a care experience which is structured to provide opportunity for real repair of the sense of self. The child, and carer too, may come to experience in a different way the feeling: I Am.

I have not, however, managed to capture the subtlety or ambience or whole mood either of each individual child or of a substitute care setting. Yet ultimately it is this which is perhaps the most important. A creative core attitude can be discovered within the child and in the act of caring, founded on a sense of relatedness with others, expressed both through feelings of hate and love, which can be survived.

This was so in the work with Dibs, with whom this chapter began, until after much work:

The feelings of hostility and revenge ... still flared up briefly, but they did not burn with hatred or fear. He had exchanged the little, immature, frightened Dibs for a self-concept strengthened by feelings of adequacy, security, and courage. He had learned to understand his feelings. He had learned how to cope with them and to control them. Dibs was no longer submerged under his feelings of fear and anger and guilt. He had become a person in his own right. He had found a sense of dignity and self-respect. With this confidence and security, he could learn to accept and respect other people in his world. He was no longer afraid to be himself. (Axline 1964)

References

Asper, K. (1987) *The Abandoned Child Within*, Fromm International Publishing Corporation.
Axline, V.M. (1964) *Dibs in Search of Self*, Penguin.
Davis M. and Wallbridge D. (1981) *Boundary and Space*, Penguin.
Department of Health (1989) *The Children Act* Vol. 4, HMSO.
Schwartz-Salant, N. (1990) 'The Abandonment Depression', *Journal of Analytical Psychology*, 35: 143–59.
Winnicott, D.W. (1965) *The Maturational Processes and the Facilitating Environment*, Hogarth Press.

2 Making sense of symbolic communication

Christine Bradley

Introduction

> Of course, there must be lots of Magic in the world, he said wisely one day. But people don't know what it is like or how to make it. Perhaps the beginning is just to say nice things aren't going to happen until you make them happen. (Hodgson Burnett, *The Secret Garden*)

In this chapter Christine Bradley addresses the problems faced by children who have real difficulties in communicating with grown-ups about their unhappiness. We expect too much of our children and young people. We expect them to sit down and talk to us, to discuss their problems with us rationally and calmly while we make soothing and approving noises. We hold totally unrealistic expectations of them – to join an adult world long before they are ready to do so or indeed should even think about doing so.

As Christine points out, many young people suffered at the hands of adults either before they had discovered words, or their suffering is literally unspeakable. And yet they all 'speak' to us in their own ways and we have to develop our skills of listening, responding and initiating helpful interventions which are not perceived as persecutory or annihilating, a sophisticated and sensitive task.

Making sense of symbolic
communication

Christine Bradley

In *The Secret Garden*, the statement quoted on p. 23 was made by Colin, a sickly child, whose recovery and increasing physical strength coincides with his discovery of the secret life in the garden. Through this experience he finds his own secret inner life, which has the potential for spontaneity, joy and creativity, and which is unique to him. It is important for all of us to discover a way of living in which we do not feel persecuted or overwhelmed by external factors. We should be at ease with our inner worlds and exist in quiet union with those around us where communication, both verbal and non-verbal, occurs in a natural and meaningful way.

Because of his illness Colin had been overprotected and had never been allowed to find the joys of childhood adventure and discovery. He had never learned to communicate his feelings. Helped by his more ebullient friends, Mary and Dickon, to find the Secret Garden, he found, in doing so, a lost part of himself and he exclaims:

> The sun is shining – the sun is shining. That is the Magic. The flowers are growing – the roots are stirring. That is the Magic. Being alive is the Magic – being strong is the Magic. The Magic is in me – the Magic is in me. It is in me – it is in me. It's in every one of us. (Hodgson Burnett, *The Secret Garden*)

Early trauma and words

Children who have suffered severe emotional trauma have rarely felt that they have been heard or understood by another person who they could trust to bear the pain of what they have to say. Words spoken to them can be experienced as annihilating as the original trauma. Grown-ups who rely on words and react to behaviour with the words of grown-ups very often fail to appreciate the pain that is being communicated by the child in other ways. Verbal communication must be combined with an understanding of the non-verbal and symbolic efforts made by children. Superficial, verbal interactions deny the true pain of the child. As a result, children are not helped to cope with the suffering of their real self and they feel abandoned. They give up and create an unhealthy defence against the outside and especially the adults who inhabit it. In this world of their own they are no longer able to experience spontaneity, creativity and a belief in the kind of magic that Colin was able eventually to experience.

In my early work I was fortunate to be part of a pioneering project to develop new and exciting ways of helping troubled and delinquent young people. What became clear was that, however well-versed we became in talking to them individually and in groups, there were a number who seemed unable to take in the experiences we were offering to them. We realised that the reason for this was that so many of the children we were looking after felt trapped in a world where either there were no words, or words were simply not adequate or sufficiently explicit to reach the adults. For some, the emotional hurt had taken place before they had learned to use words while others had developed their own words for dealing with it. For many of these children anti-social acting-out had been the only escape from their inner turmoil and despair, only to discover that the external world responded in its ignorance in the same way as the monsters from which they were trying to escape. How often do we hear workers say 'But I stayed for two hours last night talking to him and he is just as difficult as ever today'? It can be disheartening when we realise that all our efforts to engage with the young person have had little effect.

Non-verbal communication – using a third object

We have to find ways of communicating with our troubled young people in a non-verbal, non-threatening and playful way. By using a third object as the focus of our work together we can engage with them and allow them the opportunity to express their need to be looked after. This encourages the development of a relationship and needs can be communicated through a symbolic object – a teddy bear, a favourite toy or toys, play items which are non-threatening and which may hold deeply personal meaning for the young people. The adult response to them enabled a communication to be established which carried meaning for all three of us. As time passes, with continued sensitive responses from the grown-up, the child no longer needs the use of a third object. Words are found and a more direct communication about worries and fears established.

Recently, I revisited the project and met a 14-year-old boy. As he was explaining how the unit now worked, he introduced me to two finger puppets he was wearing on his hand. He explained that one was aged two years but the other was only six months, that he was in charge of them and that sometimes they went with him everywhere. At other times they stayed in their room because they needed to be tucked up and safe. I asked him if they would ever be able to look after themselves. He said that he hoped so, but at this moment they needed other people to look after them. It was apparent to me that he was talking about his own self, who had perhaps not experienced the necessary containment and nurture as a baby. Through his finger puppets, an example of symbolic communication, he was able to experience and express this need to be looked after. Those looking after him were sensitive to those needs and provided him, through the finger puppets, with the appropriate care. One hopes that in time, he will be able to realise what has happened and to talk more directly about himself. Now his personality is so fragile that he could experience attempts at direct communication as an attack.

The inner world experience of young people

Margaret and Michael Rustin in their book, *Narratives of Love and Loss* (1987), write:

> The starting point is the idea that there is an internal dimension of children's experience. In the inner world of unconscious phantasy to which we have access in dreaming and through the part of our personality which responds to symbolic or cultural experiences, the primary focus is on our intimate emotional experiences.

For many of the young people who are in need of residential care their experiences have been so traumatic and abusive that they are unable to have access to their dreams, only the nightmares, which continue to haunt them.

Children who have experienced abuse, neglect and deprivation find the idea of intimate relationships, of the kind that ordinary families engage in, a terrifying concept which makes them panic. Their aim is to destroy anything that appears to come in the way of their attempts to survive the overwhelming inner anxiety, which has been created by a sense of abandonment during their earliest years. How can you describe what has felt indescribable for years to suit the needs of a worker who thinks she can help? Nobody else has helped over the years, so why should it change now?

These are some of the thoughts the children will be having whilst we are talking at them. We cannot give a new life to them, but, by helping them to identify the areas which make them feel worse, we can perhaps give them the feeling that we are prepared to attempt to take notice of the true pain. As Sarah Adams writes:

> Whatever the injuries of abused children they can never be taken away. The dragon cannot be slain! But by gradually naming the wild things within and beginning to make sense of the pain evoked, the child can begin to tame the dragon, to put a lead around its neck and put it behind. It is in this way that children begin to take an authority over their lives and can allow real relationships to develop and a positive sense of self to grow. (Adams 1996)

Of course, to do this successfully is easier said than done when faced with a child in rage and fury. We tend to react negatively rather than find an appropriate response to the frightening behaviour. We have to have a thorough knowledge of the child so that we can spot anxiety building up and offer a way out and the possibility of communication. This is where we can use the third object, the teddy bear, for example, who can receive the feelings of the young person. Later the young person may be able to share the feelings with a grown-up over a favourite mug of hot chocolate. This is one way of making useful contact with the child's chaotic inner world.

A boy in a state of panic and rage one day threw two eggs at me. Another worker I was with at the time said that I should punish him for doing such a thing. I felt otherwise. I was beginning to develop a relationship with him and he had always found it extremely difficult to communicate in any way. Perhaps the egg throwing was a communication, which I should attempt to understand. The feeling invested in the incident seemed to be one of desperation, rather than wanting to hurt me. To the wrath of my colleague I asked him if there was something he was trying to say to me. At first he denied any need, but, when I suggested that, as he had thrown the eggs at me, I should provide him an egg to eat, he appeared very relieved. Rather than react to his actions, I was able to respond. During the rest of his stay with us, I made him a boiled egg each day. This provision became very important to him. It was interesting to note that while he had the egg his behaviour became far more manageable. He did not need to act out his intense feeling of deprivation. Even my disapproving colleague acknowledged that this provision seemed to make him more accessible. Eventually he left us, but I gave him an alabaster egg to take with him, as a representation of that experience. This egg became a transitional object and meant that he could remember the experience and value it, rather than destroy it, as so many children need to do when they leave their residential establishment. It is all too easy when in such a situation as I originally found myself in with this boy to be incensed and react with sanctions. We must consider the impact of our reactions on the inner world of the young person.

While I am not advocating that every piece of anti-social behaviour should be excused it is often helpful to take some time to absorb what has happened and to understand it before coming back to the child. It may be that a very important piece of communication is in danger of being missed. Children who have never been able to communicate consider it a huge risk to attempt to do so. If they are not heard the first time, they may never take the risk again. This is so painfully and beautifully expressed in the following poem, which was written by a child in care before he made a suicide attempt.

He always
He always wanted to explain things, but no one cared,
So he drew.
Sometimes he would just draw and it wasn't anything.
He wanted to carve it in stone or write it in the sky.
He would lie out on the grass and look up in the sky,
It would be only the sky and the things inside him that needed saying.
And it was after that he drew the picture,
It was a beautiful picture. He kept it under his pillow and
Would let no one see it.
And when it was dark and his eyes were closed
He could see it still.
And it was all of him and he loved it.
When he started school he brought it with him,
Not to show anyone, but just to have it with him like a friend.
It was funny about school.
He sat in a square brown desk like all the other square desks and he thought it would be red,
And his room was a square brown room, like all these other rooms.
And it was tight and close. And stiff.
He hated to hold the pencil or chalk, with his arms still and his feet flat on the floor, stiff, with the teacher
Watching and watching.
The teacher came and spoke to him.
She told him to wear a tie like all the other boys. He said he didn't like them and she said it didn't matter.
After that they drew, and he drew all yellow and it was what he felt about morning?
And it was beautiful.
The teacher came and smiled at him. 'What's this?' she said
'Why don't you draw something like Ken's drawing? Isn't it beautiful?'
After that his mother bought him a tie and he always drew airplanes and rocket ships

like everyone else, and he threw the old picture away.
And when he lay out alone looking at the sky, it was big and blue, and all of everything that he wasn't anymore,
Any more.
He was square and brown inside and his hands were stiff. And he was like everyone else –
All the things that needed saying didn't need it any more.
It had stopped pushing. It was crushed. Stiff. Like everything else.

The despair at the end of this poem so vividly portrays how easy it is for grown-ups to destroy in the child any hope of becoming identified with colourful and happy thoughts. This is because we do not respond to the sometimes obscure attempts that our young people make to express themselves. In the poem the picture represented an attempt to create an illusion for him, which had been denied him in his earliest emotional experiences. It is difficult for us to imagine just how desolate children feel who have no access to their inner creativity, where darkness so easily comes to reign inside them. Enid Balint (1993) paraphrasing Ferenzci writes that this state belongs to a time when the infant lived in a world where there was 'Feeling without thinking and thinking without feeling'. The infant tries to communicate, but receives no response – nothing comes back. It is a lifeless relationship, which continues, until it breaks down.

Catch the moment

We have to remember that, because of their deprivation and abusive experiences, these children live emotionally in an 'upside down' world. It is important that we are able to appreciate this and try to create situations where they feel able to share this world with us. What we must not do is block that sharing with our expectations of what they should be saying. We must not be like the teacher in the poem.

In the normal course of events, where early infantile experiences have been good enough, the child is able to feel at ease with their own creativity and imagination. Donald Winnicott (1982) writes, 'In every individual there is the capacity for creative living.' Early experiences of abuse and severe deprivation block such capacity as the main energy is put into surviving rather than living. Work with these children should therefore stimulate their potential creativity. An understanding of symbolic communication will ensure that we are able to catch the moment.

The Frozen Child

Dockar-Drysdale describes the Frozen Child as one 'who, although presenting as charming and apparently friendly with little inhibition' hides a state of panic and rage which can erupt for no apparent reason. This can be very disturbing to those around them. They are unable to show remorse or any concern. Effective communication is difficult to establish. These young people have not achieved the capacity to symbolise in a relaxing, rewarding way because neglect and abuse – a total lack of warmth – marked their earliest interactions with 'caring' adults. The emotionally distorted and over-defensive personality, which is formed, cannot take in what we offer them in a natural and straightforward way. These young people need sensitive adaptation to fill in some of their emotional gaps and spaces, perhaps even to give them an emotional beginning. It requires both intuitive and well thought-out provision on the part of the worker if they are to reach the point of helping them to symbolise and thus help them on the road to verbal communication.

From non-verbal to verbal communication

The process, from non-verbal communication to verbal communication is known as realisation, symbolisation and conceptualisation. This simply means that when the child has had a good experience which has filled them up emotionally they store the good feeling the experience has given them and this becomes an important symbol of the potential for good feelings in the outside world. With the beginnings of safety in their inner reality, they are more able to explore the bounds of external reality through play of various kinds. They are now in a position to think about what this means to them, and with support can find a way of putting this into words, that is, conceptualisation. I am now going to give you an example of how this can work.

J. was 13 years old. His parents' relationship was violent and abusive. They separated when J. was aged one year. Eventually his mother remarried, and the father disappeared completely. Before she remarried, she had been depressed and vulnerable and had been unable to respond to J., as he needed. She began another family with her new husband who was also hostile to J. J. found himself emotionally excluded from this family, and he became an isolated and lonely little boy. By the time he was ten he had been excluded from several schools for aggression, fighting and cruelty to animals. J. had also become very identified with his local delinquent subculture; in order to have some feeling of belonging. It became impossible for anybody to reach J. in an emotional way. His life seemed to be dominated by what Dockar-Drysdale (1993) describes as the 'outer circle' of feelings, namely despair, agony, frenzy and despair. She describes these children as having no 'barrier against stimuli' never having experienced the 'inner circle' of feelings such as sorrow, pain and fear which are supported by the primary carer in ordinary good maternal care. Because of this, he was unable to look towards the future, or think about the past. It was all too painful. As a result he lived life completely in the present and was unable to take any responsibility for his actions or experience guilt or remorse. In fact any confrontation of what he had done by those looking after him produced a violent reaction.

Eventually his behaviour became so difficult that he was sent to a community home for adolescents, as it was decided that he needed specialist help. I was responsible for J. and was often at the receiving end of his rage. This was manifested one day when J. picked up some money on the desk right in front of me. He walked out of the room with the money which did not belong to him. I followed him and challenged him only seconds later. He denied he had ever taken it even though it was in his hand. The fury I provoked in him through this confrontation forced him to throw a pot at me (I ducked just in time). By that time, though only a minute later, he truly believed he had not taken the money. Such is the level of dissociation in unintegrated children, who in crisis fear total emotional annihilation.

Perseverance with J. paid off. With support I was able to survive his onslaughts and help him to accept primary provision from me. J. had always denied he had any emotional need, but eventually he was able to ask me to read him a story and produced a book for me to read. It was *The Little Prince* by Antoine De Saint-Exupéry. It is the story of a little boy who, disappointed in the grown-ups who are not able to respond to his drawings as he had wished, abandons the idea of ever growing up and living in such a boring and uninteresting world as he imagines it to be: 'So I lived my life alone, without anyone I could really talk to, until I had my accident with my plane in the Desert of Sahara, six years ago.'

Here he meets the 'Little Prince' (a projection of his own desire for eternal childhood) who lived on another planet and had come to earth, via other planets where people lived. Gradually he discovers the story of life on the Little Prince's planet, and his struggle to keep down the baobabs – bad seeds which 'sleep deep in the heart of the earth's darkness, until someone among them is seized with the desire to awaken' so that the beautiful rose bushes could continue to grow as he wanted them to, without invasion from the baobabs. The rest of the book is a moving and sensitive dialogue between the pilot and the Little Prince, full of symbolic material representing the fears and anxieties of children about the task of growing up.

Even though J. insisted on being read to whilst he was wearing his 'bovver boots' as he called them, the story and the continuity of the story increased in importance to him. After listening intently for several nights without saying a word, J. suddenly identified himself with the Little Prince and his recognition of the 'good and bad' parts within himself that needed care. It was at the point where we read:

> Now there were some terrible seeds on the planet that was the home of the little prince; and these were the seeds of the baobab. The soil of that planet was infested with them. A baobab is something you will never, never be able to get rid of if you attend to it too late. It spreads over the entire planet. It bores clear through it with its roots. And if the planet is too small, and the baobabs are too many, they split it in pieces. (Saint-Exupéry, *The Little Prince*).

'I have baobabs inside me don't I? They grow and grow and then nothing feels good or worth living for': this was the first J. had ever referred to his own inner state. I asked him if he had any ideas what we could do to help the baobabs in him not to take him over so that he splits into pieces, as in the story. He asked me if I would provide him with a cuddly toy. I bought him a lamb. He took the lamb everywhere with him, albeit hidden under his large overcoat. He was not quite ready to relinquish his delinquent image which had been his only identity for such a long time. Gradually J. was able to allow himself to become dependent on the provision I gave to him, and his 'frozen' self began to melt. He became more communicative and was able to express remorse for some of his past deeds. We finished the story of the Little Prince and J. asked if he could have a copy for himself. He said he felt as though he was at the beginning of his life.

Clearly, the experience of the story and the provision he was able to accept as a result of this, and the symbolic associations he made for himself through the book, gave him an idea that this experience was unconditionally for himself and one that he was able to value, rather than devalue it and destroy it as having no meaning. Work with the family helped them to be more responsive to his needs. Eventually he was able to go back home and manage in mainstream education without breaking down.

Having the confidence to respond at a symbolic level

The symbolic gesture is crucial for meaningful communication with the children and young people we work with. It is important that we are able to be responsive to it, however bizarre and eccentric it may appear to us.

Behaviour which is constantly repeated is usually an indication that there is an important message in the communication which needs understanding. It is only with this attitude from the worker that the child will truly experience someone who is genuinely attempting to reach the self which has been locked and inaccessible for some time. Children whose 'false self' has been their only way of surviving will not be able to relinquish that with ease. However, except in the most extreme of cases, where pathological defences have become rigid and fixed, there will be some clue given out which, if the worker is able to pick it up, will allow them to gain access through a symbolic gesture to understanding and communicating with some of the child's emotional needs. A student who was a member of a training group I was working with recently asked about a boy who was in care in the children's home she worked in. She told me that the staff were most concerned about him, and spent endless time in meetings discussing him. The difficulty with him was that although he was 15 years old and fairly independent he was never able to tie his shoelaces up. The staff had attempted numerous ways of helping him to achieve this task, all to no avail. It had reached a stage where the staff, out of frustration, had found themselves becoming punitive with him. Of course, this only fuelled him to become angry and confrontational, still with the shoelaces not tied! When she shared this difficulty with me, I suggested that perhaps he would like her to tie the shoelaces for him. This would be a recognition that although he was 15 years old there was a still a part of him which needed looking after by a grown-up. A young person of this age who has experienced the breakdown of the continuity of care needed as a small child will have endured painful and abusive emotional experiences. He will not mature in the same way as a 15-year-old who has had more nurturing experiences. He will need a more adaptive programme of care, taking into account that bits of him will have been 'left behind' emotionally. The worker must realise that unless they can respond to these and recognise the 'little self' who still needs his shoelaces tied, whilst functioning as a 15-year-old in other areas, it is more likely that he will break down at a later date. It is so vital that we are able to live with the young person's pain if we are to understand how to meet their needs and offer them the chance of creative living.

Recently I came across a poem a very delinquent and angry adolescent I had once taken care of had written to me. This boy had made my life at work particularly difficult. He had been abusive and at times quite violent, yet the relationship had always been tinged with ambivalence, on both our parts. It is very difficult always to like children who are directing hatred, rejection and abuse at you a great deal of the time. I rather take the view that it is perfectly fine to hate the children at times – they do have some very hateful feelings inside them. We must acknowledge those feelings inside us and then will be able to reach the love and concern we have for them. It took this boy many hours to sleep at nighttime. Sometimes he did not sleep at all. My fantasy was that he was planning the next attack on me!

However, one morning he left a poem for me to read which he had written during the night:

The Silent Hour

I lay me down my head to sleep,
And wonder where I've been,
A trip to Mars, a football match, or
    on the Ocean Queen
My eyes they close, I cannot sleep,
The early hours come,
The depth of night, the stars they blink,
I cry out loud for Mum,
Where is she now, I wonder if her
    hair is turning grey,
Or if at last she has met her lovely
    flower of May,
The daylight comes, and I have slept,
    for only a short while,
When at my door a knock awakes the
    boy who cannot smile.

Anon

To my friend and enemy. Good luck.

As you can imagine, the poem touched me deeply. It made me realise that the volume of anger he expressed at me sometimes was only seeking to hide the depth of despair and loss he felt about the absence of his mother who had abandoned him in his early years. For him the pain of that experience had left him with only an unrealistic fantasy about her, rather than being able to discover the 'magic' which Colin discovered in the Secret Garden. By ensuring a regular time when we played together I found much of his anger diminished and I was able to facilitate for him a way in which we could communciate some of the more confusing and frightening feelings which lay behind the rage.

The examples that I have given in this chapter indicate that children communicate all the time to us. In most cases, the grown-ups miss that communication. It is in listening, true therapeutic listening in a way which takes in the whole child, where we are able to notice some of the communication I have described. Not only listening to their words, but more often to their actions, the feeling behind their actions, and to their internal poetry. It is from this awareness that the opportunities for symbolic communication occur.

It is perfectly possible for sensitive intuitive workers who are able to think about some of these concepts to undertaken important symbolic work with children. I am not here talking about child psychotherapy. That is different and requires a long detailed training together with personal analysis. I am suggesting that therapeutic understanding and support can be given to children by workers who are prepared to invest and involve themselves in the young person's world without becoming over-identified with them. For this to be effective it is important that adequate support and supervision is provided.

My final example in this chapter has been prepared by a group of students I was teaching recently, most of whom were working in Family Centres and Residential Centres for children with disability. They were asked to write a story which would make internal sense to an emotionally abused child. This group of students had only worked together for a few days, but the story they put together shows how imaginative we can be given the opportunity and a facilitating environment. It is as follows:

Once upon a time there was a little girl who lived in a world full of people but she felt unnoticed. What the people didn't know was that she had a secret – she could fly. She went flying on the most amazing journeys to a place full of colours and warmth, where the sun shone and people laughed and smiled and everybody had somebody who noticed them.

One day the little girl had been on a very special journey. She tried hard to tell the people she lived with, but everybody was too busy to listen. She stamped up the stairs to her room, sat on her bed and cried. 'Why does no-one listen and not care about my world?' Sobbing quietly she felt a little nudge. There was her favourite lion looking at her who said: 'I will always listen to you – Will you take care of me on your journey?'

The little girl said, 'You really want to go with me?'

'It sounds such a nice place, I would really like to see it. Please take me with you,' said the lion.

A bit scared, the lion asked the little girl to hold his paw as he had never been flying before.

'What,' said the girl, 'you are a lion, but you are not afraid of anything, are you?'

'Everybody is afraid of something; some lions are scared of lots of things,' said the lion. So the little girl took his paw and held it tightly. She was a bit afraid of flying too. So off they flew together to see the little girl's world.

What was in the little girl's world? Only the little girl and the lion know.

Perhaps you would like to imagine what was in the little girl's world? Maybe you would like to ask some of the children you are responsible for to imagine what was in the world?

References

Adams, S. (1996) 'The Meaning of Stories and Metaphors in the Education of Disturbed Children', Unpublished paper.
Balint, E. (1993) *Before I was I*, Free Association.
Dockar-Drysdale, B. (1993) *Therapy and Consultation in Child Care*, Free Association.
Rustin, M. and M. (1987) *Narratives of Love and Loss*, Verso.
Winnicott, D. (1982) *Playing and Reality*, Routledge.

The two novels quoted – *The Little Prince* by Antoine Saint-Exupéry and *The Secret Garden* by Frances Hodgson Burnett – are widely available in libraries and bookshops.

3 Whose feelings am I feeling? Using the concept of projective identification

Robin Shohet

Introduction

> It seems to me that the exit of a belief from the mind is either voluntary or involuntary. Voluntary is the departure of the false belief......, involuntary that of every true belief. (Plato, *Republic*, Book 3, line 412)

It is not our job to argue whether Plato or Melanie Klein gave us the concept of Projective Identification but to emphasise its importance. If we were to draw up the contents of the toolkit required to work with troubled young people then we would have to put understanding high on the list, understanding, that is, of a helpful theoretical framework. Skilled and experienced practitioners can use projective identification to diagnose aspects of the emotional world and to discuss them. We are not proposing deep interpretations, rather an understanding which can inform thinking and practice. If we know what is going on we can also offer some useful advice to our colleagues.

The problem which is not often recognised is that what is going on is some message unconsciously transmitted to us from the unconscious of our client and we are not initially conscious of having received it. Now that sounds tricky and does not usually appear on the list of competencies of a social worker or teacher. Robin Shohet understands this and using carefully chosen case material has provided us with some signposts to insight.

Supervision is vital if we are to be helped to understand how the phenomenon works and how we can use it in our practice. It is vital because it is happening all the time and to begin with we do not recognise it. The process of reflection on our practice in the light of theory is a discipline that must be learned if we are to be successful in helping our young clients.

3 Whose feelings am I feeling? Using the concept of projective identification

Robin Shohet

I remember the first time I ran a training day on projective identification. It was with a group of residential social workers. The term meant little to them, and if it had not been a module on their training course, I doubt whether many of them would have turned up. I noticed myself beginning to feel weary, and feeling frustrated that I was not able to express myself clearly. Had I not been so enthusiastic and wanting to teach what has been one of the most important concepts in my work as a residential social worker and psychotherapist, I could have easily been disheartened. It dawned on me that perhaps this is how they were feeling – tired, frustrated, their enthusiasm dimmed, wanting to give up. Many of them nodded. The concept was in the room in a very real way. I had an inkling of how they felt, because I was beginning to feel it myself.

Definition

The term 'projective identification' may seem quite daunting, but in fact I think we all intuitively have an understanding of the term, although we might not call it that. The simplest way of describing it is that we induce feelings in others that are in ourselves. So, in the above example, the training group were beginning to induce feelings in me that *they* had been feeling. In popular language we have the expression 'he gets under your skin'. We know usually when we are in the presence of someone who intimidates us or makes us feel uneasy. It can sometimes be very helpful to speculate that perhaps it is how they are feeling inside themselves, and they are passing those feelings on to us.

Sandler (1991) defines projective identification as 'Parts of the self are

41

projected onto another, who becomes possessed by, controlled and identified with the projected parts'.

Ogden defines the purpose of projective identification in the following terms:

> The projector has the primarily unconscious fantasy of ridding himself of unwanted aspects of the self, depositing those unwanted parts in another person, with the hope that the other person will be able to process what the projector couldn't for himself. (1982: 11)

It is as if, as recipients, we have been given stage directions as to how to feel, think and sometimes act. The projector does this unconsciously, almost invariably because the feeling they are trying to get rid of is too painful. The job of the recipients is to notice that they are beginning to think, feel, behave or relate in ways they would not consciously intend, and then begin to make sense of what is happening to them in terms of an unconscious communication from the other. The more disturbed the client group, the more likely this form of communication is to happen, because the feelings cannot be communicated explicitly. So, in the above example, it was relatively easy for me to notice what was happening to me, and ask if that was happening to members of the group. Feelings of being overwhelmed, common in residential social work, are not so easy to notice and feed back, because the very intense, often stressful nature of the work makes it harder to make the space for reflection that is vital in identifying projective identification.

In this chapter I will describe two case studies that illustrate the functions that projective identification serves; how to work with it; how it manifests in institutions, and its prevalence in all aspects of our lives. I also link it with countertransference and the importance of supervision and consultancy in being able to work effectively with what is inevitably disturbing material.

Two examples: J. and V.

Recently I was teaching a supervision course, and explaining how we ourselves are a very important resource. The hypothesis I was asking them to consider is that if they feel, say, angry, with someone, then maybe that person is asking them to feel their anger which is too difficult for them to accept. We have all had experience of being with someone who appears quite calm while we get more and more irritated and frustrated. I explained that my world view is that one of the best ways of understanding another is by noticing very carefully the effect s/he has on you. I asked them to entertain the hypothesis that we do to others what has been done to us. So, someone who terrorises others has probably been terrorised themselves, and is unconsciously trying to make others feel what it is like. I asked them to think of someone, past or present, who has frightened them – teachers, parents, colleagues, bosses, clients. I asked them to imagine that this person has been terrified and they are constantly trying to make you feel what they have experienced but cannot allow into consciousness. They are saying 'You feel the terror which once was too much for me to bear.' (Of course they are not saying this consciously.) There is a gasp in the group. A woman is almost in tears. She tells her story. She works with mentally handicapped young adults, one of whom is a 25-year-old woman who terrorises the staff when she gets into a rage. The woman in my group has been bitten and assaulted and had to have time off work which was never explored in the team. The idea that this girl could be terrified has never occurred to her. It makes sense. From seeing her as an unpredictable, moody, aggressive girl she suddenly saw the possibility that she was frightened. Here is her story.

J. came to our unit in 1987 as a 17-year-old with severe mental handicap. Her continued violent outbursts were managed with a helmet with a metal visor – to avoid biting – and boxing gloves to avoid pinching, hair pulling. She sleeps alone in a single room which the staff lock. There has been a reduction in staff on night duty, and few staff will go in alone in case of an outburst, with no back-up staff. J. continues to have outbursts with no apparent reason. These are managed by physical restraint. She is placed in her room for 'time out', and to allow her to cool down. These attacks are traumatic for the staff who are justifiably afraid of her – myself included, although I wouldn't readily admit it. As time passed I have even neglected to see her as a person in her own right.

On hearing about projective identification, a term I had never heard before, and the example of people communicating fear by making others feel it, I suddenly realised that Jean might be afraid of the staff and me. I told Robin, the tutor, a little about her and the more we talked, the more certain I became. She had been abandoned by her parents, put with strangers, locked up in unfamiliar surroundings. If it happened to my 17-year-old son, he would be frightened.

This information both stunned and appalled me. J. is as afraid of us as we are of her. She could only communicate her fears through violence, as she had no appreciable language skills. This realisation brought a heavy heart in me, as I realised that I was part of a regime that had contributed to her unmanageable behaviour. My feelings turned to frustration: what was I to do with this insight? How could I let J. know that she had no need to be afraid of me? Robin asked me what she liked most, and on learning it was having her back rubbed, suggested I did it and talked soothingly to her, telling her not to be afraid, and how this was much better than fighting and so on.

One of the difficulties I had was to communicate my insight and this approach to other seasoned, cynical staff on the unit. Yet whatever they thought, I knew I was committed to a new approach. I started her day gently in tone, routine and approach; in the past this has often been a flashpoint. I stroked and reassured, recognising the likely tension and fear and acknowledging my own. I have been doing this for three months with success. The outbursts have decreased markedly and staffs' attitude is more open. She is more relaxed and open, and when I find out she is tense I take a chance – a leap of faith – and continue to stroke and reassure. I have discovered a profound affection for her and fear that I might become territorial. The staff say 'you have a wonderful way with her, she'll let you do anything for her'. I am still aware of the potential for violence, but even if she were to attack me, I feel our relationship would not be irreparably damaged. My attitude to her now is bigger than the violent expression of fear and frustration, as I can understand that she is expressing herself by making us feel her feelings.

I would like to give another example from a completely different context, that of one-to-one psychotherapy given by a colleague, Jochen Encke (1993). He writes

A woman – I will call her V. – has been in therapy for a number of years. Through all that time the relationship with me was the only relationship she had. For months, while she was unemployed, I was the only contact with the outer world. That is why it was especially distressing to me when I began to hardly be able to stay awake in her sessions. The moment the doorbell rang an overwhelming feeling of tiredness took hold of me and did not lose its grip till the end of the session. I became increasingly desperate, changing the times of her sessions, and drinking strong coffee before she arrived, trying anything to conquer my tiredness. However, the harder I tried, the more tired I seemed to become. I sought help from supervision, worked on my countertransference, especially my fear of being so depended upon. The tiredness remained, increased, became an obsession and physically painful. Images appeared of being tortured by withholding sleep. I literally would have given anything to be allowed to fall asleep. I kept dozing off, only to be woken by V. There were moments when I was so deeply asleep, that it took me a while to recognise where I was. I even started speaking to her in German. We spoke about my tiredness. She shared her feelings about it, her rejection, her parents, yet it grew to such a strength I considered terminating the therapy. Each session became a struggle to survive while my feelings of guilt intensified. Until one session, suddenly and totally unexpectedly, everything changed. What I knew intellectually suddenly sank in: my painful struggle to stay awake was Val's painful struggle to stay in this world. She had always been living in the twilight of day and night, consciousness and unconsciousness, life and death. She could never rest, never give up the fight. I now not only understood intellectually, but felt what she was going through. I actually and physically experienced her pain of living. No interpretation, no supervision should have spared me the experience. It had to be lived through. The moment this had sunk in my tiredness disappeared, and I was able to be with her; I think for the first time in her life she had someone who knew the immense pain she was carrying.

He continues,

> It is a remarkable thing that those clients whose psychological damage is severe and very early, or are going through a phase in which they feel depersonalised, affect us much more and on a much deeper and unconscious level than those who have a stronger ego and are more in control of their lives. Those distressed and depersonalised clients, whose boundaries are weak and for whom a true separateness between persons had not been established, or has temporarily broken down, need the containment of the therapist's ego, and his or her separateness. But this separateness would become the main obstacle to growth if the communication remained purely on the level of interpretation or an empathic listening. I wonder how V. could have communicated her state of mind, her feelings differently. Any verbal clarification, any interpretation would not have helped her (or me). The only way to communicate with me was to make me feel her feelings – only by joining her could I reach her. We therapists need to be pushed from our safe place and spend some time in our clients' world. What they need is more than interpretations. What moves them on is our ability to join them without being overwhelmed, to dive into their world without drowning.

He quotes Field,

> It is not just rage, or loss or frustration that distresses the patient; it is the fact that he feels so utterly alone in it. If we subscribe to the view that to be human is to be related, and without this connection life is felt to be meaningless, then the core of the problem is alienation. For the therapist to enter the state of identification with the patient, to acknowledge it and endure it and yet maintain his own boundaries, is to restore the preexisting, intrinsic, vital connection between one human being and another. (1991: 105)

The purpose of projective identification

At its most basic, projective identification is a form of communication, a means by which the infant can feel understood by making the mother feel what her child is feeling. The infant cannot verbalise feelings so instead must induce those feelings in the mother. The student on my supervision course who wrote about Jean understood this intuitively. She wrote about her young adult communicating feelings because she did not have the words. I think that we are putting bits of ourselves into others much of the time, and if they are well received we feel understood.

As well as a form of communication, I believe there are many other purposes of projective identification. Most obviously it is an attempt to eliminate frightening, bad or unacceptable parts of the self by putting them into someone else. If a group does this, it leads to scapegoating. This is why it is crucial that a group owns that it has displaced onto the scapegoated person. If this does not occur, a new scapegoat will be elected to carry the disavowed feelings when the old one has left. The scapegoating has the attraction of giving the group a sense of power and cohesion, but this will be a very brittle unity if feelings are not integrated.

Some people are more willing recipients than others of projective identification. I think this has its roots in early history. The infant is dependent upon its parents for life support and has no alternatives or options. As a result, the infant feels unsafe to make the parent bad as this would evoke a terror of being separate and/or abandoned. To avoid this the child takes on the parents' pathology as their basic mark. The child feels that unless they take on this pathology, they could cease to exist for the parent.

> In her desperate attempts to deny her perception of separateness, she took the mother's pathology (communicated by means of projective identification) as the basic mark of herself. The anxiety underlying the fiercely stubborn allegiance to the character structures that evolved in this way is the terror of re-experiencing the feeling of being prematurely separate from the mother. (Ogden 1982: 107)

I think this is important in understanding why some defences are particularly difficult to change: they represent a connection with a parent which is too painful to let go.

There is another purpose of projective identification which could be easy to miss: idealisation. I think this is where someone puts their good (as opposed to the usual bad or unacceptable) feelings into the other, almost as it were for safekeeping. On the receiving end we feel special, without realising that this too is a form of projective identification which needs to be understood. This form of projective identification can all too easily happen because people who have been badly damaged might otherwise want to attack their own good qualities.

Finally, we can see projective identification as an attempt to reprocess feelings through the container. This is very relevant for our work, as we are being asked to receive unacceptable feelings, process them and give them back in an acceptable form, rather than reacting defensively. This brings me to the next section – working with projective identification.

Technique

We have seen how difficult it is to be on the receiving end of projective identification. Indeed, that is often its purpose, to make it as difficult for the worker as it is for the client. Little wonder then that we go to great lengths to avoid being recipients of it. In this section I want to look at how we can recognise it and accept it, not defend against it and use it.

One of the advantages of working as an analyst is that there is a very definite framework – when the boundaries of a session are breached (for example, giving extra time, less time, cancellations, interruptions), the analyst can be alerted to the possibility of projective identification. In residential social work there is less of a fixed framework, so that many of the defensive manoeuvres can be missed. However, I can give examples from my own and other's work.

One example of an aberration to the framework is shortening the session. When I was a residential social worker an hour-long weekly counselling session was part of the house programme. This particular resident made out that it was a complete waste of time, and I felt useless, even to the extent of wondering if in her case counselling perhaps wasn't relevant. I suddenly realised that perhaps she did not feel important and was communicating her worthlessness to me. If I allowed her to shorten the sessions I was in fact agreeing with her. I managed to communicate that she was important to me (which was true), and subsequently we had no trouble. Allied to this is terminating therapy or counselling which I was close to doing; changing ways of working; making sessions less frequent on the grounds that this is all the client can manage (that is, all the therapist can manage).

There are many ways in which we can be driven to retaliate unconsciously against the feelings of powerlessness put into us. Offering deep interpretation which a client is not ready for, accidental lateness, breaches of confidentiality, or increasing medication are all possible indications. Getting a patient to stop their behaviour (because it is too much for the therapist) by rewards and punishments is another. The list of feelings is endless – sleepiness, envy, deadness, confusion, feeling overwhelmed, managing a person's life, dread, loneliness. On training courses I really try and encourage people to accept these feelings – to be curious, to say to themselves something like, 'I can hardly stay awake – I wonder what that means' as opposed to 'I can hardly stay awake. Oh my God I'm burnt out.' As soon as one gets into a feeling of I should not be like this, or hating the client for eliciting discomfort, then the focus turns onto one's own self judgement or on protecting oneself, rather than looking at possible projective identification:

> When the patient is feeling hopelessly unlovable and untreatable, the therapist
> must be able to bear the feeling that the therapist and the therapy are worthless
> for this hopeless patient, and yet at the same time not act on the feelings by
> terminating therapy. (Ogden 1982: 30)

In terms of technique, the example of my colleague, Jochen Encke,
demonstrates that you cannot avoid feeling discomfort. The role, as we have
seen is to enter their water but not to be drowned; to absorb, recognise,
digest and eventually give back what has been taken in. The timing has to be
focused on the client and not the therapist, who must show that he or she can
bear the feelings. Most often the awareness that projective identification has
happened is only realised in retrospect, or as in the case of my colleague
known only intellectually. The temptation to defend against uncomfortable
feelings as we have seen is enormous. However, if the therapist cannot
contain, but acts upon, the projective identifications, he or she becomes
dangerous and must be destroyed. It is as if the client's omnipotent fantasies
of being dangerous and destructive, their worst fears, are confirmed.

In one example described by Ogden, a patient had successfully escaped
several times, causing the staff much anxiety. However, though they were
worried that he might commit suicide, the staff were lax in their precautions,
for example, leaving around the key to the locked ward thus demonstrating
their ambivalence: they wanted rid of him as well as being worried for his
safety. They failed to act as a container for the feelings that the patient was
putting into them by wishing to get rid of him, which terrified the patient:

> It is one thing to fantasise control over another Person, and quite another to
> receive confirmation of the fantasy. Once they had acted out their wishes to get rid
> of him they no longer were useful containers for his destructive fantasies.

Grotstein (1986) puts it in another way:

> When the infant has reason to believe that its mother has been transformed by its
> projections, then the maternal object is experienced as having undergone a
> frightening transformation into a victim. Thereafter this object becomes spoiled,
> unclean, profane, unholy, dangerous. It's as if the infant's protests to his mother
> are urgent announcements that it is about to fall prey to some internal predator. A
> mother's failure to hear the cry confirms upon her infant the suspicion that she
> has been spoiled by this fear and has become transformed by it, and therefore is
> not only no longer a useful object but now a dangerous one. Both omnipotence
> and badness are confirmed in a terrifying way.

There are no easy guidelines in terms of techniques. Because projective
identifications are usually only known in retrospect, then one has to be alert

to anything unusual happening both in the therapeutic framework and in oneself. It is important to be able to be honest about how one is feeling. If there is shame or secrecy or a climate of blame in a staff team, then the valuable information contained in the projective identification is lost, as the person is left struggling on their own, or even scapegoated for their feelings. Regular supervision, where the worker feels safe to admit to unusual and chaotic feelings is very important. What can so easily happen is that the supervision session can mirror the dynamics of the worker–client relationship, so that it can be avoided by either or both parties, for very plausible reasons. In other words, the feeling of being too much can be passed up from client to worker to supervisor. If one wants to take on board the idea of working with projective identification, supervision in which it is safe to explore difficult feelings is essential. In the next section I shall be suggesting that the same is true of the organisation, that projective identification operates here, too. A worker or a team within an organisation can easily be made the recipient of projective identification in the same way as a child in a family.

On being the recipient of projective identification, it is important that one has a certain degree of self-knowledge and honesty, and that it is not used as a defence: 'Oh, it is not my anger, I am just picking up from him.' There is always an element of countertransference involved because not everyone has identical reactions to even the most difficult of clients. The capacity to hear the message accurately requires the ability to pay attention to all aspects of one's experience, which includes admitting there are parts of oneself that are similar to the difficult client. As a generalisation, the less we have worked through an issue in ourselves, the less we are comfortable recipients of projective identification. How often we have seen working with clients, that behaviour that will wind up one person will be easily managed by another. The more open the receiver is to accepting the projective identification, the more they are able to absorb it and just sit with it, which may be sufficient. In the case of Jean at the beginning, the understanding was enough to change the relationship. If there is a need to share what has been evoked in the worker, they can do this in a way that the client feels received and understood, not blamed or interpreted. This means that we must constantly be on the look-out for our possible defensive countertransference reactions, or less technically, know our darker self, so that we do not leave that darker self with our clients.

Projective identification in organisations

In the previous section we looked at how feelings can be transmitted from client groups through the staff and into the organisation. It is also possible that the feelings get passed on the other way from the top downwards. Whichever way, one of the main vehicles is projective identification.

As a consultant working with teams, my job is to not personalise any of the dysfunction that is happening in the team or the organisation. This can be very hard when an individual is obviously behaving in a disruptive fashion. The temptation to collude with the team and make this person out to be the problem can be very great. In one team, one person was so obviously resistant – to the group, to me, to being there – that I was finding her presence frustrating, and actually wishing she would not be there so we could get on with the work. Timely supervision reminded me that this person was carrying the resistance for the whole team – chosen because she had a valency to express negativity certainly, but carrying probably more than her fair share. When I fed this back to the team at the next meeting, the difficult person sat up, very interested. From then on, her attitude changed and it was the team that became less cooperative. Even after many years of working, I can still forget the extent to which one person can carry disowned feelings for a group.

I have seen this happen when a team carries something for an organisation. One team I worked with was one of the most disruptive I had ever seen, with people attacking each other viciously. I came home upset after my initial contracting session – far more than if they had attacked me, and resolved not to work with them. This was mirroring their feelings about not be able to work with each other. I had allowed myself to identify with feelings of the team being impossible to work with, and had it not been for supervision, I have to confess that I would have acted out my feelings by abandoning them. My supervisor said 'Human beings do not act like that for no reason. I am sure they don't want to hurt each other, so perhaps they are being hurt in the organisation. My guess is that they are carrying something disowned in the organisation.' I fed this back to them in the next meeting, and it turned out that the counselling team was in fact seen as a waste of time and resources in the Institute. They responded warmly and were able to see how they were acting out what had been put onto them. There was some individual work to do with the team leader and why she was letting it happen to her team, but we bought enough time through the understanding to keep the team together, in fact very successfully.

In *The Unconscious at Work*, the consultant Chris Mawson describes being bitterly attacked – made to feel worse than useless, almost destructive for bringing up things that were quote 'best left alone' or maybe even 'creating things that weren't there'. The impulse to retaliate for these attacks on his consultancy was very strong. It was not until it emerged that the whole team had been criticised recently by management that he could make sense of his feelings, and could help the group understand their own feelings of being attacked and undermined, communicated to him through projective identification. What was particularly interesting in this case was that he was able to identify the feelings of wanting to retaliate or give up from many directions: the team's reaction to management, the parents' feelings of failure around their children in allowing them to be institutionalised, and the children who were making the workers feel like giving up on them as their parents had done. By withstanding the onslaught the consultant showed it was possible to survive, not give up or be provoked into retaliation.

There are various ways one can identify the mechanism of projective identification happening. Supervision for individuals and consultancy for teams, as mentioned, are crucial: knowing patterns of how projective identification works in individuals, teams and organisations helps. A climate where it is safe to admit to disturbing feelings, seeing this as an integral part of the work, is also important and finally, to keep reminding oneself of the primary task. This may seem obvious but it is surprising how often survival needs block out the task of working creatively with the people we are looking after. We often mirror our client group's inability to think clearly because of our distress.

I have mentioned earlier in the chapter that the more disturbed the client group, the more the unconscious communications are likely to predominate. It is here that more time to reflect is vital, but the very nature of the client group often means there is little time to do this, as one is reacting to crises. Burn-out is therefore higher than it needs to be if a good support system were in place. This reinforces the client group's fantasies that have been invoked in the staff, that are not being contained or processed. It is for this reason that agency, team and individual need to commit themselves to putting in place a structure capable of working effectively with projective identification.

Wider applications

What excites me so much about the concept is that it is relevant for all walks of life. For example, couples regularly evoke feelings in each other, in fact often choose each other to be willing recipients of their disowned selves.

Grotstein argues, and I think convincingly, that all forms of manipulation, persuasion, ingratiation and seduction are attempts to control the other with fantasies of entering their body, which is another way of describing projective identification. All forms of image are this to some extent – clothes, cars, homes. One person is trying to make the other feel something about them through the image. Propaganda, advertising, drama, film, and pornography all come into this category. We are being invited to feel in certain ways what the author, producer, playwright, advertiser wants us to feel. In these cases the projective indentification is more deliberate, but is there nonetheless, and explains our strong reactions to certain events.

I would like to end with a quote from Grotstein who writes very movingly.

> All human beings have the need to be ... relieved of the burden of unknown, unknowable figures by being able to express them, literally as well as figuratively into the flesh, so to speak, of the other, so that this other person can know how one felt. We each are projectors and ultimately wish the other to know the experience we cannot communicate or unburden ourselves of until we have been convinced that the other understands. We cannot be convinced they understand until we are convinced that they now contain the experience ... Ultimately, projective identification in its most basic communicative form is the cry of agony of the infant who must put its experience into the caretaking object so that the object can know how the infant feels ... By the same token, parents do likewise with each other and with their children. It is as if all human beings, parents and children alike, are really children who wish someone to know their agony so that the tale can be told. The transmission of this message is projective identification. Existentially it is that state of mind (or mindlessness) in which we conduct most of our lives – for we are all sleepwalkers more than we realise, and, in the act of trying to be our separate individual selves, we forget how much we walk in the shadow or even in the substance of others.

References

Encke, J. (1994) 'Beyond Boundaries', Unpublished paper.
Field, N. (1991) 'Projective Identification, Mechanism or Mystery', *Journal of Analytical Psychology*, 3(6): 93–109.
Grotstein, J. (1986) *Splitting and Projective Identification*, New York: Jason Aronson.
Mawson, C. (1994) 'Containing Anxiety in Work with Damaged Children' in Obholzer, A. and Roberts, V.Z. (eds) (1994) *The Unconscious at Work*, London: Routledge.
Ogden, T. (1982) *Projective Identification and Psychotherapeutic Technique*, New York: Jason Aronson.
Sandler, J. (1991) *Projection, Identification and Projective Identification*, London: Karnack.
Searles H.F. (1979) *Countertransference and Related Subjects*, International Universities Press.

Salzberger Wittenberg I. (1970) *Psychoanalytic Insight and Relationships: a Kleinian Approach*, Routledge.

Yalom I. (1995) 'Interpersonal Learning' and 'The Therapist: transference and transparency' in *The Theory and Practice of Group Psychotherapy*, Basic Books.

4 Exploring the language: a practice-based glossary

Andrew Collie

Introduction

> Words, like ideas, are not merely created – they have a fate: they may fall into
> disuse or lose their currency, giving way to others which are better suited to the
> needs of fresh orientations in research and theory. (Daniel Lagache 1988)

Criticism has often been levelled against the language used by practitioners, who work from a largely psychodynamic perspective. The very word 'psychodynamic' is ugly and although we know it relates to working with an awareness of both conscious and unconscious parts of the personality, it is by no means a commonplace adjective. The Caldecott researchers, breathing their own draught of healthy scepticism about the therapeutic tradition, posed the challenge to explain 'ideas ... advanced in a language which few could understand' (Little 1994). Winnicott, writing in 1952, thought that people should choose 'their own way of presenting what they discover in their own language' (Rodman 1987).

Reflective consideration of case material lies at the heart of our model of learning and so we asked Andrew Collie to consider some of the central features of the psychodynamic framework and to illustrate them not simply by definition in our own language but with a short piece of explanatory case material. For pure definition and description Judith Trowell's summary is excellent (Trowell and Bower 1994) and we could not improve on it. What Andrew Collie has done is to try a more practical, graphically explicit explanation in a child care context in the hope that practitioners who read his glossary will recognise something of their own experience.

4 Exploring the language: a practice-based glossary

Andrew Collie

Acting-out

The teenage girl was unable to express in words the distress and rage she had experienced when her parents abandoned her at the age of eight. She acted out her rage by setting fire to the house while her parents were asleep, almost killing them. After therapeutic help she began to get in touch with the emotional pain of the abandonment, first by further acting out her distress by cutting herself for several months, then by bitter weeping. She was finally able to describe her feelings to the therapist and the acting-out reduced and eventually stopped.

Adaptation

In a therapeutic setting, children and young people with limited personality development may require nurturing experiences from their special person in order to re-start emotional development. A bedtime ritual, special food or drink or some other adaptation of the environment to the child's needs replicates the original maternal adaptation that was lacking in infancy. A twelve-year-old boy needed to have a bedtime story from his caseworker in order to settle, and the other children were able to tolerate this as they sensed his need for this adaptation even though they had to miss out on the staff member's attention. These are the kind of experiences which will meet a young person's primary needs, one of the conditions for good residential care outlined in a number of Dartington papers – see Little 1994.

Ambivalence

The teenage boy had begun to trust his keyworker after months of testing behaviour. He allowed himself to be emotionally vulnerable by telling her that he liked her. Minutes later he was raging at her and demanding a new keyworker. Although this unpredictable behaviour was exhausting, the keyworker was pleased because she knew that he was showing signs of being able to tolerate ambivalent feelings – an emotional step forward from his previous denigration of her. A few months later, the boy was able to begin to talk about how hard it was to have good and bad feelings all at the same time about his keyworker.

Boundaries

Young people coming in to substitute care have chaotic inner worlds. This is partly due to coming from families where rules were non-existent, erratic, or enforced violently. To help young people to bring order to their internal chaos, the external environment is very highly structured. Bedtimes are very precise times, for example. Dinner tables are always laid out in the same way, and meals not served until the tables are ready. New people often find these procedures difficult, and there are constant attempts to subvert them. Older adolescents, who have internalised and valued these social boundaries help younger children to live within these boundaries and so internalise them for themselves as part of the process of ego development. A well-structured 24-hour management programme is a vital aid to good practice in the provision of boundaries. See also Chapter 1.

Collusive anxiety

The teacher in the community home was new to the job, having worked previously in a comprehensive school. He found the aggressiveness of the group of adolescents a little intimidating. One day, he and a residential social worker were taking a group swimming as part of the school activity programme. On the way, the group asked if they could go bowling instead, as this was another sport and therefore an acceptable change. The adults at first said no, but the young people asked again, this time more aggressively. The teacher persuaded himself that they had a point, and agreed to take them to the bowling alley, after conferring with the social worker. In their anxiety, caused by the aggression of the young people, the two adults colluded with them to change the nature of the trip. The trip cost twice as much as it was supposed to, and when the group returned they were very rowdy and disturbed all that evening.

Communication

Following a series of violent incidents the previous evening, the group meeting was a very tense affair. One of the boys who had been involved in the violence refused to talk about it but instead began to flick a cigarette lighter on and off. Another boy began to do the same. At this point one of the younger girls got up and left the group despite staff attempts to persuade her to stay. She said afterwards that the behaviour with the cigarette lighters had terrified her. The group leader correctly interpreted the lighters as threatening behaviour and a symbolic communication about the explosive and inflamed emotional state of the two boys.

Concern

P. was 18 and had been at the Centre for five years. He had a long history of violence, having himself been treated violently by his stepfather. After a long struggle he had begun to keep his anger under control, and was beginning to come to terms with his own vulnerability, which his violence had defended him against. His caseworker had tolerated a great deal of abusive behaviour and their relationship was now more friendly and constructive, but still a little superficial. It was approaching the time for P. to leave, and he was becoming more and more tense. One day he suddenly flew into a rage with his caseworker over a trivial incident and almost assaulted him. In the following group meeting P. talked movingly of his remorse at his actions, and linked his rage to a particular traumatic childhood incident with his father. His concern for the keyworker had been a spur to facing very deep and distressing childhood memories.

Containment

Daily large group meetings of staff and young people are designed to provide a forum for discussing difficult feelings and behaviour so that the rest of the day can proceed with a reasonable degree of stability. On a more symbolic level these groups replicate the mother's containment of the infant's primitive feelings and phantasies – a task which the infant is unable to perform until later stages of emotional development. In one group a very violent 14-year-old boy was refusing to answer questions about an assault on a member of staff the previous evening. He suddenly leapt up and attempted to run out of the group room. He was prevented from doing so by two other boys and an adult. He struggled and swore for a few seconds and then burst into tears. The people who had been restraining him were now holding him gently as he cried. He was able to apologise to the person he had hit, and to say a little about his violent and unhappy upbringing. The containment was both physical and emotional, and enabled him to face painful and frightening feelings.

Countertransference

The staff member, John, was discussing with his casework supervisor a particularly difficult child. He was the caseworker of a 14-year-old girl who had suffered serious sexual abuse. As he described his feelings about the girl, the supervisor noticed that John was leaning forward in his seat and jabbing his finger in the air. His voice sounded harsh and angry. These signals did not match his words. John was describing what a positive relationship he felt he had with the girl, and how he felt that he was really 'getting somewhere' with her. The supervisor found himself feeling quite angry with John, and wondered to himself whether he, John, was experiencing a countertransference. He suggested that John might be quite angry with the girl underneath the positive feelings, and that this anger might be to do with his discomfort at sexual feelings she was arousing in him. John found this hard to hear at first, but gradually realised that in fact she was in control of the relationship, and that he had been feeling flattered that she seemed to like him so much. His unconscious anger arose from feelings of being sexually manipulated by the girl. Having identified these feelings he was able to be aware of the need to keep more of an emotional distance from the girl at this stage in her treatment programme.

Defence mechanisms

John, (in the example above, 'Countertransference') had been unaware of the feelings that were being generated in him in his work with the teenage girl. They were a source of anxiety, and he had avoided them by the defence mechanism of denial (see below). He had split off his angry feelings (another defence mechanism) and projected them into his supervisor. Until the supervisor identified John's defence mechanisms operating, John himself was unable to identify and make sense of the teenage girl's defensive patterns.

Denial

M. was 14, and had been severely physically abused by his drunken father throughout most of his life. He developed a fantasy life based on morbid thoughts and a fascination with death. He used to carve model coffins, and dead animal and bird parts were found in his room. The staff in the children's home told him off for being naughty when these things came to light, but did not think they were very important. One member of staff felt very uncomfortable about M.'s behaviour and disagreed with her colleagues about their refusal to take him seriously enough. Finally it was agreed that M. should see a psychotherapist, who quickly got in touch with the children's home to say that he considered M. to be at serious risk of self-harm. A few weeks later, M. very nearly died from a paracetamol overdose, and was referred for psychiatric in-patient care. The children's home staff were stunned by these events, and felt guilty for failing to recognise the warning signs. Their collective denial of the warning signs (arising from their anxiety at the depth of his disturbance) could have contributed to M. coming to serious harm.

Depression

Following the death of her father, K. began to cut herself with increasing frequency and severity. She had been at the Centre for eight months, and though she had shown signs of depression before, she had not harmed herself in this way. Her depression grew deeper and deeper, until she was finally admitted for psychiatric assessment. She was able to continue at the Centre under psychiatric supervision and on anti-depressants. Slowly K. was able to face the fact that she hated her father for his failure as a parent. She was able to recognise that her depression had been partly to do with guilt about having wished for his death. She was eventually able to mourn his loss and the depression lifted over the following months. Though she remained prone to episodes of depression, she was able to talk these through with her caseworker, and they were never as severe or as prolonged as they had been. Depression in young people very often has the feeling of mourning a loss, rather than a clinical depression. When the depression turns into violent despair, as in K.'s case, then clinical help must be sought.

Depressive position

The staff group of a children's home were facing major changes in their working practices. The group had been split into warring factions for a number of weeks, and there appeared to be no hope of a resolution. Some wanted to adopt a more therapeutic approach to the children. Others were reluctant to give up their more traditional working practices. A consultant was called in to assist the new manager, who had tried to introduce these new practices. The consultant observed that the group seemed quite happy to go on fighting and to blame colleagues when things went wrong. Despite the consultant's intervention the atmosphere of hostility continued and the numbers of children fell as a result of the staff team's preoccupations with its own problems. Eventually the manager had to announce that unless there were dramatic improvements the children's home would have to close for financial reasons. This large and unavoidable reality forced the staff group to face their problems in other ways. The group became thoughtful, sad and aware of how dysfunctional they were. Gradually the group began to think constructively about how to reconcile its differences. Some of the staff members who found this depression too threatening left. The group was eventually able to move on to a more constructive, task-centred way of operating and the home was saved from closure.

Destruction

The adolescent centre had as part of its education service a 'foundation studio' where new arrivals and young people who were at a pre-school phase in their educational development could go during school time. The studio had play materials of all kinds, and a very informal atmosphere. D., a 16-year-old who had suffered systematic physical abuse since infancy from both his parents was a regular attender. At first he would come in and disrupt the activities of others, and sometimes would threaten violence. Gradually he began to get involved in craft activities. His early efforts always followed the same pattern. He would begin to build a balsa wood model in a very absorbed way, refusing all offers of help. At some stage he would become frustrated because it was not working out the way he had thought. He would fly into a rage, smash the model violently, and then start smashing up the studio. Following a restraint and holding by staff he would collapse into a defeated heap. After several months of this the final stage was a collapse into tears as he appeared to mourn for the broken part of himself that had been smashed by his parents.

Ego functioning

Before the weekend trip to the seaside, the senior member of staff on duty would look at the group of children and run an 'ego count'. This was his guess at the group's overall capacity to manage the activity and get back in one piece without some form of breakdown. Depending on whether he thought the ego count was low, medium or high he would allocate staff to the trip. If the ego count was low, he would go himself with an experienced colleague. If the count was medium he would send two experienced staff. If high, he would send an experienced staff member and a newer staff member because he felt that the group could probably manage its self with minimum support from staff. He included staff skill and experience in his ego count.

Emotional deprivation

E.'s mother had been a prostitute and had psychiatric problems. Little was known of his infancy but he first came to the notice of Social Services aged 14 months when he was found wandering the street outside his house. His mother was nowhere to be found and he was taken into care. He was fostered and then adopted by a childless couple, who then had two children after E. E.'s very early emotional deprivation was not significantly ameliorated by the adoption and in his early teens he was a compulsive car thief. By the age of 15, he was stealing cars on a daily basis, and had numerous convictions. On the day that he was released from youth custody he stole three cars and was immediately re-arrested. The compulsive nature of the offending pointed strongly to an explanation in terms of emotional deprivation. E. was constantly attempting to steal the good things he had missed as an infant. Breaking into the locked cars was a symbolic representation of his attempts to get inside his mother and get access to the good things he believed were in there and which had been denied to him.

Empathy

Jane, a member of staff, was very distressed after being assaulted by a teenage boy. She went to see her supervisor who listened attentively to her. The supervisor had similar experiences herself and was able to understand what the staff member must have been feeling. Even though the supervisor said very little, Jane felt that her feelings had been shared and understood. She felt relieved and able to resume her relationship with the boy who had hit her. She was also able to separate her own feelings from those of the boy, and empathise with the distress which lay behind his violent outburst.

Facilitating environment

S. had been abandoned repeatedly when an infant. She was ten years old when referred to the therapeutic community. She very quickly formed a highly dependent relationship with her caseworker as she began the process of repairing the emotional damage which had been done. The caseworker realised that for a time S. would need to take up most of her time and thoughts. It was therapeutically essential that S. was able to feel 'held in mind' by her. The caseworker thought through every minute of S.'s day to ensure that she had the environment she needed. S. was given special foods when she needed it, and her caseworker gave her a soft toy so that in her absence a part of her could be invested in the toy, and S. would not feel alone. The caseworker did not take more than a few days off for a six-month period when S. needed an almost perfect adaptation from the keyworker. When she did take a holiday she sent S. a card every day, and ensured that another member of staff became S.'s special person during her absence. By going to these lengths she tried as much as possible to replicate the facilitating environment which S.'s mother had not been able to provide.

False self

T. had witnessed horrific family violence, including the murder of her mother by her stepfather. Despite these terrible experiences she had been captain of the hockey team and a model student according to her teachers. She was referred for treatment because of her suicidal behaviour, but apart from this she gave neither her school nor her foster parents any other problems. Her therapist found her to be compliant but emotionally flat, and felt that she needed a more intensive form of treatment if she was to be able to progress. The therapist felt that T. had a false-self personality which needed a much more supportive environment if she was to feel safe enough to let it go. She came to the therapeutic community and within six weeks the veneer of compliant shyness had been replaced by manifestations of her underlying terror and rage. She swore, threatened, bullied and demanded impossible levels of care from staff all day and every day. This continued for two years with almost no let-up, except that a very few adults were regarded as trustworthy and therefore free from her attacks. A new member of staff reacted with incredulity when told that T. had once been regarded as a model pupil.

Good enough mothering

In the example of a facilitating environment (see above) the caseworker was providing S. with good enough parenting. Although she could not perfectly replicate the perfectly adapted environment required of the very small infant, she was able to give S. an experience which was good enough to enable her to make emotional progress. Even though S. demanded perfection, and was enraged when perfection was not possible (as many damaged children do), such perfection was neither desirable nor necessary for her emotional development. A degree of tolerable frustration was in fact a necessary part of her development to eventual autonomy, when she had the ego strength to adapt to frustrations and to survive them emotionally.

Greed

There was a weekly group for new people at the Centre. There were four boys and four girls, aged between 13 and 15, with a male and a female member of staff as facilitators. This group was dominated by greedy feelings, which were acted out in a variety of ways. It was traditional in such groups to provide a bowl of sweets on the table for people to take as they arrived. This group was quite unable to manage the sharing of sweets. The boys would rush in, grab the sweets and rush out again, leaving the girls with none. The staff then held onto the sweets and gave them out as people arrived, which enraged two of the boys who tried to snatch the sweets from the facilitator. Eventually there was a grudging acceptance that the sweets had to be shared. Greed also manifested itself by the group preventing any one member having any time to themselves. If anyone tried to say anything constructive, several others would intervene before the staff could respond, thus denying anyone individual staff attention. The level of greed was so great that group members could not tolerate anyone having any attention.

The staff members experienced the group as being murderously greedy, with each group member unconsciously trying to kill off all the rest so that they could have the staff to themselves. After a year, the group functioning had matured somewhat, and it became possible for a limited degree of sharing to take place. The groupwork supervisor had commented that the greed was potentially healthy as it suggested a primitive hope for good things from adults, and the prospect of emotional development.

Integration

S. (see above under 'Good enough mothering') eventually was able to develop a level of social functioning in which she was able to contain many of her chaotic feelings. She was able to develop an interest in horse-riding, and gradually was able to assume enough competence to be able to work for the riding stables on a part-time basis. The fragments of her personality slowly came together as her ego developed and she was able to tolerate frustration and to accept authority. The process was slow and painful, taking several years, but she left treatment successfully and now works in a livery stable where she is successful, settled and well liked.

Identification

Unconscious identifications can be counter-therapeutic, and can affect adults as well as young people. Judy worked for a number of years in a special school as a residential social worker. Her own background, although not as unhappy as those of the children she worked with, was nevertheless less than ideal. Her mother had been somewhat cold and rejecting of her, and her father had been a strict disciplinarian. She had not done well in school, even though she was of above average intelligence. She was keyworker to B., a 15-year-old with learning difficulties and behavioural problems, who had been physically abused by her father. Judy formed an unconscious identification with B., and became determined to try and right the wrongs she felt that B. had suffered. In fact, Judy was unconsciously attempting to right the wrong in her own life, through B., and as a result her professional judgement was seriously impaired. When B. complained to Judy about other members of staff treating her unfairly, Judy believed her without first checking to see if the complaints were true. As a result, Judy became unpopular with many of her colleagues, and was challenged about her over-involvement with B. It was extremely difficult for Judy to acknowledge either to herself or her colleagues that she had blurred appropriate professional boundaries. None of this was helpful to B., who felt that her own needs were being ignored.

Introjection

P. was 15, and had been obliged to look after his depressed mother from an early age. His father was living at home, but contributed little to his wife's care. P. was required to be the devoted carer, which necessitated a denial of his feelings of rage towards his father (for leaving him with so much responsibility), and towards his mother (for being unavailable to him emotionally). P. turned this rage inwards onto the imagined bad part of himself that failed to live up both to his parents' and his own impossibly high expectations. He became increasingly depressed and suicidal, and then became even more depressed at his failure to remain cheerful and positive. When his mother committed suicide, P. attacked his father and became very threatening to teachers at school. He was referred first for psychotherapy and then to a therapeutic community. It was an essential part of his therapy that the staff were able to tolerate months of hostility and abuse from P. as he began to externalise what had previously been an internalised rage. P. had also internalised his damaged and unavailable mother, his weak and absent father, and his parents' impoverished relationship.

Limits

Sometimes the external limits of the therapeutic setting (such as time limits) are not containing enough for those young people who have little or no capacity for separating reality from fantasy. One-to-one psychotherapy will often not work, for example, with an adolescent whose reaction to frustration is to become violent. Stronger limits in a more structured setting will need to be provided. He may receive residential treatment (if he is lucky) or eventual institutional containment in prison or psychiatric hospital if not given appropriate help. A 17-year-old boy, C., was quite unable to contain his delinquent and violent impulses, and the therapeutic community had to impose tighter and tighter limits on his behaviour. One day he and a friend robbed a local pensioner, assaulting him in the process. Both received custodial sentences. Contact with C. was maintained while he was in prison, and he eventually returned to the community. The prison experience had transformed him, confronting his defences with the harsh reality and limits he needed. He was able to resume treatment having internalised the limits prison had imposed. Outer reality had to be extreme to impinge on his powerful anti-social defences.

Merger

A. and F. were 12-year-old boys from similarly deprived backgrounds, who arrived at the Centre at about the same time. They both had a history of burglary and car theft, and found the therapeutic environment threatening to their delinquent identities. They were a delinquent pair, and would go out together in the middle of the night and break into the office or the larder, causing damage and stealing food and money. They behaved as if they were one person, and flew into a rage if they were separated. Separation was in fact the only strategy which worked in controlling this behaviour, and they always made strenuous efforts to reunite as quickly as possible. The staff experienced their pairing as a shared, crazy world-view, in which actions have no consequences. A. was eventually excluded after a further series of criminal acts, many of them with F. F. was deeply shocked and guilty at A.'s expulsion, and became first very angry, and then very depressed. The depression was a much healthier position as he was more in touch with reality. From there he was able to begin to establish a therapeutic relationship with significant adults.

Narcissism

L. was the son of a rock musician and his second wife. They divorced when L. was three, and his father had only intermittent and unreliable contact. His mother was unreliable and frequently left L. with a succession of nannies. L. had almost no sense of other people's needs and was utterly self-absorbed. He was unable to tolerate frustration and was frequently violent when forced to face even simple realities such as doing the washing up, or tidying his bedroom. One day he hit a member of staff, Bill, when he was already on a warning for a previous act of violence, and had a conditional discharge for assault still hanging over him. His caseworker persuaded him that if he apologised to the staff member he might not press charges. The conversation went as follows:

L: 'I've come to apologise for hitting you.'
B: 'I'm still pretty angry with you. How do I know you mean it?'
L: 'Please don't report me to the police. I'm too good looking to go to prison.'
B: 'I thought you might be sorry that you'd hurt me.'
L: 'I don't know what you're talking about. Are you going to let me off, or not?'

L. could only consider the well-being of his narcissistic self, and his overriding need to preserve it from damage. At that stage he had no capacity for empathy at all, and the damage he had done to Bill simply did not register in his consciousness. L.'s infant experience of the absence of the mother led to him turn his longing for relationship inwards.

Object relations

L.'s (see above, 'Narcissism') emotional development was disrupted by early parental failure, and he was developmentally still an infant. He saw himself as the centre of the universe and was unable to see others as separate individuals with their own feelings. He had been unable to develop normal relationships as a result of a failure to develop from a state of primary fusion with his mother, and as a consequence he could not develop normal object relations. His object relations were intra-psychic rather than inter-personal because he had not had a satisfactory external object on which to project his love. L. had to go through a long phase of attacking external objects (other people, or rather his projections onto other people) before he could begin to develop the capacity for mature empathetic relationships.

Oedipus complex and family dynamics

Family dynamics are often replayed in the group living setting – see Chapter 16. Groups offer the opportunity for children and young people to re-experience unsatisfactory family experiences and if they are handled by the adults in an appropriate way, young people can resolve and relinquish stuck patterns of behaviour. Group living often throws up Oedipal behaviour in particularly difficult forms. For example, a residential social worker was keyworker to two adolescents, a boy and a girl, both of whom lived at the children's home.

The boy, W., had been at the children's home for two years and was strongly attached to his keyworker. The girl, M., had been there for only six months, and was very envious of the boy's relationship. She was an adopted child with an elder brother, also adopted. She had been her father's favourite and there had been a great deal of hostility between her and her brother, over whom she had felt triumphant. She had also felt triumphant over her mother, who felt pushed out by her daughter.

This Oedipal family conflict was re-enacted. M. and W. began a sexual relationship, against the rules of the children's home. They were very defiant, particularly against the keyworker, who could see that the relationship was a destructive one. M. and W. mocked the keyworker, who was made to feel excluded. Although W. appeared to be enjoying the power he felt the relationship gave him, he was in fact suffering because he was attacking the keyworker who had been meeting many of his emotional needs. These conflicts in W. expressed themselves in violent outbursts and he eventually hit his keyworker. W. absconded after this incident and refused to return. At an unconscious level he was protecting his keyworker from his violence. M. showed no remorse at W.'s departure, and refused to accept that she had a significant part to play in his going.

Omnipotence

N. was a severely damaged teenager, who had suffered serious neglect and abuse from birth. He could not tolerate frustration and was driven by impulsive behaviour. He came to the therapeutic community as a last resort, having been impossible to contain in a variety of other placements. Although he was 16, he operated emotionally at the level of a very small child. N. liked to play the drums, though he did not have much capacity to learn from experience, and so was not very good at it. He easily became frustrated, and would frequently storm out of the music room in a rage. One morning he came into the group meeting with the pieces of one of the drums, which had been smashed violently. He demanded to know who was responsible, and was clearly very upset that his precious drums had been treated so badly. At first people were very sympathetic, but no one owned up to the damage. One by one each of the other young people accounted for their whereabouts and it became very difficult to understand what could have happened. Finally, another boy who shared a room with N. said that he thought N. had done it himself. N. was furious and attacked the other boy. He had to be restrained by adults. He vehemently denied that he had done it himself, and continued to deny it for the rest of the meeting.

Afterwards the staff reflected that N. had convinced himself, within minutes of destroying the drums, that he had not touched them – a process often called dissociation. His omnipotence was such that he believed that by wishing something was so, it was so. Reality was not external, but an extension of his own inner reality over which he phantasised that he had complete control.

Paranoid

K. could not tolerate frustration of any kind. If a member of staff refused to give him something he wanted, he became furious and would accuse the member of staff of 'torturing' him. The calmer and more reasonably the adult behaved, the more K.'s response was to behave as if the adult was attacking him. This state would frequently escalate, until K. was convinced that he was being physically abused by the adult. He made many allegations against staff members, even though incidents he cited were actually fed by his violence towards his alleged persecutors. K. rarely had these outbursts with more authoritarian male staff members. It was as if the absence of aggression in an adult triggered his paranoia.

Primary provision

Primary provision is a cornerstone of a 'Facilitating environment' (see above). Children and young people in residential therapeutic care who have not had sufficient primary provision to allow satisfactory ego development need a substitute experience from their significant carer and other trusted adults. Experiences which fit the culture of the institution and which replicate or symbolise good maternal nurturing experiences are necessary as the first therapeutic step. For example H., a 14-year-old boy, would frequently have raging temper tantrums in which he would be held by adults until he dissolved into tears. He would then cry to be given a drink. The only drink he wanted was milk, and he would frequently drink two pints in one go and then a third, more slowly. After this he would be calm and was able to function well for the rest of the day. He would only take the milk from his caseworker or the female head of care.

Projection

The P. family were referred for family therapy because A., aged 15, had been stealing from school and getting into fights. The family therapist observed that the family was scapegoating A. and that he was acting out a wider family problem originating from a failure of parental authority. Mr P. was a quiet, rather passive man, whilst Mrs P. was always shouting at the children, especially A. She had asked for A. to be taken into care, and was furious with Social Services because of the family therapy referral. She was convinced that if A. could be 'sorted out' that the family would be all right. During the course of the therapy the family was helped to see that in fact A. was not the problem, rather he was the family member who expressed the family problem. Mr P. was helped to be more assertive and to exercise the authority that the others wanted from him. Mr and Mrs P. were helped to be more open about the problems in their relationship (and so less likely to project them into A.). Mrs P. was helped to be less confrontational in her exercise of authority, a task made easier by her husband's increasing involvement in the upholding of discipline. As the projections were lifted from A., he was no longer compelled to act out the family's problems at school.

Projective identification

See Chapter 3 on this topic.

Reality

One of the therapeutic functions of the group meeting is to provide an environment in which reality can be presented to emotionally damaged young people in a way which they can receive it. Anti-social behaviour must be challenged not only for the preservation of social order and therapeutic values, but also because many young people have not been exposed to a positive external reality which they can internalise. For example, W. had hit another boy the previous evening, and was refusing to apologise or even discuss the event. It was clear that he expected to be punished, and this was his way of delaying and deflecting the harsh criticism he assumed would come his way. In the group meeting his caseworker and the director were gently insistent that he consider the consequences of his actions and that he begin to take some responsibility for his violence. W. was either sullenly silent or abusive, unconsciously trying to bring about the criticism he expected. When the staff avoided this trap, he became increasingly anxious, and attempted to run out of the room. He was stopped and held gently as he struggled to escape, and he finally broke down in tears. He was then able to begin to think about his behaviour and to connect it with his own violent upbringing. W. had tried to deflect reality in the form of the gentle challenges of his caseworker, and when the defences failed he was able to experience and transform some of his own painful inner reality. After this, and other similar experiences, W. was increasingly able to recognise that the rage he was experiencing came from within himself, and not from external sources.

Regression

G. had been adopted aged 16 months from a nursery in eastern Europe. Although her adoptive parents did their best, the early damage to G.'s emotional development had been severe, and she became increasingly difficult as she got older. At the age of 15 she was referred to an adolescent unit. G. at first behaved as if she was a normal 15-year-old, though her lack of emotional warmth and rigid defences suggested that she was operating a false self as a defence against a very distressing inner world. Eventually she became very antisocial and hostile to adults, before finally regressing to a highly dependent state. Her caseworker took the brunt of her dependency, as she became more and more distressed by his absence. Her anger became uncontrollable when she could not get her way. Finally she regressed to a point where she was unable to leave her bed for several days and had to be cared for as if she were a baby. Although it was unclear how much this behaviour was manipulative, it was at least partly an attempt to return to that point in her development where the environment had failed her, in an attempt to overcome the damage of that initial experience.

Reparation

Twelve-year-old A. was angry because he was not allowed to go into town for new shoes. He flew at his caseworker and punched her on the breast. Another member of staff and an older boy held onto him whilst he screamed abuse at her. Afterwards, A. was devastated by what he had done, but was unable to say much in the group meeting. He looked helpless and griefstricken. It was clear that he did not have any means of repairing the damage he had done to his relationship with his caseworker. A. needed help from others to find a means of making reparation. An older girl talked to him about how she had been in his position, and how she did not know how to put things right. She said that her caseworker had forgiven her, and she had not been able to believe that forgiveness was possible. Now she knew that if she hurt someone, she could often make amends by apologising and meaning it. The Director suggested that A. should say sorry to his caseworker even if he was not sure why he was doing it. At first A. refused, but after further persuasion he apologised. His caseworker said that she was still upset, but would talk to A. later when she felt more forgiving. A. started to cry, and his caseworker moved over to him and put her arm around him. He was amazed that he could have such an experience in which a relationship could survive his rage, and that he could contribute to that process.

Repression

S. had repressed her rage at her mother's ill treatment of her, and as a result she appeared to staff as almost too well-behaved. She did everything that was asked of her and was never abusive to adults. The other children could not stand her. She was always winding them up in some way, and she was bullied continuously. After she had been at the children's home for some months the façade began to crack, as the upward pressure of her repressed fury was slowly forcing its way past her defences. Unconsciously, she was aware that it was safe to begin to reveal some of her hidden anger and she became increasingly abusive and had temper tantrums more and more readily. Several members of staff commented that it was as if someone had taken the lid off a pressure cooker. When visitors came and S. was asked to show them round (something she loved to do), she was again able to repress her anger and appear as a polite, well-behaved teenager.

Separating out

S. had formed a very dependent relationship with her keyworker, M., after many months of testing behaviour. She went through a phase of being unable to tolerate her keyworker's absence for more than a few minutes, and was very difficult to manage when M. was off duty. 'When you're away, she just falls apart' was a frequent comment to M. from her colleagues. M. needed a great deal of support during this phase, as S.'s demands were incessant and seemingly endless. It helped her to understand that S. was creating an experience of primary dependency as part of a process of ego development. After a year of this intense dependency, S. began to develop a sense that she could survive M.'s absence provided the duration was less than a few days. Several months later, she was able for the first time to tolerate (with help) M. taking a two-week holiday. By this stage the process of separating out was well advanced as S.'s sense of self was now quite strong.

Splitting

An internal case conference on V. began with the staff team describing how he made each of them feel. The male members of staff gave a generally favourable impression of him, describing their reactions as warm or neutral. The women, on the other hand, had very strong reactions, some saying they loathed him, or feared him or both. Others said they felt very maternal towards him, or they found him endearing and felt protective of him. The dramatic contrast within the female staff group, and between the sexes, provided a great deal of information about V.'s internal objects. He had split the women into representations of his idealised and denigrated maternal objects and then evoked corresponding feelings in them. Some staff members became aware of colluding with the positive aspects of the split. Those receiving the negative aspects were able to be more careful not to respond to him in hostile ways. The staff were better able to avoid their own splitting mechanisms.

Subculture

It is almost inevitable in group living environments that a group of young people will develop a set of values in opposition to those of the staff team and older adolescents. The expectation that adults will fail them is a strong motivating factor in young people attempting to develop their own solutions to unmet emotional needs. Subcultures are characterised by searches for excitement – usually delinquent excitement – as a substitute for care and concern from adults whom they do not fully trust. The subculture is by definition counter-therapeutic and must be addressed if it is not to undermine therapeutic goals. Attempts to suppress subcultural activities (by rigid enforcement of rules, backed up with punitive responses to rule breaking) will only drive the subculture further underground. A more useful approach is to work with the subculture, for example, by offering more productive alternatives to delinquent excitement. Outward Bound activities, enjoyable games, recreational and creative activities and other strategies will not eliminate delinquent behaviour but will reduce it, provided it takes place as part of an ethos that responds to young people's emotional needs.

Sublimation

Outward Bound and other activities are familiar to residential social workers as means of diverting young people's attention away from less socially acceptable forms of discharge of energy. A group of 14- and 15-year-old boys were becoming increasingly delinquent. They were enjoying the thrill of shoplifting and illicit drinking at night. Their behaviour was deteriorating, and so it was agreed that they needed some alternative excitement which did not lead them into trouble. The ringleader, P., liked fishing but had never been sea fishing before. A trip was arranged, and all five members of the group were keen to go. They all caught several large fish, and had a really good day. The members of staff who took them discovered that *they* had become honorary gang leaders who were allowed to lead them into sublimatory activity. The fishing trips quickly became more attractive than stealing, and when a trip was cancelled because one of the boys had been caught stealing from the office, he was condemned most loudly by the other group members.

Superego

When a 15-year-old boy was accused by a 13-year-old girl of raping her, the other young people in the therapeutic community were outraged, and went in search of the boy to beat him up. They became like a lynching party, and were willing to mete out very harsh punishment for a crime that had not been proved to have taken place. The staff managed to contain the group but only just. The girl subsequently admitted that she had made the accusation up. When the situation was discussed in a staff meeting, the staff realised that the harsh superegos of the young people had come together in group outrage. When young people had been included in discussions about how to deal with anti-social behaviour by their peers, they were always far more punitive in their attitudes than the staff.

Suppression

A community meeting was called after a member of staff had been hit by one of the boys. She was very upset and shocked by the attack, but was determined to be in the meeting to confront the boy in a responsible way. With a great effort she managed to suppress her feelings of distress sufficiently to come into the meeting in a reasonable composed state. She was able to be very effective in the meeting, and after it was over she went to the staff room and immediately burst into tears.

Symbolic communication

A boy who had recently arrived at the therapeutic community had suffered three close bereavements in the last year. Outwardly he seemed in control of himself though he was somewhat aggressive, and kept people at a distance. He liked going to the woodwork room, and was one day discovered to be making a model coffin, which he showed to the woodwork teacher. The teacher quickly realised that this was a symbolic communication, and asked the boy if he still thought about his friend who had died. The boy looked sad for a moment, and then became very angry, smashing the coffin violently. He started to cry, and talked about how close he had been to his friend, and how he blamed himself (quite unreasonably) for his death. The woodwork teacher reported this to the staff team and it was agreed that the coffin-making was a worrying communication about the boy's suicidal feelings.

Transference

A 12-year-old boy had suffered serious physical and sexual abuse from his father over a number of years. The boy had transferred his feelings of fear and anger about his father onto his male caseworker. He was always angry with the caseworker for one thing or another, and the caseworker was at his wit's end. Whatever he did was experienced by the boy as rubbish. The caseworker increasingly felt that he was not good enough, useless, and that he would never be able to get it right. His interactions with the boy always included a high level of verbal abuse from the boy which left the caseworker shaken and despairing. With good supervision, the caseworker was helped to understand these feelings as communications from the boy's unconscious about how he had been made to feel by his own father. The split-off and denied parts of his experience were being transferred into the caseworker as part of the therapeutic relationship. He had become the container for these unbearable feelings, allowing the boy some respite from them and offering the possibility of a future recovery.

Transitional object

It is a sign of emotional progress when a child accepts a special, personal ever-present object because it means he is moving from a state of primary dependency on his caseworker. In one centre a visitor was shown round a house in which most of the children were at this stage. The visitor did not talk directly to a single child during the hour he was there. Rather he had a variety of interesting conversations with toy hippos, teddy bears and rag dolls who spoke on behalf of their owners. The visitor was not clear if this phenomenon was because he was a stranger, or because this was the normal mode of communication for children at the point of separation.

References

Lagache, D. (1988) 'Introduction', in Laplanche, J. and Pontalis, J.-B., *The Language of Psychoanalysis*, Karnac.
Little, M. (1994) *A Life Without Problems?*, Arena.
Rodman, E.R. (1987) *The Spontaneous Gesture*, Harvard University Press.
Trowell, J. and Bower, M. (eds) (1995) *The Emotional Needs of Young Children and their Families*, Routledge.

Bibliography

Bateman, A. and Holmes, J. (1995) ' Introduction: history and controversy', 'Models of the Mind' and 'Origins of the Internal World', in *Introduction to Psychoanalysis*, Routledge.

Copley, B. and Forryan, B. (1987) 'Inner world, phantasy and primitive communication', in *Therapeutic Work with Children and Young People*, Robert Royce.

Trowell, J. (1995) 'Key Psychoanalytic concepts' in, Trowell, J. and Bower, M. *The Emotional Needs of Young Children and their Families*, Routledge.

Further reading

Alvarez, A. (1992) 'Making the Thought Thinkable: perspective on introjection and projection', in *Live Company: psychoanalytic psychotherapy with Autistic, Borderline, Deprived and Abused Children*, Routledge.

Dockar-Drysdale, B. (1990) 'Reality', in *The Provision of Primary Experience*, Free Association Books.

Gomez, L. (1997) *An Introduction to Object Relations*, Free Association Books.

Greenhalgh, P. (1994) *Emotional Growth and Learning*, Routledge.

Hinshelwood R.D. (1987) 'Raw experience' and 'The Individual's own community' in *What Happens in Groups*, Free Association Books.

Menzies-Lyth, I. (1987) 'Bion's contribution to thinking. about groups', in *The Dynamics of the Social*, Free Association Books.

Salzberger-Wittenberg, I. (1973) *Psycho-Analytic Insight into Relationships. A Kleinian Approach*, Routledge.

Sayers, J. (1991) *Mothering Psychoanalysis*, Penguin.

Segal, H. (1988) *Introduction to the Work of Melanie Klein*, Karnac Books.

Winnicott, D.W. (1990) *The Maturational Processes and the Facilitating Environment*, Karnac Maresfield Library.

Defence mechanisms

Bateman, A. and Holmes, J. (1995) 'Models of the Mind' and 'Mechanisms of Defence', in *Introduction to Psychoanalysis Part 1*, Routledge.

Salzberger-Wittenberg, I. (1972) 'Conflict, Anxieties and Defences', in *Psycho-analytic Insight and Relationships: a Kleinian Approach*, Routledge.

Further reading

Boucher, J. (1996) 'The inner life of children with Autistic difficulties', in *The Inner Life of Children with Special Needs*, Whurr Publishers.

Copley, B. and Forryan, B. (1987) 'The individual and the institution' and 'Development in the inner world', in *Therapeutic Work with Children and Young People*, Robert Royce.

Greenhalgh P. (1994) 'Enemies of emotional growth and learning', 'Strengthening the personality', 'Working with the group dimension' and 'Managing the organisation', in *Emotional Growth and Learning*, Routledge.

Menzies-Lyth, I. (1988) 'The Functioning of Social Systems as a defence against anxiety', 'Staff support systems task and anti-task in adolescent institutions', and

'The Development of the self in children in institutions', in *Containing Anxiety in Institutions*, Free Association Books.

Morris, A. (1996) 'The Art of Communicating with Secretive Children', in *The Inner Life of Children with Special Needs*, Whurr Publishers.

Sinason V. (1992) 'The Sense in Stupidity', 'Primary and Secondary Handicap: Steven', and 'The Handicapped Smile: Ali's defence against trauma', in *Mental Handicap and the Human Condition*, Free Association Books.

5 Support and supervision

David Challender

Introduction

> The conflict between care and control is endemic to organisational life, and particularly the organisational life of agencies that exist to serve people in trouble. Managers need to balance the two, particularly in supervising the work staff do with their clients. Supervision can and should be a major source of support and learning. It is also an essential mechanism for monitoring the quality of a service. (C. Clulow in *The Unconscious at Work* (Obholzer and Roberts 1996))

Here we pose a serious challenge to both management and staff in children's facilities. We have become aware that the problems of supervision – irregular, poor quality – highlighted in reports to the Government following scandals in child care have not gone away. Practice which is unsupervised is private practice and that is absolutely unacceptable. The old chestnuts keep cropping up, such as 'we are short-staffed and there is no time for it'. We would say that this is when you need supervision most – when the stress levels are rising – and when support from supervision can make a real difference, for example, keeping a staff team together rather than watch them fade away in disillusion.

We challenge management to provide, regular, supportive supervision for all staff and this is particularly important for those on training programmes. Without it much learning is wasted. At a professional level, staff require help and advice in putting what they learn into practice, reflecting on their outcomes; more practically, they will need help in the vital task of completing assignments for assessment.

Too often the supervisor is seen as the guilty party when a supervisee complains about their supervision. In this situation there are two sides with equal responsibilities. There must be a detailed supervision contract coupled to a mutual determination to make it work. We would recommend Chapter 3 in Hawkins and Shohet (1984) where they consider the role of the supervisee and emphasise its importance.

David Challender knows this aspect of work with young people well and he uses his experience of supervising and supporting staff teams and individuals to outline a model of good practice.

5 Support and supervision

David Challender

The title of this book *Loving, Hating and Survival,* is taken from Donald Winnicott's 1970 David Wills Lecture, and powerfully conveys the noble struggle which workers in substitute care engage in when they grapple with the often potentially overwhelming needs of troubled children and young people. Survival is indeed the key word and a great many workers in this field have drawn strength and comfort from this insight which Winnicott arrived at during his own outstanding clinical work with literally thousands of children. Working with children who have experienced trauma, deprivation and environmental failure is an extremely demanding occupation which will threaten the emotional stability and resilience of even the most mature and well-integrated adults. It is not possible to undertake such a task without adequate attention to the needs of the worker and this chapter will explore some of the important issues associated with support and supervision. First, consideration will be given to underlying motivation in this field of work. Secondly, the nature of stress inherent in working with children will be explored. Thirdly, the support and supervision needs of the worker are investigated with an emphasis on the importance of helping the worker to bring to awareness some of the unconscious processes that arise in the task of helping troubled children.

Motivation of the worker

Many workers in this field begin their involvement in caring for children at quite a young age. Nannies have often sought their first positions in families on leaving school themselves and 21-year-old young adults seek work with children as a prelude to entering into the caring professions. Many of these

81

recruits have barely emerged from their own adolescence and certainly in the ordinary course of events would not necessarily be psychologically ready to have their own children. What, then, motivates them to engage in such demanding work at such a young age? If asked this question at interview many reply that they have always wanted to work with people. Others say that they have always loved being with children and now wish to make a career of it. Only a minority appear to look deeper at what is urging them to select this particular path as opposed to all the other avenues that may be open to them. Psychodynamic theory indicates that there are very good reasons why someone makes a career choice and this is likely to be highly significant in the arena of looking after and trying to repair the damage sustained by troubled children. Most workers have a long and often painful personal journey in recognising some of these more unconscious motivations. Many will undertake personal therapy or counselling which will contribute to the process of uncovering these underlying processes. It is beneficial for the worker to have to consider this early on in their work and to be able to apply theory to themselves as well as to the children and young persons in their care.

Exercise 5.1 Reflecting on personal motivation

Consider the following questions:

- What reasons do I tend to give in interviews or applications for wanting to work with children or adolescents?
- If I gave up working with children what other type of work would I choose?
- Do I view this work as just a job or as a vocation or way of life?
- Which aspects of my work are most satisfying to me?
- What aspects of my own childhood experience connect most frequently with issues arising in work with children?
- Am I prepared to explore my own needs to make restitution for early destructive fantasies, or my need to resolve some of my own conflicts through involvement with those of others? (These are examples of some of the possible deeper aspects of motivation I need to consider.)

There is an obvious parallel in the work engaged in by child care workers and their own early-life experiences of caretakers. In other words there is likely to be a re-enactment or a resurrection of this formative period in the worker's own personal development. Psychoanalytic theory, especially the object relations school, has formulated useful concepts to illuminate the early interactions between caretaker and infant. The infant initially splits good and bad aspects of the mother (or caretaker) and will love the good, and hate and attack the bad. Later comes the realisation that Mother is but one person for whom both love and hate can be experienced. This advance brings with it the possibility of guilt and remorse for the damage done through greed and aggression and thereby arises the wish to pursue reparation and to express gratitude for being given good care. In favourable conditions the infant comes to trust that love predominates over hate and that their attempts at reparation have been successful. For the worker who is carrying out reparative activities with children, there is every chance that there will be a personal reworking of early-life experiences that are still being dealt with (or not) at an unconscious level. Another important feature of what is going on for the worker is that they are using their own self as the main means of benefiting the child in their care. By choosing to make this very personal investment of themselves in the well-being of children the worker unconsciously hopes to demonstrate that they have enough internal goodness or worth to repair the damage sustained by the child. It is obvious that in this situation success will be deeply rewarding and failure will bring with it considerable anxiety and personal stress. Thus, for many if not most child care workers, the outcome of their work is crucial to their own sense of well-being and yet they work in a field where signs of success can be very elusive.

There is obviously a variety of motivations for entering the field of child care. Unfortunately, it has become all too obvious in recent years that for some it is connected with paedophilic orientation and a deliberate seeking-out of situations where close contact with children is required. All the more reason, therefore, that there should be well-informed management of child care agencies and closer and more effective selection and supervision of staff. Finkelhor has argued in his Four Preconditions Model (Finkelhor 1986) that a key precondition for abuse of children is 'emotional congruence' with them. This emotional fit may be present in many workers in the field and does not mean they will abuse unless they go on to override what Finkelhor calls internal and external inhibitors. All workers with children need to be able to consider themselves in this respect in terms of their own potential to abuse rather than projecting this practice on a few so-called 'evil perverts'.

Fortunately, workers in child care are for the most part dedicated and committed persons who have a very genuine concern and are keen to use themselves and their personal resources to benefit the children in their care. Idealism coupled with dedication and concern are positive motivating forces which sustain workers in very stressful circumstances and over long periods of time (Vander Ven 1979). It is, however, this very idealism which, in effect, is a two-edged sword and can contribute to a negative outcome for the worker. This is usually referred to as the 'self-assigned impossible task' (Roberts 1994) and, for example, could take the form of attempting to give children the ideal parenting they have never had. Such an idealistic task is further promoted by the keyworking system that is common in child care settings and through which workers may find themselves in a situation where they are over-identifying with the children they are paid to care for.

Clearly, the danger inherent in this impossible task mechanism is that workers who may not be clear of the way in which their own unmet needs are influencing their motivation for close contact with children in their care unwittingly set themselves up for disappointment and frustration when the hoped-for progress does not materialise. Having taken on an impossible task and failed, there is then every possibility that the workers will project failure onto the agency and blame lack of resources and insufficient staffing. It is important, too, to be aware that this does not just operate at the level of the individual worker but that there is also a group dynamic dimension. After all, child care settings will tend to attract staff with similar internal needs. There will also be a certain fit between the staff in terms of their defence mechanisms, a tendency which Bion (1961) termed 'valency', and which has been helpfully elaborated by Hinshelwood (1987). Thus collective defences arise among the workers directed against the anxieties stirred up by the day-to-day work with the children and unless understood and worked with these processes will form a considerable obstacle to productive work. It is vital for staff to have access to support and to consultancy to assist them in gaining awareness and understanding these processes.

Stress and the worker

Traditionally, child care workers have worked long hours and been poorly paid. Furthermore, they have entered their work with little in the way of training and qualifications or opportunities to acquire them. Yet even in settings where this is less true the work remains essentially stressful and demanding because of the very nature of the commitment given to children who are in considerable emotional pain. It is common for workers to feel drained and exhausted and to feel despairing about bringing about a worthwhile difference in the children's lives. Not surprisingly there is often a high turnover rate in staff in agencies working with children and this can further add to despondency among the staff who remain. There is also the 'burnout syndrome' (Maslach 1976) which is not uncommon among workers in settings where there is intense interpersonal involvement and not least involvement with children. It has to be remembered, however, that not all dedicated workers in child care become burnt out and that individuals experience stress in their own way. Part of the process of becoming an effective worker with children is to acquire more awareness of the nature of stress as it affects any particular individual and to adopt strategies to deal with it.

Exercise 5.2 Identifying personal stress in work with children

- How often am I taking home worries about work?
- Do I become ill on my leave days?
- Am I constantly fatigued?
- Do I have frequent headaches, tension in my neck or other physical signs of stress?
- Do I have a life outside work which is equally, if not more, sustaining to me?
- Am I regularly looking at my work and personal reactions in supervision?

Frequently, stress is also related to the agency setting where the worker is located. Often this will be a closed system with a tradition of doing things in a certain way and where there is a strong investment in maintaining the status quo. If the agency is administered by a cumbersome bureaucracy there may be little flexibility in the system and a potential for rigid responses to individual needs and circumstances. Regrettably these factors often result in processes which disadvantage well-motivated workers and effectively diminish the support and supervision provision which is vital in such demanding work.

Exercise 5.3 Checklist of agency as a system

- In my agency is there a clear view of the primary task?
- Is the authority structure clear?
- How far can I participate in and contribute to the agency and its development?
- Is there a child-centred approach at the core?
- Are staff valued and clearly contracted?

Morale and job satisfaction are important considerations for child care agencies just as they are for any work setting. They will tend to decline from the top downwards in an agency hierarchy and child care workers will vary in relation to their perceived ability to have an influence on decisions affecting their work with the children in their care. Where the worker is poorly remunerated and given little value or regarded as dispensable and easily replaced there is very little scope for job satisfaction other than the dedication to children which may hold the worker in what is otherwise an unsatisfactory employment contract. This undesirable situation is compounded when there is an increasing expectation of the central role of the child care worker to deliver quality care for children but when also there is no extra provision for training and career development. Job performance has interesting linkages to job satisfaction and job stress but this has not been clearly understood in relation to working with children and more research and awareness are indicated (Challender 1986).

Support for child care workers

It is difficult to underestimate the stresses and strains on the worker who engages in the demanding occupation of helping deeply troubled children. On first entering the work someone may see themselves as concerned and helpful and offering a service that their clients and possibly society will value. Most workers will experience friends, relatives and acquaintances who will assure them that they could not possibly contemplate the work for themselves usually because they would get too emotionally involved. What many workers are not prepared for are confrontations with aggressive young people and prolonged contact with messy and demanding children and often ungrateful families. Their idealised view of care work is soon exploded as a myth. Each worker has to endure a difficult and testing time before beginning to integrate their idealistic view with everyday realities. There are frequent attacks on the worker's self-esteem with consequent threats to the worker's perception of his or her helping ability. In favourable conditions there may be some very sustaining experiences which confirm the worker's desire to be in child care work. However, it is quite common for such experiences to be inconsistent and to happen apparently randomly. If workers move on to another job fairly quickly they do not see much changing in the children they have tried so hard to help. For these reasons job satisfaction in this type of work is elusive (Van Eck 1990). Clearly, child care workers will need considerable support in performing their demanding and often unrewarding work.

One useful principle for child care agencies to follow is the rather obvious but often neglected one of maintaining a balance between meeting the needs of the clients and those of the staff (Hood 1985). This approach implies placing a high priority on offering support to workers and taking cognisance of their needs in relation to the stressful nature of the work. The following model of support is recommended as good practice.

Exercise 5.4 Checklist for a good practice model of support

Support objectives:

- facilitating understanding of the task
- maintaining focus on the task
- mitigating stress
- finding solutions to problems encountered in everyday living
- assisting professional development.

Support provision:

- effective management
- good and regular supervision
- administrative support
- consultant support
- membership of professional groups and associations.

Workers joining residential and intensive child care facilities will need support from the time of recruitment through induction and on throughout their ongoing commitment to the children in their care. Providing access to appropriate training opportunities is crucial to enable individuals to gain the necessary understanding to be able to fulfil their task. Many new recruits are quite surprised to discover that ordinary common-sense responses to children and young people are not effective and they can become rapidly de-skilled and discouraged in their first few months of work when children are testing them out to see if they will survive. Workers in this phase of development are vulnerable and it is important early on to develop support systems for them that facilitate individual development and initiative. They will need some degree of protection in their role and safety in what they undertake but with scope for progressively taking on more and learning from experience.

> **Exercise 5.5 Checking my support system:**
>
> - Am I clear what my support needs are?
> - Do I have access to a staff support group?
> - Do I seek out support or do I try to be all competent?
> - Which consultants do I have access to?
> - What can I do to ensure I get adequate support?

Team work and team support

One of the key aspects of support for child care workers is that which is supplied by colleagues. Many workers will also have been drawn to the work through a desire to be a member of a closely-knit team. Teamwork that is well-managed and maintained will offer a great deal of reward and job satisfaction to hard-pressed workers and, of course, helps individuals to keep a sense of perspective within the intensity of the attachments which children form with them. In many residential settings, especially where milieu therapy is used, the way in which the team works together to provide high-quality care and treatment is a crucial factor in determining the outcome for the children and young people who are in residence. High staff turnover is often related to the inability of staff belonging to teams to resolve interpersonal conflicts and disputes. Within caring organisations where the work is emotionally demanding and stressful there is likely to be the development of institutionalised social defence systems (Menzies 1970) which on the one hand may defend a worker from the painful nature of their work but will also on the other hand inhibit the good functioning of the team and the interactions with the children. Such mechanisms point to the necessity for well-functioning teams to work at their own group processes and to do so with external facilitation. As Collins and Bruce (1984) argue:

> As most new staff are presumably well motivated to become included in their new work group, and because they will possess a natural desire to be recognised for the personal and professional levels of expertise they are bringing to the group, the climate of the residential team, in both structural and psychological terms, needs to be constantly monitored by the members themselves as well as outside consultants so that the most beneficial learning atmosphere for residential staff can be developed.

It is, in fact, crucial for teams in these settings to seek external facilitation in working on team maintenance and to work regularly on the interpersonal issues and group dynamics which are an inevitable accompaniment to residential work. Nor is this exclusive to the residential situation since professional networks involving, for example, foster parents and social workers will need to provide for awareness of the quality of their communication and interactions around children.

Exercise 5.6 Characteristics of a well-functioning team

- Clear objectives accepted by all members.
- Acknowledge each member's particular skills.
- Systems to facilitate effective communication.
- A shared belief and value system.
- Good and appropriate leadership along with an appropriate mix of individuals to assume other roles in the team.
- An effective regulator or gatekeeper between the team and wider organisation.
- Recognition and facilitation of transitions when members join or leave.

One important feature of the functioning of teams that merits further mention is their capacity for innovation and proactive work. It is crucial that a team can accept and welcome new ideas both from established staff and from newer members. In fact, this is just the area that commonly leads to difficulty in child care agencies. Innovation can be a powerful source of anxiety amongst established workers since, after all, they have already created their own frame of reference for task performance based upon their understanding of and contribution to the status quo. This well-known mechanism has been very clearly elucidated by Menzies (1970) and by Jaques (1955). Part of the reason for working in teams is to contain work-related anxiety (Hobbs 1973) and so it follows that teams will function more effectively in relation to their task if anxiety is reduced through the provision of adequate support. There are fine balances involved in these team processes if the team is to handle anxiety effectively and be proactive in pursuing its objectives. New recruits have to learn to accommodate to some consistency within the team and they have to learn how to implement the policies and intervention methods as well as the philosophies of the children's facilities they are joining. Part of the balancing act that needs to go on, however, is to ensure that this induction process for new staff does not relate to an inflexible pattern that inhibits the creativity and effectiveness of the team's work with children. The need to monitor and evaluate treatment programmes in residential facilities is vital and is dealt with in Chapter 7 of this book. It is hardly surprising that residential workers join together to work through the medium of teams. Douglas (1978) has described teams as human groups that acknowledge membership and the clear value and the necessity of shared experience and cooperation. These features are highly consonant with the overall task of creating a meaningful social setting in which to help deeply troubled children who have previously experienced families which are often abusive, neglectful or fractured. If such teams are to remain cohesive and creative and deliver effective treatment programmes to highly needy and damaged children then they will need support and maintenance on a regular basis. Furthermore, the members of the team will need access to good-quality supervision which enables them to understand clearly the nature of the processes in which they are involved and it is to this vital area that we now turn.

Supervision

In contrast to behavioural approaches to treatment the psychodynamic model takes into account the inner world of the child and the operation of unconscious mechanisms both in the child and in those working with the child. This accounts for the emphasis placed on regular process-oriented supervision in agencies using this model. Without such supervision it is most likely that child care workers will become caught up in difficult feelings and be uncertain of their origin. Only through reflection in supervision are workers likely to process for themselves their often complicated feelings arising through the operation of projective identification. Working therapeutically with children and young people is a difficult and demanding process and requires the ability of the worker to apply thinking in a creative way to what is being expressed through the child's actions and feelings both owned and not owned by the child. This in turn depends on a readiness by the worker to look at him or herself in regard to actions and feelings. The challenge inherent in this process has been clearly stated in an important paper on residential treatment:

> The essence of the residential treatment process is that as each child projects his inner world against the macrocosm of the residence by and large the staff will find within itself the strength to resist stepping into the projected transference roles. For clearly, to the extent that the child succeeds in evoking from the resident or hospital staff the response which he evoked within his own family, the treatment will founder ... the greater the child's disturbance, the more difficult it becomes to restrain the push of counter-fantasies and counter-behaviour and to resist entanglements. (Ekstein et al. 1959)

This last concept of entanglement is very expressive of what may develop and it is, of course, just as likely to happen to professional foster parents and others working closely with children. Through engaging in effective and regular supervision, workers can be enabled to disentangle their own reactions and feelings from those of the child. Such provision for workers is absolutely essential for those who are endeavouring to work with the psychodynamic model and who seek to establish effective therapeutic work with children. In spite of this clear requirement it is all too often the worker who has to initiate supervision sessions (Nelson 1978). There may also be collusion between supervisor and worker in avoidance of supervision sessions. Both parties may feel they have reasons to avoid the situation. Supervisors, for example, may experience the 'Emperor's new clothes' phenomenon whereby they fear their ignorance is being revealed in supervision with less experienced colleagues.

Supervision is often thought of as a three-way process which involves the child, the supervisee and the supervisor. When this triangular situation works well the worker is enabled to stand back and to decode communications occurring within the supervision and, thereby, to offset the tendency to replicate their clients' enactments rather than processing them. It helps to bring a fourth dimension into supervision and that is the agency, or work context, within which it is situated. In good conditions, supervision will permit the unravelling of the transactions with the children and with the agency and provide a major source of support and learning. In this respect supervision is inextricably linked to the worker's capacity to fulfil their task and also to the quality of the care and therapy provided to the child.

Supervision within the sphere of social work has been conceived of as having three major functions (Kadushin cited in Hawkins and Shohet 1989) and these are as follows.

1) Educative – This is also called formative and is mainly concerned with the development of the worker's skills, understanding and abilities.
2) Supportive – In this aspect of supervision the worker is enabled to reflect on his or her own reactions to the distressing and painful emotions and processes which are involved in working with children and young people.
3) Managerial – All workers, but especially those who are lacking training or experience, will need supervision in the sense of someone more qualified and experienced looking at their work and helping to ensure that good standards are maintained and that ethical codes are observed.

It is good practice for supervisors and workers to enter into supervision contracts whereby both parties are quite clear about the frequency of supervision sessions and the boundaries of confidentiality. Naturally, workers will not expose their own vulnerabilities and anxieties if they are not guaranteed a safe confidential setting for supervision. Contracts can also helpfully specify what educative, supportive and managerial functions the supervisor is holding. Child care workers who are engaged in demanding therapeutic work with very troubled children have every right to expect good-quality, reliable and confidential supervision from an experienced supervisor. In fact, this is a minimum requirement for embarking on this kind of specialised work. For those working with the psychodynamic model, supervision provides an essential and invaluable resource for exploring and understanding transference and countertransference issues that will be present in therapeutic work with children and adolescents. A process model of supervision (Hawkins and Shohet 1989) is well suited to this context and enables supervisor and supervisee to acknowledge and work with their transference and countertransference issues. These fundamental psychodynamic concepts are defined and elaborated elsewhere in this book.

Conclusion

In this chapter consideration has been given to the stresses and demands on child care workers in their everyday work of being with children and young people and of attempting to work therapeutically with them in different contexts to bring about change, healing and growth. However idyllic some of the settings where this work takes place may appear, there is no disguising the raw reality of Donald Winnicott's 'Loving, Hating and Surviving' theme taken as the title of this book. It is crucial in the interests of the troubled child that the child care worker does survive the child's pain and the child's acted-out expression of pain. For this to be achieved it is vital to ensure the provision of well-conceived support and supervision. Through such provision workers begin to make sense of the complex unconscious processes which develop in their relationships with children, young people and families as well as with other workers in their agency setting.

References

Berry, J. (1975) *Daily Experience in Residential Life*, Routledge and Kegan Paul.

Bion, W.R. (1961) *Experiences in Groups*. New York: Basic Books.

Bloor, M., McKeganey, N. and Fonkert, D. (1988) *One Foot in Eden*, Routledge.

Challender, D. (1986) 'Job Characteristics, Job Satisfaction and Job Performance: an Investigation of Residential Workers in a Care Agency', Unpublished MSc Thesis, University of Surrey.

Challender, D.G. (1992) 'Support Issues and Coping Mechanisms in Residential Staff' in van der Ploeg, J.D. et al. (eds), *Vulnerable Youth in Residential Care*, Part 11, Leuven/Apeldorn-Garant.

Cherniss, C. (1980) *Staff Burnout*, Sage.

Douglas, T. (1978), *Basic Groupwork*, Tavistock.

Ekstein, R. (1959) 'Countertransference in the Residential Treatment of Children', in *Psychoanalytic Study of the Child*, 14: 186–218, New York: International University Press.

Finkelhor, D. (1986) *A Sourcebook on Child Sexual Abuse*, Sage.

Gibson, F., McGrath, A. and Reid, N. (1989) 'Occupational Stress in Social Work', *British Journal of Social Work*, 19: 1–16.

Hackman, J. and Oldham, G. (1980) *Work Redesign*, Addison-Wesley.

Hawkins, P. and Shohet, R. (1989) *Supervision in the Helping Professions*, Open University Press.

Hinshelwood, R. (1987) *What Happens in Groups*, Free Association Books.

Hobbs, M. (1973) 'Long Term Care', Parts 1, 2 and 3, *Residential Social Work*, 13(4): 196–201; 13(5): 241–46; 13(6): 296–300.

Hood, S. (1985) 'Staff Needs, Staff Organisation and Effective Primary Performance in the Residential Setting', *International Journal of Therapeutic Communities*, 6(1).

Jaques, E. (1955) 'Social Systems as a Defense against Persecutory and Depressive Anxiety', in Klein, M., Heimann, P. and Money-Kyrle, R. (eds) *New Directions in Psychoanalysis*, Tavistock.

Ledger, R. (1980) 'Residential Turnover', *Social Work Today*, 2(39).

Maslach, C. (1976) 'Burned-out', *Human Behaviour*, 5 (September).

Mattingly, M. (1981) 'Occupational Stress for Group Care Personnel', in F. Ainsworth and L. Fulcher (eds) *Group Care for Children*, Tavistock.

Menzies, I. (1970) *The Functioning of the Social Systems as a Defence against Anxiety*, Tavistock Institute of Human Relations.

Menzies-Lyth, I. (1985) 'The Development of the Self in Children in Institutions', *Journal of Child Psychotherapy*, 11(2).

Mutzack, W. (1991) *Group Consultation. Personnel Supervision in Residential Care*, Leuven/Amersfoort: Acco.

Nelson, J.E. (1978) 'Child Care Crises and the Role of the Supervisor', *Child Care Quarterly*, 7(4): 318–26.

Roberts, V.Z. (1994) 'The Self-assigned Impossible Task', in Obholzer, A. and Roberts, V.R. (eds) *The Unconscious at Work*, Routledge.

Utting, W. (1991) *Children in the Public Care*, HMSO.

Van der Ven, K.D. (1979) 'Development Characteristics of Child Care Workers and Design of Training Programmes', *Child Care Quarterly*, 8(2): 100–112.

Van Eck, L. (1990) 'Leadership and management in Psychiatric Organisations', *International Journal of Therapeutic Communities*, 11(3).

6 Understanding the research

Michael Little

Introduction

As an introduction to Michael Little's chapter we reproduce here the Five Conditions from Research for Good Standards in Residential Care which his organisation, the Dartington Social Research Unit, has uncovered during the last ten years of assiduous research into the field of residential care for children and young people:

- Young people feel enriched by their residential experience in which they should perceive some caring role.
- The young people see themselves as acquiring clear instrumental skills during their stay.
- The pursuit by the institution of a set of goals which are matched to the primary rather than the secondary needs of children; that is to the needs which necessitated absence from home rather than those brought about by living away. These aims should be reiterated in a wide variety of ways and permeate the whole control process.
- Effective institutions demonstrate some consensus amongst staff, children and parents about what these goals should be and how they should be achieved. To maintain this consensus, leadership should be clear and consistent. Staff should be reminded of the strengths of residential care as well as warned against its weaknesses.
- The institutions should make efforts to fragment the informal world of the children by a variety of structural features. This may be by creating small group situations, by giving children responsibility or by encouraging close staff/child relationships. (Little and Kelly 1995)

6 Understanding the research

Michael Little

Residential care which has a psychotherapeutic base has been little troubled by research. Residential care for children in need is little better endowed and if the results from other service contexts were added, they would be but a drop in the ocean of knowledge now accumulated on other aspects of children's lives, their health, education or even their spiritual well-being. This lack of research is not necessarily calamitous. It is true that residential care for children and the psychotherapeutic section in particular has declined alarmingly in the last three decades. But its decline would not have been hindered by evidence. Rather, research is likely to contribute to the changing face of residential care. So why is evidence important?

At a simple level, we are more trusting in services proven by several independent studies to be successful. Most of us hardly comprehend the mechanics of medical care but, while we remain anxious, we are happy to expose our own children to the ministering – even where there is the prospect of a surgeon's knife – because we believe the evidence that shows that it works. Children in need of support from what we today call the personal social services form only a small subset of the population, so they are seldom exposed to arguments which set out how we might behave with our own children. But they are no less deserving of robust evidence on what works, for whom, when and why.

Even where its value is accepted, research evidence is often taken by professionals in the personal social services to be somebody else's problem. This stance has been particularly true of the psychotherapeutic tradition. While the beliefs in the doctrines described in this book took for granted the benefits of their approach, research evidence was being used by policy makers in central government (and later by managers in local government) to transform services for children in need in England and Wales (with Scotland and Northern Ireland following quickly behind).

As well as mapping the resistance to research, these opening words say something of the difficulties of incorporating its results into practice with difficult children. Supporting the young casualties of our society requires considerable belief in one's actions and a certainty that it can do some good. Knowing how little is known about the effects of sexual abuse is not necessarily helpful when faced with a potentially suicidal adolescent.

Much of the research that has been available has not been useful to the residential sector. A lot of it has been service based. It is only recently that we have come to recognise that a service does not define a child. Residential care is offered to a range of children – from those who need to stay away from home for just a night while Mother recovers from a minor operation, right through to children whose grave crimes demand secure accommodation and therapeutic work. The best remedy for this service-based malady is research which starts with the child. But even then there are problems since so few children in broad cohorts of those in need go anywhere near residential care.

A further handicap has been the reticence of researchers to define their own business. People who work from a university, especially if they carry the title 'Dr' or 'Professor' are often confused as purveyors of evidence, even when they have never met a child in need, never mind worked with one. I cannot speak for my peers but I can set out a definition of evidence that will suffice for this chapter. I am interested here in empirical research, facts and figures about actual children, about all areas of their lives, health, education, social behaviour, family relations and living situations – which tell us something about their circumstances, how the state typically responds and importantly what kinds of interventions appear to be effective.

As such, the chapter bypasses theories unsupported by evidence. But the sum of evidence just defined is beginning to suggest theories of children in need which incorporate some of the ideas set out in this book.

Context

One contribution of evidence is to tell us something about the context in which different interventions for children in need operate. It is estimated, for example, that there are about 600,000 children in need in England and Wales (Department of Health 1995). These are children with multiple and interacting problems that could benefit from some kind of intervention from a personal social services professional; for example, health visitors, social workers, teachers. In fact, only some 350,000 children receive an intervention. Nearly all of these remain at home with their relatives.

About 30,000 children each year have problems that require that they are looked after away from home by social services departments (Department of Health, annual statistics). But most of these children are reunited with relatives within six weeks of departure and only 3,400 of the 15,000 experiencing such short stays go into any form of residential placement (Department of Health 1998). Of the 15,000 who stay longer – that is for seven or more weeks – 3,500 will stay only in residential settings with another 750 moving between residential and foster homes.

It is important to bear in mind that 92 per cent of separated children return home to live with their relatives. Of the eight per cent who do not go back, half find a stable alternative to the natural family – usually in foster or adoptive homes – but half continue to have difficulties and are the most prone to homelessness, imprisonment and social exclusion in adulthood (Bullock et al. 1998).

Some children in need live away from home in settings not organised by social services departments. Each year 21,000 children live in special boarding schools. Each night 12,000 children are in hospital – 5,000 more than are in children's homes. Another 2,000 young people are sentenced or remanded to prison custody with about 2,000 coming into local authority secure units (Gooch 1996). There are about 150 extremely difficult and disturbed young people who, either sentenced for grave crimes or failing to respond to a range of specialist interventions, are locked up each night, often in an institution which boasts some kind of treatment philosophy (Bullock et al. 1998).

Much of the research in the 1980s and early 1990s in England focused on patterns of need and interventions for children looked after by social services departments (DHSS 1985; Department of Health 1991). Of the 30,000 coming into care (by court order) or accommodation (by agreement between local authority and parent) each year, less than 2,000 will be exposed to interventions grounded in the ideas set out in this book (Little and Kelly 1995). It is not possible to be precise, but a typical profile of this group would be:

- multiple and interacting needs that have not responded to interventions attempted while the child remained at home
- an extended period away from home often comprising some breakdown in a residential and/or foster placement
- placement in specialist psychotherapeutic contexts for a period of two to three years
- return to relatives for the majority, continued support in the community for the remainder

- continued relationship problems as well as education and employment instability in early adulthood.

Of young children placed in long-term residential psycho-therapeutic communities, clear patterns of changing needs have been established (Little and Kelly 1995):

- young children from fragmented families who have suffered prolonged emotional maltreatment and endured difficult family circumstances, including several moves between relatives
- victims of chronic sexual abuse long known to social services and who will have suffered disrupted education
- children with behavioural difficulties principally manifest in an education context and
- children whose homes are chaotic, inadequate and neglectful, and whose family situation is so poor they have become long-term protection cases experiencing disruption away from home as well as within it.

Putting global statements in a context

The evidence just described begins to help a practitioner see where the child in need for whom they are particularly responsible sits in relation to other children in need. How long a child has been known to the personal social services, their previous experiences of being looked after and their patterns of movement while away from home can be as definitive an experience as maltreatment, displays of misbehaviour and evidence of fractured family relationships (Bullock et al. 1995). As research results accumulate alongside practical wisdom about children in need, it should be possible to identify much clearer patterns of difficulty, service response and optimum activities.

At present, the field is still dogged by global statements which very often are disproved by research or are better understood in the context of other results. Take some common examples.

All children placed in therapeutic communities have been sexually abused.   This is certainly untrue. Evidence of incidence of child maltreatment is notoriously difficult since different researchers use different thresholds. Using a similar measure Dartington researchers have found that about 12 per cent of new referrals to social services are thought by practitioners to be sexually abused. Farmer and Pollock (1998) report that among two-fifths (38 per cent) of children looked after there is a concern about sexual abuse or abusing behaviour. Little and Kelly (1995) estimate that 40 per cent of these in Caldecott therapeutic community in the early 1990s had been sexually maltreated. So a child in a residential treatment context is many times more likely to have been sexually abused than other children or other children in need, but it is helpful to remember:

(1) most victims of sexual abuse are unknown to children's services;
(2) more children known by agencies to have been sexually abused are supported at home than are treated away from home (about 40,000 compared with about 12,000);
(3) most children in long-stay settings have not been sexually abused; and
(4) those that have been so maltreated will certainly have other needs just as pressing as those created by the abuse, sometimes more pressing.

Most children needing a therapeutic intervention have no families to which they can return and most experience periods of homelessness or imprisonment in adulthood. Again, this is untrue. The rate of reunion with relatives for children looked after has already been given: 92 per cent. Of course, the more entrenched the family problems the less likely return becomes, but 70 per cent of leavers from Caldecott went back to relatives within two years of departure. Seventy-three per cent of the children in Sinclair and Gibb's (1998) sample of children in children's homes are thought to have gone back to relatives, as did over three-fifths of the most difficult and disturbed young people in the country (including those convicted of murder, arson or rape) (Bullock et al. 1998).

These results are not to suggest that children looked after *should* go home – rather they indicate that most *do* go home. This is vital contextual information for those working therapeutically with very damaged youngsters.

It is, of course, true that the most damaged children in society are at greatest risk of homelessness, imprisonment and other difficulties during adulthood. Stein and colleagues (1995) estimate that about a third of the single homeless have been in care accommodation and Home Office studies estimate that about 40 per cent of adult prisoners have been known when they were children to social services departments.

These results are a cause for concern. But they arise from taking just one perspective, that of taking a snapshot of troubled people and looking back over their life events. Now take another perspective. If we follow up all looked-after children into adulthood, fewer than five per cent are ever homeless or imprisoned. Of course, most children in care or accommodation return home quickly and are relatively little troubled again as they grow up so it is unsurprising that they do not have severe problems in adulthood. But take a very high risk group. Of a sample of 204 of the most difficult and disturbed young people in society (all of whom had to be locked up and all of whom were exposed to sophisticated treatment programmes), just seven per cent experienced a period of homelessness before their twenty-fifth birthday. Eighty-five per cent of these children had been convicted of offences prior to entering a secure treatment context with two-thirds sentenced for serious crimes of violence or violent intent, yet only 25% were imprisoned again on release to the community.

Much of this evidence is a reminder of the necessity of forming a good diagnosis of children's needs and likely outcomes and using that information to fashion realistic professional expectations about what can and cannot be achieved. There has been a tendency while evidence has been thin on the ground to both talk up and down the life chances of children in need. Outcomes are predicted to be marvellously good, for example in the hope that the child will achieve ordinary levels of adjustment – or dreadful, for instance, that homelessness or imprisonment are inevitable. A realistic programme nearly always lies somewhere in between these two extremes.

Only specialist therapy can help children like this.   The organisation of modern children's services makes this proposition false. Children in need have multiple problems. Take the run-of-the-mill referral to social services. A third (31 per cent) will have poor relations with their mother; nine per cent live in poor housing; 16 per cent will live in households where there are unusual levels of family discord, and in 15 per cent of cases there will be domestic violence. Nine per cent of these children will be violent at home and one in ten will suffer chronic physical ill health. Ten per cent of the adults in the households of these children will be dependent on alcohol or drugs and two per cent will be identified as suicide risks (Little et al. 1998). If it is multiple needs that get children to the notice of specialist services, then this requires specialist services to be multiple in response.

It is true that some children can benefit from the treatment ideas espoused in this book better than others and – while the evidence on this point remains sketchy – probably at certain moments in their lives more than others.

In *A Life Without Problems?*, the experiences of one child, Siobhan Kelly, who undoubtedly benefited from residentially based psychotherapy of a particular sort, is described in depth alongside less detailed information on 60 others. Siobhan stayed in residence much longer than most children in need and had been placed in other children's homes prior to coming to the Caldecott Community. At the time of writing, Siobhan is just celebrating her 20th year and did as well as could be expected given her circumstances on referral.

But to achieve this outcome several interventions other than the therapeutic community came into play. In total, less than a quarter of Siobhan's life so far has been spent in a residential institution. About the same proportion has been spent with foster families. She has benefited greatly from high-quality mainstream education, first at grammar school, then at university. Then there have been hospital services for overdoses and community-based psychotherapy in young adulthood. Siobhan's natural family has been in receipt of a host of services to help keep them afloat and this has ensured continued contact between mother and siblings.

Findings from the Department of Health programme of research

Prior to the 1980s, there was hardly any research on children in need. The Department of Health and the Economic and Social Research Council began to commission new investigations. Soon the body of knowledge accumulated to the extent that practitioners relatively unused to reading research reports found it difficult to keep up. As a consequence, the Department of Health began to produce overviews of the evidence. To date, three have emerged: *Social Work Decisions in Child Care* (1985), *Patterns and Outcomes in Child Placements* (1991) and *Child Protection: Messages from Research* (1995). A fourth, *Caring for Children Away From Home* (1998), has been launched at the same time as this book and deals with recent programmes of research on residential care.

It captures just a small proportion of the findings of ten authoritative studies on residence. A few pages in this chapter can capture just a small proportion of the overview. Those who feel inspired to know more about what actually happens to children in need and how residence can contribute to improving their situation will wish to read the publications in full.

Initially, the bad news: there is still much wrong with residential services as they are currently organised. Sinclair and Gibbs (1998) found that two-fifths (44 per cent) of children in residence were bullied during their stay and that one in seven (14 per cent) had been taken advantage of sexually. Farmer and Pollock's (1998) evidence is a reminder – at a time when scandals about abuse by adults is high on the public agenda – that it is children, not adults, who are most likely to be perpetrators of abuse. It is surely disquieting that Sinclair and Gibbs found that many children in residence were unhappier than they were prior to being looked after. Two-thirds of residents were regarded as being miserable or unhappy and nearly two-thirds have contemplated suicide. These findings are echoed by Farmer and Pollock.

Not only do some children suffer in residence, but some children's homes rock from crisis to crisis. Using different types of measures, Berridge and Brodie (1998), Sinclair and Gibbs (1998), as well as Brown and colleagues (1998), found that a third of children's homes were poor, a third of medium standard and a third were good. Whittaker and colleagues (1998), along with Dartington, found considerable fluctuation in the fortunes of homes. When Goffman studied asylums 40 years previously, the residential context was fixed and the inmates changed; this situation is in danger of reversing.

The overview begins with this parlous nature of residential care and sets out a model that might lead to general improvements, more consistent standards and a context in which our knowledge about children in need can steadily increase. This model should be applicable to both managers planning an entire service and practitioners working with the individual child.

Establish the needs of the child

Traditionally, local authorities have had 100 children in residential centres because there were 100 residential beds. If they had opened another 50, the demand for places would follow accordingly, On the whole the number of places has been decreasing for three decades, from 41,000 in 1971 to 7,000 in 1996. Practitioners similarly turn to those residential placements that have a vacancy. If there was a place they used it; if there was not then an alternative, usually foster care or support at home, was found.

Caring for Children Away from Home suggests a different route. It is better for a local authority to work out the needs of children for whom it is responsible and to design services – including in some cases residence and including in some cases the methods described in this book – to meet these needs. Better it says for professionals to do much the same for individual cases. Needs should be explored in all areas of the child's life and, for children looked after the Department of Health, *Looking After Children* tools are ideal for the task.

Where this approach has been tried by local authorities fewer children come into care or accommodation, a greater proportion of those separated are placed in residential contexts and there is much greater cooperation between agencies at the point of service delivery. Children go into residence because it is needed rather than because it is available.

Be clear about the aims and objectives of residence

Several studies in the Department of Health programme tried to predict what factors are associated with a children's home being of high quality. All agreed that a fundamental factor was clarity about aims and objectives.

Brown and colleagues (1998) found a residential centre that asked:

- what does society expect of this placement?
- what can this home achieve given the needs of children it is being asked to support?
- what does the manager and staff really think is possible given available resources?

and achieves some agreement in the answers to the questions intended to provide better-quality care.

Bullock and colleagues (1998) offer a similar test for individual children. They ask practitioners to set out what is likely to happen in all areas of a child's life – living situations, family and social relationships, social and anti-social behaviour, physical and psychological health, education and employment – over the next two years both at best and at worst. They then ask practitioners to list those services that will lead to the best scenario being achieved. By this mechanism, clear objectives with respect to all residents can be established and monitored.

Ensure homes are healthy places to live

Whittaker and colleagues (1998) at York, along with Brown and colleagues (1998) at Dartington extended a long tradition in residential care researched by scrutinising the culture of children's homes. The York team were principally interested in group dynamics – how staff and children got on with each other. Dartington asked staff and residents how they would respond to typical events in children's homes for example:

- when a new resident arrives
- how to deal with a parent's visit to the children's home
- what to do if one resident hits another.

If there was agreement on how to respond, a culture was said to exist. Culture defined in this way could be either positive or negative. So, staff or children could be uniformly warm or cold on the arrival of a new resident. This test can be used individually by practitioners and for the children's home as a whole.

The evidence would seem to suggest that where:

- local authorities and individual practitioners are clear about the needs of children (step 1)
- congruent aims and objectives (step 2) are more likely, which produce

- a healthy staff culture (step 3) which, in turn
- creates a stable and positive house, and most importantly,
- has beneficial outcomes for children and families.

Conclusion

A century ago there were hardly any services for children in need. Today, over 350,000 are supported in some way. A small proportion of these children will continue to be supported in residential settings. A small proportion of those will benefit from the psychotherapeutic methods described in this book. We know much more today about what works, for whom, when and why but we still know very little compared to other children's services.

Winnicott, Bowlby, Bettelheim, Erickson and others hypothesised about the benefits of the psychotherapeutic tradition for needy children. All four explored their ideas in clinical practice and write eloquently if inconclusively about their gains and losses. Others have taken this tradition forward but with less enthusiasm for clarity about the ideas or research into their effectiveness.

If the psychotherapeutic tradition is to keep a foothold on the mountain that is today's personal social services for children, it will have to right this wrong. This book can help in as much as it can clear the now muddy waters of psychotherapeutic language. Others then must continue the task by studying what works.

The answer is likely to be complicated. It is likely to be the case that therapeutic communities can hold some children but not others; at certain moments in time but not at others; in some areas of the child's life but not in others. But such a complicated answer would advance our understanding of children in need beyond all recognition and must be a primary aspiration of our work, wherever we operate in the system of personal social services.

References

Berridge, D. and Brodie, I. (1998) *Children's Homes Revisited*, London: Jessica Kingsley.

Brown, E., Bullock, R., Hobson, C. and Little, M. (1998), *Making Residential Care Work*, Aldershot: Ashgate.

Bullock, R., Gooch, D. and Little, M. (1998) *Children Going Home*, Aldershot: Ashgate.

Bullock, R., Little, M. and Millham, S. (1998) *Secure Treatment Outcomes*, Aldershot: Ashgate.

Bullock, R., Little, M. and Mount, K. (1995) *Matching Needs and Services*, Dartington: Support Force for Children's Residential Care.

Department of Health (1998) *Caring for Children Away from Home*, Chichester: Wiley.

Department of Health (1995) *Child Protection: Messages from Research*, London: HMSO.

Department of Health (1991) *Patterns and Outcomes in Child Placement*, London: HMSO.

DHSS (1985) *Social Work Decisions in Child Care*, London: HMSO.

Farmer, E. and Pollock, S. (1998) *Substitute Care for Sexually Abused and Abusing Children*, Chichester: Wiley.

Gooch, D. (1996) 'Home and away: the residential care, education and control of children in historical and political context', *Child and Family Social Work*, 1: 19–32.

Little, M. and Kelly, S. (1995) *A Life Without Problems?*, Aldershot: Arena.

Little, M., Ryan, M. and Tunnard, J. (1998) *Matching Needs and Services for All Children in Need*, Dartington.

Sinclair, I. and Gibbs, I. (1998) *Children's Homes: A Study in Diversity*, Chichester: Wiley.

Stein, M., Biehal, N., Clayden, J. and Wade, J. (1995) *Moving On*, London: HMSO.

Ward, H. (1995) *Looking After Children: Research into Practice*, London: HMSO.

Whittaker, D., Archer, L. and Hicks, L. (1998) *Working in Children's Homes: Challenges and Complexities*, Chichester: Wiley.

Part Two

Direct Work

7 Assessing the emotional needs of children and young people: using a need assessment programme

Christine Bradley and Andrew Hardwick

Introduction

'What we need is a plan,' said Pooh. (A.A. Milne)

At the outset we only intended to produce in this chapter a system for assessing the emotional needs of young people which would promote sound therapeutic practice but we think it has wider potential in the assessment and matching of children's needs to future placements.

We must also bear in mind that most practitioners do not have access to skilled external consultants. We recommend that, wherever possible, initiatives in the care of troubled young people should be checked with consultants. At the very least, regular supervision by experienced practitioners must be in place. If you are responsible for the delivery of care and/or education to young people with emotional and behavioural difficulties either in management or working with groups or individuals, this programme is for you.

A special acknowledgement to senior colleagues at the Caldecott Community for their advice and to the many managers and staff members in other organisations who are using the programme and who have given us useful feedback.

7 Assessing the emotional needs of children and young people: using a need assessment programme

Christine Bradley and Andrew Hardwick

An assessment programme for substitute care

In addition to the above basic objective, we are now certain that the Caldecott College Assessment Programme can be used as an accurate guide to the success or failure of individual placements in substitute care such as adoption and fostering. Utting (1991) identified a group of young people who require expert and sophisticated treatment in a residential setting which is not a family.

Many residential establishments are shocked by the number of young people referred who have already suffered multiple breakdowns in substitute care which simply compound the earlier traumas which resulted in removal from the birth family. It would help if we could identify those children least likely to survive in a substitute family at the start of their careers in the care system. There would be a better chance of helping these very damaged young people and we hardly dare mention the possibility of real cash savings through better use of social work time.

Many residential homes offer a preparation-for-fostering service. They need an accurate assessment guide so that they can commit to a future placement with confidence. Social workers whose job it is to try to find permanent homes for challenging young people will be helped enormously if they have access to more accurate assessments.

Do not ignore the basics: *Looking After Children*

The Department of Health assessment system *Looking After Children* should be in use in your agency or facility. It provides a comprehensive, broadly-based assessment, regularly updated, for each young person. It collates all the basic data required by those who seek to make decisions about or work with young people in care. The Caldecott College Assessment Programme starts where *Looking After Children* finishes and focuses on the young person's emotional world, that part of the personality which, through chronic suffering, triggers anti-social behaviour and problems of care and management. But therapeutic intervention has to be informed by understanding not just of useful theory but by an understanding of what has happened to the young person, when, why and how and where are we now? *Looking After Children* delivers this overview for us across seven developmental dimensions:

- Health
- Education
- Identity
- Family and social relations
- Social presentation
- Emotional and behavioural development
- Self-care skills

Personal identity

Although the Caldecott College Assessment Programme which follows concentrates on working with individual young people in residential and other group settings, it is absolutely vital that we understand what external factors and experiences have contributed to their personal development thus far. *Looking After Children* recognises the role played by identity in personal growth and the extent to which elements in society have had a negative or positive impact. The impact of poverty, poor housing, unemployment, discrimination and unsympathetic educational provision all need to be understood if we are to make helpful assessments and design programmes of care which have a good chance of leading to good outcomes.

The family context

It is equally important to consider the role of the young person in their family, the family dynamics and the affects of chronic dysfunction and abuse. The vast majority of looked-after children return to their families and therefore we must build into our assessments and plans mechanisms for contact, opportunities for reflection and the possibility of an acceptance of family reality that the young person can survive. This is not an easy task. The young person's identification with the abuser, the idealisation of the 'caring family' often at its height around Christmas and the ambivalence inherent in relationships conditioned by the transient nature of earlier models push personal and professional resources to their limits. (See also the ways in which children in substitute care bring about re-enactments of the dysfunctional family system described in Chapter 17.)

Why do we need another form of assessment?

The breakdown of the personality into pathological acting-out is triggered in the here and now by something often quite inoffensive, but is caused at root by traumatic events in early life – neglect, abuse, premature separation(s) from the primary carer. If this emotional deprivation is not addressed, then we can confidently predict a journey through life marked by regular contact with either the criminal justice or mental health systems or both, accompanied by another set of family problems. Research undertaken by the Dartington Social Research Unit (see Chapter 6) assists us in forecasting careers through care based on earlier experience. It also helps us to identify the kinds of intervention which make a difference if initiated soon enough along the way.

Our assessment programme is designed to provide diagnosis and practical signposts for practitioners: teachers, residential and field social workers, day centre staff, foster carers and nurses. Child protection is a skilled discipline which requires sophisticated tools for both assessment and intervention. The decision to remove a young person from home for their own safety triggers another set of decisions about the best placement in a form of substitute care. The Caldecott College Assessment Programme assists this process because it will guide both decision making about placement and about suitable treatment/education.

How does the programme work?

We have identified 20 dimensions of a young person's personality which we think must be addressed if we are to intervene successfully. These are grouped into three sections. Section One comprises those dimensions which lie at the heart of a healthy personality. If the assessment score is low, mainly types A and B, then the young person must not be fostered or adopted except by skilled therapists capable of providing 24-hour therapeutic management. These are very ill children who must have their primary needs met to make good what they missed or suffered in early childhood. Similarly, if residential care seems to be a positive choice in the light of A and B scores, then it is vital that the residential facility operates a treatment regime based on Dartington's five conditions (see Chapter 6). See also *A Life*

Without Problems (Little 1995: 116) which this assessment programme helps to satisfy.

Section Two consists of those dimensions which can take us forward as practitioners but also provide further help in diagnosing problems and suggesting practical methods. For example, if a young person cannot play, that may not be a reason for rejecting fostering as a placement but it is one of the most important parts of our practice if we are to help them to grow. And the same can be said for communication. Failure to communicate verbally would not block a foster placement, communication by other means such as smashing or burning property must.

Section Three offers a number of dimensions which are very much part of the way forward and must be among the objectives of a treatment programme.

Theoretical underpinning

This Assessment Programme, as well as being the distillation of 25 years' work, relies on research and clinical experience. Modern research in this field has been spearheaded by the Dartington Social Research Unit and the findings and implications provided by Professor Millham and his team over thirty years inform our thinking. Clinical studies of Winnicott, Dockar-Drysdale and the Tavistock clinicians are equally important. We also offer some useful Kleinian insights. We have made suggestions for connected reading at the end of the chapter. This is not an exhaustive list but we have found it stimulating when thinking about our assessments and translating thoughts into therapeutic action. We hope that our readers and users will add to the lists from their own reading and thinking. We are certain that regular reading and reflection form an essential part of a practitioner's working life. We totally reject the idea that we are too busy or too exhausted to do any reading. Our young people will not always thank us for our efforts. They will never thank us for our ignorance.

Stabilising and integrating

One of the key findings of the Dartington Study of the Caldecott Community (Little 1994) was that despairing and violent children and young people were effectively stabilised and work towards rehabilitation started. The outcome for Siobhan would have been far from positive had the Caldecott Community not been able to help her settle down and face up to the future and her problems. Repressive regimes used to claim that they stabilised young people but institutionalisation does not last outside the walls of the institution. What has to be recognised is the extent to which the personality of the young person is 'in bits' so that a more permanent repair can be effected. Then use can be made of family work and other forms of creative intervention including, for example, education, personal therapies, anger management programmes and work experience.

The young person who is 'in bits', suffering from distortion of many aspects of their personality, some split off in the unconscious, is certainly not a whole person. There probably is no such thing. But we are all more or less integrated, that is, the parts of our personality are more or less stuck together. This assessment programme points to those crucial aspects of the personality which determine how far a young person is integrated and can cope with life and make relationships. The A type is the least integrated, the most 'in bits', which Dockar-Drysdale called the 'frozen child', and is totally unable to manage life without constant adult management. The E type is coming together nicely and will be expected to take more responsibility for their own life with adult support, guidance and counselling; they may even help with the cooking and cleaning and go to school, college or work experience. Attachment theory is useful when considering this young person.

The programme seeks to provide a route for practice which can take the least integrated young person through to a fragile integration when they should be stable and more whole as a person. Stable and integrated are but two sides of the same coin. Working towards a stronger integration through use of this assessment programme is creating a more stable young person better able to cope with problems from the past and those still to be faced.

Using the programme

The Programme is designed to be flexible and easy to use:

1 **Familiarisation**: With any assessment system it is crucial that you are familiar with the structure and its content. Ideally you should dip into some of the references. These are really helpful and explain the theory which underpins the assessment programme. Try to find your way round the three sections and see how they inter-relate. The Sections are listed below.

2 **Start small**: Choose one aspect of the young person which worries the team the most to start with and then work on that. Start in Section One. For example if you are especially concerned about the way in which the young person merges with other children and disrupts the functioning of others then you should look at the section on 'Boundaries'. Follow this with consideration of other important dimensions in Section One.

3   **Your first decision**: Decide which of the types A to E your young person fits into and whether he is best described by the Initial team view or by one of the 'Signs of progress'. Remember assessment is a team exercise. No one person can assess a young person. It is also important to involve other significant colleagues, for example, the teacher, as in the *Looking After Children* programme.

4   **Two hints**: a) If you find that 'Signs of progress' are strong then you should also look at type E because progress towards integration is being made quite quickly. b) At the outset you will spend most time in Section One but gradually you will want to make more use of Sections Two and Three as you expand your confidence and you recognise treatment possibilities.

5   **Draw up guidelines**: Jot down the guidelines for each heading – we suggest you use the left-hand side of a page. Then on the right-hand side personalise the guidelines to suit the young person under discussion.

6   **Derive**:

- A set of guidelines for practice in relation to behaviour and emotional development.
- A 24-hour management programme.
- A Set of Objectives for Keyworking including family contact.
- A consistent agreed general approach to the young person for the whole team. This could be encapsulated in a 24-hour management programme.
- An example of this method is provided towards the end of the chapter.

7   **Alert**:

- The class teacher or FE college so that your deliberations can be taken account of in the Educational Need Assessment.
- Others who may be involved in the next review so that new, realistic objectives can be set and agreed.
- Parents if contact is approved and sufficiently strong.

8   **Use the Helpline**: Contact Caldecott College for help if you have encountered an intractable problem.

9   **Do not neglect the positive**: We sometimes tend to focus on the problem areas – they seem so huge. But, while we are trying to provide for areas of deprivation, lack of functioning and acting out, we should also watch for signs of potential or actual good functioning and change and build on them. Our young people have very low self-esteem, we should try to raise it wherever possible.

10 **Do not ignore compliance**: We are often consumed by the anxiety created by those young people who present serious management

problems. However, types C and D often seem to be able to cope and we feel we can concentrate our efforts on the most difficult. This will backfire. If you have C or D types in your client group then spend just as much time on them because they will break down catastrophically later if we do not help them as soon as we can.

11 **The masculine form is used throughout and denotes children and young people both masculine and feminine.**

Section one

- Boundaries
- Capacity for concern, empathy, remorse, etc.
- Containing emotion, anxiety, anger, stress
- Delinquent excitement
- Communication
- Dissociation
- Self-destruction
- Separation/loss
- Violence/aggression
- Play

Boundaries: A

1) Initial team view: Merges and disrupts the functioning of others. (A merger is the joining together of two or more young people in anti-social/destructive activity which is exceedingly hard to interrupt. It is an unconscious process but may appear premeditated)

2) Action:

Needs to have one person who is preoccupied with him. Adults need to be in touch with him the whole time; they cannot afford to lose track of this child and must provide him with CLEAR expectations and boundaries. Disruption and lack of boundaries need to be seen as a breakdown of communication and uncommunicated primary needs which must be met by primary provision: nurturing experiences which are the essence throughout the day, but special thought needed at bedtimes. Needs a very clear 24-hour management programme, or similar in day centres and schools, which the whole staff team accepts and works within. This Programme is only therapeutic if there is the opportunity for the young person to have his dependency needs met in a relationship with one grown-up.

Signs of progress: Adults are able to supply boundaries and interrupt mergers and disruption.

3) Action:

As the young person responds to the above method, the special adult (for example, the keyworker) has to help the young person understand the reasons why he is this way and take some responsibility for it, but it may be some time before the move from Stage Two to Stage Three can happen.

Signs of progress: Able to supply own boundaries generally.

Boundaries: B

1) Initial team view: Has areas of functioning but help is needed when functioning breaks down

2) Action:

Needs a 24-hour management programme which allows for the vulnerable areas to be provided for and contained by grown-ups. When functioning breaks down his needs must be met with primary provision and nurturing. Support functioning areas. Expect different kinds of attachment – B. uses different people for different things, not necessarily absolute dependence. Support creativity.

Signs of progress: Less frequent break down of functioning.

3) Action:

Primary carer converts provision into communication, for example, is able to talk about breaking down and its causes before it happens. Adults 'shout through' that all is well in many areas when he seems to be falling apart. Keep creativity going. Prefers doing rather than imagining – do not expect too much play, for example.

Signs of progress: Possible breakdown under stress but generally manages own boundaries.

Boundaries: C

1) Initial team view: Under stress merges and disrupts the functioning of others

2) Action:

The grown-up has to 'fight' to provide care for the small ego. The defensive shell that the young person has built will resist and will only dare to hand over real care to the grown-up when he feels safe enough to do so. The grown-up has to prove their reliability and consistency and unshakeability and accept the fairly violent reaction and try to make provision for it.

Signs of progress: Keeps more within own boundary but merges when anxious. Lot of non-verbal communication.

3) Action:

Gradually and often through symbolic gestures the young person comes to realise that the grown-up can be trusted with his unresolved infantile needs. There will be small instances of 'handing over' of care, for example, wanting the worker always to wash his hair or look after some special possession. Continue with the play.

Signs of progress: Rarely merges; accepts provision, a lot of communication, mainly symbolic.

Boundaries: D

1) Initial team view: Disruptive, stirs things up and then disappears

2) Action:

Confront the falseness and the compliance, which hides subculture, with reality and expect rage/fury in return. This way the disruption becomes less subcultural and more in the open with potential for meaningful communication.

Signs of progress: Still stirs up but less underhand.

3) Action:

Compliance gives way under confrontation. Help is needed from grown-ups to bear the pain and rage. One grown-up to provide nurturing experience. The young person can be so very over self-reliant – he must be persuaded to accept provision for the pain. Then there should be the start of some sadness for experiences which have been missed.

Signs of progress: Holding boundaries well, very little underhand stuff.

Boundaries: E

1) Initial team view: Pushes boundaries in an anti-authority, non-panicky way, especially under stress

2) Action:

The realities of shared living, education and the expectations of the outside world must be presented. Support from adults is needed in taking responsibility and coping with both emotional and external stress. Help the young person to differentiate between the two as they are felt on the inside, for example, using opportunities for communication to explore where anxiety and stress result in getting things out of proportion and perspective. Take care to take this approach in a non-punitive yet positive way. The young person will need to see results and rewards for living this way. Recognition from close adults is very important. The combination of his fragile ego and the onset of adolescence results in challenges to authority which have to be met 'like a lighthouse' pointing the way but remaining firm.

Signs of progress: Adolescent challenges to boundaries given, yet less frequent.

3) Action:

Opportunities for joining in the outside world with support. Communication about the stresses and strains. Expect young person to give up or find ways of wriggling out. Keep the communication open about the difficulties. Aim for milestones of achievement not millstones of 'ought to dos'.

Signs of progress: Well-internalised boundaries, only occasional challenge under stress.

Capacity for concern, empathy, remorse, etc.: A

1) Initial team view: Very low

2) Action:

Concern emerges through a relationship with a grown-up who has met the young person's needs to be dependent. If the grown-up is able to meet the young person's needs at a deep level, the young person is able to be more separate rather than go looking for mergers. A healthy concern is developed when the young person is able to see the grown-up as a person in his own right who they value. Reparation may take an obscure form, for example, much later than the incident for which reparation is being made and in a small way.

Signs of progress: Beginning to show signs of capacity for remorse/reparation.

3) Action:

Further growth in these areas depends on the degree of inter-dependency facilitated by the adult i.e. separating out from the total dependency.

Signs of progress: Now also showing signs of capacity for concern and empathy.

Capacity for concern, empathy, remorse, etc.: B

1) Initial team view: It is growing but is poor when not functioning

2) Action:

Maintaining the reliability will allow the young person gradually to value the grown-up and out of this stems the beginnings of concern, etc. The young person diverts his focus from the tiny self onto the grown-up and starts to show concern often through symbolic communication and the use of a third object.

Signs of progress: Expect non-verbal reparation.

3) Action:

The concern moves from the symbolic third object into the relationship with the grown-up as the young person learns about reparation.

Signs of progress: A growing ability to express concern and empathy but needs adult support for confirmation that they are okay.

Capacity for concern, empathy, remorse, etc.: C

1) Initial team view: Little capacity for accepting personal responsibility

2) Action:

Maintaining reliability will allow the young person gradually to value the grown-up and out of this stems the beginnings of concern, etc. The young person diverts his focus from the tiny self onto the grown-up and starts to show concern often through symbolic communication involving an actual object.

Signs of progress: Communicates by symbols, starts to make a relationship but is precarious and can become violent or depressed/despairing when continuity breaks down.

3) Action:

The concern moves from the symbolic third object into the relationship with the grown-up as he learns about reparation.

Signs of progress: Begins to show concern, etc. as relationship develops – feels precarious (see 2) but usually has a strong caring side.

Capacity for concern, empathy, remorse, etc.: D

1) Initial team view: Falsely presents as accepting personal responsibility

2) Action:

Guilt and concern is rarely genuine and the young person must be challenged. But this must be done (it's tricky) in such a way that he does not feel annihilated or attacked. This was his greatest fear when he was very young and this is what produced the false veneer as protection.

Sign of progress: Starting to feel real, not false.

3) Action:

These young persons will feel real when they allow themselves to experience their pain and anger. Depression is a factor and verbal communication is absolutely essential.

Signs of progress: Much more real feel in these areas.

Capacity for concern, empathy, remorse, etc.: E

1) Initial team view: Some willingness to make reparation and express concern, not much empathy

2) Action:

Awareness can be increased by sharing in talking groups issues about difference, other people's problems, current issues at home and abroad and how they could affect us. Young person may be able to use a creative medium – play, art, drama – to explore some of this before he can talk about them.

Signs of progress: Can make reparation and express concern.

3) Action:

High adult expectations in this area coupled with straight talking. Adults working with his own disappointment when things do not work out and not showing too many hurt feelings. Communication vital, often in relation to the needs and problems of others in the group whose programme may be different. Young person needs convincing that we are committed to meeting his needs and the adult remains confident that concern will gradually be mirrored back.

Signs of progress: Can empathise.

Containing emotion, anxiety, anger, stress: A

1) Initial team view: Cannot contain emotions, acts out violently

2) Action:

Grown-ups with care confront the young person with reality – the effect of which may well mean physically holding. The young person needs one grown-up to stay with the rage and explosions, accept them and to be able to cope with the despair and emptiness that follows the breakdown. Through this the young person should be able to recognise the depth of his own emotional needs which will help to accept the grown-up providing the nurture needed to move on. There is a possibility of communication about the rage and emptiness accompanying the nurture. Acting-out is reduced through communication.

Signs of progress: Reduction in acting-out both in frequency and intensity.

3) Action:

Growing dependency and communicaton will help both grown-up and young person to face the pain inside. A better reality on the outside will promote depression but it will often break down into despair accompanied by the beginnings of holding on to his own inner dreadful feelings using play and opportunities for communication.

Signs of progress:　Further reduction in acting out.

Containing emotion, anxiety, anger, stress: B

1) Initial team view: Will act out violently under stress

2) Action:

The young person needs to feel that the violent chaos inside can be contained by a grown-up and through that he begins to take responsibility for it himself. The grown-up has to stay with the despair and self-destructiveness and to protect the young person from his own primitive impulses until he starts to settle.

Signs of progress:　Working towards pulling together areas of functioning. Commitment to regular meetings with key worker, signs of communication. Will start need containment although is now less violent.

3) Action:

The development of the young person's functioning areas begins to be able to support the potential violence. Despair becomes depression which can lead to communication and the violence diminishes. Likely to return to despair when very anxious or stressed – need for adult anticipation and early communication. Development of creativity and creative functioning very important.

Signs of progress:　Will get very depressed and despairing and will need adult support, anticipation and support with creativity.

Containing emotion, anxiety, anger, stress: C

1) Initial team view: Reacts violently under pressure or assumed stress

2) Action:

The violence needs to be understood as the temper tantrums of a very little person which, as long as there is a grown-up standing by, will work itself through. Nurturing can help the before and after.

Signs of progress: Less frequent and intense violence as relationship develops, not always towards people, for example, destroys own room.

3) Action:

Gradually the young person is able to hold together using symbols, play and the grown-up where trust and a small dependency is growing.

Signs of progress: Can contain feelings – uses provision well.

Containing emotion, anxiety, anger, stress: D

1) Initial team view: When confronted with reality can act out violently

2) Action:

Maximise the amount of opportunity for communication – See under 'Communication'.

Signs of progress: Beginning to accept confrontation of reality with less acting-out.

3) Action:

Continue with 2 above.

Signs of progress: Can accept confrontation of reality without acting out. Copes with stress better – See under 'Communication'.

Containing emotion, anxiety, anger, stress: E

1) Initial team view: Disintegrates when very anxious and finds it difficult to talk about stress

2) Action:

Uses keyworker and the group for this more than acting-out. Begins to talk about difficulties in coping and can be depressed. Promote creativity to help cope with depression and avoid flight and delinquency when pain becomes too great.

Signs of progress: Generally attending and using keytime to express areas of stress. Some insights into transference relationships. Still some incidents of disintegration.

3) Action:

Needs help to ensure that depression does not overwhelm. Forward-looking planning and functioning is important. Adults very supportive of education and creativity. Grown-ups need to promote both by enjoying their own creative pursuits in the group as well as supporting a particular young person or group of young persons in theirs.

Signs of progress: Able to talk in an insightful way about stress, transference and anxiety. Rare outbursts under stress.

Delinquent excitement: A

Initial team view: Finds delinquent excitement very satisfying

2) Action:

The grown-ups must be able to understand the excitement in terms of what the young person is looking for emotionally and to be able to provide for it in more socially acceptable ways, for example, to encourage greed so that the young person accepts special food provision rather than needing to act out the excitement.

Signs of progress: Reduction in delinquent excitement through relationships and adaptations.

3) Action:

As the small ego grows, stress will cause it to regress and seek excitement. This can be met by localised provision, for example, regressive experiences such as staying in bed for a morning.

Signs of progress: Further progress, excitement only present in times of stress.

Delinquent excitement: B

1) Initial team view: Can be put in touch with a better alternative

2) Action:

Young person really does not like getting involved but will do so to avoid the pain. Imaginative use of provision to head off/convert excitement into something more acceptable. If it goes wrong apply a lot of care afterwards.

Signs of progress: Accepting of anticipation by staff and interruption in advance.

3) Action:

Watch for signs of anxiety and stress. Usually gives us clues and will then need support and opportunity for communication.

Signs of progress: With an increase in creativity less likely to be drawn in.

Delinquent excitement: C

1) Initial team view: Uses it as a defence

2) Action:

The grown-up has to identify the emotional need that is being acted out through the delinquent excitement. Find a way of offering provision to 'fill the hole' – this could be food, regressive experience or just the grown-up being with them.

Signs of progress: Reducing, more rage directed at co-workers/relationships and environment as a reaction to developing self.

3) Action:

As the young person accepts the provision and its continuity he begins to depend upon the grown-up for that and other experiences. At this stage the transference comes into being and the young person can displace hostility and other conflicts into the grown-up. Difficult for the grown-up but important for the young person's emotional development.

Signs of progress: Excitement under stress only, now better communication and acceptance of provision.

Delinquent excitement: D

1) Initial team view: Sets excitement up for others

2) Action:

The only way to prevent delinquent excitement is to stay with the confrontation of the compliance and help the young person move into depression.

Signs of progress: Starting to accept anticipation/interruption, but when involved not so underhand.

3) Action:

With awareness evolving through provision and depression, the young person sees situations which can cause excitement. He will allow himself to re-focus onto a different activity or way of thinking, for example, play or other activity which enables sublimation.

Signs of progress: Less likely to occur, easily interrupted.

Delinquent excitement: E

1) Initial team view: Gets involved when under stress/out of communication

2) Action:

See under 'Defence mechanisms'.

Signs of progress: Occasionally, usually at times of high anxiety or stress.

3) Action:

See under 'Defence mechanisms'.

Signs of progress: Delinquent excitement is now rare.

Communication: A

(1) Initial team view: Not in a one-to-one situation – tends to chatter

2) Action:

Through the primary provision made for the young person he begins to trust the primary carer and allows them into his inner world which is full of anxiety, fears and pain. The adult must respond to this without being seduced, so that an understanding and developing consciousness can be arrived at together. That becomes the foundation stone of true communication. Encourage non-verbal communication through squiggles, play, etc.

Signs of progress: Non-verbal and symbolic communication expressed.

3) Action:

A developing consciousness enables the young person to be aware of anxious and stressful times which penetrate his vulnerability. Because of this he begins to accept an element of personal responsibility for his actions with considerable help and support from grown-ups. Continue with non-verbal approaches.

Signs of progress: Should be able to communicate verbally with one person.

Communiation: B

1) Initial team view: Potential for communication but backs off when anxious or stressed

2) Action:

Starts to accept help with communication but finds it very painful. Despair often very close. Will communicate non-verbally/symbolically and not always at the time the grown-up wants. For example, will make symbolic gestures of reparation sometime after an incident or will make a present seemingly unconnected with grown-up's attempts to communicate.

Signs of progress: Beginning to communicate.

3) Action:

Still finds verbal communication difficult but do not despair. Will tend to communicate with and through activity/creativity. Copes better with non-verbal methods, for example, squiggles. If self-esteem improving will talk more freely. Try to anticipate stressful times like anniversaries.

Signs of progress: More able to communicate when anxious or stressed.

Communication: C

1) Initial team view: Communication that is not easily understood – often symbolic

2) *Action:*

Look for the symbols and respond in the language of symbols. A lot of play. Grown-ups must not repress the spontaneity nor allow it to be acted out but converted into creative play and creative thinking.

Signs of progress: Much symbolic communication, some verbal, mainly through play and adaptation.

3) *Action:*

Finds verbal communication difficult but do not despair. The young person takes quite a while to adapt to our reality after being 'locked into' his protective shell. First verbal communication will be talking in symbols and substitutes. Do not force the issue on talking.

Signs of progress: A lot of communication particularly with primary carer though often finds reality difficult to adapt to.

Communciation: D

1) Initial team view: Contrived compliant communication

2) *Action:*

As the compliant self is confronted and the young person expresses the real deprivation, which in the past has been split off by the compliant personality, there is the possibility of getting in touch with real painful feelings which can lead to creativity. Look for the symbolic, the ability to play and then verbal communication. This last is vital.

Signs of progress: Symbolic communication, occasionally leading to real verbal communication.

3) Action:

With the awareness and insight brought about by the play and capacity to symbolise, the young person begins to free up and is able to trust the adult enough to talk about early anxieties without feeling that he will be attacked.

Signs of progress: Starting to talk about self – what stresses him and makes him anxious, also his history.

Communication: E

1) Initial team view: Little emotional investment and rare symbolic communication; reluctant to talk about reality; acts of delinquency when out of communication

2) Action

Two routes out of delinquency are communication and creativity/creative living. Communication should be both structured/timetabled for working over the longer term and spontaneous to pick up an issue or incident as it arises. Still look for the symbolic and non-verbal communication and acknowledge it. Transference can distort communication. Adults keep in tune.

Signs of progress: Signs of investment in communication. Often able to communicate with adults. Struggling to come to terms with reality. Can still revert to delinquent acts.

3) Action

Young person talks a lot both about the world of feeling and the world of living and education. Uses grown-ups well, often more than one to share different parts of life.

Signs of progress: In good, healthy communication with adults. Generally in touch with reality.

Dissociation: A

1) Initial team view: Conscience-free misbehaviour, for example, stealing, soiling

2) Action:

A creative and playful way has to be found of responding to the despair and helplessness which has become separated from the young person's ego, for example, providing special possessions/trinkets for someone who steals and denies it. It helps not to call the action 'stealing' – there is no morality here yet.

Signs of progress: More able to accept provision of symbolic nurture. The behaviour may reduce but not necessarily.

3) Action:

Look for rationalisation as evidence of the end of dissociation.

Signs of progress: Making use of play and other opportunities for communication and provision.

Dissociation: B

1) Initial team view: Splits off experience but can be made aware of it

2) Action:

Does have split-off bits which are more likely to overwhelm than be dissociated. Some use of the imagination in providing for these areas will really help.

Signs of progress: Much less splitting off.

3) Action:

Should be able to talk about the painful areas but let it come gently in the context of a relationship. Often will communicate in shared activities.

Signs of progress: More in communication about these areas.

Dissociation: C

1) Initial team view: Dissociates until there is a safe resolution of problem: dissociation is a protection

2) Action:

Primary carer has to make the relationship within which the young person can feel safe enough to accept provision and make communication, often symbolic.

Signs of progress: Letting the primary carer in – dissociation diminishes.

3) Action:

Maintain high level of communication.

Signs of progress: Does not dissociate.

Dissociation: D

1) Initial team view: Unaware of their own falseness

2) Action:

Vital that falseness is tackled, otherwise the false area will haunt the young person well into adulthood, bringing psychotic problems.

Signs of progress: Getting into communication with a grown-up. Confronted by reality, the falseness will gradually break down. Pain and rage can accompany this process.

3) Action:

Confrontation of falseness. Grown-ups need to be confident in not accepting falseness and saying so in a way which can be accepted by the young person. Remember that this kind of young person often does not present a behaviour management problem and so we can easily be lulled into a complacent feeling that all is well.

Signs of progress: More in tune with falseness but unhappy with being confronted with reality. Still likely to be delinquent and resort to false veneer.

Dissociation: E

1) Initial team view: Unaware of some behaviours and attitudes (for example, anti-authority)

2) Action:

In presenting reality it is important to point out those areas where the young person is unaware of negative/destructive attitudes which affect others and the life of the group. Also, denial is often a part of this and the grown-up must help the young person to bring these areas into consciousness and devise ways of coping and converting them into more socially acceptable activity.

Signs of progress: Awareness of own behaviours and attitudes and links them to feelings.

3) Action:

Keep above going until the areas are more fully integrated into the personality.

Signs of progress: Manages these areas, or they cease to exist.

Self-destruction: A

1) Initial team view: Very low self-esteem

2) Action:

Imaginative provision to prop up low self-esteem. Primary carer needs to show unshakeable preoccupation which helps the young person to be able to accept provision. This in turn gives the young person a stronger value and belief in himself. Monitor impact of stress and anticipate.

Signs of progress: Accepts care from staff.

3) Action:

Continue above until young person is free from destructive impulses.

Signs of progress: Less self-destructive.

Self-destruction: B

1) Initial team view: Range of symptoms from self-mutilation and suicidal gestures to normality

2) Action:

Needs grown-ups to insist on providing care during and after breakdowns. The young person relies on the grown-up's unwavering determination to look after him.

Signs of progress: Allows grown-ups to help and provide care following breakdown.

3) Action:

Gradually will rely less on the provision as they come to value themselves. Remember the potential for self-destruction is there. Grown-ups need to be in touch and anticipate.

Signs of progress: Less likely but always a potential.

Self destruction: C

1) Initial team view: Protects themselves

2) Action:

The potential for self-destruction is in the tiny ego if it remains hidden, and uncared for. He has to allow the grown-up to meet the hidden self, and to protect it. No easy task for either worker or the young person, but very necessary.

Signs of progress: Although 'protector' breaking down, still no self-destruction.

3) Action:

As the ego gains confidence and greater belief in the self, he feels able to take better care of himself. His developing creativity combats the destructive impulses but it remains fragile.

Signs of progress: Not deliberately self-destructive.

Self-destruction: D

1) Initial team view: No overt self-destruction; narcissistic

2) Action:

The falseness of the personality carries with it potential for self-destructive behaviour which is often unconscious. The challenge to compliant behaviour and pseudo-adulthood will often produce a violent response if handled with insufficient sensitivity. But this is preferable to the unthinkable longer-term consequences of allowing the young person to go unchallenged.

Signs of progress: Showing signs of discomfort with the internal conflict between reality and falseness.

3) Action:

As above.

Signs of progress: Is in more communication and uses adults, depression and insight – can see that falseness is potentially self-destructive.

Self-destruction: E

1) Initial team view: Can revert to self-destructive behaviour particularly if a feature of the past

2) Action:

Unambiguous sign of breakdown. Get consultant/psychiatric help. Otherwise there should be no self-destruction. May be talked about under stress and we should be aware of past history and anticipate.

Signs of progress: Very rare instances.

Separation/loss: A

1) Initial team view: Full of raw hate. May panic at violent inner reaction

2) Action:

Adults provide space and time, not questioning, probing or providing sympathy/interpretation. Grown-ups need to be with the young person, helping to hold the despair for which there may well be no words.

Signs of progress: Starting to mourn and real crying. Reduction in frequency, intensity and duration of raw hate.

3) Action:

Primary carer gives the young person permission to feel absolutely awful and provide opportunities for communication both verbal and symbolic. Help the young person to move from the loss by creating something in reality which is satisfying. Grown-ups must make tentative efforts to communicate about the pain and sadness so that the young person can process some of the feelings, survive them and want to move on.

Signs of progress: Further reduction of violent reaction: communicating feelings of loss and sadness.

Separation/loss: B

1) Initial team view: Disintegrates into panic and despair

2) Action:

Can only face the early deprivation around the original loss when there is enough consistency, reliability and continuity established in his present reality. The panic that surrounds these early feelings needs to be contained by the grown-ups and he needs to know it.

Signs of progress: Becoming more in touch with his loss and less panicking, more despair and anger.

3) Action:

The panic begins to subside as the young person is able to talk about his early losses and stops idealising parents; although depressed, a better sense of reality is established.

Signs of progress: More communication, less displaced anger/more depression.

Separation/loss: C

1) Initial team view: Symbolism and non-verbal communication, also acting-out

2) Action:

The grown-up has to 'fight' to provide care for the small ego. The defensive shell that the young person has built will resist and will only dare to hand over real care to the grown-up when he feels safe enough to do so. The grown-up has to prove his reliability and consistency and unshakeability and accept the fairly violent reaction and try to make provision for it. Remember that the young person has to be able at some point to recognise feelings associated with loss and move on from them. Cannot be rushed.

Signs of progress: Anger as defences break down and realisation dawns.

3) Action:

Gradually and often through symbolic gestures the young person comes to realise that the grown-up can be trusted with his unresolved infantile needs. There will be small instances of 'handing over' of care like wanting the worker always to wash his hair or look after some special possession. Continue with play.

Signs of progress: Uses opportunities for play and communiation and dependency. Freedom of depression.

Separation/loss: D

1) Initial team view: Appearance of independence

2) Action:

Confronting the denial of the pain and loss of original carer. Great rage but can lead to communication providing the grown-up stays with it. This is the heart of the problem and it will take some time before treatment is effective.

Signs of progress: Starting to communicate, verbally and non-verbally. Primary carer will move into the transference and must be supported in it by the team. All the early feelings in the child's life begin to emerge and the carer has to receive and survive the pain.

3) Action:

Continue as in 2 above.

Signs of progress: Good communication and good use of new relationships plus depression.

Separation/loss: E

1) Initial team view: Unable to transfer unresolved feelings onto keyworker

2) Action:

Working still with the transference when anxiety/stress are high. Vital importance of encouraging discussion of the family and what went wrong. The wounds are still fairly raw for all our efforts and one person may still be required to absorb quite a bit of negativity and anger.

Signs of progress: Aware of transference relationships, interest in and discussion on family, past, etc.

3) Action:

Good time to start life-story work and plan for the future, that is, look back to help further processing of pain while looking forward in growing self-esteem to build on achievements to date.

Signs of progress: Life-story work.

Violence/aggression: A

1) Initial team view: Acts out violently – difficult to locate cause

2) Action:

Anticipation of acting-out, recognising the signs – met with appropriate provision, for example, sitting quietly with the young person before crescendo of acting-out rather than leaving him on his own.

Signs of progress: Is able to accept early interruption and primary provision.

3) Action:

Continuation of above. The young person will be able to recognise the feelings that cause the acting-out and can talk about it before it becomes uncontrollable.

Signs of progress: Can communicate violent and angry feelings and accept adaptation and symbolism.

Violence/aggression: B

1) Initial team view: Acts out anger, stress, anxiety

2) Action:

Grown-ups have to help the young person to find an outlet for his violence so that it does not become internalised and self-destructive. Imaginative provision and creative thinking needed.

Signs of progress: Reduction of violence in intensity and frequency particularly to adults.

3) Action:

As the young person learns to sublimate his anger and communicate about his feelings, the need to be violent is reduced. But the potential is still there.

Signs of progress: Rare but when it occurs, attacks self rather than grown-ups.

Violence/aggression: C

1) Initial team view: Acts out violently as response to perceived threat to inner self

2) Action:

Responsibility of grown-up for holding the transference and for recognising own feelings of countertransference so that the young person is protected from impingement by the adult.

Signs of progress: Aggressive towards carer and environment but reducing as provision meets needs.

3) Action:

Grown-ups must accept that this can be a very lengthy process and can be interrupted by further losses when the young person may well repeat earlier traumas and react badly. Violent acting-out is the breakdown in communication past or present and this needs to be understood and identified by the grown-up in the debriefing which should follow such outbursts.

Signs of progress: Aggressive when under stress or out of communication.

Violence/aggression: D

1) Initial team view: Violence in response to reality confrontation

2) Action:

Violence will only subside as young person gets into communication and depression. Channelling aggression into play and adaptations.

Signs of progress: Less prone to violence when confronted.

3) Action:

As the identification evolves, although the aggression subsides, the transition period is fraught with 'recidivism' and inappropriate alliances. Sensitive but no-nonsense communication, play and creativity are vital weapons in the armoury here.

Signs of progress: Less aggressive when confronted but could get drawn in to fight other people's battles.

Violence/aggression: E

1) Initial team view: Occasionally violent, often displaces or uses indirect forms to express his aggression

2) Action:

Grown-ups work imaginatively to convert any lingering hate and violence through healthy channels: communication, creativity, recognition of worth, management of feelings; now it is time to leave it behind and move forward.

Clear beams from the lighthouse and strategies for coping when the pain threatens.

Signs of progress: Fewer outbursts of violence. Beginning to find other channels to express aggression such as sport, creative pursuits.

3) Action:

Lots and lots of opportunities for socially acceptable channelling and sublimation of aggression through sports, gardening, riding and other more cerebral activities.

Signs of progress: In touch with feelings, generally able to contain. Channels aggression into creativity/activity.

Play: A

1) Initial team view: Never learned how to play

2) Action:

A lot of tactile play at a very primary level.

Signs of progress: Engages in play sessions with primary carer.

3) Action:

Regular play sessions with primary carer in which the adult is able to respond to the young person's playing world and thus create an interaction through which the young person can grow. Then they will move on to more sophisticated play.

Signs of progress: Can keep to rules, plays in a group.

Play: B

1) Initial team view: Can play but easily distracted and sometimes destructive – needs total adult preoccupation

2) Action:

Fluctuates between creative and destructive feelings. Is able to symbolise but do not expect too much too soon. Encourage play: it may be quite creative but hard to understand.

Signs of progress: Capacity to symbolise and more commitment to sessions.

3) Action:

The aim is socialisation and integrating with other young people and his play. Help them to join in and share without envy.

Signs of progress: Able to make good use of all play opportunities.

Play: C

1) Initial team view: Very infantile

2) Action:

Understanding of transitional objects and transitional experiences combined with as much opportunity for play on an experiential and constructive basis.

Signs of progress: Lot of symbolic play.

3) Action:

Play and communication will be populated by transitional milestones, for example, important play material and possessions become projected with the young person's fantasies about past and present experiences. It is important that the grown-up can come to understand and communicate with the young person the nature of, and the anxieties associated with, these fantasies so that the young person can grow and develop and can then move on leaving the material behind.

Signs of progress: Makes good use of play.

Play: D

1) Initial team view: Usually cannot play, blocked

2) Action:

As the compliance breaks down, if the environment is holding, the young person feels able to become more free and more spontaneous. Staff have to spot the moment and offer very basic, tactile experiences through which the young person can develop some freedom to play and learn about his potential.

Signs of progress: Starting to play, needs a lot of help, reluctant to get messy.

3) Action:

With the development of play, communication should also be established and this continues to enrich the young person's inner world from which the more genuine real self is becoming established.

Signs of progress: Continues to play, needs opportunities but less help. Play more reflective of genuine self.

Play: E

1) Initial team view: Poor response to range of play opportunities

2) Action:

Much can be achieved by making the everyday things playful. Grown-ups often have to take the lead and show that they can play thus giving the young people permission to play. Certainly anything that stimulates non-verbal and verbal communication is fine and the deliberate promotion of sublimation through creativity/creative living and functioning is a must.

Signs of progress: Able to enjoy some play although at times inhibited.

3) Action:

Remember this useful thought: 'We do not stop playing when we grow old, we grow old because we stop playing.'

Signs of progress: Enjoys playing – delightful small boy/girl inside.

Section two

- Defence mechanisms
- Depression
- Meeting primary needs
- Potential psychotic areas
- Self-perservation

Defence mechanisms: A

1) Initial team view: All defences pathological – uses own tactics to defend against relationships

2) Action:

Adults provide constant, reliable, predictable management and provision (for example, play sessions) so that the young person feels safe and can start to trust a grown-up or grown-ups. Cannot accept help without trust developing first.

Signs of progress: Starting to accept help – entering a dependency.

3) Action:

Symbolic communication recognised by grown-ups and responded to, not interpreted. Play should start and be maintained along with other regular opportunities for communication. Look for the beginnings of concern as the young person's need to maintain provision develops.

Signs of progress: In better communication with an adult and defences are less distorted.

Defence mechanisms: B

1) Initial team view: Under stress and anxiety they collapse into panic and chaos

2) Action:

Grown-ups must anticipate breakdown: learn what are the major stress points for the young person. Develop good nurturing and provision which can be used instead of breakdown. Strong support of functioning/creativity. Lot of sensitive care following breakdown which young person might try to reject – grown-ups must hang in there.

Signs of progress: Getting into communication and dependency – accepting of primary provision.

3) Action:

As the young person comes together and can start to talk about the areas of panic and rage, then convert provision into communication. Pay particular attention round cyclical events which may resurrect early trauma – again, importance of anticipation, for example, anniversaries.

Signs of progress: Better at coping with stress and anxiety; less destructive.

Defence mechanisms: C

1) Initial team view: Passionate denial, self-protection, blames others

2) Action:

The defensive shell can only give up when a trusting relationship develops. The young person uses the grown-up for provision but the process can be quite long-winded because the defensive shell has been in place for a long time.

Signs of progress: Letting the primary carer in – use of provision. Same paranoid reaction and beginnings of depression.

3) Action:

As the young person 'hands over' the defensive shell to the grown-up, the small sense of self that is left seeks to be looked after and through nurturing experiences is able to bear the pain of talking about the original deprivation. A stronger sense of self emerges.

Signs of progress: More communication, depression and dependent.

Defence mechanisms: D

1) Initial team view: False veneer of normality which breaks down under pressure of reality and stress

2) Action:

As compliance breaks down, the adult in touch needs to be able to produce the necessary primary provision, often localised nurturing experiences like staying in bed and receiving care and attention, which the young person finds acceptable.

Signs of progress: Becoming more dependent on adults, more age appropriate.

3) Action:

Through the provision comes a true appreciation of what adult relationships can offer and that allows the young person to move on and eventually accept genuine personal responsibility.

Signs of progress: Still uses adult relationships but to help with fragility, not falseness.

Defence mechanisms: E

1) Often paranoid and obsessional, low frustration threshold, psychosomatic

2) Action:

Combination of firm and clear guidelines, opportunities for creativity and communication and recognition of progress. The job is to convert paranoia and aggression into socially acceptable forms. Help young people to develop strategies for coping/taking responsibility when under stress or escaping the depression. What to do if you feel like ...?

Signs of progress: Reduction in use of anti-social defence mechanisms, beginning to channel aggression into acceptable forms.

3) Action:

Sublimation is a key component in developing survival defences. This mechanism for converting raw, primitive impulses and feelings needs to be consciously promoted by grown-ups at all times. Satisfying moments in relationships, stimulating intellectual and practical activity and self-esteem-building achievements are absolutely vital.

Signs of progress: Able to channel (sublimate) aggression and respond in socially acceptable ways.

Depression*: A

(* Depression here is not a clinical form of depression but rather a feeling of loss and sadness for what the young person has missed in earlier life.)

1) Initial team view: Cannot reach a healthy mourning

2) Action:

In order for the young person to be depressed there has to be a recognition of some good experience (a healthy dependency) to contrast with what the young person has missed. The level of communication is very important.

Signs of progress: Can be depressed but will lapse into either despair or acting-out.

3) Action:

The young person will have to give up the dependency – depression implies loss – but the young person can now cope with this because of the recognition of the value of the dependency and the need to grow. Emphasis on all forms of communication.

Signs of progress: Can be depressed for a significant period of time, using verbal or non-verbal communication.

Depression: B

1) Initial team view: Can be depressed but despairs. Needs localised 'regressive' experiences and adaptations

2) Action:

By staying with the young person through breakdown and beyond into making things better, he will start to appreciate the grown-up(s) and this will bring on the depression but not easily and there will be a lot of despair, possibly self-harm. Localised nurturing experiences, often spontaneous, will help – not long-lasting nurturing experiences.

Signs of progress: Can begin to be depressed but needs support.

3) Action:

Will need opportunities for communication and creative functioning – watch for symbolic communication in functioning and acknowledge positively. Likely to break down into despair – needs reminding how well he copes so much of the time and equally when functioning well may be able to talk about the bad times and their causes.

Signs of progress: Depression and functioning more in balance. May still be signs of despair.

Depression: C

1) Initial team view: Depressive feel to the young person

2) *Action:*

With the transference developing in the relationship with the grown-up, the young person begins to be able to get in touch with his depressive feelings. To manage this he will most likely regress to the point of the original breakdown. It is important that grown-ups can allow this to happen, for example, he may need to be ill and spend a few days in bed.

Signs of progress: Regressive and at times angry, depressed at times.

3) *Action:*

As he emerges from this breakdown he begins to deal with reality in more acceptable ways and can communicate about angry feelings. This leads to a greater sense of personal responsibility.

Signs of progress: Less regressed – becoming more depressed as communication improves.

Depression: D

1) Initial team view: No depression

2) *Action:*

As compliance begins to crack, a mixture of rage and depression emerges. It is very important that grown-ups are in touch with what is happening and encourage communication.

Signs of progress: Signs of depression.

3) *Action:*

Grown-ups have to respond to the degree of isolation in the young person that lies behind the compliance itself. By living closely alongside the young person, the pain and isolation can be brought into the personality.

Signs of progress: Can be depressed but needs help with it – communication, and opportunities for creativity.

Depression: E

1) Initial team view: Can get in touch with loss, sadness but unable to remain depressed

2) Action:

Depression can become despair or flight into paranoia/denial. Need plenty of opportunity for talking and doing something about those feelings that disturb the young person. It may be simply talking but it could be more concrete, for example, more work with home, more help with schooling.

Signs of progress: Able to verbalise depression and stay with it but only for short periods.

3) Action:

Maintain high level of communication and look for other ways of coping such as play and creativity.

Signs of progress: Can stay depressed. Will talk a lot. Good use made of key people.

Meeting primary needs: A

1) Initial team view: Does not trust adults

2) Action:

Stick to adult management and nurturing provision in the face of violent rage and rejection.

Signs of progress: Can allow adults to meet primary needs.

3) Action:

The emotional content of the key relationship takes on a more intimate and personal emphasis and the transference is recognisably powerful. Colleagues must be very supportive of primary carer.

Signs of progress: Greater emphasis on transference of feelings to the mother-figure than just having physical needs met.

Meeting primary needs: B

1) Initial team view: Unable to trust adults at moments of crisis

2) Action:

Provision of nurturing experiences by primary carer. Recognition in planning and management of his ability to function well and to fall apart under stress.

Signs of progress: Beginning to accept primary provision, particularly in a transferential relationship, although may be very rejecting.

3) Action:

As the relationship becomes stronger and the transference can be withstood, the hostility from previous relationships diminishes and the young person comes to see that the quality of the present relationship with the adult could have a positive outcome for him.

Signs of progress: Strong transference but more accepting of a relationship.

Meeting primary needs: C

1) Initial team view: Appearance of independence

For action see under 'Boundaries: C'

Signs of progress: Starts to use provision for the young person within –
can be nurtured. Able to regress. Allows adaptation for the young person
within; more age-appropriate.

Meeting primary needs: D

1) Initial team view: Denial of need of dependency relationship

2) Action:

Confronting the compliant self will produce rage which the primary carer
has to be able to hold and communicate with and make an adaptation which
meets the primary needs of the original deprivation, for example, being able
to wrap a young person up in a blanket with a hot water bottle to make them
feel safe in the face of his rage.

Signs of progress: Allowing an adult in to make primary provision,
needing nurturing experiences.

3) Action:

Then we should expect the young person to indicate that he wants to take
time out to have and use his own space. Adults allow them to do this rather
than continuing to impose the original provision.

Signs of progress: From time to time will make use of regressive
experiences.

Meeting primary needs: E

1) Initial team view: Independent

2) Action:

Can now begin to move away from primary provision and dependency on
one person. Now encourage the young person to use a number of people for
what they have to offer. Honour education relationships. Promote the idea of
a support network that we all need to develop to survive in a tough world –

so much more important where family support is unreliable. The concept of interdependence is similar and useful.

Signs of progress: Less dependent on one, accepting of input from others.

3) Action:

Encourage the use of the group for support, satisfying activity and the use of the grown-ups for helping hands. He will have a long time doing things on his own. Pass on to him a toolkit for survival.

Signs of progress: Interdependence: relies on different things. Uses the group.

Potential psychotic areas: A

1) Initial team view: Young person often not in touch with reality. Repeated patterns of worrying/bizarre behaviour

2) Action:

Initially the adult is in touch with the split-off areas and keeps the consciousness on behalf of the young person. Is able to make provision for the deprivation which the split-off area represents. Encourage play.

Signs of progress: Reduction in frequency, intensity and duration of worrying behavior.

3) Action:

Adults should be able to talk about split-off bits and help the young person to take responsibility for them by developing tactics/strategies with the young person.

Signs of progress: More able to develop techniques with adult help to manage with adult support.

Potential psychotic areas: B

1) Initial team view: Falls apart under stress, panics, can be violent with potential for breakdown into despair – can be helped

2) Action:

As yet the split-off bits of rage and anger are not unreal but could become so if not treated. Providing the treatment programme is adhered to, the young person should not end up with psychotic areas.

Signs of progress: Less frequent panic and for shorter periods of time.

3) Action:

Ask ourselves whether there are any 'stuck' areas. These can lead to serious problems in later life. Important that after a while the primary carer brings the subject up in communication – to keep it conscious.

Signs of progress: In good communication; less violence but always an element of despair/self-destruction.

Potential psychotic areas: C

1) Initial team view: Furious denial protects their potential for breakdown

2) Action:

The rage, if not processed through the transference, will form a psychotic area, potentially murderous, split off from the self that is able to symbolise and play. This process can take years because the damage has been so chronic and profound.

Signs of progress: Accepts provision of care and nurture – safe dependency created.

3) Action:

To maintain primary provision and play recognising symbolic communication and its importance.

Signs of progress: Symbolically hands over the young person within – to the primary carer.

Potential psychotic areas: D

1) Initial team view: Continuing falseness defends against their real inadequacy being exposed

2) Action:

Maintain the treatment programme, particularly in relation to communication so that the young person is always aware of the potential for nurturing experiences. As the young person begins to be able to take responsibility for himself, so he can defend against the potential psychotic areas and know what makes him vulnerable to acting-out.

Signs of progress: The falseness which prevents real inadequacy being exposed gradually reduces. There will always be a potential for self-destructive acting-out.

3) Action:

As he is helped to become more real and creative, so he begins to move away from his potential psychotic areas.

Signs of progress: Reducing problem as falseness decreases, but still very fragile.

Potential psychotic areas: E

1) Initial team view: Displays some worrying stuck areas, for example, dependence on infantile defence mechanisms such as splitting

2) Action:

Watch for worrying stuck areas and talk about them seriously without persecution. Sell the benefits of extra help from outside experts. See Laufer (1973).

Signs of progress: Reduction in display of stuck areas.

3) Action:

Devise strategies for the stuck area. But do not leave it alone, especially if there is more than one.

Signs of progress: Beginning to manage own difficult bits and signal stress.

Self-preservation: A

1) Initial team view: Careless awareness of self

2) Action:

Grown-ups take care of and respond to the crumpled young person. Make the young person feel loved and appreciated.

Signs of progress: Accepts care from staff, with increase in self-esteem.

3) Action:

Young person is encouraged to take on his own care as he appreciates himself for his own qualities.

Signs of progress: Able to accept positive aspects of self, and care for self with occasional support.

Self-preservation: B

1) Initial team view: Careful except when not functioning then careless

2) Action:

Needs grown-ups to insist on providing care during and after breakdowns. The young person relies on the grown-ups' unwavering determination to look after him.

Signs of progress: Own carefulness increasing. Can vary according to level of stress.

3) Action:

Gradually will rely less on the provision as they come to value themselves. Remember the potential for self-destruction is there. Grown-ups need to be in touch and anticipate.

Signs of progress: Much greater sense of self, both good and bad.

Self-preservation: C

1) Initial team view: Poor real self-preservation

2) Action:

Preoccupation of the young person on the inside can make them neglect themselves on the outside. See under 'Boundaries' for guidance.

Signs of progress: Accepts help with care.

3) Action:

Through the adult's value of the young person they are able eventually to take care of and value themselves.

Signs of progress: Improving sense of self.

Self-preservation: D

1) Initial team view: Very narcissistic

2) Action:

The young person tends to be far too focused on his self and its survival. Therefore self-preservation is over-determined and is used as a denial – 'I cope very well, don't I?' A hopeful sign would be getting messy and getting into tactile play.

Signs of progress: Less narcissistic.

3) Action:

Being able to allow illness and to be looked after – not being so self-reliant and allowing depression and dependence.

Signs of progress: Might become messy, in other words, more real.

Self-preservation: E

1) Initial team view: Lacking in self-esteem and personal care

2) Action: Grown-ups provide strong support here. Training for living and coping with personal matters in times of stress. Remember how it was for us and we had a lot of help.

Signs of progress: Deteriorates at times of stress and anxiety.

3) Action:

Continue as above.

Signs of progress: Generally good.

Section three

- Creativity
- Ego functioning
- Environment: making use of and contributing to one's own
- Identification
- Learning from experience/learning-school

Creativity: A

1) Initial team view: No healthy creativity

2) Action:

Opportunities for play, art, doing things with a grown-up. Using the imagination: stories, spontaneity as an antidote to acting-out.

Signs of progress: Able to participate in creative pursuits with an adult.

3) Action:

Constant offering of creative opportunities by grown-ups so that the young person is able to take something of that for themselves. We are trying to promote enthusiasm.

Signs of progress: Can follow creative pursuits alone. Still may need a little adult support occasionally. Gains self-esteem.

Creativity: B

1) Initial team view: When functioning and settled can be creative

2) Action:

The adults must recognise the creative areas of the young person and must support these as a counter to the self-destructive urges.

Signs of progress: Regular creativity developing – needs a lot of support.

3) Action:

The creativity allows for sublimation (see Chapter 4) of the self-destructiveness and a greater integration of the split-off areas of the personality.

Signs of progress: Regular creative pursuits alone.

Creativity: C

1) Initial team view: Potential for creativity but it is short-lived, often ends in destruction

2) Action:

All experiences that the young person has from the primary carer must be complete, for example, you do not give him a bit of apple, he has a whole one. Time spent with him must have a beginning, a middle and an end. This goes on until he realises that provision is unconditional and cannot be threatened.

Signs of progress: Creativity in play/symbols; less destructive.

3) Action

As he internalises the good experience he becomes more confident with his own creativity and involves grown-ups and other young persons in his play without disruption. As his play develops he can communicate about his anxieties, particularly around separation and loss.

Signs of progress: Long periods of good functioning, often creative, uses grown-ups.

Creativity: D

1) Initial team view: Not age-appropriate creativity – done to conform

2) Action:

Encourage creativity in all its forms. The more the depression holds and the young person comes through it, the more creative they can be.

Signs of progress: Signs of self-motivated functioning, more age-appropriate.

3) Action:

Maintain encouragement.

Signs of progress: Much more self-motivated and genuine functioning.

Creativity: E

1) Initial team view: Able to pursue creative pursuits alongside an adult

2) Action:

Very important. What stands between children and delinquency, promiscuity, etc., is a rich, self-actuating inner world of imagination, getting involved, planning for the future, ambition and training, creative activity and living, all activities which encourage sublimation at one level and increase self-esteem at another.

Adults must promote this in every way possible – by example, by stimulus and by recognition of achievement in this area.

Signs of progress: Once initiated is able to pursue creative activities alone with encouragement.

3) Action:

More of the same as in 2.

Signs of progress: Has individual creative pursuits. Initiates creative activities.

Ego functioning: A

1) Initial team view: Little sense of self. Total reliance on others to provide ego strengths

2) Action:

Young person begins to live alongside and interrelate with others, not wholly preoccupied now with his own survival.

Signs of progress: Main functioning with and through adults.

3) Action:

Recognise small achievements and steps – to boost self-esteem.

Signs of progress: Periods of survival without adult support.

Ego functioning: B

1) Initial team view: Capable of periods of functioning with total adult support

2) Action:

Needs a lot of support both when functioning well and when he 'falls apart'. Will use more than one adult and they should quietly let him know that he is talked about – adults pulling together are a mirror for the young person. Still likely to try to reject adult help – hang in there.

Signs of progress: More functioning with less adult support.

3) Action:

Stimulate functioning and creativity, also recognise the young person's own initiatives. Needs self-esteem boosting and communication.

Signs of progress: More self-generated functioning and ability to accept help in breakdown/despair.

Ego functioning: C

1) Initial team view: Over-determined sense of right and wrong, fairness and 'holier than thou' attitude (often known in shorthand as the super-ego), responds mainly to external stimuli

2) Action:

As the young person perceives that the grown-ups determine the environment, the reality created by the young person becomes precarious and makes him react violently to this culture. As the young person comes to realise that there is something in it for him, the super ego diminishes and the primary carer is allowed to get in touch with the fragile ego and feed it through numerous play experiences.

Signs of progress: Starts to use provision and becomes dependent for functioning on adults.

3) Action:

Through that process as the ego strengthens the young person becomes less dependent on the provision of the grown-up and begins to be more self-motivated.

Signs of progress: Begins to function on own.

Ego functioning: D

1) Initial team view: Very superficial based on their idea of what others want – age inappropriate, no creative flair

2) Action:

The capacity of the grown-up to confront the compliance/falseness and hold on to feelings which emerge enables the young person to develop a new basis for his experience. The grown-up offers as part of the provision more appropriate experiences and activities.

Signs of progress: More age-appropriate, more real feel to ego functioning.

3) Action:

The young person is able to make use of experience offered and to make a contribution to the culture they are involved in rather than identify with subculture.

Signs of progress: Good progress – educationally and creatively real contributions, not just to conform.

Ego functioning: E

1) Initial team view: Needs a lot of support and encouragement

2) Action:

We start by moving from primary provision to support of the fragile ego. Getting the young person involved more in doing things to help make group living tick. Develop genuine enthusiasm for the tasks of living while teaching skills for living. Massive support for education and future planning, must have goals, achievements and growing feelings of self-worth.

Signs of progress: Less dependent on support from others. Is it genuine or compliance?

3) Action:

Encourage more self-motivated functioning – creativity, outside interests, contributing to the household environment. Talking about problems at school, planning for making things happen both there and at home. Recognise and celebrate milestones.

Signs of progress: Still a concern, more ego developed, is more genuine, for example, is working towards an objective.

Environment: making use of and contributing to one's own: A

1) Initial team view: Not aware of self, only superficial interest, obsessional hobby likely

2) Action:

The young person identifies with the adult and adult surroundings through the dependency. Help the young person to see the outer reality as non-persecutory.

Signs of progress: Accepting of milieu. Stops damaging environment.

3) Action:

Young person is helped to share the world they are in and is encouraged and is able to contribute to it. Is the culture experienced as pleasurable?

Signs of progress: Contributes to milieu. Attributes and sense of self apparent through this contribution.

Environment: making use of and contributing to one's own: B

1) Initial team view: Their appreciation is a double-edged sword – it has capacity to destroy as well as contribute

2) Action:

Enormous capacity to destroy both self and surroundings. Has great capacity for contributing as well: give opportunities. They do get better!

Signs of progress: More accepting of environment – more destructive to themselves than environment.

3) Action:

Less self-harm through being valued by grown-ups and will value surroundings more if needs are being met.

Signs of progress: Destructiveness to self abates, also more of an appreciation and contribution to environment

Environment: making use of and contributing to one's own: C

1) Initial team view: Not rejecting of whole environment and will contribute to their own

2) Action:

Grown-ups helping the young person to be less panicky about the outside world and his close environment – he will naturally tend to see it as threatening and impinging on his reality. A very sensitive moving-in by the primary carer.

Signs of progress: Growing awareness of his wider environment.

3) Action:

Gradually the young person will 'join' as the defensive shell gives way but very much with adults in the centre of life providing for the little ego.

Signs of progress: Is able to share environment with others and contribute to the group life.

Environment: making use of and contributing to one's own: D

1) Initial team view: Pseudo appreciation – what others want them to accept

2) Action:

When the child is able to afford dependency and accept provision he feels that he can contribute to the group culture without being envious of what other people have to offer. He is satisfied with his individual creativity as his instinctual life deepens.

Signs of progress: Not quite so conformist, could be challenging.

3) Action:

Maintain the challenge and aim for more age-appropriate initiatives.

Signs of progress: More positive and developing individuality.

Environment: making use of and contributing to one's own: E

1) Initial team view: Only contributes to subculture. Lethargic air about him

2) Action:

Keep closely in touch – individual sessions, talking groups, lots of purposeful planning, satisfying creative activity. Challenge negativity and unearth the subculture and bring it into the open for discussion and learning. Keep boundaries clear and remember the lighthouse.

Signs of progress: Involved in creating, developing environment and joins in activities.

3) Action:

Encourage the taking of initiative by individuals and groups to improve the quality of life and celebrate the achievements.

Signs of progress: Often initiates activities, developments in the group.

Identification: A

1) Initial team view: Merges rather than identifies

2) Action:

The young person through the dependency recognises a sense of his own value and rejects the merger.

Signs of progress: Healthy recognition of self.

3) Action:

Watch for signs of separation from the dependency and allow it to happen. Primary carer must be very aware of his own feelings – colleagues on the outside may be more sensitive to the signs.

Signs of progress: Healthy identification with peers or adults and a self-identification.

Identification: B

1) Initial team view: Can identify with adult or young person but will also merge

2) Action:

When 'falling apart' will merge but through adults will start to identify with peers and grown-ups, the latter through functioning and creativity.

Signs of progress: Can identify with others, often a link through creativity.

3) Action:

Will move away from other young persons for focus and will use grown-ups. Can be a loner. Needs reassurance that he is OK because own family adult models often unhelpful in this area.

Signs of progress: More adult identification and possibly a 'loner'.

Identification: C

1) Initial team view : Identifies with someone who has cared for them at some time in their life

2) Action:

Strong adult role models offered in all areas of functioning. Take care to avoid stereotypes within the team organisation.

Signs of progress: Starting to make good contact with a grown-up and handing over care.

3) Action:

Key worker prepared to take on primary care of small ego. Use symbols and play creatively.

Signs of progress: A more genuine identification with role models.

Identification: D

1) Initial team view: The pseudo-adult

2) Action:

The more he is able to get in touch with pain and process it through an adult the more able he is to form more realistic relationships. This is a lengthy process and has to be sensitively helped along by both primary carer and others.

Signs of progress: Not quite so idolatrous, less pseudo-adult – possibly inappropriate idealisation of adults and peers.

3) Action:

Continue as in 2 above.

Signs of progress: Beginning to make more age-appropriate relationships and use adult models for support.

Identification: E

1) Initial team view: Immature or unhealthy identification. Could appear pseudo-adult

2) Action:

Difficult to get the balance right between age-appropriate and emotional age-appropriate identity. Uses grown-ups not so closely involved for his opinions, for example, teachers and those who meet them in outside interests. Challenge without being punitive and talk about it a lot. Do not expect instant success. Much revolves round his own peers rather than grown-ups. But the metaphor of the grown-up as a lighthouse is a useful one.

Signs of progress: Identification with role-models and bits of others.

3) Action:

It may not appear so sometimes but young people do use us as role models and so the lighthouse is a useful symbol for us to follow.

Signs of progress: Individual identity developing.

Learning from experience/learning-school: A

1) Initial team view: Does not learn from experience, possible school phobic, excluded, very behind for age

2) Action:

Emphasis here is on adults as role models so that the young person has a mirror with which he can identify reliable/predictable incidents of cause and effect. Play very important in this process.

Signs of progress: Developing basic trust, understands cause and effect.

3) Action:

Adults confirm and support the young person's view of themselves as worthwhile people. Play should be very constructive and creative.

Signs of progress: Can make positive choices.

Learning from experience/learning-school: B

1) Initial team view : Potential both cognitively and emotionally through communication but will lose it under stress

2) Action:

Has had a pretty terrible early experience and this conditions and colours his responses. Expect repeated failure to avoid breakdown but grown-ups make themselves available positively both for the pain and for the functioning.

Signs of progress: Starts to learn from experience and makes use of school.

3) Action:

Despair is the problem. Often understands 'too well' what is causing problems but cannot escape. Wait for communication to start and also recognise small non-verbal signals of change. Essentially is capable of both understanding and change with adult support.

Signs of progress: Is learning from experience but becomes stuck in despair occasionally.

Learning from experience/learning-school: C

1) Initial team view: Finds learning from experience difficult. Huge support needed at school

2) Action:

Cannot learn easily as reality is so threatening to the small ego. Allow time and the persistence of the nurturing grown-up to enable the young person to make the dependent relationship in which learning can take place safely. Play very helpful because it helps the young person to order reality.

Signs of progress: Starts to learn through relationship and provision. Symbolic infant emerging.

3) Action:

Promote communication and more age-appropriate activity in a sensitive supportive way so that the young person does not perceive the world as threatening/persecutory.

Signs of progress: Can learn generally and able to grow from the exploration of a strong transference over a long period of time.

Learning from experience/learning-school: D

1) Initial team view: Learns with enormous difficulty – what they think others want of them

2) Action:

The young person needs to feel secure in the environment so that the breakdown of the compliance into reality is held and he can make the transition to healthy ego development and learning. Very painful because the appreciation of what has caused them to be what they are like is upsetting.

Signs of progress: More real reflection of the young person in school and group – possible breakdown in formal education.

3) Action:

Continue to provide opportunities for learning and communication.

Signs of progress: Still learning and changing, still sometimes reluctant. Better use of school/educational opportunities.

Learning from experience/learning school: E

1) Initial team view: Commitment to school generally. Poor progress, repeating past mistakes

2) Action:

Expanding communication and encouraging a variety of functioning helps here. Life-story work can be valuable allowing for supported reflection and a chance to improve the pay-off from more profound communication. Planning again to cope with those events which have proved so difficult in the past. Using what we have learned to plan for the future realistically.

Signs of progress: Less repeating of past mistakes, commitment to school.

3) Action:

Provide help with mapping support network and planning for those times when stress and anxiety are high, for example, anger management programmes.

Signs of progress: Can reflect on experience and values education.

Using the need assessment

We suggest the use of a chart for each dimension on which is recorded the team's views, what action is to be taken and where this is to be recorded. We have to ensure that the assessment is a live, working document and so vital information is transferred and key people alerted to the current programme. The chart could look something like this:

DIMENSION	GUIDANCE	ACTION TO BE TAKEN	ALERT AND/OR TRANSFER
			24-hour management programme Care Plan
INITIAL TEAM VIEW			Social Worker Family School Consultant Child protection Training dept Health Children's services Other

Once the chart for each dimension has been designed in the way you want it then it can be used to record the team's assessment.

As a guide we have included below a sample of a real assessment of a twelve-year-old girl, S. The team looked at eight dimensions and from that adjusted the 24-hour management programme, amended the care plan and improved her contact with both school and family.

As the team becomes more familiar with the process and the material, assessments will speed up but to begin with do not try to do too much. The team whose assessment we present as a sample managed to consider eight dimensions in the time available but they were those dimensions which concerned them most at that time.

Name: S.   Age: 12   Assessment No. 1   23.06.97

DIMENSION	GUIDANCE	ACTION TO BE TAKEN	ALERT AND/OR TRANSFER
Boundaries – **C**	Fight to provide care for small ego. Keyworker to provide reliability	Mike – keyworker to 'fight' to provide care and needs help of whole team	24-hour management **X** programme Care Plan **X**
INITIAL TEAM VIEW	consistency and unshakeability. Make provision for violent reaction.	to be reliable and to make special provision – chocolate Freddos.	Social Worker Family School
From C 'Under stress merges and disrupts the functioning of others'.			Consultant Child protection Training dept Health Children's services Other

DIMENSION	GUIDANCE	ACTION TO BE TAKEN	ALERT AND/OR TRANSFER
Capacity for concern, empathy, remorse, etc. – C INITIAL TEAM VIEW	Communicates by symbols. Starts to make a relationship but it is precarious and can become violent or depressed when continuity breaks down.	Continue communicating with the wrestlers* until S. is able to transfer to grown-ups. Encourage reparation and recognise it. * She has some dolls – wrestlers.	24-hour management X programme Care Plan X Social Worker Family School Consultant Child protection Training dept Health Children's services Other

DIMENSION	GUIDANCE	ACTION TO BE TAKEN	ALERT AND/OR TRANSFER
Dissociation – C	Primary carer has to make the relationship.	Mike to hang in there promoting communication and trust.	24-hour management X programme
	S. must feel safe enough to		Care Plan
INITIAL TEAM VIEW	communicate, often symbolic, and accept		Social Worker
	provision.		Family School Consultant Child protection Training dept Health Children's services Other
Dissociates until there is a resolution of the problem, that is dissociation is a protection.			

DIMENSION	GUIDANCE	ACTION TO BE TAKEN	ALERT AND/OR TRANSFER
Self-destruction – C	Can allow certain grown-ups to get close.	Mike to continue to make the relationship, to help S. hand over more of	24-hour management X programme
INITIAL TEAM VIEW		her care to the grown-ups.	Care Plan Social Worker Family School Consultant Child protection
Protects herself.			Training dept Health Children's services Other

DIMENSION	GUIDANCE	ACTION TO BE TAKEN	ALERT AND/OR TRANSFER
Communication – C	Takes a while to adapt to our reality.	Play to be encouraged at all times. Care with forcing talk.	24-hour management X programme
	Keep up play and responding to symbols.	Offer variety of play art,	Care Plan X
INITIAL TEAM VIEW	Don't force the issue on talking.	modelling, toys and games	Social Worker Family School Consultant Child protection Training dept Health
Symbolic communication, some verbal, play and adaptation.			Children's services Other

DIMENSION	GUIDANCE	ACTION TO BE TAKEN	ALERT AND/OR TRANSFER
Defence Mechanisms – C	The defensive shell can only be given up when a trusting relationship develops.	Mike to work as in section on Boundaries. Ensure support while in group situations.	24-hour management X programme
			Care Plan X
INITIAL TEAM VIEW	It has been there for a long time. It's a slow process.		Social Worker Family School Consultant Child protection Training dept Health Children's services Other
Passionate Denial Self protection Blames others			

DIMENSION	GUIDANCE	ACTION TO BE TAKEN	ALERT AND/OR TRANSFER
Play – C	Past and present fantasies communicated through play. Vital that the grown-up comes to	Play to be encouraged. Mike to play alongside S. to enter her world of fantasy.	24-hour management X programme Care Plan Social Worker Family
INITIAL TEAM VIEW Lots of symbolic play.	understand and communicate with S. the nature of her fantasies and the anxiety associated with them so S. can grow and move on.		School X Consultant Child protection Training dept Health Children's services Other

DIMENSION	GUIDANCE	ACTION TO BE TAKEN	ALERT AND/OR TRANSFER
Potential Psychotic Areas – C	The rage, if not processed through the transference, will form a psychotic area.*	Work as for 'Boundaries'.	24-hour management **X** programme
			Care Plan
INITIAL TEAM VIEW	*Editor's note; Chronic 'stuckness' merits a consultation with a psychiatrist.		Social Worker Family School Consultant Child protection
Furious denial protects her potential for breakdown.			Training dept Health **X** Children's services Other

DIMENSION	GUIDANCE	ACTION TO BE TAKEN	ALERT AND/OR TRANSFER
Identification – C	Strong adult role models offered in all areas of functioning. Avoid stereotypes.	Family contact to be maintained and encouraged.	24-hour management X programme
			Care Plan X
			Social Worker X
			Family X
INITIAL TEAM VIEW			School
			Consultant
Identifies with someone who has cared for them at sometime in her life.			Child protection
			Training dept
			Health
			Children's services
			Other

DIMENSION	GUIDANCE	ACTION TO BE TAKEN	ALERT AND/OR TRANSFER
Learning from experience, etc. – C	Cannot learn easily as reality is threatening to the small ego.	Mike to offer support at school.	24-hour management **X** programme
		Encourage lots of play and symbolic	Care Plan **X**
INITIAL TEAM VIEW		communication.	Social Worker Family
		Introduce this concept to	
Finds learning from experience difficult. Huge support needed in school.		school.	School **X** Consultant Child protection Training dept Health Children's services Other

Part of a sound therapeutic programme is the 24-hour management programme. This is constructed by the team to ensure consistent and reliable parenting, plus those vital individual pieces of provision or support. Much of the data will come from the Need Assessment. The team which completed the assessment above produced the 24-hour programme which follows. It is also possible to produce shorter plans for day centres and schools.

It is the responsibility of the shift leader or equivalent to remind staff of the details of the 24-hour programmes for that period of the day. Changes and updates are only agreed by a team meeting. Without showing the actual 24-hour piece of paper, it should be possible to discuss the contents of the programme with the young person. Major changes need to be part of the care plan and it is vital that interested parties are kept informed.

Key workers should make a summary of objectives and methods and this should form part of the care plan and be attached to the Looking After Children records. Documentation is vital so that new staff can check things out, inspectors can check practice almost at a glance and parents and social workers receive clear, helpful review papers.

24-Hour Management Programme

Name: S.   **Date: 23 June 97**

Waking/getting up	Meal Times	In Between Times
S. to be allowed to remain in bed if she claims to be ill. Give encouragement and support. Help S. get up by getting her clothes ready and dressing her if needs be.	S. needs encouragement to eat. Either with the group or on a one to one.	Adults standing by for violent outbursts. Use distractions and staff with some relationship with S. to interrupt when she becomes excited.
Behaviour in Groups	**Communication**	**To and From School**
Mike to offer support whenever S. is in a group. Mike to support during art therapy.	Watch for signs of stress, e.g. building camps. Watch for transference and staff countertransference. Encourage play.	S. to be supported to and from school. Staff to offer support in school.
Bed-time and Night-times	**Special needs and Adaptations**	**Needs Assessments**
Mike to make provision for play. Also S. to choose about her door and light.	Mike to provide Freddos. Mike to play with S. on a regular basis to support functioning.	Encourage reparation, watch for dissociation and denial. Communication with school imperative.

Bibliography

Start here

Dockar-Drysdale, B. (1993) 'Needs Assessment I – Finding a basis', 'Needs Assessment II – making an assessment' and 'Needs Assessments and Context Profiles', in *Therapy and Consultation in Child Care*, Free Association Books.
'Looking after children: understanding the assessment and action records' from 'The Looking After Children Training Pack', HMSO 1991.

Further reading

Ahmed, S., Cheetham, J. and Small, J. (1986) *Social Work with Black Children and Their Families*, Batsford.
Alvarez, A. (1995) 'Motiveless Malignity: Problems in the Psychotherapy of Psychopathic Patients', *Journal of Child Psychotherapy*, 10(2).
Balbernie, R. (1973) 'Un-integration, integration and level of ego functioning as the determinants of planned "cover therapy" of unit task, and of placement', Paper presented at the University of Reading, available from Caldecott College.
Balbernie, R. (1989) 'Looking at what professional carers do', *Maladjustment and Therapeutic Education*, 1989.
Barrett, M. and Trevitt, J. (1984) *Attachment Behaviour and the School Child*, Routledge.
Bentovim, A. et al. (1991) *Children and Young People as Abusers*, National Children's Bureau.
Berger, M. (1994) 'Psychological Tests and Assessment', in Rutter M., Taylor, E., and Herzov, L., *Child and Adolescent Psychiatry: modern approaches* 3rd edn, Blackwell.
Bick, E. (1987) 'The experience of the skin in early object relations', in Harris Williams, M. (ed.) *Collected Papers of Martha Harris and Esther Bick*, The Clunie Press.
Bradley, C. (1995) 'Issues in residential work' in Trowell, J. and Bower, M. (eds) *The Emotional Needs of Young Children and their Families*, Routledge.
Brandon, M. and Lewis, A. (1996) 'Significant harm and children's experiences of domestic violence', *Child and Family Social Work*, Blackwells.
Bruggen, P. and O'Brian, T. (1986) *Surviving Adolescence*, Faber and Faber.
Copley, B. and Forryan, B. (1987) 'Inner world phantasy and primitive communication', in *Therapeutic Work with Children and Young People*, Robert Royce.
Davis, M. and Wallbridge, D. (1981) 'Adapting to shared reality' from *Boundary and Space: an introduction to the work of D.W. Winnicott*, Penguin Books.
De Zulueta, F. (1993) *From Pain to Violence*, Whurr.
Dockar-Drysdale, B. (1993) 'Residential treatment of 'frozen' children', 'The provision of primary experience in a therapeutic school', 'Play as therapy in child care', 'Integration and un-integration', 'Meeting children's emotional needs', 'Syndrome', in *Therapy and Consultation in Child Care*, Free Association Books.
Dockar-Drysdale B. (1990) 'Staff consultation in an evolving care system', in *The Provision of Primary Experience*, Free Association Books.
Finkelhor, D. et al. (1986) *Initial and Long Term Effects of Sexual Abuse: A Conceptual Framework*, Sage.

Graham H. (1993) 'Caring for Children in Poverty', in Fergusson, H., Gilligan, R. and Torode, R. (eds) *Surviving Childhood Adversity: Issues for Policy and Practice*, Dublin: Social Studies Press.

Greenhalgh, P. (1994) *Emotional Growth and Learning*, Routledge.

Hoghughi, M. (1992) *Assessing Child and Adolescent Disorders*, Sage.

Jewett, C. (1982) *Helping Children Cope with Separation and Loss*, Batsford.

Laufer, M. (1975) *Adolescent Disturbance and Breakdown*, Pelican.

McMahon, L. (1992) *The Handbook of Play Therapy*, Routledge.

Menzies Lyth, I. (1994) 'The Development of the Self in Children in Institutions' in Trowell, J. and Bower, M. (eds) *The Emotional Needs of Young Children and Their Families*, Routledge.

Mirza, H. (1992) *Young, Female and Black*, Routledge.

O'Flaherty J. (1995) 'High/Scope', *Highlight*, 131, London: N.C.B.

Parker R., Ward H., Jackson S., Aldgate J. and Wedge P. (eds) (1991) *Looking After Children: Assessing Outcomes in Child Care*, London: HMSO.

Salzberger-Wittenberg, I. (1970) *Psychoanalytic Insight and Relationships*, Routledge.

Trowell, J. and Bower, M. (1995) 'Introduction: the social context', in *The Emotional Needs of Young Children and their Families*, Routledge.

Varma, V. (ed.) (1996) *The Inner Life of Children with Special Needs*, Whurr.

Ward, H. (ed.) (1995) *Looking After Children: Research into Practice*, London: HMSO.

Ward, H. (1992) 'Assessment and the Children Act 1989: the Looking After Children Project' in Fergusson, H., Gilligan, R. and Torode, R. (eds) *Surviving Childhood Adversity*, Dublin: Social Studies Press.

Winnicott D.W. (1990) 'Ego distortion in terms of True and False Self', in *The Maturational Processes and the Facilitating Environment*, Karnac Books.

Winnicott, D.W. (1990) 'The Theory of the Parent-Infant Relationship', 'Ego-integration in Child Development' and 'Ego Distortion in terms of True and False self' in *The Maturational Processes and the Facilitating Environment*, Karnac Books.

Winnicott, D.W. (1990) *Deprivation and Delinquency*, Routledge.

8 Using a therapeutic model of thought and practice

Anna Maher

'Grown-ups never understand anything for themselves, and it is tiresome for children to be always and forever explaining things to them.' (Saint-Exupéry, *The Little Prince*)

For those who are involved in residential care – in a boarding school, foster care, secure accommodation or children's home – Dartington's five conditions (see Chapter 6) are an elegant and simply stated set of commandments. However, we are left to work out the full implications of putting each condition into practice. Take, for example their third condition:

> The pursuit by the institution of a set of goals which are matched to the primary rather than the secondary needs of children; that is to the needs which necessitated absence from home rather than those brought about by living away. These aims should be re-iterated in a wide variety of ways and permeate the whole control process. (Little and Kelly 1995: 116)

'Meeting primary needs' are the key words. Those vital moments of the early years when the primary carer expresses Winnicott's maternal preoccupation, is the good enough mother and allows the baby to move from a state of oneness with the mother into an integrated, separate person. But if it all goes horribly wrong and a substitute has to be found, then how do we make good the missing primary needs? The chapter which follows written by Anna Maher addresses this third Dartington condition and demonstrates the thinking needed both by the child therapist and by those who live with and care for the young person.

What is so striking about Anna Maher's chapter is her unflagging attempt to accept the communication from the child in whatever form it takes –

difficult behaviour (C.'s rejection of fairness or D.'s taking what does not belong to him which is not stealing*), symbolism and non-verbal interaction which often lead to the most significant verbal exchanges.

These are ways in which primary needs are communicated and met in the child's world. Fail to meet these needs and we spend much of our time in policing trying to interrupt mergers and delinquent excitement, and coping with panic.

The model of thinking and practice that Anna Maher presents is a sophisticated one but must be understood and practised if the findings of Dartington's useful research are to be used to benefit children in substitute care.

*See also Chapter 28 in *Deprivation and Delinquency* where Winnicott (1984) describes dissociation and a model for dealing with it.

8 Using a therapeutic model of thought and practice

Anna Maher

In this chapter I am exploring the role of the therapist in terms of the relationship with the child within the boundaries of the therapy sessions, and the wider aspects of the role as a resource to others working with and caring for the child. My focus is on what is meant by a therapeutic response and the issues surrounding its development. It is written within the theoretical framework of psychoanalytic ideas, with the use of case material. One central issue runs through the chapter: knowledge and understanding of the development of individual children accompany the growth of self-knowledge in those who work with and care for the child.

By a therapeutic response I mean thinking about what the child is trying to communicate through words and behaviour, and responding in a way that is helpful and can be understood by the child. To achieve this, it is necessary to try to understand what may be the feelings underlying what the child is communicating, and to respond in a way that both acknowledges and contains them. This means taking into account the child's inner world and stage of emotional development, as well as the reality of what is happening in the environment, and one's own response to it. This chapter will expand on and clarify the complex issues involved in achieving this in a way which aims to be helpful to those who endeavour to develop a therapeutic response.

The setting and its boundaries

The use of case material has been made possible by my work at two small therapeutic units where I see the children directly for individual therapy work and also supervise the staff who care for them. The combination of the two roles of course raises questions as to how I am perceived by the children, as it is inevitable they see me in the units when fulfilling my supervisory role. This means that the boundaries between the two roles have to be strictly adhered to, and fully understood by both the children and staff, and that all my interactions with the children outside the therapy room are kept to a minimum. I play no part in their everyday care. If present during a confrontation between a child and a member of staff, I remain neutral and do not intervene in any way, and leave the scene as quickly as possible.

Discussion about appropriate intervention and therapeutic practice are kept strictly within the boundaries of supervision sessions, as strictly as the relationship with the child is kept within the boundaries of the therapy session. Because the boundaries are so strictly observed by the staff and myself, the children come to have a clear understanding of my role in the overall function of the unit.

An example of a child's understanding of the difference between the role of the therapist and the care staff was nine-year-old R., who was fully engaged in her work with me during her therapy sessions. R. was standing by herself in the kitchen as I was passing through, struggling to do up her skirt which she said was about to fall down, and obviously needing some adult help. R. did not expect me to undertake the nurturing role, and did not ask for any help, seeing my function in relation to her as separate from those involved in her everyday life. I told her I could hear someone coming who I thought would be able to help her. As soon as the member of staff entered the room, R. ran towards her, asking for and receiving the help she needed.

The therapist provides a reliable time and place, within safe limits and boundaries, so as to attempt with the child to understand thoughts and feelings, whether conscious or unconscious, expressed through words, play and body language, and to translate the understanding into words. The countertransference feelings evoked in the therapist by the material presented plays a significant part in the development of this understanding, and will be a continuing theme throughout the chapter as of course it also applies to those looking after the child in its everyday environment.

The boundary between the role of the therapist and the child's carers is important. As the therapist does not take a parental stance, this helps the child to experience the session as a time and a place in which to express difficult and angry feelings towards previous parental figures, and to have them contained within it. This can help to defuse some of the hostile feelings that can be aimed at those undertaking the essential task of everyday care and nurturing within the unit. The child's perception of nurturing can be very different from the spirit in which it is being offered to them, so that beneficial intentions can be perceived as threatening or abusive. At the opposite extreme the child may have unrealistic expectations as to what the carer is able or prepared to offer in terms of attention and commitment. They are likely to transfer feelings experienced in earlier relationships onto someone else in the present, which makes sense since we all learn about other people by our experience of them from infancy onwards.

An important function of the therapist is to be able to contain the sometimes intolerable anxieties and feelings of pain, loss and rage expressed by the child, and to have a 'space in the mind' (Hoxter 1990) in which to receive and reflect on them, in order to respond in a way that has helpful meaning for the child. In this way the therapist is able to gain insights into the child's world, which when combined with a body of knowledge obtained through training and practice, can be used creatively to develop further understanding of the complex issues which arise. Both carers and therapists develop the ability to observe and listen to the communications which underlie the specific words and behaviour, some of which can be puzzling, inappropriate in the given circumstances and at times extremely frightening. This requires consideration of the feelings evoked in the adult by what is being presented by the child, sometimes resurrecting feelings from their own childhood, supposedly long-forgotten or discarded. It is important to become aware of them and when possible convert them to positive use.

It is important to acknowledge our own vulnerability, that when faced with a child's distress, we would rather be rid of feelings from our own past experience, which may sometimes be similar to the child's. These can come to the surface to muddy the waters and hinder our ability to think clearly. But to become aware of this, and to put it to positive use can help to clear the waters and contribute towards the ability to think about what the child is communicating. We need to respond creatively in a way that is helpful to the child, rather than giving an immediate emotional reaction, based on personal feelings and long-held attitudes and assumptions.

The necessity of acquiring self-knowledge has been spoken and written about throughout human history. In 400 BC Socrates stated that 'the unexamined life is not worth living' and his words are as potent now as they were then. Of course the degree of self-examination is up to the individual concerned, but also needs to be informed by practical considerations when working with troubled children. For example, to become a psychoanalytic psychotherapist it is necessary to undergo personal training analysis. Self-development and understanding can be a painful process as well as a liberating one, and working with troubled children can sometimes become so disorientating that the temptation to hide behind familiar 'safe' attitudes and responses can be overwhelming. This can lead to a negative and unhelpful interaction for the child, and often an unsatisfying and frustrating one for the adult.

Foremost among the reasons for choosing to work with troubled children is the wish to relieve their mental pain as swiftly as possible, to help them make sense of their past experiences and its effects on their present predicament, and the belief in having the skills and commitment to undertake the task. Macbeth asks the physician to provide for his wife a 'sweet, oblivious antidote', to 'pluck from the memory a rooted sorrow'. These words epitomise both the wish and the difficulties inherent in bringing it about. It is not possible to 'pluck away pain'. One might provide a temporary antidote by giving a great deal of attention, treats and material goods, even love, but the pain remains 'rooted' and can continue to inhibit the child's emotional development and ability to function, and could persist into adult life. It is better to attempt to understand the child's actual feelings, which may be different from your expectation of what they might be, to work through and to bear them with the child and to modify and relieve them by a therapeutic response.

Freud, (1914) in *Remembering, Repeating and Working Through* observed that his patients required time to 'work through' defences before change could take place. Intellectual insight is not sufficient until emotional insight takes place. There needs to be an internal acknowledgement of the underlying causes of emotional pain and suffering which can happen via the interpretations of the therapist, and, in the context of this chapter, by the interventions of those caring for the child.

Case Study – C.

C., aged nine years, had suffered abuse and neglect and multiple placements before and after being placed in care at an early age. He needed to experience over a period of time the therapeutic responses to him to know that his predicament was understood. Only then could he begin to assimilate them into his internal world structure and feel safe enough to relax his defence system and to risk experimenting with new ways of relating to others. But 'working through' conjures up feelings of pain and loss, feelings which C. defended himself from experiencing again, requiring continual support in the process by those caring for him.

It can be frustrating for those involved with a child to observe them repeating behaviours which are detrimental to them and only increase their difficulties. This was true for the staff of the Unit where C. was living, and also had an effect on the other children living there. His justified feelings of having been unfairly treated permeated his present life to such an extent that his continual dissatisfaction became difficult to tolerate. Every effort was made to be scrupulously fair to him. His share of breakfast toast was put on a separate plate in order to alleviate his constant anxiety that the other children would eat it all, and to the extent of measuring the breakfast toast to show him that they were all the same size, because he felt others had larger pieces. But this fell on stony ground and he still felt hard done by. He was unable to accept what his eyes could see and his feelings of being unfairly treated persisted.

How was C.'s everyday behaviour reflected in therapy with me? During one of his therapy sessions with me, C. went over to the bag of clay and pulled out a large lump and brought it over to the table where I was sitting. He banged it down on the table in front of him and began to pummel it into a circular shape, breaking off a tiny piece and putting it to one side. He continued to pummel the clay for two to three minutes, looking up at me as he did so, with a rather sly expression on his face. He then stood up and lifted the piece of clay, saying 'This is a huge apple pie, and it's all for me', opening his mouth wide and pretending to bite it. He then sat down and pushed the tiny piece of clay until it was in front of me, saying 'Ha, ha, ha, that one's for you!' He was watching my face intently, and I needed to think carefully about my response as my feelings of being belittled were very strong. I commented that I thought he wanted to make me feel how horrible it was to feel so empty, when everyone else was so greedy and got what they wanted, and that he felt he never stood a chance. The expression on his face changed, the moment of triumph had passed. C. picked up his pie and banged it down again onto the table, saying 'It's a horrible pie anyway!' I said that perhaps having a huge pie and me a tiny one had not made him feel any better, that he still felt hungry and the apple pie had not filled him up. This has been a continuing theme throughout his therapy. Whenever C. gets what he thinks he wants it never fills the emptiness inside. C. then kicked a ball around the room in a desultory way, twice walking towards the sand tray, each time deciding against playing with it, despite his use of it in previous sessions as a means of communication.

C.'s emotional needs were so great that he was unable to contemplate the needs of others, and if he saw them being met it felt like a further impoverishment of himself. Because of this, C. had great difficulty in relating to the other children. He had built up a system of defences in order to survive his life experiences, and to protect himself from experiencing them again. This meant that all his mental energy was concentrated on being constantly vigilant, guarding against the next catastrophe, leaving no space for emotional growth to take place. In terms of his relationships with both adults and children, he remained at the emotional level of a much younger child – at the stage of being the centre of the world before the development of a capacity for concern for others (see Winnicott 1964).

The staff realised that their feelings of frustration and helplessness in the face of C.'s continual dissatisfaction could lead to a cycle of negative responses from them. It would be difficult not to say things like 'What's the use of doing anything for you, you're never satisfied', leading to further difficulties in communication and continuing anguish for C. His continual need for adult attention, and difficulty in relating to his peers, could be frustrating and time-consuming, sometimes leading to unhelpful responses. These responses were understandable, and could be helpful when through supervision they revealed just how awful C.'s inner experience was.

During staff meetings C.'s emotional development and the feelings he evoked in the staff were discussed at length. Theoretical concepts were used to help make sense of what was happening and facilitate responses to C.'s primitive communications. It can sometimes be hard to envisage that emotional growth in children and the consequent ability to think does not in some way happen automatically, whatever the circumstances: it is part of a process that takes place from birth in the growth of their relationship with others in an environment which enables it to take place. It is therefore so important that a substitute care environment provides the safety and containment that allows for children to repair emotional damage.

In this connection Bion (1989) in *Learning from Experience* developed the concept of 'containment', similar to Winnicott's idea of 'holding', as an essential function of the mother (or main carer) in the relationship with her baby. Developing the concept of 'containment', Bion describes the relationship between the baby and its mother in terms of maternal 'reverie' or preoccupation, when she is able to take in what the baby communicates to her, whether good or bad, using Melanie Klein's idea of projective identification to describe this mechanism. He writes that

> the baby's behaviour is reasonably calculated to arouse in the mother feelings which the infant wishes to be rid of. If the infant feels that it is dying it can arouse feelings in the mother. A well-balanced mother can accept these and respond to them therapeutically, that is to say, in a manner that makes the infant feel it is receiving its frightened personality back again but in a form it can tolerate – the fears are manageable by the infant personality. (Bion 1989)

Thus, in normal development, the baby projects onto the mother its bad feelings, where they are modified and made bearable, and she acts as a container for the sometimes nameless dreads conveyed to her by the baby. If the mother's function as a container is good enough, the baby is able to begin to build its own internal container for its own feelings. This interaction between mother and baby from the time of birth affects all further interactions and requires continuity for satisfactory development to take place.

Of course there are circumstances when a mother is unable to care for her baby, either through death or on a temporary basis through illness or some other event, and the continuity of care must be provided by someone else. But this continuity has been so badly disrupted, or has not had the opportunity to begin, in the children written about in this chapter. That this is the case can be reasonably deduced by knowledge of their previous history, but most importantly by their present behaviour and the quality of experience in their interaction with others. It would probably be safe to say that C.'s experience of a good mother was non-existent, or at the most severely limited, and further disruptions in care consolidated and increased the emotional damage causing further developmental delay. Bion's use of projective identification in terms of normal development helps us to understand what is happening in C.'s internal world, and the feelings he aroused in others. He projected onto them the parts of himself he wished to be rid of, his feelings of frustration and hopelessness affecting their internal worlds to varying degrees, so they ended up feeling misused by him.

C. had not developed his own 'container' or 'space in the mind' to be able to deal with what was unbearable to him. This is when the concepts of 'maternal reverie' and 'containment' can be adapted for use in the development of a therapeutic response in the context of the present. It is not possible to replace the loss of adequate early emotional care. C. cannot be provided with the idealised early infancy experience he may wish for. Unrealistic expectations of ideal care have to be modified so that in what is being offered, past feelings of rejection and abandonment can also be reduced. It is important to define to yourself what your role is with the children, to maintain a clear boundary between implementing the essential nurturing tasks usually undertaken by a parent or parents, making it clear to the child that you cannot be the substitute parent they might wish you to be. Most children will come to accept this, but sometimes a particularly needy child will interpret any caring on your part as concrete evidence of you as the parent they so desperately want. Also development (however fragmented) will have already taken place, and particular people, parents, other family members and previous carers, however inadequate, or even harmful they may appear to be, remain extremely significant to the child, and can often be over-idealised. These feelings need to be handled with sensitivity, as an over-idealisation can be a defence against all the negative feelings that are too painful to think about or to express. Time is needed to allow them to come to their own, perhaps more realistic conclusions, and come to terms with their situation and with what they have and what they have lost.

For C., it is important to recognise that his feelings of being unfairly treated in the past are justified, while also acknowledging how dreadful it must be for him that these feelings dominate everything that happens to him now. It is important to be with him in his internal world in which his exactly measured piece of toast appears to him to be totally inadequate. Words such as 'It must be a horrid feeling inside (or in your tummy) which never goes away' may help. It is also essential to emphasise the external reality, letting him know that every attempt is being made to be fair to him. This sort of response would need to be repeated again and again in all sorts of situations, the adults continuing to think for him until he is able to begin to receive their benign interventions. It is useful to remember that C. is often relating on an infantile level, an infant whose experience was of his needs never being adequately met. If a baby's need for a feed is responded to in 'good enough' time, it will learn to deal with the frustration of not always receiving it immediately, *because he knows it is coming.* And when it does come, to be able to internalise feelings of satisfaction and the beginnings of a sense of self. Children like C. need to have their emotional needs met at their developmental level, while also responding when necessary to their chronological age-appropriate wishes.

For a long time C. remained suspended in a state of dissatisfaction and frustration and, as previously stated, often projected these feelings into those caring for him. This was recognised by the staff, and recognised as an infantile need for them to be contained, thought about and acknowledged, helping C. begin to build feelings of self-worth and hopefulness and trust in the intentions of others. This process began and developed for C. so well in the children's unit, to the extent that he has been able to move on to a permanent adoptive family, who have already adopted one of his natural siblings.

In one of his last sessions with me, shortly before his leaving party, C. made a parcel for the children to play 'Pass the parcel'. He launched into this immediately with great enthusiasm, putting a large pile of newspapers in front of him on the table, some black paint and a large paintbrush. He screwed up one piece of paper, and then splodged black paint all over it, then rolled another piece of newspaper over that, smiling broadly and saying, 'Everyone that opens it will get covered with black paint.' He continued this process six times until the parcel was quite big, all the time saying how funny it was going to be when they played the game, that only he would know that they would get covered in black paint. He then sat back in his chair, looking rather dejectedly at the parcel. I said that perhaps he did not want to be the only one to know that he was sad and frightened as well as looking forward to going to his new family. Moving on meant he had all sorts of difficult mixed feelings, and I suggested that maybe he was sometimes angry with the other children who would be staying with people they knew and would also continue to see me. C. acknowledged that he had good and bad feelings about leaving, and was able to talk about what he would miss and what he was looking forward to in his move. At the end of the session he put his parcel briskly into the bin, with an air of finality.

After a year, C. became an integral part of his new family. But he is still a child who is difficult to care for. Some of his defences against further rejection and pain remain with him. In particular, his capacity to respond with spontaneity to the physical affection given to him by his family is still limited. They feel that any physical gestures from him are false and put on. But his progress continues, albeit slowly, as does the growth of the family's affection for him.

Case Study – D.

D. was placed in the unit at the age of ten years because of parental neglect and fears for his own safety and the safety of others. He had already been seriously injured in a road accident. D. had been living on a large estate with his mother. His father left home when he was a baby, but continued to live on the same estate and saw his son occasionally, but took no part in his care. D. had been out of the control of his mother since he was a small child, being out on the estate all day and sometimes most of the night in the company of older children and teenagers, and supposedly adults as well. Because of this it was difficult to know what abuse he may have been prey to, or had witnessed, and the criminal activities he could have become involved in. D. talked about seeing his mother 'having sex' with her boyfriend, and how it made him feel angry and upset; often his speech and behaviour had sexual connotations that were inappropriate for his age and unacceptable to other people. But within this bleak picture there were people on the estate who tried to help D. and his mother, but to no avail and he slipped through their fingers like a latter-day Artful Dodger.

Nevertheless, there is an attachment between D. and his mother and regular contact was maintained while he was living in the unit, and she continues to be a significant part of his life. This is in spite of the fact that he is not able to live with her. D. was helped to begin to understand and accept this by the staff, with the cooperation of his mother, who also had the painful experience of facing the reality of her inability to care for him. I think it is a vital ingredient of the therapeutic model that, where appropriate, any significant relationships within the natural family are maintained at a level that is considered to be in the child's best interests. Whenever possible, work should be undertaken with them and the child, to help modify the range of feelings they are all left with by the experiences which have led to their present predicament. This is an arena which provides an opportunity for some reparation to take place, and in the view of Melanie Klein, is the most important source of mental growth and creativity (see Segal 1973).

It is sometimes very hard to accept a parent or relative who is known to have been harmful to the child through abuse or neglect. It can be a struggle to have any compassion or understanding of people whose lifestyle and behaviour appears to be so alien to one's own values and beliefs. It would be easy, and understandable, to feel that the child would be better served by having been completely removed from their lives, than to face the fact that they will always play some part externally to a greater or lesser degree according to the particular circumstances. But whatever the external situation, they cannot be erased from the child's inner world. If there is an opportunity to help to modify the destructive and frightening elements attached to early experiences, it can begin to open the door to the emotional growth and development that is necessary to form relationships in the future. As previously stated, unsatisfactory early relationships can stunt emotional growth, and unless worked through and some insight gained can continually intrude into the present and impinge on how we relate to others. It can help to illuminate the whole child, and inform our responses to it, and perhaps give some understanding of the parents' position without condoning in any way the abuse or neglect.

D. presented as a child with serious developmental delay, which particularly affected his ability to think, to retain information and his capacity to learn from experience. But this was overlaid by some of his delinquent behaviour and the language he used which was the norm in the culture and lifestyle he had been plucked from but was not in the milieu of the unit. At first this could cloud a true recognition of the enormity of his all-round deprivation. D. had great difficulty in differentiating thought from action, so if something came into his head, he could rarely stop himself from doing it, unless under the close supervision of an adult. His aggressive thoughts and feelings caused him particular anxiety. He was afraid they might actually happen and become out of his control. Shortly before he left the unit, in one of his last sessions with me, he was setting out a tray for the meal he had prepared for us on the toy stove. He began to talk about what he would miss when he moved on from the unit. Suddenly he picked up the toy plastic knife and brought it down with some force onto the back of my hand (the knife bent and it hardly hurt). He then cried out 'Anna, Anna, your hand's bleeding, it's bleeding' and threw the knife across the room with a look of panic on his face. It took him several seconds to realise that he had not injured me and that there was no blood on me or the knife. D. told me that he had had to stop talking about leaving, and had suddenly found himself stabbing my hand with the plastic knife, 'to make it all stop'. He was not able to tolerate the feelings that had suddenly surfaced surrounding ending, and had to banish them from his mind with a violent piece of acting-out.

It was evident that for D. every day was a question of survival, in which he had to protect himself against what he perceived to be the persecution of others. This meant he was unable to play with his peers without an adult present. If someone threw a ball in play and it happened to hit him, he would see this as an attack, and would often retaliate by physically attacking the thrower of the ball. D. had not developed his own internal 'container' (with similarities to C.) and had minimal boundaries between thought and action. His life on the estate meant that he had had to be eternally vigilant to protect himself from external danger, and his own internal fear of annihilation. The lack of adult care and protection, alongside the mental energy required in this enterprise, left no space in his mind for emotional development to take place, or to acquire the ability to learn from experience. D. was like a very small child who had to be told, and helped to carry out, over and over again, even everyday things a child of his age would be expected to do. At first this was very hard for the staff to take fully on board, because superficially D. had a streetwise demeanour, which belied his actual stage of emotional development. This struggle was discussed at length during supervision and the staff learned from the experience of living with D. the true nature of his difficulties. D. projected his feelings of hopelessness and despair into others, adding, to the staff's own feelings of frustration and sometimes despair, that despite what they saw as their own best efforts, his progress was so slow and painstaking.

As previously stated, at first D.'s descriptive language and swearing was inappropriate in the unit, and it was sometimes very upsetting for the other children and staff to hear particular words, especially when addressed to and about them. D. was helped to understand that there were different ways in which he could express himself and different words he could use. I think this illustrates the enormous power of words and the effect that they can have on people, and how sometimes they can remain indelibly on the mind. It emphasises how important it is to think about the words we use when responding to what a child says or does. When not under close supervision, D. would go into other children's rooms and take sweets and belongings. They were always left in a place where they could be easily found. They were not things he wanted or needed or for personal gain and he obtained no apparent pleasure from them, but he could not stop himself from doing it. It is not productive to talk about stealing or calling him a thief, it would only compound his already strong feelings of being bad. It is also important not to collude with what he has done. It would not be helpful to him or to the other children in the group. It would be easy and understandable to do this, to excuse him and let it go because he is such a deprived child and because he is so heavily influenced by the criminal connotations of his home environment. It would be more helpful to confront him in a non-punitive way, by using words which describe what he had done, such as pointing out to him that he had taken something that did not belong to him without them knowing, and that it was something that people did not like happening to them, although D. himself had little or no concern about his own possessions. He must return what he had taken to the owner and apologise to them. This D. always did but the behaviour continued.

I want to reiterate D.'s stage of development. He was like a very small child who, if he saw something he liked, would pick it up, and if there was no adult present to say something like 'put it back, it is not yours' would take it away. He had not reached the state of taking responsibility for his actions, and the responses of the staff had to be repeated and repeated and repeated. This was of course extremely time-consuming and sometimes extremely frustrating for them, that they sometimes nearly gave up in despair. One aspect of D. made his behaviour more understandable, and therefore easier to respond to in a way that was helpful to him. He had not reached the stage of 'I am' and therefore had no comprehension of something belonging to him. The staff recognised this in the way he treated his belongings. He did not mind what happened to them. If they broke, or disappeared he expressed no concern and he would give them away if anyone asked for them. D. needed to develop a sense of self before he could say 'It's mine' and begin to comprehend the rights of others, and their rights over their possessions, and to care about and make decisions about his own. D. was always in jeopardy of becoming the scapegoat for anything bad that happened in the unit; added to this his lack of a sense of self led him to believe that anything bad that happened must be due to him, and he would readily confess to things he had not done.

It also follows that to say to a child that they are lying, or to call them a liar, only compounds their negative feelings about themselves and in some cases makes them live up to what they believe to be your perception of them. The reasons why children do not tell the truth are complex, one being not understanding what is true and what is not true, and they may need help in differentiating between the two. Also they have a desperate need for approval, and they fear what the consequences might be if they admit to doing something wrong. To use the words 'lie' and 'liar' can cloud the issue as stated above. To say something like 'I don't think what you are telling me is what really happened' or, in the case of D, 'I think you did take R.'s sweets from her room, perhaps you can tell me where they are, or we could look for them together.' It can also be hurtful if a child you have been working with appears not to trust you enough to tell you the truth – to respond by letting them know how hurt you are, is like asking them to contain and reflect upon your feelings when they are not yet in the position of being able to contain their own.

During his last few months at the unit, D. often played what he called his 'baby game' in his sessions with me. He would lie on the cushions on the floor and put a rug over him, making a bed for himself. He filled the toy baby's bottle with water and put it beside him. He then said 'I'm the baby, and you're my Mum.' He made baby noises and then said 'I made my first burp, and you're pleased about it', burping straight afterwards, continuing to make baby noises. He picked up the bottle and drank from the teat, again saying that I was pleased that he was drinking from his bottle. After a short time he said 'I can crawl now and you're pleased about it', followed by him sitting on the sand bucket and repeating that I was pleased about him doing a poo in his pot. Then he went round the room like a toddler, staggering and falling over, saying that I was pleased that he could walk. This was always followed by D. getting back into the bed after putting the plastic knife, some pencils and a toy cup beside him: 'I'm the baby, and you're the Mum. You're asleep and you don't know what the baby's doing.' He would make baby noises, and pick up one of the pencils and put it in his mouth and pretended to smoke. Then he would drink out of the cup and say 'The baby's getting drunk, but you don't know.' On one occasion he crawled out of bed with the plastic knife, saying 'You don't know that the baby's gone out with a knife.' It seemed that on these occasions he split me in two, as the 'good' and the 'bad' mother, one that cared for him and watched his progress with pleasure, and one whose mind had no space in which to think about and care for him, or to protect him from his own frightening feelings and external dangers. These sessions took place over the period when work was being done with him and his mother, and, alongside this, his growing realisation that he would not return to live with her, which at first had been his most fervent wish.

In the sessions it was plain that he wished he could start all over again, to be born to his mother who would have been able to look after him properly and to have his Dad living at home.

During his time at the unit all the staff became fond of him, and within the structured environment which was essential to him and constant adult supervision, he caused no management problems and could be a pleasure to be with. The staff gained enormous insight into the complexities of emotional deprivation and damage through caring for him, and in developing their responses in a way that he understood and was helpful to him. D. moved on to a residential unit with education on the premises, where he can stay if necessary until he is 19. While there, he has occasionally evaded the supervision he requires and has then run away, and outside his known environment. D. still loses control of what he is doing to the extent that his actions have required the intervention of the police. Nevertheless it has been proved that in the right setting D. can manage his life without causing danger to himself and others, and to make some developmental progress. But this provision is hard to find and maintain, and the prognosis for D.'s long-term future still remains in the balance.

I have tried in this chapter to show that it is possible to work with what the children are and what they bring with them both in therapy sessions and in their living situations. Success hinges on the development of insight generally and then being able to apply it and vary it in individual cases. The distortions in the development of personality in individuals usually have a similar root but a wide range of unique behavioural symptoms. There are no ready-made competencies for dealing with them. Each new child provides new challenges, demands fresh approaches and the willingness to relearn what we thought we already knew. C. and D. through their own growth and development were responsible for new growth and development in the staff team of a children's unit and in one therapist.

References

Bion, W. (1989) *Learning from Experience*, Routledge.

Freud, S. (1914) 'Remembering, Repeating and Working Through (Further Recollections on the Technique of Psychoanalysis II)', in *The Complete Psychological Works of Sigmund Freud*, Vol. 12, p. 145 (1975), The Hogarth Press.

Hoxter S. (1990) 'Some feelings aroused in working with severely deprived children' in Boston, M., Little, M. and Kelly, S. (1995) *A Life Without Problems?*, Aldershot: Arena.

Segal, H. (1973) *Introduction to the Work of Melanie Klein*, Karnac.

Szur, R. (eds), *Psychotherapy with Severely Deprived Children*, Karnac Maresfield Library.

Winnicott, D. (1964) *The Child, The Family and the Outside World*, Penguin.

Winnicott, D. (1984) *Deprivation and Delinquency*, Routledge.

9 Healing play

Linnet McMahon

Introduction

'It is playing and only in playing that the individual child is able to be creative and to use the whole personality, and it is only in being creative that the individual discovers the self.' (Winnicott 1971: 54)

Adults have a real problem when they try to work with troubled children and young people. We are enthusiastic keyworkers, co-workers, foster carers and teachers and we all want to help. We believe that it helps to talk about our anxieties, counselling is a growth industry and all we have to do is to get into a one-to-one with our young people and life will improve. Communication is everything, acting-out is a breakdown in communication and it is a professional affront to be told that your child is out of communication.

Recently, a course member requested help in working with a young person for whom multiple separations and losses of important figures were causing serious difficulties. What was wanted was a book or books which would enable her to start discussing the problems with the young person.

Some of our children and young people suffered traumatic events, for example abuse or loss, at such an early point in their life, before they had learned to talk. It is unlikely that they will be able to talk about them for many years, if ever. For the majority of our children their experiences have been quite simply unspeakable and to be encouraged to talk about them is often to ask them to do the one thing they do not want to do and often cannot do. So adults have a problem – they want to talk, that is their medium for helping, but children are definitely not keen.

One of the reasons Winnicott is an inspiration for this book is that he understood the difficulty children and young people have in communicating with adults and he developed techniques to help. Play is such a powerful yet sensitive tool. It offers a non-intrusive starting point for adults and children, allowing trust to develop which in turn promotes verbal communication. 'I work with adolescents – they don't play': how often have we heard this?! They do, they want to and they enjoy it. Stuck for a way in? Then start playing 'Squiggles', Winnicott's drawing game – everyone can play.

Linnet McMahon, whose own book (McMahon 1992) we highly recommend has given us an introductory chapter on play to remind us that it is best not to start with books – start with play. Adults talk too much, listen badly and play too little.

9 Healing play

Linnet McMahon, with case study by
Ros Fanshawe

In this chapter I consider what is special about play and why play can contribute so much to a child's therapeutic progress. I then explore some of the different ways in which we can help emotionally damaged children through therapeutic play and play therapy. In particular I will explore ways of providing primary experience through play, symbolic play therapy, and play in focused therapeutic work or 'counselling'. Ros Fanshawe's case study demonstrates some of these ideas in practice.

What is play?

Ask a child what she has been doing and the likely reply is 'just playing'. As adults we may well leave it at that, going along with the idea that play is not an important matter compared with the real business of work. I want to put the opposite view and argue that play is essential, for children and adults alike, not simply as a way of relaxing but as a way of helping us make sense of the world and of having some feeling of control over our lives.

Grown-ups' play

As adults, most of us look forward to having time when we can choose what we do rather than having demands made of us. We think of it as a breathing space, a time to relax, to unwind, to recharge our batteries, to 'sort out our heads'. Some of these metaphors suggest simply that play is time off from work, others indicate a more active process. We know that we feel better for it. For example, we have ways of looking after ourselves after a hard day, perhaps having a bath, eating a cream cake, or reading the newspaper undisturbed in the loo; we may play sports, go out to the pub or an evening class, watch our favourite programme or listen to music. These activities tend to feel most satisfying when some inner need has been met, a reaffirmation of our inner self, a more creative process than just 'unwinding' has been going on.

Probably we can recall an experience of having something explained to us – for example, how to programme. the video or use the new washing machine – and we feel more and more muddled; we can't wait for the person to go away so that we can 'play' on our own and gradually become more familiar with this new thing. We know too that if we stop consciously thinking or worrying about a particular question we are often surprised by the answer popping unexpectedly into our heads; our unconscious has been left to play and has come up with the answer.

When we have heard some bad news we can feel quite mentally numb and want time on our own to 'digest' it, to 'chew it over', to understand what has happened, to think about how we would like to respond and to rehearse in our own mind how we will actually respond. We tend not to think of this as play, but play is not always happy and like this can be a serious business. Maybe later on we will want to tell someone else and talk it through at length, sometimes repeatedly; this is like Winnicott's play 'in the presence of someone', and offers an insight into the connection between adult counselling and play therapy.

So we have different kinds of play, some more obviously playful in feeling than others. All are to do with ways in which we consciously or unconsciously process our experiences, integrating them into our inner world. This brings a renewed feeling of things making sense, which in turn gives us a sense of autonomy – of things being manageable and under our control, at least as far as our own actions and responses are concerned.

Children's play

As for adults so for children. But children have less autonomy than adults, and they are often less able to find the words to express their thoughts and feelings. So play has a crucial significance for them. Let us consider a child's version of the situations I have just described.

After a hard day and 'periods of rough going in the social seas' (Erikson's phrase) children, like us, need some play space when they can reassert control over what they do and who they are. For example, when my daughter was finding school stressful she would come home in a temper, disappear upstairs to play for an hour and re-emerge feeling much more settled.

Like us, when we cannot take in an explanation of how to work a new machine, children often ignore the instructions (or your directions) that come with toys such as Lego and play on their own – exploring, trying something, finding it doesn't work, having another go. They are thinking and learning through becoming familiar with the materials and making them their own, a more creative and ultimately more satisfying process.

Children who have had a difficult or distressing time, or suffered a painful separation or loss, may use pretend play to help them come to terms with their experiences. Unlike adults who can run things over in their mind, children need to externalise their thoughts through play. In pretend play children can safely bash, bury and throw away the people they are angry with or frightened of, or re-enact something which has happened, perhaps changing the outcome, and sometimes then feel better.

So play is a way in which children assimilate experience of the real world, making it part of the self. In play, children have an opportunity to be themselves, and to explore different ways of being.

If we draw out the common elements of the scenarios described, the essentials for play to take place are:

- *Safe boundaries* – the need for the player to feel safe within a physical boundary of time and space, where the rules of everyday life do not apply, and to feel well enough held emotionally
- *Autonomy* – the need for the player to feel in control of the play and the direction it takes, whether or not another person is present or playing
- *No consequences* – playing matters more than any results of play. Mistakes do not have serious consequences, so risks can be taken in play.
- *Creativity* – when the first three conditions are met then there is the possibility for play to be a creative exploration. The excitement and importance of play lie in the way it links the real world with the inner world of fantasy.

Before continuing you may like to do the 'Good Play Memories' exercise: Think back to your earliest childhood. What good memories of play do you have? What were the feelings involved? Think about how the play essentials listed above match your memories. It may be that you have some memories of play that are not good ones, perhaps being bossed around by other children or a game where something went frighteningly wrong. Such experiences are not so much play as real-life encounters, and you will probably find that at least one of the four essentials of play was missing.

For many children such healing play takes place in the normal course of events, probably without adults being aware. The opportunity to play may be enough for the child whose life is not overwhelmingly disrupted or distressing, and when there is also someone around who holds the child in mind, providing the mental containment which helps them manage their anxiety. Children who have had too much going on in their lives can benefit from the active involvement in the play process of a concerned and aware adult; this is where therapeutic play or specific play therapy sessions may help.

When we are offering therapeutic play and play therapy we need to think carefully about our provision and management of each of the essentials of play. How we provide them varies, depending on our assessment of the child's needs. We will return to these questions. First we need a way of understanding the way in which normal play develops, in order to assess the child's developmental stage and to be able to match play provision to the child's need.

The development of play

In providing a framework for thinking about therapeutic play I have drawn on some of Winnicott's (1971) ideas about the development of play.

Stage 1 – Primary experience: maternal preoccupation and sensory play

The beginning of play is in the safe space between the baby and the mother. The baby uses all its senses to experience the world and to find its own 'edges', not only physical but also emotional. It responds with its whole body to sounds such as a rhythmical heartbeat, to being spoken or sung to, to touch and smell and taste of the mother's milk and her body, to being held, or exposed through being changed or undressed, or immersed in the bath. The baby goes on to explore the world using first its mouth, then finding its hands and feet and using them in sensory motor play.

Initially, the mother's attunement to the needs of her baby (Winnicott's primary maternal preoccupation) enables her to make spaces for her baby to have a magical experience of feeling in control, as 'she makes actual what he is ready to find'. Winnicott calls this the area of 'illusion'; when hungry the baby is fed, when wet and uncomfortable it is changed. The mother imitates and reflects the baby's noises and facial expressions, and plays games like peep-bo, which the baby finds very exciting. Later, the mother may bounce her baby on her lap, perhaps singing 'Pop goes the Weasel'. As she reaches the 'Pop' she stills and pauses; after repeated experience the child delightedly awaits the 'Pop', and in due course manages its own.

These kinds of interactive and sensory play with the mother are part of the normal baby's primary experience. The deprived child who has missed this good experience does not know what is 'me and not me', and so has little sense of being a real person in a world that is comprehensible and responsive.

Stage 2 – Symbolic play

As a baby develops and becomes more aware of the difference between self, others, and the world around, she becomes more aware of her dependence on others. From about the age of about six months, she becomes fearful if her carers go out of sight – the beginning of separation anxiety. Symbolic or pretend play which develops subsequently helps her to link the outside world (of people, objects, toys and other things) to inner experience (her own thoughts, feelings, fears and fantasies). This play is immensely exciting and offers a sense of mastery which relieves anxiety. This bridging of outer and inner reality is illustrated by a child's creation of a transitional object, the teddy, soft toy or cloth which is both a real object and one which has an emotional meaning to the child. Winnicott calls this the child's first symbolic creation and the beginning of symbolic play. It supports the child 'engaged in the perpetual human task of keeping inner and outer reality separate yet interrelated' (Winnicott 1971: 2). The transitional object is used as a symbolic way of managing the anxiety of separations, from the brief separation of going to sleep to the longer one of being looked after by someone else. It should thus be clear how important it is for children, at any age, who are entering substitute care or moving between places to keep with them belongings which have such symbolic value.

Exercise 9.1: Transitional object

Think about a special object which was very important to you as a small child. When did you use it and need it? Do you remember not needing it any more? Do you know what happened to it – maybe even where it is now? Talk to other people about their memories of this. (Not every one has a transitional object – some cultures and some families manage things differently, and equally well.)

Play at this stage takes place when the young child is 'alone in the presence of someone', someone who is reliably there when needed and who may reflect back what happens in the playing. The child who is ready for symbolic play is developing a sense of self, with the capacity to hold on to experiences good and bad, which Winnicott calls the beginning of integration.

A child whose very early primary experience was 'good enough' but who later in infancy experienced damaging separations or losses may find that symbolic play in play therapy can offer a measure of healing.

Stage 3 – Playing together

Winnicott's third stage is for the child to allow and enjoy the overlap of two play areas – child and mother (or therapist) paving the way for playing together in a relationship. For example, the peep-bo game of infancy turns into hide-and-seek, in which the child herself instigates the hiding game. Symbolic play may take the form of cooperative role play. Play with other children, often initially with siblings or older children, later on with peers, allows for the development of increasingly complex socio-dramatic play and games with rules. Alongside this, many children still preserve a space for solitary pretend play.

Children whose early childhood has been emotionally satisfactory but who have suffered a separation or loss, or other traumatic events, later in childhood may be able to benefit from focused play or counselling approaches (often called 'direct work'). Such playing together with a helpful adult draws on the integrated child's ability to think and be reflective.

Matching therapeutic play provision to developmental stage

In order to decide what kind of play provision will be appropriate it is important to have an assessment of the child's developmental stage. The child's case history, especially information about the child's experience in the first year or two of life, will give important indications. Barbara Dockar-Drysdale's Need Assessment (1968) is a helpful way of thinking about present observations of how the child is in everyday situations (see also Chapter 7). Observations of play will give some indication of the child's capacity to use symbolic play. Assessment needs to be an ongoing process.

Winnicott's stages of normal play development can be matched to Dockar-Drysdale's account of the series of therapeutic processes which a child must go through in order to reach integration. Experience and realisation are comparable to stage one maternal preoccupation and sensory play, symbolisation to stage two symbolic play, and conceptualisation to stage three playing together. Dockar-Drysdale explains:

By this I mean that a child may have a good experience provided by his therapist, but this will be of no value to him until he is able, eventually, to realize it; that is to say, to feel that this good thing has really happened to him. Then he must find a way of storing the good thing inside him, which he does by means of symbolizing the experience. Last in the series of processes comes conceptualization, which is understanding intellectually what has happened to him in the course of the experience and being able to think this in words. (Dockar-Drysdale 1990: 98–9, see also Chapter 3)

This outline of the process is a useful guide in helping us keep track of the therapeutic processes involved in play, helping us decide where to start and recognizing how far there is to go.

Providing play as primary experience in daily life

Much therapeutic work today is about helping children who are unintegrated to a greater or lesser degree. Sometimes the children are in residential homes or schools, sometimes in foster care, and sometimes at home with parents and perhaps attending school or family centre. They need a complete holding environment in which they can develop their sense of self and so begin to play.

The child who needs primary experience requires this throughout all aspects of their daily life, from waking to sleeping. As with the baby, sensory and interactive play are part of everyday activities, so having meals, playtime, bath and bedtimes provide their own opportunities for good experience.

Provision needs to be reliable, giving a complete and uninterrupted experience. For example, a mealtime which is planned and the child given warning beforehand so that he has time to bring what he is doing to a close, appealing food offered in a quiet and attentive setting with awareness of the child's responses to different foods including cultural differences in what is familiar in smell and taste – and with time for the child to enjoy it, even play with it, is a very different experience from a noisy, pressured mealtime. It provides an appropriate version of a good infant feeding experience – see also Chapter 1.

The sensory responsiveness of the whole environment matters. For example, are there comfortable chairs or sofas to sink into, are smells homely rather than institutional, is the sound around harsh or companionable – with familiar and relaxing music? Do the surroundings look attractive and welcoming? Are there appealing toys and play equipment, including cuddly toys, rocking and swinging things, books and story-telling? Is there access to the natural world of sun, wind, water and trees?

Sensory play can help restore the often blunted senses – of sound, sight, touch, taste and smell – of an emotionally deprived child. It can be offered in many ways, some in everyday life, others in special play sessions, perhaps providing the material to stimulate one sense at a time, for example, one day a 'feely' bag of objects, another listening to different sounds and music. We need to match the provision to the child, taking account of what is appropriate and familiar for the child's age and culture.

Physical play might include walking, riding or climbing, swimming and playing in water, or adventure trips and sports. 'Messy' play can be provided in a playroom or through everyday activities, such as cooking, washing up and bathing, as well as outdoor pursuits. One group of children who were bought ice-creams on an outing delighted in rubbing them all over their faces! Another child, playing in a paddling pool on a hot day, revelled in becoming wet and muddy all over.

A special play area for a group or class of children, a nurture group for example, can pay particular attention to the sensory qualities of its whole environment, and can offer play activities such as sand, water, painting, clay and dough, pretend play, cooking, singing and music. While it is easy enough to provide such a play-group environment for young children it becomes more of a challenge to make such activities feel acceptable and age-appropriate to adolescents. Then play activities may be presented, for example, as art, cooking, music making, drama, or adventure activities.

Regressive or baby play needs careful thought and management. It should be only at the instigation of and under the control of the child, with adults paying careful attention to localising such a regression to a play therapy time or an individual provision or special time. For example, in play sessions one child decided she was a puppy, wanting a bowl of food and water and a basket to curl up in, which her worker provided, although at all other times she was expected to behave 'normally'. In this way she was enabled to have an experience both real and symbolic of being taken care of. Pets provide a way of having safe cuddles. For example, an adolescent girl, separated from the siblings she had cared for, looked after a rabbit in her room.

We need to plan for play times but also seize the many opportunities for play in daily life. Such opportunity-led work can be a spontaneous game with a child on a walk, in a between-time – in fact, at any time. It does not need special play provision, although there does need to be protection from interruption, which can be provided by a team of workers attentive to the importance of what is taking place.

Many of these activities also lend themselves to interactive play with a responsive adult who can provide the equivalent of the fine-tuned play of a mother with her infant. Reciprocal play and turn-taking games, including action songs or games, often involve body movement and contact. (The role of touch is complex when so many damaged children have experienced abusive touching, and the worker needs to give it careful thought. The question is further discussed in Chapter 15.) In such play the rules of the game matter less than using play to support a developing relationship. This may sometimes involve careful 'reaching out' by the worker to draw the child lost in her own world back into communication, a version of animated baby play (Alvarez 1992).

The adult role may on occasion involve 'socially unobtrusive object play' where the worker who is watching the child playing quietly moves into view the next piece of jigsaw, Lego, and so on. This can help a child sustain or develop playing, and therefore thinking, at a time when they cannot tolerate greater adult contact.

Like the 'good enough' mother, the task of the therapeutic worker has emotional as well as physical aspects. Emotionally the mother's preoccupation or reverie has its equivalent in the worker's provision of an inner mental space. This is not easy. Sometimes a child's terrifying feelings threaten to overwhelm us and make us want to reject the child, but the task is to survive and to bear the rage or fear without putting up defences against it. Only then can the child start to believe that their feelings are not entirely destructive but can be borne.

Symbolic play therapy

The child's first therapeutic symbolic experiences are likely to take the form of symbolic equations, in which the symbolic experience is itself the real primary experience. For example, in a 'special time' or individual provision a child may want the worker to feed her and play like a really messy baby or perhaps, as we have seen, be a puppy needing to be looked after. As the child achieves a more integrated sense of self, true symbolic play becomes possible. In symbolic play the play situation is a way of representing or symbolising some other experience.

Planning playroom sessions

In addition to opportunity-led occasions for therapeutic play, a child may be offered regular times with a particular therapeutic worker, perhaps their keyworker or a specialist therapist. These often take place in a special playroom, ideally in a room designed for the purpose, but often one used for a hundred and one other things. The child needs a playroom that is familiar, so it needs to be the same each time the child comes. This is not too difficult in a setting with a designated playroom but a real challenge for a peripatetic worker who may find herself moving furniture each time before setting out play materials. The well-equipped playroom can offer more variety (but also more possibility of distraction) from the room (or even mat) to which the worker carries equipment in boxes or bags. Mess is usually more acceptable in a designated playroom; the worker's anxiety about mess and damage may well necessitate limiting the kinds of play, such as water, that she makes available elsewhere.

What play materials are offered depends not only on the setting but also on the child. The child able to make use of one-to-one sessions has usually developed some capacity for symbolic play. Provision for this can include 'pretend play' materials, puppets, dressing-up materials (hats and pieces of material rather than specific costumes), dolls and teddies, and dolls' houses, domestic and wild animals, dinosaurs, monsters, witches, policemen, cars and vans, and so on. Miniatures seem to be most easily used by more nearly-integrated children; the less integrated need the larger-size dolls and puppets, or use themselves as actors. Using miniatures of all sorts in a sand tray can be helpful in providing a non-structured but clearly bounded setting which facilitates play. A telephone (or two) can make it easier to say things which are hard to say directly. Medical and hospital equipment offers a way of re-enacting some painful experiences.

Art materials, such as clay, dough and plasticene, and materials for drawing and painting, cutting and pasting, offer further opportunities for symbolic communication. Some children are quite wary about drawing, having being asked to draw in previous assessments by 'experts'. Others delight in it, or in writing stories and poems. Books and stories can be carefully selected to match the child.

Symbolic play is the main tool of probably the majority of play therapists, and particularly those who use a non-directive approach, who reflect Winnicott's view that play must be spontaneous: 'The significant moment is that at which the child surprises himself or herself. It is not the moment of my clever interpretation that is significant' (Winnicott 1971:51).

The worker's task is to tune in to the child's feelings, to bear and think about them until they become modified, in such a way that they can in due course be taken back by the child in a more manageable form. Such emotional containment (Bion's term) enables the child to integrate both good and bad feelings into the self. The child in turn becomes a container for his feelings, able to hold on to them and think about them (rather than get rid of them onto others), first through symbolic play and then by putting them into words that can be thought about, so reaching a measure of integration.

Exercise 9.2: Winnicott's squiggle game

As a way of tuning in to a child Winnicott would ask them to draw a squiggle on a piece of paper and he would then turn the drawing into something. Then he would draw a squiggle and the child would complete it. The game continued with each taking their turn. As they played they talked about their drawings. Try this playful exercise with a partner (it need not be a child). You may well find that you are getting to know something about one another's 'inner worlds' in a way which would not happen in an ordinary conversation.

The worker's skills include reflective listening. We need to be attentive and responsive to what the child is communicating. This means emptying our mind of our own thoughts and making a mental space to focus on the child. We may start by recapping (Pinney 1990), a gentle running commentary describing what the child is doing, for example, 'You're burying the monster in the sand – you've got rid of it.' To reflect back to the child what she is doing is not so easy as it sounds. It takes practice both to stop asking questions and to make non-judgemental comments, avoiding praise as well as criticism. The next stage is to reflect back tentatively the feelings which the child is communicating, for example, 'Maybe you don't like the monster – you look angry with it – you seem pleased that you have got rid of it.' We are staying with the metaphor or symbolism of play, not rushing to make interpretations such as 'That may be how you feel about your stepdad', although we might consider asking, 'Does it remind you of anything?' This non-directive approach avoids exposing feelings which the child may not feel ready to handle. (Sometimes a trained and experienced therapist may make a tentative and carefully timed interpretation which can move the therapeutic process on. However, an ill-judged interpretation risks intrusion on the child's autonomy in play.)

Sometimes it is clear from the child's play what he is feeling. At times when it is less obvious it can be helpful to attend to the worker's own feelings. For example, the child who makes us feel bored may be projecting her own feelings of depression and anger. The child who pointedly ignores us may make us feel useless and hopeless, and this may be exactly what the child is feeling. This transference can *help* us understand. However, as we examine our own feelings as we play with a child – the countertransference – we need to be able to distinguish between the feelings projected into us by the child (diagnostic countertransference) and those feelings arising out of our own life experience (personal countertransference). Confusion can ensue especially when these coincide, and supervision for the worker is crucial in helping sort out what belongs where.

The child's game as an exercise in reflective listening?

Ask a child to play a special game with you for a few minutes, so that they expect something different from usual. Have some play materials ready or join the child at something they are playing.

1.   *Child's activity.* Allow your child to choose what to play. Do not introduce anything new into their play. If your child changes activities follow this but do not change the play yourself.
2.   *Follow.* Watch carefully what your child is doing. You may find you are 'shadowing' their movements and becoming aware of their mood.
3.   *Attend.* Describe aloud what your child is doing. This is a bit like giving a running commentary.
4.   *Join in and copy.* Participate in your child's play, by handing them materials or by taking a turn. You may also join in by imitating your child's play. Be careful not to direct or structure play yourself. Remember that your child's play is to be the centre of your attention, so continue to describe their activity and not yours.
5.   *No questions or commands.* Do not ask any questions or give any orders. (This is not as easy as it sounds.) These interrupt and structure your child's play.
6.   *No teaching.* Do not use this time to teach your child or to test what they know. Play for just five minutes at first. If you find your child enjoys it you can play for longer after a few times.

This game can help also parents play with their child without taking over. The worker plays it alone with the child at first, then demonstrates it to the parent and asks them to play for five minutes, at first with the worker's containing presence and then later at home.

It may be that the child will invite us to join in play, often in role play in which the child allocates us the role, often either of the victim or the 'baddie' – 'You be the child and I'll be the teacher.' For example I have been told to be asleep while the robber comes in the night and steals my new birthday presents; I then have to wake up next morning and be distressed at their loss, while the robber dances with glee. The symbolic significance of having had something which is then taken away is clear; the child made me experience and articulate his feelings of loss.

Engaging in role play is a delicate and difficult balancing act involving following the child's lead (so as to enable him to explore his feelings) but without getting drawn in to collusion and so losing the sense of our adult self and with it the ability to think.

The case study at the end of the chapter gives a fuller example of role play.

Focused play in therapeutic work and counselling: making sense of past, present and future

There is growing evidence (Fonagy et al. 1994) that the child's capacity for resilience to adverse experiences is enhanced by the development of a reflective self-function. This means that a child is able to think or conceptualise rather than simply act or react. It appears that this reflective ability grows out of the child being held in mind by someone, in the emotional containment already described. A consequence of this containment is that the child becomes able to reflect on and make sense of their past, and able to consider the future, that is to become a 'container' themselves. In fact, one measure of the child's progress is seen as the extent to which a child can construct a coherent self-narrative, that is, give an account of their life so far that hangs together and makes sense.

We can help the child understand their life story and think about the future, through a variety of non-directive and more focused approaches. Children may develop their own ways of doing this with their worker, making their own books, games or writing their stories. There are also commercially produced board and card games available, such as Barnados 'All About Me'. The game provides the 'third thing' (Winnicott 1968) between child and worker which eases the communication and enables the encounter to go at the child's pace, so sustaining the conditions for play.

Tools include genograms (family trees), ecomaps and mind maps, flow charts, life-story work, play materials and games. There is abundant literature to help the worker, for example, Redgrave 1987, Oaklander 1978, Owen and Curtis 1988, Ryan and Walker 1993, Jewett 1994, Cipolla et al. 1992.

This work can arouse powerful and painful feelings in the child, which the worker needs to be able to accept and bear as well as judging 'how much the child can cope with at any one time'. The worker who has had experience of using focused tools to think about her own life will be aware of their potential power, as the next exercise may reveal.

Exercise 9.3: Family trees/flow chart

Find a partner with whom you feel comfortable working. Draw your family trees and take turns discussing the feelings which arise. Or draw a flow chart of the different places where you have lived, and discuss this together. Make sure that you have listened to one another carefully.

Since some of this work is moving away from the non-directive approach of symbolic play, consideration therefore needs to be given to who does this work with the child – should it be the same person who has been involved in non-directive work? The answer is likely to vary according to particular circumstances. Whoever helps the child at this stage still needs to bear in mind the basic principles of creative play, that the child should be in control, going at their own pace, in a situation that feels safe and contained.

Issues in managing play within the wider context

Play therapy for a child at any age is only effective when it is set in the context of work with the whole system, family and professional, of which the child is a part. When we are thinking about primary provision it becomes obvious that all the activities of everyday living form the child's therapeutic experience. However the individual play therapy session also needs to be considered within the wider context. Parents or carers envious of the attention the child is receiving, or professionals who do not understand the process of play therapy, may wittingly or unconsciously sabotage the work. It can be a struggle to ensure the regularity and continuity of sessions, for example, when a school event suddenly is given precedence.

It can seem very hard for a carer who is coping probably with several children at once for a long stretch of time to recognise that the individual session is not just a luxury but a time for hard work involving painful feelings for the worker as well as the child. It can be even harder if the carer finds that they are having to deal with even more difficult behaviour. As Kegerries (1995) has pointed out, as children emotionally get better their behaviour may for a time become worse, as long-repressed feelings start to surface where they can be worked with. Unless the carers, and more crucially the managers who have the power to make decisions, understand what is happening the risk is that the child's placement or therapy will be ended prematurely as the child is whisked off elsewhere.

The therapeutic play worker can feel isolated, inadequate, and at times threatened. She risks ending up defensively colluding with the powerless child, angry with the outside world which does not understand and either attacking it or withdrawing. The challenge is to recognise such feelings but not to act directly on them. The task is to understand what is going on, to explain, without blame, to the child and to those outside, and to liaise carefully with others in the best interest of the child, giving thought to what is confidential and what needs to be shared. This is rarely easy, partly because of the damaged child's capacity for 'splitting', to make one person all good and another all bad. This is catching, especially when the worker feels the same. Supervision is important in helping sort out whose feelings belong where.

Play in family work

Working with the whole family present is normal in family therapy and family centres but is also a developing area in residential and foster care. Good play provision, such as engaging together in an art or play activity, or telling and enacting stories, can help the whole family relax and feel more at home, perhaps able to play with difficult new ideas. Or the children's play, perhaps a drawing or arrangement of miniature dolls or animals, may give an important clue to how they are thinking and feeling.

It helps if the child is able to get help from their family with constructing a coherent self-narrative. For instance when the child is on the verge of being looked after, changing placements, or leaving to make their way in the world, in a family session with the child the family can be asked to tell their story of the child. This can enable important pieces of knowledge and understanding to fall into place.

A case study in play therapy in a residential setting

The following case study from Ros Fanshawe at the Caldecott College illustrates the way in which individual play therapy sessions can contribute to the therapeutic treatment of a child in a residential setting. It demonstrates how an emotionally damaged adolescent can use an individual time with his key worker to re-create aspects of primary experience.

For a very long time N., an adolescent boy, had been looked after in the group in which I was working, and for most of this time I had been his keyworker. Playroom time had been an established part of his treatment.

N. had been looked after as a result of multiple hospitalisations for non-accidental injury before he was four, and for which his father was prosecuted and imprisoned. In addition to gross physical injury he suffered emotional abuse and neglect by his mother (as well as suspicions of sexual abuse). The family lived in squalid conditions and the household was riven with arguments and fighting. After numerous attempts to rehabilitate N. and several short-term foster placements, he was placed with another foster family ostensibly for the short term and stayed for four years until the birth of a younger sister put such strain on the family that they requested his removal.

In the playroom, N. devised the following game of hide-and-seek; he would select an object, usually a piece of 'fool's gold' and I would cover my eyes and count to ten whilst he hid it, although on many occasions N. gave me the first go. I think that if the playroom had more hidey holes or N. and I had been smaller it would have been the people who hid instead of their hiding an object. Together we had made rules to the game: the object could be hidden anywhere in the room, and the 'hider' could give the 'seeker' clues as to how close they were to finding the object by saying 'hot' or 'cold'. The object could be hidden on the hider themselves in their clothes with the exception of areas of the body which would be wrong to invite search of (such as in my breast pocket or in underwear) and there was no time limit to the search. The game was very playful and humorous in mood – finding the object was often accompanied by cries from N. of 'oh damn, I knew you'd find it' and much laughter between us.

What was striking was the persistence with which N. wanted to play this game; I would always ask, on going into the playroom, what did he want to do and often he would find the piece of fool's gold and give me a knowing smile.

It seemed that there were two themes in the game: first, 'knowing' in the sense of knowing what he wanted to play by presenting me with the object, knowing where he had hidden it, really 'knowing' N. I was rapidly led to connect this to his very poor early experiences of abuse and neglect where he was not sufficiently well-'known' and held in mind by his parent. Certainly his father's abuse of him seemed connected to feeling frustrated by not being able to meet (beginning in knowing and understanding) his son's needs. Also there was 'knowing' in the sense that N. could be very delinquent and when found out would be angry but also relieved that grown-ups 'knew'. His secrets made him feel very unsafe, powerful and anxious – if he was not 'found out' he would become increasingly omnipotent. It seemed to be important in the game that I knew what N. was doing even when I could not see him, and it felt very important to be able to find the object.

A second very important theme was relating to touch and being touchable and 'in touch' with him, which was important for several reasons. One was N.'s age – he was over 14 when we were playing this game. Touch was an area laden with negative meaning for him because of his experience of being very severely battered as a baby. He was not a child who sought physical contact and his ability to distinguish good physical contact from pain was severely impaired – he would laugh maniacally when in severe physical pain. Secondly, N.'s encopresis and enuresis often made physical contact with him an unattractive idea. Thirdly, N. was developing physically and the game provided an excuse to touch one another, so there was an element of what was almost physical exploration, something which he never abused.

This account shows how the worker provided primary experience akin to a mother's play with her infant. N. was able symbolically in the game (and probably also concretely in daily living) to have those good experiences with his keyworker which he had missed in infancy. However the worker's reflection on the meaning of that play for N. meant that she offered a more powerful emotional containment; her search for 'knowing' could offer N. the hope not only that he would be 'known' and 'touchable' but also that he too might become someone who 'knows'.

Conclusion

Many people who become interested in play therapy were initially inspired by Virginia Axline's *Dibs – In Search of Self* (1964) and her book *Play Therapy* (1947 and 1989). In recent years there has been a growth of interest in play therapy with a number of books appearing in the UK, including West (1996), Wilson et al. (1992), McMahon (1992), and Carroll (forthcoming). There are increasing numbers of courses offering training in play therapy, notably at the University of York. The British Association of Play Therapists has been formed and provides information about training and supervision, both essential to anyone undertaking play therapy.

Bibliography and references

The psychodynamic and attachment theory base for play therapy

Alvarez, A. (1992) *Live Company – Psychoanalytic Psychotherapy with Autistic, Borderline, Deprived and Abused Children*, London: Routledge.
Bowlby, J. (1973) *Separation*, London: Penguin.
Bowlby, J. (1984) *Attachment*, London: Penguin.
Copley, B and Forryan, B. (1987) *Therapeutic Work With Children and Young People*, London: Robert Royce.
Dockar-Drysdale, B. (1968) *Therapy in Child Care*, London: Longman.
Dockar-Drysdale, B. (1990) *The Provision of Primary Experience*, London: Free Association Books.

Fonagy, P. et al. (1994) 'The Theory and Practice of Resilience', *Journal of Child Psychology and Psychiatry*, 35(2): 23–257.

Kegerries, S. (1995) 'Getting Better Makes it Worse', in Trowell, J. and Bower, M. (eds) *The Emotional Needs of Young Children and their Families*, London: Routledge.

Winnicott, D.W. (1965) *The Maturational Processes and the Facilitating Environment*, London: Hogarth Press and the Institute of Psycho-Analysis.

Winnicott, D.W. (1971) *Playing and Reality*. London: Tavistock.

General play therapy texts

Axline, V. (1947 & 1989) *Play Therapy*, Edinburgh: Churchill Livingstone.

Axline, V. (1964) *Dibs: In Search of Self*, Harmondsworth: Penguin.

Carroll, J. (forthcoming) *Introduction to Therapy Through Play: Practical Help for Troubled Children*, Oxford: Blackwell Scientific.

Cattanach, A. (1992) *Play Therapy With Abused Children*, London: Jessica Kingsley.

Erikson, E. (1965) *Childhood and Society*, Harmondsworth: Penguin.

McMahon, L. (1992) *The Handbook of Play Therapy*, London: Routledge.

Pinney, R. (1990) *Children's Hours*, Children's Hours Trust, 28 Whitehouse, Clapham Park Estate, London SW4 8HD.

Ryan, V. and Wilson, K. (1996) *Case Studies in Non-Directive Play Therapy*, London: Baillicere Tindall.

West, J. (1996) *Child-Centred Play Therapy*, London: Arnold.

Wilson, K., Kendrick, P. and Ryan, V. (1992) *Play Therapy. a non-directive approach for Children and Adolescents*, London: Bailliere Tindall.

Focused play techniques

Cipolla, J., McGown, D. and Yanulis, M. (1992) *Communicating Through Play. Techniques for assessing and preparing children for adoption*, London: BAAF.

Jewett, C. (1994) *Helping Children Cope With Separation and Loss*, London: Batsford/BAAF.

Oaklander, V. (1978) *Windows to Our Children*, Utah: Real People Press.

Owen, P. and Curtis, P (1988) *Techniques for Working With Children*, Chorley, Lancs.

Redgrave, K. (1987) *Child's Play – Direct Work with the Deprived Child*, Tilde: Boys and Girls Welfare Society.

Ryan, T. and Walker, R. (1993) *Making Life Story Books*, London: BAAF.

Winnicott, C. (1968) 'Communicating with Children', in Todd, R. (ed.) *Disturbed Children*, London: Longman.

British Association of Play Therapists, PO Box 98, Americium, Bucks HP6 5BL.

10 Adolescence: a time of transitions

Kevin Healy

Introduction

> The variations of behaviour during adolescence are so numerous that it is often difficult to decide what is due to temporary stress and what has to be viewed as a sign of the presence of or vulnerability to more serious mental disturbance. (Moses Laufer 1975)

Kevin Healy's chapter reminds us just how difficult adolescents at the point of breakdown are, both to manage and to help. As he leads us through his case examples, he raises many of the issues which are the subject matter of other chapters. The quotation above highlights the importance of skilled assessment of emotional needs and informed supervision of both the assessment process and the treatment which follows. The understanding of, and sensitivity to, communication from the unconscious is an essential tool. We are also challenged to deal with identity, anxiety, relationships and the behaviours associated with them. What Kevin Healy emphasises is the importance of the ordinary member of staff as keyworker who will take on the challenge of relating to a very unstable young person. Yes, they will have their special therapy sessions with a special therapist for very short periods only. That leaves the hundreds of humdrum everyday interactions and activities available and here there is enormous therapeutic potential. We often forget this in an age when, thanks to the media, we constantly look to specialists and experts for help, explanations and answers.

10 Adolescence: a time of transitions

Kevin Healy

In this chapter I propose to explore adolescence as a transition from childhood to young adult life. I will

- Outline the psychodynamic principles underlying my work with adolescents in a specialised in-patient adolescent service
- Use appropriately disguised clinical material to highlight the transitions of adolescence relating to identity, attachments, sexuality, love and hate, and the inner fantasy lives of adolescents
- Endeavour to highlight the impact on others working with and living with young people in transition
- Emphasise the rightful concerns when young people become stuck in their developmental journey
- Outline ways of working with adolescents that may enable them to move on from their stuckness.

Adolescence is a time of transition. The Oxford Reference Dictionary defines transit (from the Latin *transire* to go across) as the process of going, conveying or being conveyed across, over, or through. Transition itself is defined as the process of changing from one state or subject to another. The adjective 'transitory' defines the quality of 'not lasting or existing only for a time'. This terminology is very relevant to the journey of adolescence from childhood to young adult life. Donald Winnicott, psychoanalyst and paediatrician, developed the concept of a transitional object in childhood that helps a child move from a state of being dependent on another person, usually his/her mother, to a state of using and relating to others differently. Young people in their journey through adolescence may create either individually or collectively a range of transitional objects to help them on this journey. We can think of peer relationships, the first loves of adolescence, the culture of adolescence whether music, art, rebellion and the use of legal or illegal substances as transitional objects to help on this emotional journey. Adolescence is not always a time of angst and turmoil. Rutter and Rutter (1993) have highlighted the dangers of generalising to all adolescents from the issues that arise in the treatments of disturbed adolescents. However, this does not deny the impact of the major biological, psychological and social changes that are central to the transitions of adolescence.

Some of the services provided to help adolescents and their families on this journey reflect the particular needs of adolescents. Educational provision, in secondary schools, sixth-form colleges and universities, usually recognises the role of education in helping young people on their journey. There is an increasing emphasis within government and amongst policy makers on the significance of training and employment to all our lives, and on the crucial part this plays in the lives of young people seeking an identity and a role for themselves in society. Social services and health services often provide poorly for the needs of adolescents. Adolescents are often expected to move on from situations of care to independent living without the emotional and social support necessary to achieve this. Health services for adolescents are non-existent in many parts of the country. Children's services and adult services exist. The needs of young people who fall between these services often go unrecognised and unmet.

The Adolescent Service I work in was set up specifically to cater for the clinical needs of 16 to 20-year-olds who fell between child and adult health and social services, and who were unable to face the transitions of adolescence. It is an internationally renowned in-patient psychotherapeutic community. Psychoanalytic principles and understanding are applied in each of the three in-patient units; the Families Unit, the Adult Unit, and the Adolescent Unit, that together form the working community. Patients come for treatment at times in their lives when they are feeling desperate, despairing, hopeless, self-destructive and suicidal. They will often have harmed themselves or others in a number of serious ways and are usually very stuck in their lives on referral. All who come to work in treatment must have a wish to risk facing change and to begin to look at and explore their emotional and social worlds.

Psychodynamic principles in practice

R. is 16 years old, and is placed in a social services secure unit. She cuts herself, she overdoses, she is violent, she lashes out at herself and at others. She uses her body promiscuously. She has hung herself a number of times and at the time of her referral to the adolescent service here we were told that she is being restrained by staff up to five times a day to control her. I will follow through on R.'s story as I explore some of the psychodynamic principles that guide my work.

Actions have meaning

What we hear about now on a daily basis in the secure unit is something that has been repeated over and over in R.'s lifetime. She has been looked after since she was three, and has had a succession of children's homes, foster homes and a therapeutic community placement, all leading to breakdown. There are usually scenes of violence leading to her exclusion from the setting and being moved on to somewhere else. R. herself is able to explain an incident of violence on the basis of somebody annoying her, somebody saying something they shouldn't have, or somebody taking something of hers. She feels she is only asserting her rights. This may be her conscious way of understanding what is actually happening at any particular point. However, I think that the word 'secure' actually has a lot of meaning at an unconscious level for her. As we get to know more about R. we find that there is a sense of security engendered in her when someone else can sit and try and control the violent rages that she has to face within herself. There is a sense of security when people restrain her, hold her and take responsibility for the stuff that's within her. However this is for much of the time 'known' at a more unconscious level within R.

Understanding the meaning of actions is usually helpful

Understanding the meaning of actions can be an intense process. It can be painful and difficult and may itself stir up more disturbed behaviour. However it is usually helpful for an individual to have some sense of why they do what they do, and to be able to think about themselves rather than just act without capacity to think. It is almost always helpful for families and friends to have some sense of what is going on when a loved one is behaving in a strange way. The process of grieving is an example that we all know about. The death of a loved one is a huge loss and can lead to the saying and doing of strange things. Understanding grieving makes it possible for others to live through it with us. For professionals working with disturbed young adults, understanding does provide a framework in which to continue to be in contact with an individual whose disturbance may be very severe and worrying. A sense of understanding can often make possible what Winnicott has termed '*holding*' and Bion has named as '*containing*'.

Relationships are central to understanding

Relationships do provide containment for all of us when in distress. Most of us get our containment through families, parents, children, friends, peers, colleagues or loved ones. Disturbed adolescents may often rely for some sort of containment on professional workers. R. was at times kept alive by her social worker, who worked alongside her very intensively for a number of years. He was the one who was there from placement to placement, to pick things up, to hold things, to be around and to provide some thinking space around her. Therapeutic relationships provide a setting within which there is a re-enacting or repetition of themes that have arisen from past relationships of an individual. This is known as *transference*. R., for example, expected to be rejected all the time. That had been the pattern in her life and that is what she often times elicited in her relationships.

The feelings elicited in workers in response to R.'s behaviours and interactions are known as *countertransference*. Exploring such feelings can lead to a fuller understanding of her psychological world. The exploration of such feelings is a central part of the 'culture of enquiry' at the Cassel Hospital which makes possible psychological work with disturbed and disturbing individuals.

Workers need holding and containing

It can be very painful and traumatic to get in touch with the traumas of another person's life. We need as workers to be sure of our own containment for the work that we do, of our own clarity about management structures where we work, about adequate supervision, and about having a space just to share with colleagues when we have had a difficult time. I have phrased this paragraph in terms of what we as workers need to ensure for ourselves. This is putting an onus and responsibility on us to seek adequate support for our work.

I recognise however that most of us are only a part of the institution within which we work and are reliant on others within the institution to provide an overall thinking space within the organisation.

Anxiety is a feature of living

Anxiety is a feature of life and is contained and managed in different ways at different stages of life. Physical discomfort, the fear of falling apart, and other specific anxieties of infancy are usually contained by a 'good enough' environment or environmental mother who is preoccupied with her child's welfare. Bion has written of the importance of the containing of a child's distress by another who can take on board that distress, not be overwhelmed by it, but provide a soothing comforting response in return.

Childhood raises a lot of anxieties linked with separations, starting school, making new friends, and often with the arrival of siblings. These anxieties are mostly contained by relationships within the family, with parents, with siblings. They are also contained by relationships with peers and friends, through the passage of time and through the experience of difficult situations being survived and life continuing. Adult life often involves dealing with the breakdown of relationships, moving jobs, moving home, the impact of the death of loved ones, the birth of children, stressful/relaxing holidays. Such anxieties are usually once more dealt with within supportive relationships with others. Such relationships are part of family life, and part of working life. Relationships generally make the work of living possible.

What are the anxiety-making issues that face adolescents? The main work of adolescence is trying to discover an identity. This occurs in the external world in terms of career plans, a place within a peer group and with friends, and within the increasingly intimate and sexual relationships that are now possible. Alongside this is the search for identity within oneself. It is a time when a sense of identity can be fickle and unstable.

Feelings are often intense. Adolescents are moving from particularly intense attachments to family and establishing new attachments with friends and with intimate sexual partners. Moving away from the family and establishing one's self in the larger world is a major cause of anxiety. Adolescents often have many doubts about their sexuality following on the reawakening of sexual feelings early in adolescence. The period of adolescence is both a difficult and also a very exciting time: there is so much to be thought about, the world is at their feet and everything is in one sense still before them. How will an adolescent deal with their love, hate, and aggression? The internal world of the adolescent remains a rich world of fantastical imagery.

The transitions of adolescence

Identity

Since running away from her family one year previously, M. had 16 placements and several assessments in various treatment facilities. She was referred to the unit after other attempts to treat her had broken down. M. was an emotionally damaged young woman who described having been sexually abused by her father for many years. She herself abused substances, mutilated herself by cutting, and had attempted to strangle herself more than once. M.'s surname and address were unknown. She had refused to disclose this information to any of her carers. There appeared to have been a rivalrous relationship between M. and her older sister for the major place in their father's affections. At the age of 14, M. ran away to London hoping that life would be better and safer for her. Instead she found herself on the streets, cold, frightened and abusing any substance she could get hold of. When she first came to the attention of Social Services she had been found unconscious after sniffing glue in a London train station.

M.'s physical appearance was striking. Her left arm was heavily scarred from repeated self-cutting. She constantly carried a teddy bear with her. She needed to use crutches to get around and to support her knee which had been dislocated in an attempt to restrain her from harming herself in a previous hospital. In her treatment, at times M. received enormous input and support from other patients and staff. She found this support very containing, yet ironically this often meant that in the process she became more childlike in herself. Her greatest difficulties were in contributing and giving to others. She found it impossible to take on ongoing responsibilities within the therapeutic community. The breakdown in this area left her feeling overwhelmed by ongoing exploration of her past abusive relationships and unable to contain inevitably difficult feelings.

M. had decided that all men were bad. If she were going to have relationships they would have to be with women. She couldn't understand why she had a male pop group poster on her wall, or why she trusted Robert, her male nurse. These sorts of confusions often filled her mind, and made her uncomfortable. She could be far more comfortable when things seemed clear-cut, either good or bad. She began to think about her confusion of love and hatred for her father. This made her feel terrible about herself. She was discharged to a more secure psychiatric hospital.

M. clearly had major identity problems. She had given up her place in the real external world, going by a false name with an untraceable background. She moved from acute placement settings to acute psychiatric settings without forming any ongoing relationships. She was not in school, in training, or working towards any career or future. Her use of crutches made it appear as if she 'hadn't a leg to stand on'. Her internal world was in a mess. She recognised that her great neediness often provoked abusive responses in others. She seemed comfortable at times with such relationships as if that was the best she could expect for herself. However there were glimmers of a self who was interested in music. M. was also interested in animals and recalled having a cat for most of her childhood years. It may well be safer for some people to build relationships with animals rather than risk the hurts of human relationships. Overall M.'s search for an identity was very difficult for her. She was unclear as to what she had come from, what she would wish to leave behind, what she couldn't leave behind. She was equally unclear as to what she was going to do, what she wished to make of her life. It is not surprising that the transitional period was so problematic. Nor is it surprising that M. was more connected to a transitional object of childhood, her teddy bear, giving her the incongruous appearance of a large very small child.

Attachment

P. was born ten months after her sister S., who occupied all of their mother's available space. She was filled with hatred for S., and for her mother whom she described with great contempt as having been a whore, a drunk, and physically abusive to her. She told of times when her mother had beaten her. Once her mother had held P.'s thumb in the door and slammed it. P. felt that her father loved her and raised her while her mother was busy with her sister. Her parents separated when she was five years old. Her mother refused to allow their father to contact the girls.

When her mother remarried, P. became very close to her stepfather. She was 16 when he became ill with cancer. When it became obvious that he would die and 'leave her', she left first and fled to Greece. There she welcomed the oblivion of a life of drugs. Her drug habit was expensive. She became a prostitute to pay for it. When she returned to England she lived with a drug-dealing boyfriend in a stormy and violent relationship. Both of them were promiscuous. P. often physically attacked him.

I will describe in this section some of the work undertaken by P. and her nurse D. around the issue of weekends. Typically patients are expected to return to their own homes at weekends, having discussed practical arrangements with their nurse and with other patients before hand. There is a strong emphasis on facilitating patients' capacities to help one another. In this way patients come to view themselves not only as people with problems but also as individuals with resources.

Early in treatment, P. would depict, in a manner that was mocking of her nurse, that she delighted to get away from the hospital for the weekend. There were friends to see and parties to attend. Any attempt by D. to reflect upon particular difficulties, and how these may encroach upon her weekends, was wildly dismissed. She would convey that her nurse D. was neither wanted or needed. It became increasingly clear that such experiences were a powerful communication of how she herself could feel at a time of impending separation. She herself could feel pushed out, unwanted and uncared for. Any rapport that was built up over the week between D. and P.

was demolished as the end of the week approached. She would behave rudely and belligerently towards him, leaving him feeling exasperated and humiliated. On her return to the hospital at the beginning of the week, she would typically not turn up for meetings and D. would find himself searching for her throughout the hospital in an attempt to make contact with her.

P. did however manage to return to treatment each week. There was over time an increasing sense of her ability to think with D. about her experiences. This enabled her to reach a stage where feelings about the weekend could be anticipated. This seemed to represent a shift in her, from excessively evacuating painful feelings to being more able to find a space inside herself for such feelings, to hold on to them, and to give them thought. This was followed by a period in which P. allowed D. to care and show concern for her. There was also a shift in P.'s capacity to show some concern for herself. She began to share the emptiness and loneliness that she experienced at home away from the hospital. She depicted staying in bed for whole weekends and eating little. This showed in a concrete way how the mental image of a caring relationship evaporated with the separation.

Soon she began to leave treatment early and return late without negotiation. D. was the one who now had the experience of what it felt like to be left behind. P. recognised that her comings and goings were a way of her having some control over feelings of loss. She revealed that she often spent her weekends getting high on drugs and selling herself for sex, as a way of escaping the emptiness. She felt that by selling herself for sex she could maintain the idea that somebody was interested in her. It was also a re-enactment of her sense of being denigrated.

In their ongoing relationships with R., staff and patients showed their persistent concern for her. Through an explicit statement that her self-abuse was not acceptable, she was able to experience a genuine concern from others towards her. She slowly began to adopt a similar attitude of concern towards herself.

P. was encouraged to take on a job within the hospital which involved managing an annual fund-raising event. She poured weeks of concentrated effort into this job which she managed very successfully. This job inspired a wide range of networks and relationships within the hospital which she experienced as very containing. She was connected up to others in the pursuit of something creative. Through this work she was able to gain more of a sense of her inner resources. She planned her weekends and structured them in a way that provided more containment. She planned to shop and cook for herself, visit friends, and explored ordinary means of obtaining pleasure.

Other important work with P. centred around her body. With a female member of staff, P. visited the local well woman's clinic for support and health education. Though streetwise she had never used protective measures within sexual relationships. This work was a concrete way of caring for her, which in turn encouraged her to look after her body in a concrete, practical and healthy way. Through such work P. was able to develop some internal as well as external resources to help her negotiate the powerful conflicts aroused by separations. There was more of a sense of her utilising the care that she had received, of her having more confidence in her ability to tolerate such care, and indeed taking the risk to care for herself when carers were absent. There was more of a sense of P. making space for herself within which she could live and where nurturing could be experienced.

The above example on one level is all about the capacity to be separate and to continue to care for oneself while separate. What is however most striking in the clinical material is the development of P.'s capacity to get alongside others and allow them alongside her in the showing of care and concern. Having such an attachment makes separation possible. Attachment provides in John Bowlby's phrase *'a secure base'* from which to explore the world. There is a more concrete equivalent observable in all children striving to walk for the first time. Walking independently can only happen when an infant feels secure enough about falling over. Separation likewise is only possible when an individual feels secure enough about attachments.

Sexuality

C. was referred for treatment because of ongoing serious depression and suicidal acting-out. She was the only child of elderly parents. C.'s depression dated from the age of eleven. C. recalled her father doing her homework for her for many years. She was left with no confidence in her own mind and indeed very little knowledge of it either. She was sent to a private school on secondary transfer, which was supposed to encourage individual development rather than stress academic excellence. C.'s description of this was that the students who already had some sense of themselves as individuals got on fine, but she felt increasingly at a loss as she did not have any sense of who she was in order to develop it. She also found that she could not manage without her father's continuing help with schoolwork and became very preoccupied by the idea of being 'a cheat'.

During the early months, C. often spoke of wanting to leave treatment. Her therapist found it very difficult to have an emotionally alive sense of her and found herself mechanically bringing her up in staff meetings so as to try and keep her in mind somehow. Little by little, C. described her role in her family. She saw herself as a kind of partner/protector of her father whom she felt was a victim of her mother's cruelty. She would beg them to 'just listen' to each other. She saw herself as the glue that held them together. Seeing her parents in this way was also the glue which held her together by allowing her to project any emotional mess into them. When she felt herself to be sacked from this position her life became intolerable. Her mother changed towards her father and became more concerned and caring since he developed a serious life-threatening illness, one year previously. She felt terribly betrayed by her father who turned towards her mother more. She was furious with both parents and filled with hatred and contempt for them. There was an increasing sense of desperation in her therapy sessions. As she began to value her treatment and to realise her dependence upon it, she felt vulnerable and unprotected by her superiority and coldness. There were times when she felt herself to have absolutely nothing inside and others when she felt herself to be 'a discharge, an angry stinking mess'.

Along with this increased vulnerability and anxiety came moments of increasing warmth towards particular friends and particular relations. This gave her some hope that her internal coldness might not last forever. As she became more engaged in her treatment in the hospital she also took more risks for herself. She used her sessions to think about and experience herself in a different way. She talked with other patients and in group settings in a more open way about herself. She took on a variety of jobs within the in-patient therapeutic community that allowed her to exercise responsibility for herself and to exercise an ownership of her own thoughts, feelings and actions. She became more able to express her anger and disagreements, her warmth, and increasingly her sexuality. She experimented with her life and took some risks that would allow her to experience fresh situations. Just as with her school work as a young teenager, she also 'cheated' within the hospital. She stayed up late at night talking into the small hours with some male patients. She experimented with some vodka that another patient had brought into the hospital against hospital rules. She became much more aware of her impact on others and was both provocatively sexual at times and provocatively stubborn at other times. She risked being more openly hostile to her parents and would often not let them know until the last minute whether or not she would be returning home to them for her weekends away from the hospital. She had the option also of staying with a favourite older female cousin whom she also began to treat in the same way. In one sense she was positively asserting herself as an individual, but was unable to do this in a way that left others feeling satisfied on her behalf. She also began to assert her sexuality in a similar way.

On one particular weekend, she intimated to her parents that she would be staying at her cousin's, and to her cousin that she would be staying at her parents. After leaving the hospital she then phoned her parents to say that she would in fact be staying in the flat of a young man, R., whom she knew from the unit. R. had been involved in some long talks into the night with her. They had probably begun to experiment sexually also, but had not had a full sexual relationship. C. had let her parents know of her interest in R. Her parents became concerned and frightened by what was happening. They phoned the hospital repeatedly to speak to nursing and medical staff. All the duty staff were made fully aware of C.'s predicament and of her parents worry that she might lose her virginity, become pregnant, and have her whole future destroyed as a consequence. Her parents wondered if C. was mad, or unable to think for herself in putting herself at serious risk of destructive consequences. C.'s sexuality had become a very powerful force. The creative aspects of it were lost amongst the destructive potential that might be released.

Many eminent writers see adolescence as a time for gaining contact with and coming to live within a sexual body. It is also a time of great intensity, doubt, uncertainty, experimentation, as an adolescent comes to terms with new-found sexual feelings. It is a time of transition from living with sexual feelings and fantasy within the family, to living with and experiencing such feelings in newly formed relationships outside of the family. All individuals are likely to base the intimate sexual relationships they form on their experiences of loving intimacy within their family of origin. C. rarely saw loving intimate moments between her parents as she grew up. However it is likely that there were loving intimate moments between her and her mother (and probably also with her father) around feeding, changing and bathing. She recalled her parents being very proud of her appearance as a young child. She was like their doll whom they could dress as they pleased. She was not however allowed to have or to express feelings of her own. As C.'s body began to develop into that of a young woman, her parents probably became more frightened of her developing sexuality and withdrew their admiration from her. C. as an 18-year-old was now left with some very complicated feelings about her own sexuality. On this occasion her actions seemed more driven by a desire to cause her parents to suffer than by a wish to develop her sexuality further.

Love, hate, aggression

The description above of C.'s development clearly also has intense loving, hating and aggressive qualities. It is impossible to separate off feeling states from one another in a meaningful way. I do so here only for the purpose of clarity and description. I will return now to P. and to exploring her struggle with her intense, angry, hating and loving feelings, as manifested in her individual therapy sessions. I wrote of her great difficulty with separations which included her inability to keep good and bad separate in her mind. It also included separations from her therapist at the end of sessions, and on holidays. P. often felt the separation from her therapist as a brutal rejection and cruel abandonment, which she experienced as final and irreversible. In order to protect herself from this terrible state of mind, P. had to quickly destroy her own sense of hope in her therapist's concern for her which might have been gained from session to session. Her therapist became the one who was made to feel the destruction of her hopes for P., and had a sense of being utterly thrown out and being made to experience an attack on her professional abilities which often added up to a sense of complete worthlessness. Often her therapist felt that the best she could do was survive.

In an early session P. eloquently described to her therapist her inability to believe that she had a real separate identity of her own. P. felt that she didn't ever really know what was true. When she tried to figure something out for herself, she heard her mother's voice in her mind telling her something else. She went on to talk about her feeling that inside she was her mother. In one session she said to her therapist 'I am really angry with you today for making me feel so dirty with my mum inside of me. I want to scrape off all my skin but chiefly the bones inside me, she'd like that.' Two days later she took an overdose which she said was to kill off the mother inside of her. P. may have believed that her therapist, like her stepfather, had failed to protect her from her murderous mother and so she was left to do the job herself.

She went on in sessions to describe her mind as a jumbled-up pile of drink cans. They were all mixed up and she wished she could get them separated: the good cans would be in one pile and the bad cans in another, with strings which could connect them up. There had been times when her mother had seemed good and loving only to turn quickly cruel again. P.'s relationship with her therapist was also muddled in this way. Endings of sessions, weekends, and holiday breaks and any lapse in her therapist's attention, or her not providing P. with instant relief from her distress, were ample reasons for P. to feel not cared about and to attack her therapist: 'You don't give a damn about me, you care more about your hair and your clothes, you go off to your cushy little life and leave me here with all these crazy people, you are useless, you haven't helped me at all, they must have made a mistake and sent you the wrong letter when they hired you.' She would often stamp out of the room five minutes before the end of the session slamming the door and shouting down the hall.

Very gradually P. began to think that it just might be possible to repair some of the damage that she felt she caused and to stop the internal and external warfare with her mother and with her therapist. In the beginning of this phase these attempts had a desperate and manic quality. She came to her first session after the Easter break a few minutes early. She had been frightened to find that her therapist might be dead especially given the fury of her angry attacks against her before she had left on holiday. P. asked 'Did you have a good holiday, the room looks different, you look different, your hair is permed it looks really nice that way, I missed you when you were gone, I didn't think I would, but I really did, it surprised me but I guess I must like you more than I thought but you weren't here, I was quite sad really, you weren't here when I needed you, I felt so sad.' P. noticed that there was no coat on her therapist's coat hanger and asked 'Are you cold? I'll get you a coat.' Her therapist commented that P. wanted to be sure that her therapist was all right. Her therapist commented that P. was trying hard to take care of her and that she was also trying to protect her therapist from how angry she was that her therapist had been away. P. agreed 'I won't be mean to you any more, I won't say I want another therapist, you are fine, I really like your hair that way.' In the above sessions, her therapist felt it was important to support the part of P. who was trying to be on the side of protection and repair, however 'manic' her attempt had been. Little by little P. began to establish the beginning of real separation between what was good for her and what was bad. This progress was very tentative and subject to constant setbacks.

Impact on staff

I hope it is clear from the examples given that the lives of these particular adolescents are highly charged and full of intense, rawly expressed, emotion. All those who come in contact with these young people will be undoubtedly affected. Some will allow the emotional world of disturbed adolescents to impact on their lives in a direct way, others because of their need to protect themselves from intolerable anxieties will find ways to defend against the rawness of these relationships. Most of us will move between such ways of relating. I wish to emphasise two points here, first that not all adolescents experience such emotional intensity or repeat such emotional traumas within their relationships (Rutter and Rutter 1993). The adolescents described in this chapter come from a highly selected group of individuals who have needed the containment of in-patient treatment within a therapeutic community to help them safely on their journey through adolescence. Their behaviours are extreme, their emotions are very raw, their impact on others is immense. Secondly, I wish to emphasise that within the setting described, adolescents often have their most intense relationships with each other and consequently their impact on each other can be immense. Although I have chosen to emphasise in this section the impact on staff of working with such adolescent disturbance, I wish also to recognise that each adolescent must find a way of living with the intensity, the rawness and the turmoil I am describing.

The turmoil created in the emotional lives of staff feels at times to be hugely traumatic and invasive. M.'s relationship with R. her nurse, often left him feeling totally attacked as a nurse and as a person, and hated by her. He often doubted himself, felt wiped out both in his role as her nurse and as another human being and felt very much at the receiving end of her violence. She was never actually physically violent to him as others have been to her; however, the attacks on him as a nurse and as a person were just as destructive. Likewise M.'s therapist, having initially felt very warmly towards M. and the courage she was showing in her sessions to begin to talk about herself, soon became filled up with the horrors of the abuse she was describing. In addition, M.'s therapist began to perceive herself as if she too were abusing M. through her interactions. This was the world which M. inhabited and into which she drew others. The emotional experiences of those relating to her were consequently often perceived by them as traumatic, intense and barely survivable, just as no doubt M.'s own experiences had been for her throughout her short life.

On Thursdays after P. has had her second individual therapy sessions in the week, and the final one before her weekend break, P.'s therapist often comes spinning into the staff room. You can see by the look on her face that she is terrified P. may be going home with plans to kill herself this weekend. She is filled with great anxiety. As a staff group, we need to look at both what is happening within P.'s sessions and within her life in the wider in-patient community. We need to ensure that she has been involved as far as possible in planning a safe weekend for herself. As a staff group, we can usually then take the risk of P. going ahead with her weekend plans with the likelihood that she will be able to return safely enough to treatment at the end of the weekend. Keeping the issues of self-harm and suicidal thoughts and behaviour alive in us as a staff group seems to make it more possible for her to live with her own anxieties about her destructiveness and to survive.

Helping the staff to survive emotionally is essential for this work. This psychological survival needs to happen on a day-to-day basis and over time if effective work with patients is to continue and staff burn-out is to be avoided. Containment for staff is built into the working structures of the unit. Above all it depends on the quality of relationships established in a line management and supervisory capacity within the staff team.

Supporting staff is facilitated through allowing feelings to be heard. Use is then made of these feelings to explore the psychodynamics of the interaction between adolescents and staff. Such an understanding develops within individual supervision, within joint supervision with nurse and therapist of a particular adolescent, and within the daily staff meetings involving all staff as available on the adolescent unit. In such settings, we are very aware of the process of splitting and use the fact that workers often experience very polarised feelings in relation to a patient to understand the dynamics of that patient which engage us. Being aware of these dynamics is usually helpful in bringing the world of the patient together. Treatment usually means that patients will re-enact situations from their internal world and from the past, and will test staff as to whether they can hold concern for the patient when all feel so despairing. Holding suicidal feelings, as in the case of R.'s therapist, can be easier when these are openly shared with other workers and thought about together. It is very important that one person isn't filled with all the anxiety on behalf of the team.

It is very important for the patient and for the staff group to know who will be working with the patient in the absence of their primary worker on holiday, on study leave, on sick leave, or for whatever reason. When primary workers are absent, it is important the patient actually knows who is going to be keeping them in mind and looking after them. Issues of clear authority are usually very significant within the staff team and are sometimes severely tested through the reenactment of difficulties from an adolescent's internal world. The management by senior nurse and consultant psychotherapist of the adolescent unit needs to allow a space for autonomy for the patient, for their key primary workers, and for the staff group as a whole to make autonomous and considered judgements. Against this background of respect for individuals' rights, some clear limits around what behaviours are unacceptable within the hospital need to be set and maintained. The role of the nurse at the Cassel Hospital is to work alongside patients, to interact and be with patients in an everyday way. Because of the support that is available, nurses at the unit are able to engage in relationships with patients that would be intolerable in a less supportive setting. Working as a psychosocial nurse is extremely demanding in a personal and professional way. Nurses expose themselves to all sorts of intense feelings directed towards them by the patient in order to be able to work effectively towards change. Nurses do not deny the patients' distress and disturbance but encourage patients to explore alternative ways of managing this disturbance through developing and using everyday relationships for effective support.

Way of working

There are three main strands to the treatment at the unit that are of help to patients in risking change. First there is an emphasis placed on relationships formed during treatment. Adolescents will share a room with two or three other young people and will come to know the other adolescents, the adult patients, the parents, and often importantly, the children with whom they share their lives during the working week. They will build a relationship with their primary nurse who works closely alongside them on day-to-day issues and on planning for times at home over weekends and in the longer term. They will also form relationships with their individual therapist who will see them for two 50-minute sessions each week, and with their group therapists who will see them for two one-hour group therapy sessions each week. Within all these relationships they can expect to repeat all the difficulties they have had up until now in relating. This in itself is not therapeutic but is a first step towards thinking about their difficulties, exploring them, coming to understand them and seeking ways to change them within the relationships formed.

The second main therapeutic factor is the emphasis placed on adolescents remaining responsible for themselves throughout their treatment. They will be responsible for taking the risks involved in beginning to talk about themselves at their own pace. They will be responsible for keeping themselves safe throughout their treatment and for allowing others to work alongside them to ensure their safety when they feel at particular risk of harming themselves or others. They will be responsible as treatment progresses for taking on important jobs within the therapeutic community. These jobs may be of a practical nature such as preparing meals, keeping the hospital tidy, or running various activities. Patients' jobs also include taking on roles within the adolescent unit and within the whole hospital community, chairing meetings, and acting as the responsible person to whom other patients who are distressed may go initially.

The third main therapeutic factor is the emphasis on an adolescent getting on with life and facing the ordinary things in living no matter what else is going on for them. In this way adolescents are encouraged to develop their particular skills and hobbies, to continue with their education and training towards building a career for themselves, and to carry on with the commitments they have to themselves and to others no matter what else may be troubling them or distracting them at the time. Life on the adolescent unit at the Cassel Hospital is intense and difficult, but at times can be fun. Patients live in the hospital from Sunday to Friday returning to their own home at weekends in order to continue to build their lives outside of hospital. Patients must make a continuing commitment to their treatment and can at any time choose to leave if that is what they wish. Most patients do not choose to leave and often have few viable alternatives. What keeps most people in treatment is their recognition that the process of treatment at the Cassel Hospital is usually life-changing and enables individuals to get beyond the log-jam in their lives, to build significant relationships for themselves, and to see and build some future career for themselves. Family work is an integral part of the treatment provided. Linking with the many professionals involved in the lives of these adolescents and helping to integrate the inputs of the workers, which often reflect the emotional state of the adolescent, is a crucial part of the treatment package.

The 'culture of enquiry' is evident in the above description. Through enquiry difficult experiences come to have meanings and can then be expressed in thoughts and perhaps in words as a way of avoiding the urge to repeat such experiences within current relationships and situations. Such a shift represents a huge step for the adolescent in treatment: troubled adolescents often feel very stuck in their development, and this shift reflects a freedom within the adolescent and the rediscovery of the capacity to be creative. Adolescence is often a time of great creativity as the adolescents' attentions are drawn to relationships outside of family and to the world at large. It is a time of discovery for all concerned and no less so for those of us who work with adolescents. Adolescence is a transitional space that maintains contact with the world of childhood and with the world of adult responsibility. Each of us perhaps could benefit from continuing to live our lives within such a transitional world.

References

Bowlby, J. (1988) *A Secure Base. Clinical Applications of Attachment Theory*, Routledge.
Laufer, M. and Laufer, M.E. (1984) *Adolescence and Developmental Breakdown*, Yale University Press.
Main, T. (1989) *The Ailment and other Psychoanalytic Essays*, Free Association Books.
Rutter, M. and Rutter, N. (1993) *Developing Minds, A Challenge and Continuity across the Lifespan*, Penguin Books.
Winnicott, D.W. (1965) *The Maturational Processes and the Facilitating Environment*, The Hogarth Press.
Winnicott, D.W. (1971) *Playing and Reality*, Penguin Books.

Bibliography

Copley, B. and Forryan, B. (1987) 'Mother and Baby in the First Year of Life', in *Therapeutic Work with Children and Young People*, Robert Royce.
Erikson, E. (1977) 'Eight ages of Man', in *Childhood and Society*, Paladin Books.
MacMahon, L. (1992) 'The Development of Play', in *The Handbook of Play Therapy*, Routledge.

Winnicott, D.W. (1986) 'The Child in the Family Group', in *Home is Where We Start From*, Pelican Books.

Further Reading

Alvarez, A. (1992) *Live Company: Psychoanalytic Psychotherapy with Autistic, Borderline, Deprived and Abused Children*, Routledge.

Balbernie, R. (1992) 'Adolescent Sexuality and Aggression', *Therapeutic Care and Education*, 1(3).

Blos, P. (1979) *The Adolescent Passage: Developmental Issues*, International Universities Press.

Bowlby, J. (1953) *Child Care and the Growth of Love*, Pelican Books.

Coleman, J.C. and Hendry, L. (1990) *The Nature of Adolescence*, Routledge.

Collie, A. (1996) 'The Institute as a Container of Unconscious Feelings: The Therapeutic Challenge of Adolescents in Residential Care', *Journal of Social Work Practice*, 10(2).

Copley, B. (1993) *The World of Adolescence: Literature, Society and Psychoanalytic Psychotherapy*, Free Association Books.

Dwivedi, K. (ed.) (1993) *Group Work with Children and Adolescents*, Jessica Kingsley Publishers.

Erikson, E. (1968) *Identity: Youth and Crisis*, Faber and Faber.

Erikson, E. (1977) *Childhood and Society*, Paladin Books.

Fahlberg, V. (1987) 'Adolescence', in *A Child's Journey through Placement*, BAAF.

Friedman, M.H. and Laufer, M.E. (1970) 'Problems in Working with Adolescents', from Brent Consultation Centre, London.

Freud, A. (1980) *Normality and Pathology in Childhood*, Karnac Books.

Greenberg, H. (1975) 'The Widening Gyre: Transformations of the Omnipotent Quest During Adolescence', *International Review of Psychoanalysis*, 2 (231).

Greenhalgh, P. (1994) *Emotional Growth and Learning*, Routledge.

Hendry, L.B., Shucksmith, J., Love, J.G. and Glendinning, A. (1993) *Young People's Leisure and Lifestyles*, Routledge.

Harris, H. and Lipman, A. (1984) 'Gender and the Pursuit of Respectability: Dilemmas of Daily Life in a Home for Adolescents', *British Journal of Social Work*, 14.

Hartman D. (1996) 'Cutting among young people in adolescent units', *Therapeutic Communities*, 17(1).

Hoghughi, M. (1983) *The Delinquent: Directions for Social Control*, Burnett Books.

Hoghughi, M. (1992) *Assessing Child and Adolescent Disorders*, Sage Publications.

James, O. (1995) *Juvenile Violence in a Winner–Loser Culture*, Free Association Books.

Keith, C.R. (ed.) (1984) *The Aggressive Adolescent: Clinical Perspectives*, The Free Press.

Kellmer Pringle, M. (1975) *The Needs of Children*, Unwin Hyman.

Kennedy, R., Heymans, A. and Tischler, L. (eds.) (1987) *The Family as In-Patient: Families and Adolescents at the Cassell Hospital*, Free Association Books.

Kroeger, J. (1989) *Identity in Adolescence: The Balance Between Self and Other*, Routledge.

Knibbs, S. (1994) 'Coming Out in Care', *Community Care*, 7–13 July.

Lane, D.A. and Miller, A. (1992) *Child and Adolescent Therapy: a Handbook*, Open University Press.

Laufer, M. (1975) *Adolescent Disturbance and Breakdown*, Penguin Books.

Laufer, M. (1995) *Adolescent and Developmental Breakdown*, Karnac Maresfield Library.

Laufer, M. and Laufer, E. (1989) *Developmental Breakdown and Psychoanalytic Treatment in Adolescence: Clinical Studies*, Yale University Press.

Linesch, D.G. (1988) *Adolescent Art Therapy*, Bruner/Mazel.

Mahler, M., Pine, F. and Bergman, A. (1985) *The Psychological Birth of the Human Infant*, Karnac.

Menzies-Lyth, I. (1985) 'The development of the self in children in institutions', in *Containing Anxiety in Institutions*, Free Association Books.

Mirza, S.H. (1992) *Young, Female and Black*, Routledge.

Moore, S. and Rosenthal, D. (1993) 'Sexuality and Adolescent Development', in *Sexuality in Adolescence*, Routledge.

O'Mahony, B. (1989) 'Key issues for managing adolescent sexual behaviour in residential establishments', paper delivered to the Training Advisory Group on the Sexual Abuse of Children at the National Children's Bureau.

Rose, M. (1990) *Healing Hurt Minds: the Peper Harow Experience*, Routledge.

Sandstrom, C.I. (1968) *The Psychology of Childhood and Adolescence*, Pelican Books.

Segal, H. (1988) *Introduction to the Work of Melanie Klein*, Karnac.

Shapiro, E.R. and Wesley Carr, A. (1991) 'Containing Chaotic Experience', in *Lost in Familiar Places: Creating New Connections between the Individual and Society*, Yale University Press.

Trowell, J. and Bower, M. (eds) (1995) *The Emotional Needs of Young Children and their Families*, Routledge.

Vasta, R. (1992) *Six Theories of Child Development*, Jessica Kingsley Publishers.

Wilson, P. (1986) 'Psychoanalytic Therapy and the Young Adolescent', *Maladjustment and Therapeutic Education*, 4 (3).

Winnicott, D.W. (1956) 'The anti-social tendency', *Collected Papers: Through Paediatrics to Psychoanalysis*, Tavistock.

Winnicott, D.W. (1984) *The Child, the Family and the Outside World*, Penguin.

Winnicott, D.W. (1986) *Home is Where We Start From*, Penguin.

Winnicott, D.W. (1989) 'Adolescence: Struggling Through the Doldrums', *The Family and Individual Development*, Routledge.

Winnicott, D.W. (1990) *The Maturational Processes and the Facilitating Environment*, Karnac Books.

Winnicott, D.W. (1995) *The Family and Individual Development*, Routledge.

11 The difficulties of working with violence in young people

Andrew Collie

Introduction

> That girls are raped, that two boys knife a third,
> Were axioms to him, who'd never heard
> Of any world where promises were kept
> Or one could weep because another wept.

W.H. Auden, 'The Shield of Achilles'

In this chapter Andrew Collie will look at violent behaviour from the perspective of its origins in early childhood. He will attempt to offer an understanding of violence so that it can be managed more effectively in residential or other care settings. It is important to try to understand the largely unconscious motives for most acts of violence, because without such understanding we are left only to condemn the violent persons and not to help them. Failure to manage violent behaviour is one of the most common causes of placement breakdown, and in extreme cases such failure can lead to the closure of community homes and the withdrawal of foster carers' services.

We will look at the case history of a violent teenage boy, J., who was placed at a centre in the mid-1980s. J. is an extreme but, in many ways, typical example of someone who resorts to violence frequently, but who at the same time elicited enormous sympathy and a wish to understand in the adults trying to help him. He was very untypical in that he had a capacity to articulate some of the inner forces which drove him to violent conduct. Despite the extremes of his behaviour, J. was at times able to tolerate and communicate his vulnerability. He taught those who tried to help him a great deal about the relationship between emotional pain and physical violence.

11 The difficulties of working with violence in young people

Andrew Collie

Violent behaviour can be seen as the extreme end of a continuum, and like all forms of extreme behaviour, it poses a threat to social order, individual well-being and productive relationships. I will argue that it also represents an extreme manifestation of characteristics which we all share in varying degrees. In the context of group-living environments, individual work or groupwork with children and young people, violent behaviour or the threat of violence is damaging to the helping task. In certain circumstances (some of which we will look at later), violence can threaten the very existence of the institutions or family placements created to help young people. How we understand and respond to violence, or the potential conditions where violence may occur, is often an essential part of the professional task. If we view violent young people as making conscious and deliberate decisions to act violently, then we will inevitably make a moral judgement that they, as well as their behaviour, are bad. The appropriate response from this perspective will be to punish them.

If, on the other hand, we see violent behaviour as the product of learned behaviour from earlier periods in the child's life, then the responses will be different. From this perspective we will attempt to help young people to modify their behaviour and find more constructive ways of relating to other people. The behaviour will still be condemned, and adult response may well be challenging, but they will be essentially non-punitive. This is the starting point in developing a therapeutic approach to the issue.

The therapeutic perspective I will be outlining draws on psychodynamic theories (in particular object relations theory), systems theory, social learning theories and therapeutic community theories of Kennard (1983), Hinshelwood (1987) and others. This approach rests on the following assumptions:

1. Early childhood experiences of violence and deprivation are causally connected in some way to later repeats of violent patterns of behaviour. Recent studies (in de Zulueta 1993 and James 1995) suggest that violent offenders are 20 times more likely than the population as a whole to have had violent upbringings.

2. Every infant experiences frustration and rage, and we all contain remnants of these early infant experiences which can be reactivated under certain circumstances in adulthood. Anxiety generated by stressful circumstances in the present awakens more primitive unconscious anxieties from the past which complicate our reactions and judgements of the objective reality. These anxieties are within adults as well as young people, and breakdowns in relationships which lead to violence always include contributions by the adult as well as the child or young person. There are precise concepts to understand this phenomenon, which help to explain some of the difficulties involved in working with damaged young people. (See chapters in this book where countertransference and projective identification are discussed.)

3. In group-living settings, violent behaviour by individuals is always at least partly a manifestation of disowned violent feelings in others in the group, including members of staff, and attention must be given to what is happening in the group as well as in the individual.

4. Appropriate therapeutic help for young people who have problems associated with violent behaviour must include a capacity in the helpers to tolerate such violence in the early stages of therapy. For very violent young people, this almost certainly means therapy in an institutional setting, where violence can be more effectively contained. Extremes of violence often go hand in hand with other forms of criminality, and violence is a central theme in forensic psychiatry and forensic psychotherapy (see Weldon and Van Velsen 1997).

Definition of violence

Violence can be described as an intrusion by one person across another's social, emotional, sexual or physical boundaries, with intent to cause harm. Violence is not necessarily a physical act, but can range from, at one extreme, murder and suicide (a violent act against the self), through violent assault or rape, to verbal abuse, sexual harassment and casual insults and intrusive behaviour. In the context of the care of damaged children and young people, violence by this broad definition is a daily occurrence. Examples might include:

- the child who attacks a social worker on a family visit
- the girl who hates being woken up, and reacts with violence to a persistent member of staff
- the boy who uses violence and threats of violence to get his own way with other young people and adults
- the girl who punches a male member of staff when he insists that she does her share of the household chores
- the boys who fight over a girl who plays one off against the other
- the girl who cuts herself when she feels unhappy
- the group of boys who swear at and sexually taunt a young female member of staff
- the quiet 'well-behaved' boy who is bullied persistently and sets fire to his bedroom.

In the staff group, anger and violence may express itself in less overt forms, such as cruel and humiliating jokes, impulsive retaliations to assaults from young people, hostile verbal attacks in response to anti-social behaviour from children, or a dehumanising regime. Some of these may not fall into our usual definitions of violence, but by the definition of intent to cause harm, consciously or otherwise, they deserve inclusion.

Violence must also be defined across a wider spectrum of behaviour ranging from compulsive passivity, through to assertiveness (the appropriate expression of aggression), aggression (some of which may be a legitimate response to extreme circumstances), to violent behaviour at the other extreme. Some people view violence as a distorted form of assertiveness, as, for example, when a normally shy, retiring person suddenly 'cashes in all their chips' and explodes into a violent rage, giving vent to months or years of pent-up fury.

The origins of violence are by no means universally agreed or understood, even amongst psychodynamic theorists. Some believe that human aggression is innate, whilst others believe that aggression arises from faulty child-rearing practices, especially where aggression is encouraged by male-dominated societies. It is a stark fact that gender is the single most significant variable in determining whether an individual is likely to be violent or not.

We will now attempt to give a more detailed analysis of violence and professional responses to it, through a case study of 'J.', a teenage boy who received help in an adolescent treatment centre.

Case Study – 'J.'

The mixed centre to which J. came provided care for adolescents aged between 13 and 20, coming from throughout Britain. The young people arrived with a wide range of problems, including delinquency, drug abuse, self-harm, violent conduct and occasionally bizarre behaviour patterns. Most had been through every alternative provision. Some had had custodial sentences. Extreme behaviour was expected from certain young people in the early stages of therapy, though there was a limit to the institution's capacity to absorb such behaviour. The methods of work were psychodynamic – through the development of attachment relationships and provision of primary experiences (ego nurturing), and social learning – feedback about behaviour in groups and through daily living and working together. This feedback was given in such a way that young people could hear it with a minimum risk of feeling persecuted, though such a reaction was sometimes unavoidable. Both approaches depended on the successful containment of powerful emotions and behaviours within the community. Success levels were high at approximately 33 per cent successful return to society of some of the most damaged individuals in the country.

J. was 15 when he came to the Centre in the mid-1980s, following his referral from a County Social Services Department. There was a long history of family problems which culminated in J. committing many offences including several counts of burglary and a charge of grievous bodily harm. No community home in his county held him for more than a few days and he had assaulted several social workers. J. came from a middle-class professional background. His father was described in reports as autocratic and bullying towards both J. and his mother. There were no other children in the immediate family. His father frequently used physical violence to punish J. from an early age. There were unproven suspicions that he beat his wife and that he was often vicious and sadistic in his punishment methods.

J. did not exhibit overt behavioural problems at primary school. He was reported to be quiet and withdrawn, and not achieving to his potential, which was high. When he went to secondary school, the position changed and he began to exhibit violent outbursts against other pupils and teachers. This pattern increased in severity as he got older, and by the time he was 14, he was described as being out of control at school. He spent less and less time at home, preferring to spend his time with a group of punks who hung about the town centre. He was sniffing glue on a daily basis, and using other drugs when he could get them. He began to offend regularly, mainly shoplifting and public order offences, and began to dress very aggressively in leather and torn jeans. He rarely washed. The goth-punk group he particularly identified with were anarchist, pacifist and vegetarian. Their preoccupations included morbid fantasies of death, Satanism and the macabre. J.'s pacifism and vegetarianism seemed strange when expressed by someone with his capacity for violence. The psychiatrist who assessed the family attributed this to a reaction formation – an attempt to deny unconscious wishes and fantasies by consciously espousing their opposites. His terror of his own violence and his desperate attempts to escape from these impulses led him to adopt non-violent philosophies.

During the referral process, J. committed numerous offences. Given his previous record, and warnings from the magistrates, there was a high possibility of a custodial sentence. The Centre decided to offer him a place partly because it was likely to be his last chance of escaping a downward spiral to prison or worse. The prognosis was not good, though not entirely hopeless. It was known that very violent people were hard to help in that setting (for reasons we will explore later), but on the other hand he was intelligent and had expressed a willingness to change. Additionally, he was liked by his social worker who was very committed to him, and by his prospective caseworker. For J. and the Centre it was to be a race against time, attempting to achieve a modification of his violent and self-destructive behaviour before that behaviour became so intolerable to the people who lived and worked with him (and to society in general) that he was expelled or the law intervened and administered a custodial sentence.

During the early days of his stay at the Centre, J. treated all adults as hostile intruders into his private world. Adults were either threatened or ignored – the latter being almost as disconcerting as the abuse, as it left people feeling worthless and negated. Drug abuse was not tolerated, and J. was a daily user of glue, which meant that he was in constant conflict with the adults and other young people who were attempting to help him. He was threatening and occasionally violent, and was particularly dangerous when he was high on glue. It was almost impossible to form a working relationship with him. At the same time, he formed a sexual relationship with D., a 15-year-old who had arrived a few months before J. and was as damaged as he was. She had suffered violent sexual assaults including vaginal mutilation and enforced prostitution from an early age and for many years. She also sniffed glue regularly and was part of the punk culture. She had frequent outbursts, and at times made threats against people which had to be taken very seriously. She was physically small and slight, which made her marginally less of a daily threat. D. was a frequent absconder, and she and J. formed a delinquent pair – absconding, glue sniffing, threatening and being abusive to others, and supporting each other's distorted version of reality. Their relationship became the most important thing to both of them, to be defended against intrusion with violence and threats. Only a few very experienced staff members were able to make any emotional contact with them. The question can be asked whether it was therapeutic for young people of such fragile egos to be thrown together at such a sensitive stage of their emotional development.

J. pushed the capacity of the centre to contain him to the limits and beyond. He terrorised both young people and adults – except those who were very skilled at dealing with violent young people. Through violence he became a very powerful but isolated figure. However, there were a few hopeful signs. First, he formed a strong attachment to his male caseworker, Dan, who was rarely threatened by J., and indeed J. was able to regress and play with Dan on occasions. Secondly, J. was able to communicate (at first non-verbally) the underlying terror of annihilation which his rage and violence served to protect him from. The thinly veiled vulnerability was apparent to everyone around him, and there was, despite everything, something in J. which elicited warmth, concern and a wish to help. There was a similar process going on in the other residents, who were both appalled by him, but were also anxious to see whether someone so out of control and damaged could be contained and helped by the Centre. J. represented that wild infantile part of everyone, which most people keep hidden even from themselves, but which longed to be recognised, held and helped. From the point of view of the group as a whole, it was important that the staff were seen to do their utmost to help J. – or more precisely, the J. part of everyone.

Two examples of therapeutic strategies

Of many incidents involving J., two serve to illustrate some of the issues involved in the therapeutic management of violent young people, and the different strategies that might be adopted by carers. The therapeutic task at this stage was to hold on to him, survive his attacks and manage his behaviour until he could begin to control himself.

Incident one

Every summer the whole community, staff and residents, went on summer camp, which at that time involved a choice of four or five activities in small groups of perhaps eight to ten young people and four or five members of staff. The groups would spend a week in one activity, then have a changeover day before going off with a new group on a new activity. The purpose of camp was to give group members the opportunity to experience small group living in different environments, and to expose them to transitional experiences as a means of helping them to cope with change. Some of the activities were more challenging than others. The canal boat was for those whose primary need was for safety and containment, or for those who could not cope with more challenging activities.

After considerable debate, and with great reluctance, it was decided that J. and D. would go on the canal boat together for the first week, since it was the only conceivable way that they could cope with the stresses of two weeks out of the Community. The alternative was for them to be placed elsewhere for the two weeks of camp, which would have further marginalised them – possibly resulting in the end of their placement. The changeover day, which involved the stress of a major transitional experience – the loss of one group and new membership of another – was likely to be particularly stressful for people like J., who was both very damaged and a relatively new member of the community. The weakness of his relationships reduced his sense of safety and trust that the camp could be survived.

The approach adopted by the staff team on the narrow-boat was to give J. and D. as much leeway as possible so that they could have some chance of a positive experience without major conflict with adults. Attempts were made to create possibilities for both J. and D. to form attachments to adults – a primary goal for many young people on summer camp. Even the minimum stress of a narrow-boat holiday proved to be too much for J. and D. They were exclusively preoccupied with each other, ignoring all adult attempts at communication. The staff were unable to intervene effectively without real threats of serious violence and were left as rather helpless observers of a deeply damaging relationship. (They were being made to experience what it had been like for J. as a child in relation to his parents.) D. controlled the relationship, alternatively drawing J. in and then rejecting him. J.'s rage grew over the six days of the trip. Minor outbursts were contained, and the staff held their breath, hoping that the week could be negotiated without a catastrophe.

As the narrow-boat was about to set off on the last half-mile of the journey on the final morning, the tensions that had been building all week came to a head. With perfect timing, D. told J. that she was going to finish with him. He exploded and smashed every window in the boat, and most of the crockery. The tension of the impending transition and D.'s manipulation of his feelings were the final straws in blowing the uneasy peace apart. D. had pushed J. into expressing her rage as well as his own, leaving the staff feeling helpless and ashamed at not having physically intervened, even though to have done so would have risked serious injury.

Incident two

Two months later, D. had left the Community prematurely. J. would frequently abscond to go and see her in London where she was living in a squat. At the start of a new term, J. was due to change bedrooms as part of his treatment programme. He was facing a court case for assault in his home town where the magistrates had already given him a final warning and a suspended sentence. A custodial sentence looked highly likely. He refused to change bedrooms on the grounds that he was going to get sent down the next day so what was the point. To give in to his insistence would be to collude with his defeatism, and to insist on the move would have resulted in violence. The result was a very tense stand-off. The senior member of staff on duty believed that J.'s violence should be challenged and that bullying could not be allowed to succeed. All the other residents went to bed, leaving J., the senior staff member and the sleep-in staff member downstairs. J. was highly agitated, volatile and armed with a broom handle. Both adults felt that he was capable of doing serious damage. They felt that he was capable of murder if he was not managed properly.

The stand-off continued into the early hours of the morning, in an atmosphere of extreme fear, rage and stress. Eventually J. agreed to have a coffee with the senior staff member, Alex (who had nursed him through the second week of summer camp) and the tension eased marginally. J. talked for hours about his nightmares, his sexual fantasies (many of them involving violence and death), his father and his mother. He talked of what it felt like to stab someone – how it was almost addictive, and how easy it would be to do again – about glue-sniffing, and about his longing for death. The staff member listened to him for several hours, and was shaking with tension when J. finally finished talking. Both members of staff felt that they had experienced something of what it was like to be J.

This episode enabled J. to go to court without destroying his chances. He was, to his utter astonishment, given a further suspended sentence after a member of staff made an impassioned plea on his behalf. The court was persuaded that J. was benefiting from being in treatment rather than custody. J.'s relief and gratitude was evident, and for the first time in his life he was able to accept and respond to positive help from others. For a few weeks the downward spiral was slowed and he was able to enjoy a period of calm and contentment probably for the only time in his life. He did not use drugs during this time. Ultimately his treatment terminated early, as he allowed himself to be lured back to London by D. He found the process of change unendurable, but he retained a sense of having been cared for and valued, and undoubtedly gained from the experience.

Discussion

A number of questions arise from these incidents. J. came to the Centre at a time when two significant events were still being worked through. Important staff changes had occurred and both staff and young people were in a process, some of which was unconscious, of establishing a new culture, with new directors. Authority was being challenged heavily by the young people. The staff were ambivalent about the departure of the director, and may well have unconsciously colluded with the anti-authority feelings. The second event was that what had been a boys' centre had become co-educational several months before the director's departure. In their search for emotional security and to satisfy infantile feelings of deprivation, some of the young people began to choose each other rather than adults. The normal sexual exploration of adolescence became enmeshed with their unconscious and infantile emotional needs. J. and D.'s relationship was an example of how destructive this process could be.

The two examples also illustrate how extreme behaviour from young people can push staff into behaviour which re-enacts family patterns. In the first instance, despite conscious efforts not to do so, the staff team manifested some of the qualities of helplessness of J.'s mother, and of J. himself as a child. In the second, the staff partly re-enacted his father's confrontational approach, though they did not get caught up in the violence which J.'s behaviour was threatening to produce. Although the staff were aware of and attempted to avoid such polarisations and acting-out, there was evidence that they were not entirely successful.

The senior member of staff in the second incident contributed initially to the confrontation, but then handled J. with great therapeutic skill. He survived J.'s unconscious attempts to induce a violent response ('survived' in the sense that he managed to contain the powerful feelings of rage and fear which J. was provoking, and neither retaliate nor withdraw from J.). He continued to talk to that hidden aspect which the violent front was protecting, namely, the terrified and traumatised infant self. Finally, J. was able to trust Alex's capacity to survive his rage, and to begin to reveal his acute underlying anxiety. Alex then had to demonstrate his ability to tolerate J.'s pain and distress, and to provide the containment which his parents had so manifestly failed to provide.

It may have helped J. if the magistrates had given him a custodial sentence, as it might have brought him closer to the reality of the consequences of his behaviour. The pressure not to return to custody may have given him an additional impetus to change. On the other hand, at a deeper level, custody might have been experienced as the Centre's failure to look after him at a time of his greatest need. This is a very open question.

The origins of violence

Human violence is so universal that many theories about its origins suggest that we are innately violent and that there is little to do about it other than to set up systems of rewards and punishments in an attempt to limit violent behaviour. An alternative view sees violence as arising from failures in the carer–infant relationship which generate powerful feelings of rage and frustration in the infant which later develop into the potential for violence (de Zulueta 1993). The implications of the latter view are more hopeful because they suggest that violent feelings, impulses and actions have either been learned or are the product of early deprivation, or both, and can therefore be treated therapeutically and ameliorated. The latter view is supported by the example of J., who was physically abused from an early age, and who became physically abusive in turn, in a vicious cycle. J. re-created in the forum of the centre the family dynamics – murderous, hate-filled and terrifying – of his own childhood and his own inner world. He was able to articulate some of these feelings, and to link them to his own childhood experiences. He once reported, after beating someone up, that the face of the person he was punching had suddenly become the face of his father. He actually saw his father before him. To J., every adult male was potentially violent and had to be driven off with threats and violence before they attacked him.

How can all this be understood? Although he was a 15-year-old boy, his past experiences had been so awful that they had suffused and distorted his entire personality. He carried within him his own battered infant self, an image of his violent father so real that he sometimes hallucinated and an image of his weak and helpless mother. He also contained within him all the feelings associated both with those figures, and with the relationships between them. The family drama was constantly replaying in his unconscious, distorting and dominating his perception of the external world and his own sense of self.

His effect on the external world of the centre was to project his feelings into the groups of staff and young people. In internal case conferences, female members of staff often reported feeling terrified of J., and terrorised by him, a situation interpreted as a re-enactment of his father's relationship with his mother. Male members of staff also felt terrorised but enraged as well. They reported having murderous feelings towards him. J. had aroused similar feelings in the male staff members that his father had towards him, and he towards his father. Almost everyone wished he was someone else's problem, and there was a strong wish to drive him out of the institution, which the staff had to work hard not to act out. Through careful thinking about J.'s behaviour in terms of its purpose in recreating family dynamics, the staff team became aware that he was most likely to be violent when:

- His caseworker was off duty or on holiday. He became enraged because he could not bear the underlying and more painful feelings of separation and loss, which re-awakened his terrifying memories of parental abandonment.
- When there were no female staff around. He felt under severe threat by males, but less so when women were around. It was assumed that his mother must have given him some protection or consolation.
- When his relationship with D. was challenged in any way. He could not tolerate any hint of enforced separation, and experienced the challenge as a direct threat to his masculinity.
- At points of change in the day. He found transitional experiences such as staff going off duty at the end of the day, intolerable because they evoked unbearable feelings of loss and uncertainty.
- When D. threatened, or pretended to threaten to finish with him. He was often used by D. to express her feelings of rage on her behalf as well as his own. It was not unusual for the girls to use the boys in this way, often quite unconsciously. (There are real questions to be asked about the advisability of mixed centres for adolescents. See above for further discussion on this point.)
- Whenever he was at the point of facing painful issues from his past in individual work or in therapeutic groups. J. would sometimes talk movingly of past abuses, and within minutes be in a towering rage, as he attempted to reinstate his violent defences against the underlying distress.

Taking J. as an extreme but in many ways typical example of someone for whom violence is a common feature of their behaviour, it is possible to identify a number of possible causes of violence:

- Being male. 'More than anything else, violence is caused by not being female' (James 1996: 75). Girls are more likely to turn anger inwards in the form of self-harm and depression, or in mixed settings, to engender violence in males on their behalf. Girls are usually less physically able to express rage effectively through violence, and are socialised more strongly than boys not to be violent. This pattern does seem to be changing, and girls are more willing to behave violently now than they were twenty years ago.
- A need to control a threatening environment, whether the threat is real or not. This threat may often include the 'threat' of intimacy, which

may have unpleasant connotations such as physical or sexual invasiveness. Violence is a distancing mechanism.

- A family history of violence by one or both parents. Violence is a learned behaviour pattern and is not linked to genetic inheritance (James 1996).
- Real or imagined fear of other people's violence, at least partly arising from projected rage.
- Threats to identity, especially sexual identity, which have their origins in earlier parental conflicts.
- Loss, or fear of loss, of important relationships, triggering rage as a defence against intolerably painful infantile feelings of abandonment (de Zulueta 1993; Bowlby 1985).
- An inability to cope with transitions, arising from inability to tolerate separation (Bowlby 1985).
- Failure of institutions adequately to meet emotional needs of young people and staff, or to work with unconscious processes (Dockar-Drysdale 1990).

The effects of violence in care settings

Young people in residential or foster care settings need a stable, caring and non-abusive environment in which to begin to come to terms with their psychological, social and educational problems. It is one of the ironies of therapeutic work that when offered such an opportunity many young people find it intolerable and attempt unconsciously or otherwise to undermine such stability. (Chapter 3, on projective identification, explains the mechanisms of this process.) In order to continue to offer what young people need, staff have to struggle not only with the psychological and physical assaults from young people, but also with their own wishes to retaliate or withdraw from the conflict. The power of the adolescent group in undermining caring should never be underestimated.

Looked at from this perspective, acts of violence have a number of effects. First, violence, or the threat of violence, serves to keep others at a distance. The young person both fears and longs for attachment to trustworthy adults. J. tried to resolve this dilemma, as many people do, by splitting off and projecting his violent feelings into some staff and preserving a warmer relationship with his keyworker. Those staff not favoured felt suspicious and hostile to J. and at a distance from him emotionally. He was not able to draw on the goodwill of either the majority of the staff or most of the young people, who were terrified of him. For the individual, the use of violence creates social isolation and reduces the possibility of forming the attachment relationships essential to emotional growth.

A second effect of violence is at a group level. The social stability of an institution is threatened by violence and everyone feels less secure. Adult authority is challenged, people feel intimidated and anxiety levels increase following violent episodes. Other people's violent impulses may be aroused in response to initial feelings of fear and hurt and the levels of violence can escalate. Violence begets violence.

J. had the capacity not only to intimidate others, but also to arouse their fury. He once racially insulted a senior girl and her friends in the dining room, in full view of fifty other people. He was attacked by seven or eight people, and had to be rescued by staff. The fury he managed to evoke in the others left them shaken and distressed. This incident required an emergency meeting to help everyone to recover their calm and to make sense of what had happened. J. had no conscious idea why he had done what he did, and seemed unconcerned, almost pleased, by the furore he had caused. He felt safe with violence he had controlled.

Once an institution has begun to lose control of the group and a subculture of violence and delinquency begins to take hold, it becomes extremely difficult to retrieve the situation. Staff morale declines and the risk of retaliatory behaviour by adults increases. Adults who in other settings would rarely if ever resort to violence, find themselves increasingly vulnerable to their own violent impulses, when they are in a setting where violence is out of their control. Violent young people relate to adult authority as if it is the same as their early experiences of parental authority and attempt to recreate their early experiences. They test caring to destruction.

Strategies for managing violence

A strategy for managing violence has to begin with a sound basis of good practice which addresses the emotional needs of the young people, and the staff team. Good practice must take place in a setting and a set of professional structures appropriate to the task of the organisation. These issues are covered elsewhere in this book, but they boil down to two fundamentals – clear and appropriately enforced boundaries, and opportunities for young people to form relationships with adults which meet their psychological, social and educational needs. It is especially important that staff are helped to understand both their own and the young people's unconscious impulses and motivations.

When these conditions are fulfilled and adults are both in control and working appropriately with young people towards their growth and development, violent incidents will be less likely, and when they do occur, they will be regarded as aberrations. Nevertheless, even in the best-run community home, there will be a degree of violence for which the institution must be ready.

The following are essential elements of an effective strategy:

- A culture in which the underlying anxiety of the young people is addressed so that it does not often erupt into violence, and when it does staff remain calm and stay focused on the distress behind the rage. (Bettelheim 1974)
- Written procedures for dealing with violent incidents, including appropriate restraint techniques, follow-up support for staff, follow-up with the young person, and recording of these. Written procedures must be agreed with staff and where possible with young people, and communicated clearly, especially to less experienced staff.
- Support for staff members after violent incidents. When a staff member is hurt or frightened, they are often forgotten as attention focuses on the aggressor. If their own distress is not acknowledged by their managers they will find it more difficult to process the experience, and be less effective as a result. If a member of staff retaliates, consideration must be given to how that staff member can be supported whilst also facing possible disciplinary action. Staff support must include the opportunity for detailed reflection on the nature of violence and conflict.
- Staff need to be provided with skilled support to help them make sense of their own contribution to violent episodes. It is superficial to attribute violent behaviour solely to the young person or people concerned. Dockar-Drysdale (1990) is emphatic on this point, arguing that violence results from breakdowns in communication between staff and young people, and that part of any violent episode is the child acting out denied staff anger. Our own hurt and enraged aspects can be activated in the emotionally charged setting of residential and day care of damaged people. Staff need the opportunity to explore their own difficult feelings so that they do not unthinkingly project these feelings back onto the young people. When this process is not acknowledged and worked through with staff, at least some violent behaviour can be attributed to this source.
- Children need to be helped with their angry feelings. Regular individual work, small groups and large groups (for adolescents) can help to reduce violence provided they are opportunities for young people to talk to and be listened to by adults. Translation of anger into words is the therapeutic goal in dealing with violence.

- Staff groups cannot be expected to understand violence and their own responses to it, without training and guidance. Appropriate staff training can be invaluable in reducing staff anxieties. Appropriate training should have the following elements: exploration with staff of their own experiences of violence or conflict in their families of origin; learning about the roots of violence in early childhood; training in recognising and defusing potentially violent situations by remaining calm and in emotional contact with the distressed child/young person; training in appropriate restraint techniques only in the context of the above, so as to avoid a self-defence mentality.

Adolescent sexual relations

Finally, there has been much discussion and soul-searching about the way in which looked-after young people relate to one another. Adolescent sexuality was a major factor in the lives of J. and D. and certainly confounded and challenged their carers. What follows is a document written for the staff team in a community home to try to help them work with young people who, while very disturbed indeed, wish to have exclusive, usually sexual, relationships. The establishment was attempting to adopt a longer-term approach, having been for many years a traditional short-stay 'warehouse'. Many of the staff were either confused about or hostile to notions of restricting the liberty of young people in relation to their sexual pairings. The document was an attempt to get some thinking going around this issue, prior to agreeing a set of practice guidelines. The following note was attached to the document: 'It is recognised that some staff members may feel that this approach represents an infringement of young people's rights. Others may feel that these guidelines will be difficult to enforce. Before the policy is introduced, a full staff discussion will take place in order to ensure that the policy is agreed and accepted by the whole staff team.'

Long Ridings Community Home – Staff Guidelines

Adolescent sexual relations

Introduction

The following guidelines rest on a number of assumptions about the meaning of adolescent sexual relationships *within the context of a therapeutic residential environment.*

Young people are here for the primary purpose of working on serious emotional difficulties which will lead to severely restricted lives if not addressed. Sexual relationships usually represent a flight from this difficult task.

In my experience these emotional difficulties always include profound psycho-sexual problems. Sexual relationships in such cases are an attempt to satisfy unmet primary needs – the sexual partner represents an idealised parental figure who will answer all their problems. As such, these relationships are based on unconscious fantasy and inevitably fail, usually at great emotional cost to the young people concerned.

Sexual relationships between adolescents at Long Ridings are not simply normal adolescent sexual exploration. For the reasons suggested above, these relationships are almost always abusive to some degree.

In therapeutic terms, the primary relationship is between the young person and their special staff member (keyworker or caseworker). The sexual relationship is an unconscious substitute primary relationship. It is therefore counter-therapeutic.

It is recognised that these relationships are very powerful and difficult to prevent. Crude attempts to prevent them will be experienced as persecutory and will encourage subcultural sexual activity.

The powerful Oedipal content of sexual relationships in such a public sphere creates a climate of exclusivity and envious resentment. Left unchecked, this atmosphere can become highly charged and potentially violent. Early confrontation will help to minimise the risk of aggressive reactions.

Staff guidelines and policy

Sexual relationships between young people are always to be regarded as inappropriate and should be discouraged by staff at all times. This inevitably means that staff will be experienced as persecutory and there is the potential for violence if staff challenge sexual relationships insensitively. There can be no firm rules about the level of intervention necessary in particular cases provided both individuals are over 16 (but see below for these exceptions). As a general rule, public displays of sexual behaviour must not go unchallenged by staff.

All young people coming to Long Ridings will be made aware at interview that sexual relationships are not appropriate in this setting.

If a couple persists in a relationship despite repeated challenges and offers to discuss the problem with them, it may be ultimately necessary to suspend or exclude them.

If such relationships take place between individuals aged under 16 they are illegal and the social workers of the children must be informed. There is the possibility of abuse procedures being invoked and senior staff must be informed in all such cases (see separate child to child abuse procedures).

If such relationships take place between individuals, one of whom is over 16 and the other under 16, then Abuse Procedures MUST be invoked (see separate guidelines).

References

Alvarez, A. (1992) *Live Company*, Routledge.

Bentovim, A. (1992) *Trauma Organised Systems: Physical and Sexual Abuse in Families*, Karnac.

Bettelheim, B. (1974) *A Home for the Heart*, Thames and Hudson.

Bowlby, J. (1985) *Separation: Anxiety and Anger*, Hogarth.

Collie, A. (1997) 'Damage and Survival in the Residential Care and Treatment of Adolescents', *Therapeutic Communities*, 7 (3).

Copley, B. and Forryan, B (1987) *Therapeutic Work with Children and Young People*, Robert Royce.

De Zulueta, F. (1993) *From Pain to Violence*, Whurr.

Dockar-Drysdale, B. (1990) *The Provision of Primary Experience*, Free Association Books.

Dockar-Drysdale, B. (1993) *Therapy and Consultation in Childcare*, Free Association Books.

Erikson, E. (1968) *Identity, Youth and Crisis*, Faber and Faber.

Hinshelwood, R. (1987) *What Happens in Groups*, Free Association Books.

James, O. (1995) *Juvenile Violence in a Winner-Loser Culture*, Free Association Books.

Kennard, D. (1983) *Introduction to Therapeutic Communities*, Routledge and Kegan Paul.

Klein, M. (1946) 'Notes on Some Schizoid Mechanisms', in *The Writings of Melanie Klein*, Vol. 1, Hogarth.

Mawson, C. (1993) 'Containing Anxiety in Work with Damaged Children', in Obholzer, A. and Roberts, V.Z. (eds) *The Unconscious at Work*, Routledge.

Menzies-Lyth, I. (1988) *Containing Anxiety in Institutions*, Free Association Books.

Miller, A. (1987) *For Your Own Good: The Roots of Violence in Child-rearing*, Virago.

Saltzberger-Wittenberg, I. (1973) *Psychoanalytic Insight and Relationships: a Kleinian Approach*, Routledge and Kegan Paul.

Varma, V. (1997) *Violence in Children and Adolescents*, Jessica Kingsley.

Weldon, E. and Van Velsen, C. (1997) *A Practical Guide to Forensic Psychotherapy*, Jessica Kingsley.

Bibliography

Dockar-Drysdale B. (1990) 'Panic', 'Collusive anxiety in the residential treatment of disturbed adolescents' and 'The management of violence', *The Provision of Primary Experience*, Free Association Books.

Glasser, M. (1982) 'Working with Violent Patients at the Portman Clinic', paper presented at the Analytical Psychology Club.

Winnicott D.W. (1984) 'Aggression and its roots' and 'Aggression, guilt and reparation', in *Deprivation and Delinquency*, Routledge.

Further reading

Alvarez, A. (1995) 'Motiveless malignity: problems in the psychotherapy of psychopathic patients', *Journal of Child Psychotherapy*.

Bowlby, J. (1988) 'Violence in the Family' and 'On knowing what you are not supposed to know and feeling what you are not supposed to feel', in *A Secure Base*, Routledge.

De Zulueta, F. (1996) *From Pain to Violence: the traumatic roots of destructiveness*, Whurr Publishers.

Dockar-Drysdale, B. (1990) 'Holding' and 'A note on intent to murder in adolescent boys', in *The Provision of Primary Experience*, Routledge.

Dockar-Drysdale, B. (1993) 'Some aspects of damage and restitution', 'Communication as a technique in treating disturbed children' and 'The management of violence in disturbed children', in *Therapy and Consultation in Child Care*, Free Association Books.

Hoghughi, M. (1992) 'Home and Family Problems' and 'Anti-social Behaviour', in *Assessing Child and Adolescent Disorders*, Sage Publishers.

Miller, A. (1987) *The Drama of Being a Child*, Virago.

Miller, A. (1987) *For Your Own Good: the roots of violence in child-rearing*, Virago.

Miller, A. (1990) *The Untouched Key: tracing childhood trauma in creativity and destructiveness*, Virago.

Redl, F. and Wineman, D. (1952) *Controls from Within: techniques for the treatment of the Aggressive Child*, Macmillan.

Sinason, V. (1992) 'Finding meaning without words: self injury and profound handicap', in *Mental Handicap and the Human Condition*, Routledge.

Szur, R. 'Sexuality and Aggression as related themes', in Boston, M. and Szur, R. (eds) (1990) *Psychotherapy with Severely Deprived Children*. Karnac Books.

Varma, V. (ed.) (1997) *Violence in Children and Adolescents*, Jessica Kingsley Publishers.

Welldon, E.V. and Van Velsen, C. (1997) *A Practical Guide to Forensic Psychotherapy*, Jessica Kingsley Publishers.

12 Working with sexually abused children in the context of the family

Annie Bousfield

Introduction

> Solid and usual objects are ghosts
> The furniture carries cargoes of memory,
> The staircase has corners which remember
>
> Stephen Spender, 'The Double Shame'

In the early 1990s, there was increasing awareness about sexual abuse and considerable improvements in the procedures for the investigation of sexually abused children. However, a gap in service provision could be identified as therapeutic services for sexually abused children and their families. NCH Action For Children's child sexual abuse initiative set up 15 treatment projects nationally with the aim of providing a service where previously there was none. From the setting of one such specialist treatment project, the aim of which is to provide therapy for children who have been sexually abused, this chapter proposes to demonstrate the importance and benefits of working with children in the context of their family.

12 Working with sexually abused children in the context of the family

Annie Bousfield

A family focus

Work is undertaken from the assumption that in order to understand individual behaviour it is essential to understand the significant group in which a person lives or lived, the relationships within that group and the impact of any particular person's behaviour on that group.

When there is stress in any part of the family system, this can be seen to affect all individuals within that system and equally, when the structure of the family group is transformed, the position of all family members alters accordingly.

A family focus identifies repetitive sequences of interaction. Such sequences observed in the present can often also be identified as recurring themes throughout the family's history. In the cases of families where sexual abuse has been a feature, sequences of behaviour organised around secrecy are likely to be a common but frequently dysfunctional feature. Summit (1983) identifies secrecy 'as both the source of fear and the promise of safety' in child sexual abuse within the family.

We often come into contact with families at the point when they have assessed themselves or been assessed by others as no longer able to cope or manage in a particular situation. A recent disclosure of sexual abuse may mean that family members have been dispersed. It is nevertheless important for us to recognise that a belief in the meaning of an individual's family continues for that individual in spite of family fragmentation or the radical changes in shape and structure that families may undergo after a disclosure of sexual abuse. Examples of this would be the removal of the perpetrator or the victim being accommodated. The yearning for the idealised father who never was may need to be recognised and modified before any further work can be done with a sexually abused child. It is crucial for us to recognise the internalised family patterns of relationships (fact or fantasy) in the families with whom we work.

Similarly, within the care system in which sexual abuse is such a dominant theme, therapists need to take stock of and work with the context in which the child is currently located, whether this be a substitute family or a residential unit. If carers are not aware of the aims and objectives of therapy and supportive of it, then treatment can be ineffective or indeed can be sabotaged. The child's context, past and present, provides an essential marker which the therapist cannot afford to ignore.

Definition of sexual abuse

The definition of sexual abuse used is that of Schecter and Roberge (1976):

> ... the involvement of dependent, developmentally immature children and adolescents in sexual activities that they do not truly comprehend and to which they are unable to give informed consent and that violate the sexual taboos of family roles.

The sequelae of child sexual abuse can be devastating and far-reaching for all parts of the family system, treatment focusing only on the individual child to the exclusion of other family members and possibly doomed to failure. More lucrative is treating the individual in the context of the family system or indeed sometimes through that family system or particular subsystem.

Finkelhor (1986) identifies four traumagenic dynamics in victims of sexual abuse – *powerlessness, stigmatisation, betrayal* and *traumatic sexualisation*. These themes invariably need addressing in therapy both with the sexually abused child and his or her family and/or current context. A child who feels stigmatised and powerless as a result of sexual abuse is likely to bring behaviour and belief that emanates from that into any current relationships, whether they be therapeutic or social. Similarly, abused children have experienced a betrayal of basic trust and are likely to approach any future relationship without any sense of mutual trust. Thus substitute carers and therapists should expect to have to invest considerable time, effort and patience in working towards the establishment of a relationship with developing trust. Premature and inappropriate sexualisation is likely to have traumatic consequences which often get expressed in later childhood through highly sexualised behaviour or inhibitions around sexual expression. All these issues need to be dealt with in the process in order that they can reinforce the work done in the time between sessions. Two common strands are apparent in working with sexually abused children and their families: secrecy, and safety and protection.

Secrecy

Sexual abuse, whether perpetrated by a family member or not, is likely to have taken place in a context of secrecy. Perpetrators not only groom victims to ensure their silence but also non-abusing carers and siblings, so that either they have no idea about the victim's abuse or they may be aware of it but are immobilised in the same way as the victim and so are not able to talk about it. Once disclosure has occurred, the communication system within the family or between non-abusing carer and child is likely to need to change significantly. This can be a difficult process for all family members as it is not easy to start talking openly when there are issues of guilt and when more familiar patterns lend themselves more readily to secrecy or even dishonesty. Summit (1983) demonstrates how child victims of sexual abuse face secondary trauma when they disclose. Too often the disclosure is met with disbelief and outrage by the non-abusing carer. As a result the child is frequently rejected and ostracised by other family members, so reinforcing the child's sense of self-blame and alienation. Children frequently feel responsible for the break-up of the family 'because I told'. Summit (1983: 179) shows how a child abused, for example, by a father and rejected by the mother is 'psychologically orphaned' rendering them vulnerable to further victimisation at many levels. He also indicates that when the mother or non-abusing carer can protect and advocate for the child, this can reduce the negative consequences of the abuse dramatically. Summit presents a simple model and sequence of interaction between victim, abuser and potential caretakers which he labels 'Child Sexual Abuse Accommodation Syndrome' which helps us understand the vulnerability of the child's position in the complex situations of sexual victimisation, particularly when it occurs within the family system. It is against this backdrop that clinical work takes place:

> Clinical study of large numbers of children and their parents in proven cases of sexual abuse provides emphatic contradictions to traditional views. What emerges is a typical behaviour pattern or syndrome of mutually dependent variables which allows for immediate survival of the child within the family but which tends to isolate the child from eventual acceptance, credibility or empathy within the larger society. The mythology and protective denial surrounding sexual

abuse can be seen as a natural consequence both of the stereotypic coping mechanisms of the child victim and the need of almost all adults to insulate themselves from the painful realities of childhood victimisation. (Summit 1983)

Roland Summit's *Child Sexual Abuse Accommodation Syndrome* is a five-stage process which helps to shed light on the child's experience of abuse and his or her ways of coping with it. The first two categories (1) Secrecy and (2) Helplessness are preconditions to the occurrence of sexual abuse. The remaining three categories, (3) Entrapment and accommodation (4) Delayed, unconvincing disclosure and (5) Retractions, are likely reactions to the experience of abuse.

The accommodation syndrome can be used by clinicians to improve understanding of the child's position and to challenge entrenched myths and prejudice in the field of child sexual abuse.

Safety and protection

Even if parents have not known about the abuse because, for example, the child had been silenced by the perpetrator or was simply too frightened or embarrassed to tell a parent, the child has, by definition, not been in a safe environment. It is commonly acknowledged (Smith 1995; Doyle 1990; Bannister 1992) that the starting point of therapy for the child must be the creation of a safe environment. It is often necessary to work with non-abusing family members or carers in order to do this before the child is available to the benefits that treatment can provide. If the child is not in a safe environment, the therapist could end up contributing to or colluding with an abusing system where secrets continue and the child continues to be unable to tell when they are not feeling safe. Equally, a child needs to be in a secure and stable environment before they are likely to feel safe enough to embark on any really meaningful treatment. In these cases, therapists need to be firm that therapy should not start until the child has settled in any new or re-formed environment; the therapist often needs to make an impact on the wider family and professional system in order to see that this happens for the child.

The family system may be mobilised in the interests of the abused child in a number of different ways:

1. Working with the individual child mindful of the context of their family, with or without a move to working directly with different family sub groups in due course.
2. Working through the parent or carer.

3. Working with the whole family.
4. Working with the carers in conjunction with the work done individually or in a therapy group with a child.

Working with the individual child in the context of their family

The child or young person's family context is crucial to acknowledge and work with in the course of treatment. E. is a case in point.

Case Study – E.

E. came to the Project aged 17 years – four years after she first disclosed to a teacher that her brother was abusing her. Her parents were spoken to by the school but they never discussed the matter with her and she was left feeling unbelieved and unsafe. Over the next six months, the school again became concerned about E., this time noting her extreme thinness and reluctance to eat and her self-harming (cutting). Police and Social Services were involved and E. disclosed the abuse by her brother more formally. The only discussion between her and her parents made clear the parents' view that she was at least partially to blame for whatever happened between her and her brother. A lock was put on her bedroom door and again E. reported feeling unbelieved and unsafe. Her eating remained disordered and her cutting continued. Alice Miller's (1984) words are instructive here: 'An unacknowledged trauma is like a wound that never heals over and may start to bleed again at any time. In a supportive environment the wound can become visible and finally heal completely.'

It is not surprising then that with no acknowledgement of E.'s disclosure of abuse in the immediate environment of her family after two years she overdosed badly and was admitted to a psychiatric hospital (her first admission) from where she refused to return home. At this point she was accommodated with foster carers and referred to the Project for treatment.

A great deal of work with E. has been centred around her internalised feelings about different family members and her belief system regarding what they felt about her. Although it has never been appropriate to work directly with any of her family they have been 'brought into the room' by a number of family therapy techniques. In an attempt to help her address her feelings of guilt at breaking up the family as a result of her disclosure, E. was helped to 'sculpt' her family relationships at different points in time: prior to the abuse, when the abuse occurred, at the time of disclosure, post-disclosure and now.

'Sculpture' was also used to help her examine the function her anorectic behaviour served in the family and how it served as a distance regulator. In relation to her eating, she sculpted how close or far family members have been to her: before her first hospitalisation, when in hospital, when in the Eating Disorders Unit, now and in the future.

This has been linked to a number of other axes, in particular the illness behaviour – anorexia nervosa – and her intense feelings of guilt and self-blame regarding the abuse. Within the context of her family, E. has been enabled to explore why she feels she deserves to be ill and starving. She has looked at what was happening in her family when she started to get ill and what her family seemed to notice and do about it. This has been connected with the abuse and the family reaction to her disclosure. Gradually, she has been helped to see how being ill has been functional for her, particularly in relation to her family and to examine what needs to change for her not to need to be ill. The technique of 'storying' has also been utilised. E. has been helped to speculate on the different 'scripts' written for her by her different family members. This has been linked to how other people in the family's stories or scripts about E. have affected her own version of things. In an attempt to help E. differentiate herself from the rest of her family and to help her become more self-actualising, exceptions or small incidents (unique outcomes) were identified when she was able to resist other people's stories about her and about the abuse.

Case Study – K.

K. was a ten-year-old girl abused by a 17-year-old male neighbour over a six-month period while baby-sitting. She was referred to the Project immediately after disclosure in a rather withdrawn and shocked state. It soon became evident that she experienced overwhelming relief at having disclosed, so stopping the abuse happening, but she was very troubled and confused by the rather dramatic reactions that other members of her family were having to the disclosure, for which she felt very responsible.

Work with K. was very low-key, providing a safe place for her to explore her feelings about the abuse and the disclosure. As is often the case, the incidents surrounding and after the abuse and subsequently the disclosure were more troubling to K. than the abuse itself. K.'s mother was expressing murderous feelings towards the abuser who had moved to live with a relative nearby and towards his parents, who remained living next door for a six-month period. The intensity of the mother's negative feelings was frightening to the mother herself as well as those around her, in particular, K. Sessions were therefore offered to the mother on a weekly basis to assist her to process her anger and guilt about what had happened to K. This proved cathartic for the mother and was reassuring for K. that her mother was being contained.

Shortly after the disclosure, K.'s older brother R.'s behaviour began to give cause for concern. He started running away from home, running out of lessons in school and trashing his bedroom. He too was offered weekly sessions and it became evident that he was consumed with guilt at not having known about or stopped the abuse and consumed with anger at what had been done to his sister. His mother's fury fuelled this but he felt responsible for this too. The father was clearly distressed by the upset in his family. He declined formal treatment but often brought the two children to therapy and would snatch a chat with the therapists about his concerns.

This was a situation where although K. undoubtedly needed some therapeutic time in order to help her process what had happened to her, people's reactions to it and what was happening in terms of criminal proceedings, she appeared to be much less traumatised by the situation than her mother and brother. The sessions provided to both mother and brother helped to provide the secure, supportive environment necessary for K. to embark upon her recovery. The family had become so destabilised by the disclosure that without these inputs from the Project and elsewhere it is difficult to see how a downward spiral could have been stemmed. One aim of the work with the mother and brother was to (re-)mobilise the undoubted resources within this family to help K. through to her recovery.

Working through the parent or carer

Sometimes it seems inappropriate to involve the child in treatment at all and work can more than adequately be done via the parent or carer.

Case Study – M.

M. was seven-years-old. He was a child who suffered from a life-threatening illness which resulted in many medical problems and invasive surgical procedures.

He came to the notice of the Project when his mother's ex-partner had been arrested for sexually abusing other children on the estate. M. eventually also disclosed serious sexual abuse at the hands of this man which had occurred when he was undertaking M.'s intimate physical care. M. made it clear that he could not handle thinking or talking about the abuse at the time; given that his life was already dominated by medical appointments it was felt inappropriate to introduce another regular appointment. His mother, however, was deeply distressed by what had happened and she readily accepted support for herself to help her come to terms with what had happened to M. She had three individual sessions and then joined a group for mothers of sexually abused children from which she derived considerable support and a reduction in her sense of isolation. She found ways to give vent to her understandable anger regarding M.'s abuse without burdening him further with the intense and almost immobilising rage. At times she felt so repulsed by what had happened to M. that she felt unable to offer him the nurturing she knew that he required. She worked through these intense feelings in treatment and, when M. was ready to talk about what had happened to him and the feelings it left him with, she was able to deal with it herself with the Project in the background.

Case Study – S.

S. was a seven-year-old boy who was referred to the Project because of concerns about his highly sexualised behaviour towards children and towards his foster mother. On one occasion his behaviour towards his foster mother, to whom he was devoted, was such that she commented 'If he hadn't been seven years old I would have described what he tried to do to me as attempted rape.'

It was felt that S.'s sexualised behaviour was a grave cause for concern and was likely to escalate. The treatment of choice was a 'Stop and Think' Group, due to start in three months' time. This seemed too long to wait without any direct intervention with S. and yet it was felt that the impact of the group would be diluted if individual work took place with S. in the interim. It was agreed, therefore, to work with the foster mother to help her process the impact of the highly sexualised behaviour directed towards her and to offer her coping mechanisms for dealing with his behaviour.

Case Study – J.

J. was another child who was not felt to be directly accessible to treatment. Work with and through his foster carers was, however, successfully undertaken. J. was a six-year-old boy who had alleged abuse by his mother's cohabitee. He was placed with first-time foster carers for a three-month period while arrangements were made for him to move to his father who lived out of the area. The foster carers quickly became overwhelmed by J.'s highly sexualised behaviours which included constant masturbation, sticking things up his anus and simulating sex with his teddies. The foster carers were so distressed by his behaviour that they felt they might need to have him moved. They couldn't make sense of either his sexualised behaviour or his constant lying and were aware of behaving in an increasingly punitive way towards him, which they felt was inappropriate. In view of J.'s pending move to his father, it was felt to be inappropriate to engage him in another adult relationship which could not be sustained, but it was felt that it might be possible to help him through his foster carers. They readily agreed to this and the sessions were used to offload their outrage, disgust and anxiety about J.'s behaviour.

There was also a strong educative function to help the foster carers make sense of his behaviour. As they began to do this, their anxiety levels decreased and their responses to J. became more appropriate and more positive, so enabling him to remain with them for the period planned and to move on to his father with the benefits of both a positive experience in general and a positive ending in particular.

Working with the whole family

Although children and young people are referred to the Project as a result of issues which stem from sexual abuse, sometimes a focus on the victim seems less appropriate than seeing the whole family together. This may well be the case if difficulties in the family pre-date the abuse or are magnified as a result of it.

Case Study – N.

N., aged 14 years, had been abused by a business associate of his father when he was eleven. He was investigated as a result of another child disclosing and

N. having frequently been seen in the abuser's company. N. was a very immature young man who was the subject of bullying at school. He was particularly upset at being called gay. Over recent months, he had become increasingly withdrawn and he also suffered from bad nightmares. His father was also a rather withdrawn man who expressed some guilt at having befriended the abuser and encouraged him to come round to the house. He described considerable tension and disagreement between his wife and himself. N.'s mother and both his older sisters suffered badly from pre-menstrual syndrome and this seemed to dominate family life. When pre-menstrual, N.'s mother was very violent towards her husband and recently she had twice overdosed. When agitated, she often drove off in her car – anywhere. This was understandably a source of considerable anxiety for N. On assessment it was established that much of this disturbed behaviour pre-dated N.'s disclosure of abuse and it was felt that N.'s symptoms were on the one hand developmentally and contextually appropriate and on the other were a means to get help for the family. It was therefore decided to see the family as a whole, a decision which they all readily agreed to.

Gradually, it emerged that the family's preoccupation with N. left his sisters feeling left out and his mother feeling a failure as a mother. As they felt released from such a sharp focus on N. their own symptoms of PMS diminished. It became apparent that Mum blamed Dad for having befriended the abuser and this exacerbated his own sense of guilt and left him immobilised as a parent and husband. Mum and Dad were enabled to communicate their feelings and gradually the tension between them diminished. As Mum and Dad became closer again, N. was relieved of some of his anxiety and sense of responsibility for his mother. The parents began to work together again to co-parent N. which in turn allowed him some increasing independence more appropriate for his years.

Case Study – L.

L. was sexually abused by a neighbour's son when she was twelve and he was 15. He then re-assaulted her four years later. From the start, L. was clear that she did not want individual treatment. She felt the whole family needed help and other family members agreed. The parents and elder sister felt powerless about helping L. They did not know how to talk to her about the abuse or how she was feeling. L. recognised their distress but she too was at a loss as to what to do.

Both parents were very angry and upset about what had happened to their daughter; L. wrongly perceived their anger as directed at her, so communication was skewed between them. In the struggle to deal with this, Mum had become very enmeshed with L. and, Dad feeling useless, she became more and more disengaged. Work focused on accurate communication and a return to shared parenting. Distance regulating manoeuvres brought Dad in more thus allowing Mum to move out and not be so over-protective of L.

The parents' distress at what had happened to L. had left them unsure as to how to parent her. In their effort to be protective, they were tending to impose inappropriate boundaries and deadlines – treating her like a very much younger child. Involving the elder sister had the advantage of maintaining a whole family perspective rather than the focus being on a stuck threesome organised around L.'s victim status. The elder sister helped to normalise the situation helping the family reflect on how she had been treated at this age. This helped the parents re-connect with how to parent a 17-year-old who had not been abused.

Working with the carers in conjunction with the work done individually or in a therapy group with a child

Case Study – R.

R., aged four years, was abused by his father during access visits. The parents separated after a stormy relationship dominated by the father's drug and alcohol abuse and domestic violence. R.'s mother was vociferous about her loathing and anger towards her ex-husband even before R.'s allegations of abuse by him. After the disclosure, she coped by complete denial of her ex-husband's existence. This was a source of considerable confusion for R. R. used his therapy to act out his mother's anxieties and difficulties with the perpetrator and his own inner conflict regarding the expression of his feelings, both negative and positive, for his father. Although R. clearly found the therapy sessions of considerable value, it was felt that unless work could be done with Mother alongside, a plateau would quickly be reached. Five sessions were arranged with Mum in which she was helped to acknowledge the importance of her ex-husband as a part of R.'s life. She was supported in helping R. process his very strong feelings towards his father, thus enabling him to move on.

In the group therapy for adolescent sex offenders, it has proved invaluable to work with a Carers Group alongside. This affords the therapeutic team invaluable insights into issues in the young offenders context that could inhibit or sabotage the work he is doing. Given the common themes of secrecy, grooming and creating a context of safety and protection for other potential victims, it is essential to work with carers to reinforce the work done with the boys. In the case of natural parents, it is necessary to help them work through the shame and difficulty of having a son who has committed sexual offences.

In the case of substitute carers, whether foster carer or residential workers, considerable work often needs to be done to mitigate the tendency to minimise both the serious nature of the offence and the ongoing risks for the future. Ultimately it is with considerable relief that these young offenders experience the veil of secrecy being lifted both in the therapy group and in their family-living context.

Similar processes were important with the 'Stop and Think' Groups. These treatment groups for young children under ten years of age with highly sexualised behaviour had Carers Groups running alongside. What quickly became evident was the great needs of the carers in their own right. It was found that if the carers' needs were met, the benefits were clearly demonstrated in their dealings with their children. The carers potently expressed how beneficial they found it to feel listened to and valued in the group. This was reflected in their ability to listen to and value their children and to recognise their needs.

Within the therapeutic relationship parents felt heard, valued, respected and listened to in their own right. Their own needs were enormous and therapists had to work hard to help them to connect with their children's needs and the reasons for them both attending the Project. These families often experienced multiple problems over and above their child's inappropriate sexualised behaviours. Often they suffered considerable poverty. Some were survivors of sexual abuse in their own right and others had unsupportive partners. A major difficulty for them in parenting was maintaining appropriate and consistent boundaries. Often they had difficulty in maintaining discipline, were inconsistent or over-harsh in their punishments and needed help in establishing more appropriate limits.

Another major issue for parents which reflected directly in their handling of their children was either a lack of expression of feeling or inappropriate expression of feeling arising from poor role-modelling in their own childhood and directly reflected in the role-models they too gave their children. Another major linked theme was their difficulties in dealing with issues of loss and bereavement which directly affected their ability to deal appropriately with their children's losses. Direct links could be seen with the carers getting to grips with some of these issues for themselves and being able to impact positively on their children's difficulties in these areas.

It can be seen from these examples how closely intertwined the work with parents/carers is with the treatment of the child. Without attention to the total context of the child, including their inner world and external world past and present, the work can only be defined as partially complete. The clinician requires a working knowledge of the family system(s) that the sexually abused child relates to and an understanding of the importance of mobilising different parts of the system to create a supportive environment in which any therapeutic gains can be developed and maintained. Without such a collaborative endeavour, the family or its sub-sections can sabotage or hinder the child's work with the therapist. Working with the family history, communication system, internalised feelings and belief systems provides a realistic and comprehensive context from which the wounds resulting from the trauma of sexual abuse can begin to heal.

References

Bannister, A. (1992) *From Hearing to Healing: Working with The Aftermath of Child Sexual Abuse*, London: Longman.
Doyle, C. (1990) *Working With Abused Children*, London: Macmillan.
Finkelhor, D. (1986) *A Sourcebook of Child Sexual Abuse*, London: Sage.
Miller, A. (1984) *Thou Shalt Not Be Aware: Society's Betrayal of the Child*, London: Pluto.
Schecter, M.D. and Roberge, L. (1976) 'Child Sexual Abuse' in Helper, F. and Kemper, C.H. (eds) *Child Abuse & Neglect: The Family & the Community*, Cambridge, MA: Ballinger.
Smith, G. (1995) *The Protector's Handbook*, London: Women's Press.
Summit, R. (1983) 'The Child Sexual Abuse Accommodation Syndrome', *Child Abuse & Neglect*, 7: 177–193.

Bibliography

Bray, M. (1997) *Poppies on the Rubbish Heap*, Cassell.
Finkelhor, D. (1986) *A Sourcebook on Child Sexual Abuse*, Sage.
Furniss, T. (1991) *The Multi-Professional Handbook of Child Sexual Abuse*, Routledge.
Glaser, D. and Frosh, S. (1988) *Child Sexual Abuse*, MacMillan.
Jackson, V. (1996) *Racism and Child Protection*, Cassell.
Sinason, V. (ed.) (1994) *Treating Survivors of Satanist Abuse*, Routledge.

Further reading

Alvarez, A. (1992) *Live Company*, Routledge.

Bentovim, A. et al. (1988) *Child Sexual Abuse Within the Family*, Butterworth.

De Bruga, W. and Schuman, R. (1993) *Sexual Abuse and Residential Treatment*, Haworth.

Eliot, M. (1993) *Female Sexual Abuse of Children*, Longmans.

McMahon, L. (1992) *The Handbook of Play Therapy*, Routledge.

Welldon, E. (1988) *Mother Madonna Whore*, Guildford.

Welldon, E. and Van Velsen, C. (eds) (1997) *A Practical Guide to Forensic Psychotherapy*, Jessica Kingsley.

13 Throughcare: supporting young people as they make the transition from residential care to the wider community

Mick McCarthy and Prue Hardwick

Introduction

> Where a child is being looked after by a local authority it shall be the duty of the authority to advise, assist and befriend him with a view to promoting his welfare when he ceases to be looked after by them. (From Section 24(l), Children Act 1989)

Leaving care, for example, leaving the warm tolerance of long-suffering foster carers or leaving a supportive and concerned residential home or halfway semi-independence unit, is a very big step to take. For most young people, the reality of leaving care means surviving in your late teens in a hostile environment – poor-quality housing, subsistence survival on benefit, few opportunities for work if, as is usually the case, your educational achievements are low. You are still a very volatile, vulnerable sort of person who used to rely on regular, tolerant, adult support. You do not cope with stress very well and are likely to react without thinking when something goes wrong. An all-too-large proportion of young people living on the streets and/or committing crime are products of the care system.

The idea that young people can survive on their own without adult support owes more to the political philosophy of ancient Sparta than to the caring democracies of the 1990s. However, in Sparta, the young people were only expected to last on their own for a few weeks as a rite of passage. Many of the readers of this book would have been lost without a network of family and friends during those early adult years.

Although this chapter is about what a good throughcare service does, there is a strong subtext. What must we do during a young person's career in care to try to smooth the passage into the post-care years? We are making a simple appeal on behalf of all post-care support workers that each care plan and individual programme in fostering, residential home and school should address the post-care needs of our young people while also attending to the pressing needs which brought them into the care system in the first place. An extra condition of good care to add to the Dartington Five (Little 1994: 116).

The creation of a post-care support network for our still vulnerable young people is not an optional extra. It is an absolute essential.

13 Throughcare: supporting young people as they make the transition from residential care to the wider community

Mick McCarthy and Prue Hardwick

This chapter attempts to highlight some of the essential ingredients in the mix of thinking and practice which goes into providing for young people when they leave our care to make the transition into a harsh and unforgiving world without the support network provided for the vast majority of us by parents, relatives and friends. Many of us can reflect on our own turbulent adolescence – it was not always fun! The chapter will describe the legislative framework within which our work is guided, the way in which the Caldecott Foundation has responded to these guidelines and more importantly, the messages from young people in research.

First, a case study which will help put the theory, legislation, experience and practice into context.

Case Study

J. left the Caldecott Centre aged 17. She moved into a shared house set up by Caldecott for their leavers in the local area, and was employed on a Youth Training Scheme in catering. She was surviving well at work, but other areas of her life were a struggle. She had recently been left by her boyfriend who used to hit her, she was heavily in debt and had a poor relationship with her mother. Social Services supported her through the Throughcare service until she reached 19 years old, when funding stopped. Their involvement in the early stages was valued not only by J. but also by her family in London.

At around this time it was decided to close the house in which she was living and accommodation was found for her in a flat offering greater independence. Although she had welcomed the move, it quickly became clear that she was not coping. Despite hours spent advising on money management, her debts increased. Her personal hygiene and appearance deteriorated. Food was short, and the flat became scruffy and dirty.

J.'s desire for companionship also led to problems. The high of a new boyfriend would be followed by a deep low when he used her and left her. Her friends at that time were not so much drawn to her, as to the freedom that her flat offered to them. She would not turn them away, gladly welcoming their friendship and company. Parties, late-night music and alcohol all led to extreme pressure on her by neighbours and the landlord (a local housing association). Work suffered and the full-time job that had followed the training scheme ended.

There followed a period of unemployment. As problems mounted so did her inability to face them and she was depressed for long periods. Efforts to find work were half-hearted and she did not present well at interviews. Her relationship with her mother had not improved and friends who had benefited from her generosity melted away. Even her relationship with the Caldecott and Throughcare suffered as, with no one else to turn to, she became almost too dependent.

J. needed to be taken out of the situation. Caldecott had placed her in the Housing Association flat, and we advised them that it was in her best interests to move on. She needed to come to terms with the reality of independent living and that meant seeing through the consequences of her actions. The Housing Association agreed and instigated eviction procedures for rent arrears. Meanwhile Throughcare worked with J. to find more supportive accommodation.

In April 1991, 20 months after leaving the Caldecott, she moved into lodgings away from the town centre and near genuine friends. There was a resident landlord whose tenancy rules were quite restrictive, but at least they would help to ensure that her previous experiences would not be repeated.

J. herself seemed to recognise this as a turning point. She took more pride in her appearance, looked after her room and respected the shared facilities. She took job-hunting seriously, and while not finding full-time work, successfully completed a number of short-term posts.

Her relationships with friends and even family improved. She visited home occasionally, even though it was always difficult. Her contact with Throughcare matured. Rather than expecting us to manage everything for her, she would use us to check what she had done herself.

As her sense of personal responsibility increased, the restrictions of her tenancy became increasingly irksome and it was felt that she should move. This time a room was found where the landlord lived next door. At this point a Caldecott leavers' fund agreed to pay off her debts.

Over the next two years, J. managed increasingly well. She had a regular casual job two evenings a week and with benefit, she was able to manage her money. The debts of the previous two years were still there, but they had not increased. The frequency of Throughcare contact decreased as J. became less needy. She began to use the Throughcare drop-in both socially and to see Throughcare staff. Their role was to keep in touch, listen when necessary and offer reassurance that all was well.

J. desperately wanted a regular partner and a family of her own but she still found relationships with men hard to manage. Twice she thought she was pregnant, and, although she protested her relief when the test results were negative, there was sadness in her eyes as she talked to us.

In December 1993, aged almost 22, she moved in with her boyfriend. Throughcare did not wholeheartedly support this move, but nevertheless maintained contact with her. They stayed together for over a year which showed that J. was managing better. Her debts rose a little, probably because of the man, but she is paying them off regularly and they will soon be cleared.

She is now settled in her own flat with two cats and is surviving well. Although she now needs very little support work from Throughcare, we keep in touch with her at social events like Charter Day and the Christmas supper for leavers.

There are several keys which allow children and young people access to a successful adulthood. A positive self-image brings with it the confidence to own these keys, which open doors to positive relationships, the world of work and further education and therefore mainstream society. If a young person leaves care beyond the age of 15 their opportunities are greatly diminished:

- 75% will have no qualifications
- 80% will be unemployed after 12 months
- 50% will experience homelessness
- 40% of young women aged 15–18 will become pregnant or have a child
- 54% of prisoners aged 18–24 will have been in the care system
- 66% of male prostitutes are young men out of the care system
- 50% of those begging in London will have been in care
- 80% of care leavers will experience destitution.

J.'s experience and that of the Throughcare worker supporting her encapsulate the dilemmas and failures of a 'caring' system and highlight the myths that are perpetrated which enable society to allow an estimated 10,000 young people aged 16–17 to leave care each year with inadequate support within a legal framework.

Services to younger children, particularly in the field of child protection, have benefited from the Children Act, and the levels of care and accountability have risen for those placed in residential and foster care. For those young people who are not expected to return to their families, the 1989 Act and its excellent guidance call for an increased awareness of need and emphasise the importance of preparing children for adulthood and interdependence. Attention is paid to the need for building and maintaining relationships with a variety of other children, other than those also in care. The need for stability is expressed with placements kept to a minimum, to both encourage long-term relationships and, crucially, educational stability leading to qualifications. Positive adult role models, also outside the system, should be sought, and carers should be encouraged to play a positive role after a young person has left. Where appropriate, relationships with birth families should be actively maintained and children from ethnic minorities must have contact with others from the same cultural background to ensure a sense of identity and pride. Attention is encouraged by the Children Act on sex education and in particular the emotional implications of entering into a sexual relationship. It also describes the need to recognise the implications for young people who have been sexually abused and to support those who are gay and lesbian.

We are told to enable young people to develop their self-esteem, which is often low due both to feelings of rejection by birth parents and the stigma of being in care. There are also checklists galore outlining the practical and financial skills and knowledge needed to survive. After leaving care, the local authority is responsible for providing advice and information, an interest in their welfare, assistance in cash or kind, a return to care if necessary, education and training and accommodation.

Why then do young people like J. experience the kind of difficulties narrated above? Here we believe lies the first myth, which legislators and those empowered to interpret the law use to underpin the allocation of resources. Within the system we have unrealistically high expectations of a young person's ability to manage their lives effectively. At a time when the average age for leaving home is 21 for women and 23 for men, we are evicting young people from caring and supportive environments by the time they are 18. Many young people who enter the care system at 16 are not placed with foster families but in lodgings and shared accommodation to make way for younger children whose needs are perceived to be greater in a climate of diminishing resources. Furthermore, a local authority is only required to provide advice, information and an interest in the welfare of a young person – and that can cease on their twenty-first birthday. Assistance involving cash or resources, a return to care and any service provided by housing or education is voluntary.

Other areas of social legislation support the myth that young people can cope with less support. In the mid-1980s welfare rights legislation removed the right of 16–18-year-olds to access benefits unless in 'severe hardship' and those aged 18–25 received lower amounts. The current government, in establishing a minimum wage, are considering exempting those under 25 from impending legislation. Youth employment is higher than at the time of the 1980 Child Care Act, and under the 1977 Housing (Homeless Persons) Act, local authorities had more discretion to define young people leaving care as vulnerable than under the 1990 Housing Act. Under the same act, Housing Benefit restrictions to this age group have restricted opportunity for decent housing by limiting eligible payments to a local single-room rate.

Within the core of our society, young people are encouraged if not forced, to stay within their families for longer. For J. and her peers, the opposite has happened. Furthermore, in her case, those with a responsibility to support her (the local authority) withdrew by the time she was 19. Having spent most of her life in care, she did not have the options of traditional networks to call upon.

In general, families fulfil an obligation to support their children through adolescence into adulthood and withdraw as part of a natural rather than planned process.

An independent study of the outcomes of 60 Caldecott leavers (Little and Kelly 1994) found that out of those staying on after their sixteenth birthday nearly all (93 per cent) went on to flats and bedsits locally rather than in their home towns. Two years after leaving 'All were managing to keep their heads above water', and 'the continued support of Caldecott Throughcare workers was helpful to the long-term well-being of these young people.'

The picture of Caldecott leavers at the point of leaving presented by the Dartington research team will be representative of the national pattern of care leavers. We reproduce below their chart which in its stark reality underlines the importance nationally of the Throughcare task.

Table 13.1 Summary of outcomes by career pathway

Career route	Likely outcome	Positive areas	Potential weaknesses
Children from fragmented families	Quite good if Caldecott provides stability between 14 and 17 years	Employment; ability to look after self	Drugs; petty crime
Victims of chronic sexual abuse	Generally good, danger of disruption following sexual activity network	Education; resilience; gregariousness; socially orthodox	Pregnancy; re-abuse
Children with behavioural difficulties	Mixed. Some problems endure, but most likely to integrate fully	Education; family relationships	Social isolation
Long-term protection cases	Generally poor	None	Offending leading to custody

Source: Little and Kelly 1995: 174.

Although we could question the make-up of the Dartington categories – would not victims of chronic sexual abuse also be long-term protection cases? – their findings underline the paramount need for expert and sophisticated support for leavers. Where placement in substitute care had been interrupted prematurely before the age of 17, the researchers found that outcomes were not as good as for those who were provided with stability between the ages of 14 and 17.

Adults working with children in residential care who by definition will have experienced several placements and earlier emotional, physical and sexual abuse and neglect, have a particular responsibility and duty to interpret the Children Act in the children's favour. Young people will not understand the reasons behind a withdrawal of services, and will endure further neglect if the messages sent by the statistics are not heard. We are learning that young people, if given the choice, would rather be closely supported than not, and we must confront the myth that their rejection of traditional 'leaving care packages' is due to their need to be independent of us. In the majority of cases, services are not made use of because they are offered by a new adult with a 'role' rather than from the basis of an existing relationship which has already established trust and understanding. We should not wonder why young people reject the support provided to prevent them joining the horrendous statistics mentioned earlier, when the other hand from the same 'supportive' body has just pushed them into a situation where they have little hope of surviving.

At the Caldecott Community, we have adopted a Throughcare approach. We have appointed three social workers who are involved with the three residential groups caring for young people aged 11–17. They form a new team which is encouraging the residential workers to have a young person's needs as a future leaver and young adult at the forefront of everyday life and as part of the therapeutic milieu. We are avoiding making preparation for adulthood a separate task, preferring to incorporate it within the overall task. We believe young people accept this more readily, and become less likely to reject it if it is not so obviously connected with the inevitable fear of leaving and rejection.

Our experience tells us that leavers will often call upon the Caldecott for support after having left, but only when emerging from the wilderness and after one crisis too many. To address this, the Throughcare team are involved in the planning for leaving, providing resources external to the Community to minimise institutionalisation, and will remain supportive to the young person living interdependently or within their next placement. It is this continuum of care, based on a relationship developed while still in care, which will do most to help prevent a sense of isolation. This relationship is actively encouraged, and will be maintained if necessary up to the point at which it ends through 'natural causes', usually around age 25.

To facilitate contact, we have a 'drop-in' service in Ashford, close to the Caldecott, and also in London at a foyer near Covent Garden. A trust, the Leila Rendel Fund, which was set up in memory of the Caldecott co-founder, is available to provide financial support to our leavers through grants and loans.

Some practice guidelines

J.'s case is quite illuminating and she and others in her predicament have helped shape the elements of the Throughcare model. What are the implications for practice?

- **Continuity** Most young people experience a number of changes of social worker but the Throughcare worker, who ideally will have known the young person even before he or she left care, is able to offer continuous, consistent and reliable support.
- **Consistency** Remain concerned at all times even in the face of no response through periods of depression and rebellion. Send postcards, birthday cards and Christmas cards.
- **Practical support** Decorate flats. Move furniture. Help with form filling, budgeting and debt management. In J.'s case, this help was necessary over and over again.
- **Listening** Be willing to listen to problems, no matter how small or unimportant they may seem. Remain open rather than judgemental. It is not always necessary to respond in a particular way. It is often enough for young people to feel that they have been heard.
- **Reliability** Keep appointments and carry out the tasks agreed with the young person. Never promise what cannot be done.
- **Building family links** Support the young person as they try to forge relationships within their families. Be there for them if it goes wrong: 'Those remaining at the Community beyond their sixteenth birthday, though the least likely to live with their parents, were the most likely to have frequent contact with home ... Although family and social relationships were rarely unproblematic, links were at least enduring and usually improved' (Little and Kelly 1995). J.'s relationship with her family illustrates this point very clearly.
- **Reality** By far the toughest time for J. was around her eviction. Throughcare had, in effect, initiated those consequences but took responsibility for supporting her through them. She was forced to face reality and she made the change inside herself as a result.
- **Responsibility** The Throughcare worker constantly encourages the young people to accept responsibility for their own lives. When J. was able to do this, she was able to put down roots and feel a sense of belonging to the community. Her self-esteem increased and she made friends and relationships.
- **Roots** Every year the Caldecott hosts Charter Day when Caldecott old boys and girls are welcomed with their families. The Throughcare service also offers a Christmas dinner to younger leavers in the area. These are very important events which epitomise the Caldecott's ongoing concern for its young people even if they were there fifty years ago. Charter Day brings back at least one hundred and fifty people every two years and is greatly valued, especially those for whom Caldecott was a positive life-changing experience.
- **Liaison** Throughcare is the link between Caldecott and the wider

world for young people about to leave the Community itself. Subsequently we liaise between client, landlord, social services, probation and family as required. It is important to maintain good working relations with other agencies concerned with young people.

● **Evaluation** Without adequate records, Throughcare cannot prove that it is doing a valuable job.

● **Time** There are no quick fixes. Some leavers have more serious problems than J. and Throughcare regularly visits young people in hospital or prison. But many of these gradually mature and Throughcare are there to support them as they try to put their lives together.

We must continuously be mindful of the potential we have for compounding the diminished opportunities many children have when not brought up within a loving, supportive birth family. The Throughcare model is not the answer, but will limit further damage.

References

Action on Aftercare Consortium (1996) *Too Much Too Young. The Failure of Social Policy in Meeting the Needs of Care Leavers*, Barnardo's.

Broad, R. (1997) *The Inadequate Child Care Legislation Governing Work with Young People Leaving Care: A Research Based View*, Childright.

Cathcart, J. (1997) *Preparation for Adulthood – Standards for Good Practice in Residential Care*, National Children's Bureau.

Kirby, P. (1994) *A Word from the Street. Young People who Leave Home and Become Homeless*, Centrepoint.

Little, M. and Kelly, S. (1995) *A Life Without Problems?*, Arena.

McParlin, P. (1996) *Education of Young People Looked After*, First Key.

Royal Philanthropic Society (1994) *Developing Effective Aftercare Projects*, Royal Philanthropic Society.

Social Services Inspectorate (1997) *When Leaving Home is also Leaving Care*, HMSO.

Stein, M. (1997) *What Works in Leaving Care?*, Barnardo's.

Part Three

The Carer, the Family, the Group and the Organisation

14 Working in substitute care settings with sexually abused children: issues for carers

Ros Fanshawe

Introduction

> When we consider the qualities we most admire: courage, wisdom, integrity, we implicitly acknowledge that those who possess such qualities have achieved maturity by having struggled with and being able to continue to deal with the destructive elements in their personality and that of their fellow human beings. (Isca Saltzberger-Wittenberg 1973)

This chapter has been created from several sources: working in group care with young people who have experienced sexual abuse, a small-scale piece of research into the experience of substitute carers looking after young people who have been sexually abused and experience of training substitute carers involved with young people in need, an increasing number of whom have experienced sexual abuse.

The aim of the chapter is to focus on the feelings aroused in carers working with sexually abused young people and the implications of these feelings in their practice. It is not intended to examine the many and diverse issues related to the sexual abuse of young people.

14 Working in substitute care settings with sexually abused children: issues for carers

Ros Fanshawe

For the purposes of this chapter sexual abuse is defined as

> ... the involvement of dependent, developmentally immature children and adolescents in sexual activities they do not truly comprehend, to which they do not give informed consent or that violates the taboos of family roles. (Kempe and Kempe 1979, cited in Ghate and Spencer 1995)

This chapter reports the experience of carers of young people who are deemed to be 'in need' as defined in the Children Act 1989. These young people are living away from their family of origin, for much of the time in foster or residential care.

Residential care and sexually abused children

In 1992, the Warner Committee reported on the recruitment, supervision and training of staff in children's homes and found that

> Over the past decade more and more difficult children have been placed in a shrinking number of children's homes ... Some homes have many violent, abused, abusing and self mutilating children, rather than the orphans and truants of a bygone era. (Warner 1992)

In the course of the Committee's inquiry, senior managers in children's homes were asked to estimate how many young people in their care had been sexually abused prior to placement. Responses to this enquiry revealed that in both local authority and voluntary homes, almost one-third of young people had been sexually abused and in private homes one-quarter (Warner 1992: 19). Respondents indicated that their figures were probably an underestimate.

The 1991 report *Children in the Public Care* suggested that residential placements were best allocated to children in certain circumstances:

> The characteristics of children in care suggest residential care as the preferred, best or only option in certain circumstances, where ... abuse has occurred within the natural family of such a kind that placement with another family is undesirable. A complex of personal and social difficulties indicates a need for sophisticated and expert treatment in a residential setting. (Utting 1991)

Information presented in the Utting Report (1991) and the Warner Report (1992) gives an indication of the experiences of and disturbance present in young people in residential care, reflecting a picture of young people who have experienced repeated rejections, neglect and abuse, whether physical, sexual, emotional or all of these.

In my experience of training substitute carers, it is becoming increasingly rare to meet carers who are not involved in caring for young people who have been sexually abused. Many of these young people display bizarre sexual behaviours and a significant number of them have begun to abuse other young people. Although there are no collated statistics on the experience of children in foster care, case histories often show similarities with children in residential care. It would be reasonable to suggest that there are now such a number of young people in substitute care who have experienced sexual abuse that issues related solely to their care should be debated with some urgency.

Issues and concerns in residential care

With so much written about abuses and malpractice in residential care it has to be asked how such events keep occurring: how did it happen that in children's homes in Staffordshire residential carers concluded that the most effective (and by implication 'right') way of dealing with very disruptive young people was the regime of isolation and confinement which came to be known as 'Pindown'? Whilst there is a pressing need to pursue the findings of the Utting Report into young people coming into residential care, and to establish why these young people are as troubled (and troubling) as they are, that is only half the picture. Carers need to examine their responses to young people and to understand what motivates their responses. Bullock comments:

When vulnerable staff are at their most vulnerable, they ... fall back on remedies which offer ready solutions. One of the most frightening aspects of the Pindown saga ... was its clear attraction for staff struggling to care for difficult adolescents ... Isolated and beleaguered staff placed in impossible situations can behave as drastically as the children for whom they care. (Bullock 1989)

The feelings and experience of young people who have been sexually abused are powerfully voiced by Constance Nightingale, herself a survivor of sexual abuse in childhood:

Incest is the most unloving thing that can happen to a child ... Our healing begins when we can acknowledge what has happened to us – first to ourselves and then to someone who will believe us and hear our pain ... someone listening and believing, someone caring and understanding the complex mix of our emotions ... accepting all the rage, grief and terror we have concealed for so long. (Bray 1997)

Constance Nightingale's account of her feelings and experiences is one part of an extremely complex picture of how the world view of children who have been sexually abused has been conditioned. Seen as a whole, this needs to encompass a recognition that some children who have been sexually abused have become eroticised by the sexual activities in which they were involved. In some cases, children have been abused from a very early age and their experience of being cared for and nurtured has become strongly or completely suffused with sexual memories, fantasies and feelings. Children such as these may scarcely have a 'notion of non-abuse' (Alvarez 1992). It is not uncommon to find children such as these in residential care. Their sexualised, often violent, bizarre and anti-social behaviour becomes intolerable for even the most resilient and experienced foster carers and they are unwelcome in mainstream schools. In an article which explores the experience of the abused child and the dilemmas involved in treatment of these children, Yates writes:

The assumption that children involved in incest are passive, unwilling victims is an over simplification of a complex situation. Young children may find such relationships gratifying and, when exposed over time to intense genital and extra-genital stimulation, they often become highly erotic. Foster homes are neither trained or supported in caring for these children, so serial placements are common. (Yates 1982)

Yates continues 'In fact, erotic expression may be so gratifying that it is difficult to find comparable rewards to reinforce socially acceptable behaviour.'

Such bald statements of fact are uncomfortable to contemplate. How should we respond to the 'rage, grief and terror' articulated by Constance Nightingale, or the child who has little if any concept of being protected rather than exploited, or the eroticised children described by Yates. What is the effect on the grown-ups caring for these young people? How do they bear to acknowledge, believe, hear, understand and accept the horrific truths sexually abused young people will impart to them, truths sometimes doubly shocking owing to the impact of both the content of their experiences and the feelings they induce. How can grown-ups listen with sensitivity to the child rather than react drastically to what they hear?

Processing powerful feelings

The effect on grown-ups of working with sexually abused young people has largely been documented by therapists reflecting on their experiences of sessional work. There is little written from the point of view of residential carers but it would be foolish to assume that complex conscious and unconscious interpersonal processes recognised by therapists do not exist in residential care or in foster families.

Just as in the hourly therapy session the therapist needs to be aware and constantly monitoring their response to their client, so too in the day-to-day living situation must the residential carer or foster carer in order to be receptive and open to children. Hoxter writes most perceptively:

> ... the child ... has been exposed to intense suffering ... How can we bear to be aware of such pain? ... if we are to be able to maintain our sensitivity without being overwhelmed, how can we put this to use to help the children with whom we live and work?
>
> The children ... showed that their lives were dominated by a continuing need to keep at bay the intolerable emotions of their past experiences of deprivation ... Many of them [had] a pervading pre-occupation with the complex of experiences relating to their sense of deprivation, which left little space in their lives for anything else, thus diminishing their capacity to benefit from ordinary maturational experience.
>
> Yet, despite the permeation of the effects of deprivation into every aspect of the child's development almost invariably the children had little initial capacity to feel or think about their inner suffering ... the notion of a capacity to process external events into internal experiences becomes central when considering what it means to speak of 'coming to terms with severe loss' ... this capacity depends crucially on the opportunities to identify with parents who are themselves able to feel and think.
>
> The crux of the child's deprivation may be perceived as the absence of an adult who, parent-like, shows constancy of care by being sufficiently present and

emotionally available to be receptive to the child's feelings and to 'think about them'. (Hoxter 1990)

In the group care of sexually abused young people, it is important that working with these thinking processes is not restricted to the individual but also accepted as part of the group process and actively worked with. Menzies-Lyth writes:

> The effects on staff of the human material they work with are especially great in institutions whose clients are people in trouble. The clients are likely to evoke powerful and primitive feelings and fantasies in staff ... The acknowledgement and working through of such feelings is not easy, although it is an important part of staff support and primary-task performance to do so. In so far as feelings cannot be worked with personally or institutionally, they are likely to be dealt with by the development of defences against them ... They come to be built into the structure, culture and mode of functioning of the institution and thereby impair task performance. (Menzies-Lyth 1988)

In relation to sexually abused children, it is likely that the 'feelings and fantasies' are particularly potent as they relate to sex and violence.

These intense and often painful feelings and dilemmas spoken of by the interviewees and by carers in groups at the College have important and serious implications for practice and, most importantly, for carers' ability to remain open and receptive to the communications of abused and traumatised young people, some of whose experiences and feelings may challenge carers' long-held and deep-seated beliefs. Yates confronts us with this:

> A common assumption is that children involved in incest, who are necessarily victims, are also invariably the unwilling, passive recipients of a sexual assault. It is believed that the selfish powerful adult extracts pleasure from the terrified, helpless child and that if the incest persists the victim will continue to react with fear and revulsion. This view is an oversimplification that prevents an objective approach to a relatively common problem. (Yates 1982)

From the author's experience the primary task of residential care for sexually abused young people is five-fold:

(a) understanding the child's experience of abuse in the context of their emotional development
(b) preventing a recurrence of abuse
(c) supporting the young person through the process of coming to terms with their experience of abuse

(d)   helping them to develop a positive self-image
(e)   learning to avoid future re-victimisation.

The primary task is at once preventative and facilitative. It needs to be informed by ongoing and established research and knowledge about the long- and short-term effects of sexual abuse on young people. For example, we need to know more about the vulnerability of abused young people to re-victimisation, the destructive effects of abuse on the young person's developing ego and sense of identity, as well as the potential for some young people to become abusers. (For a fuller discussion of these issues see Finklehor 1986; Bentovim 1995; Hunter 1995.)

The nature and complexity of the task of substitute care

Exploring issues relating to sexual abuse and substitute care (in particular residential care) has to involve some examination of the nature of substitute care:

> ... it is in the immediate best interests of any child to be reared by its parents as they see fit and within a family context protected against intrusion upon its privacy. However, when a family fails or the child is exposed to harm, the parents forego their rights of autonomy and privacy. The guardianship of a child then passes from its parents to the State, which guided by the best interests of the child, determines an appropriate course of action – eventual return to the parents or the reallocation of the child to new caretakers, such as a residential institution or foster parents. (Archard 1993)

The relevance of issues of privacy to substitute care of children who have experienced sexual abuse is that family life involes the numerous experiences of intimacy inherent in child rearing. Sexual abuse is a very intimate form of abuse or violence and children who have been sexually abused may have come to recognise not just physical contact but the intimacy of family life/group living as laden with sexual meaning.

Whilst there has been much attention to the idea of ritual abuse in the context of occult practices, I feel it could be argued that the 'ritual' context for many children who are sexually abused is the 'ritual' of daily life in their families. Consequently, group living is potentially fraught and referral notes do not always contain the sort of information necessary to create an accurate picture of these family rituals and routines which could help avoid potent re-enactments. As one 13-year-old girl told us: 'I always knew when it was my turn, when it would happen because he [her very violent father] would pick an argument with me [or one of her siblings] whilst the telly was on and then send me to my room.' What would happen was that her father would go to her room on the pretext of 'apologising' but instead would abuse her (or whichever sibling) had been banished.

Another child refused point blank to participate in the summer camp which occurred a few weeks after he joined the group. His refusal was desperate and protracted despite our naive and well-intentioned attempts at persuasion – no one had ever *not* wanted to go to camp before! It was many months before he could bring himself to tell us that when he was a young child his father used to take him camping with a group of friends and in the evenings he would be passed round the group to be repeatedly sexually abused.

Residential and foster care are both designed to offer a substitute family experience for children living away from their family of origin. Family life is intrinsically intimate and this experience of intimacy is important for children who need a model of intimacy with which to identify and which to identify and which can form the basis for close relationships of their own in later life.

Children who have little if any experience of 'non-abuse', where the whole of family life has become suffused with sexual meaning, may apply this template of experience to subsequent experiences of group living in whatever context. This has serious implications for substitute carers. For these children, there may be scant reason to assume that the group-living situation will not be the same as their original family group situation and they may appear to expect or anticipate abuse. Concurrently there is the certainty that in caring for the child, substitute carers will inherit these areas of intimacy which are part of child care (see also Chapter 17).

Research

I conducted research through a series of interviews with residential and foster carers experienced in working with sexually abused young people. Within the time available for the research it was possible to interview only eight carers, therefore what is presented is a 'snapshot' of carers' feelings although research yielded a rich seam of findings.

The interview questions focused on:

- the carers' experience of young people disclosing sexual abuse to them, and whether the knowledge that the young person has been sexually abused affects how the carer works with the young person

- the feelings aroused in the carer by the disclosure and in daily life with the young person
- the support needed by the carer to work with the young person.

Carers' feelings about disclosure

The main findings of the research were that most carers had experience of young people disclosing sexual abuse to them and they experienced a variety of powerful feelings – 'very upset', 'frightened', 'did not want to hear', 'very drained', 'helpless' – as well as lasting feelings of anger and sorrow. One foster mother spoke movingly of a 16-year-old girl she had cared for who continued to wet the bed and wake up screaming years after she had been raped by her father.

An important issue for carers was having or supervising contact with the young person's family where there was contact with a perpetrator. All carers reported this as very stressful and upsetting.

Knowing that the child had been sexually abused led to carers feeling anxious that the child would try to re-create an abusive relationship with the carer or would abuse other young people. In many placements, children had been told that they would be safe and carers took this undertaking very seriously. Residential carers felt they had failed if abuse occurred in their children's home and this was coupled with a feeling that they had broken their word. Where abuse had occurred, residential carers were often left feeling demoralised.

This sense of responsibility was felt by carers despite the recognition that sexually abused children may attempt to initiate a sexual relationship with another child. One residential carer referred to the behaviour of some young people as 'compulsive' (see Yates above).

The desire to protect young people from further abuse, and the recognition that for some young people seeking sexual gratification was a powerful need, were two important issues. If a residential unit was managed in a repressive way and the young people over-controlled then it would not be possible to work with these. One male residential carer said,

> ... there is the likelihood, possibility, motive, opportunity for children to wish to have sexual contact with each other and clearly the management of that is very important, because we do not want to over-control these children so that their real problems never surface. But equally we do not want to get into situations where one child abuses another in our environment, because one of the things we tell our children ... we are going to keep them safe.

In groups where work is 'opportunity led', this was complex. The problem of peer abuse was particularly difficult to manage in groups where there were children who were ambivalent about their abuse. One carer recounted the following:

> ... some of the children we work with actually 'enjoyed' the abuse. We have got one lad who was abused by his mother and he misses the cuddles and contact and all the elements of attachment of this relationship which went with this abuse ... it can be quite difficult because he cannot actually see any thing wrong with it.

It was not unusual to find carers relating similar incidents where children had become identified with their abusers and caught up in a repetition compulsion or where abuse had become synonymous with nurturing.

All carers needed clear information and discussion about what was normal sexual maturation and experience. This discussion needed to cover the whole range of sexual behaviour and activities. As one male residential carer said, 'What I find so hard to deal with in working with X is that he has had many sexual experiences I have never had and I find it hard to imagine how he may feel about these experiences.'

Several of the carers interviewed had experienced children making sexual advances to them and had reacted in a number of ways. Some carers were able to address what had happened with the young person and to make use of their experience in working with the young person. Other carers had reacted in a stronger, negative, way. One male residential carer suddenly saw an eight-year-old girl as a 'monster'. Carers who were not able to address the incident with the child tended to resort to avoiding contact with the child at the time of day or in the sort of situation in which the incident had occured.

All carers had strong feelings about the experiences of abuse children recounted to them. Carers understood some of the implications of the children's experiences and were mostly preoccupied by the possibility of re-enactment of abuse or children being abused again. Carers needed opportunities to discuss issues relating to sexuality and abuse and sexual development in children, for example, what is deemed to be normal or abusive.

Residential carers in particular were aware of the implications for the safe management of children in groups where some or all children had been sexually abused. The risk of peer abuse has implications for referrals and the selection of young people in groups. In particular, residential carers were aware of how sexual incidents begin to develop between young people and that bullying often played a very large part.

Different treatment

For all carers, knowing that a young person had been sexually abused made them anxious and consequently they treated the young person 'differently'. Carers did not experience this level of anxiety working with young people who had not been sexually abused. This different treatment occurred for three reasons.

A distorted view of child–grown-up relationships

Carers viewed sexually abused young people as having been taught distorted views and expectations of child–grown-up relationships and this was expressed in the context of relationships with carers as well as in relation to the daily routines and the environment in which the young person was living. A foster couple who lived in a small house and who had many years' experience of fostering girls related that they were very careful not to go upstairs in such a way that the young women living with them might feel that they were 'creeping up on them'.

Attention had to be paid to the environment in which the child lived, an example of this was given by an experienced male residential carer who said:

> ... trying to be aware of what things are being said or seen on television – the meanings for the abused child could well be different from those for the non-abused child ... we have for a while spent some time with the business of bathrooms ... you see a bathroom come up on a television advert ... and we maybe see it as one thing, whereas a lot of children I have seen ... were actually abused in the bathroom. It obviously has a different meaning in its entirety than it does for us.

The same was said of bedrooms and bedtime routines by all carers who recognised that these aspects of daily life were often laden with meaning and memories for young people and needed to be handled with particular sensitivity.

A hidden agenda

In carers' experience sexually abused young people often have a hidden or (delinquent) agenda motivating their actions. This was a reflection of the secretive, covert nature of sexual abuse itself and of the increased salience that sexual abuse gives to relationships, physicality and sexuality for abused children. My research revealed that these issues relate to young people and grown-ups, young people's perceptions of relationships between grown-ups and also how sexually abused young people relate to their peers, as the following examples illustrate:

I think we need to be constantly aware that what might seem like normal healthy behaviour for an eight-year-old may actually have different motives in a child who has been sexually abused. Instead of dress/make-up being about identification with adult figures and wanting to look like them and be like them, with an abused child it may well be about 'this is the way I am going to get sex', or 'this is the way the workman is going to find me attractive that is working around the corner.' You have to be aware that the motives are very different. (Male residential carer)

'S.' (who is 12 years old) believes that all male–female interactions result in sexual activity, however brief the interactions. For example Jane (female co-keyworker) was off work for two days with 'flu, coinciding with the start of my holiday. 'S.' assumed that Jane was with me. Even if adults spend ten minutes in the office, 'S.' assumes they are 'kissing'. (Male residential carer)

This 'hidden agenda' was also seen operating in relationships between young people and their peers. One residential carer spoke of this in some detail in relation to young people who are potential abusers and how they may 'groom' other young people for subsequent abuse. Carers related this to young people playing together and the high level of supervision they required because of the possibility of grooming (this was in comparison to the play of non-sexually abused children). This carer gave the example of 'playfighting' and said he would question whether play was all it was or whether it was part of a grooming process in the group of young people whereby 'winners' (dominant/abusers) were distinguished from 'losers' (passive/victims) and thus the scene is set for an abusive subculture to evolve. Yates (1992) comments: 'The highly cathected focus on sexual learning seems to detract from social learning and a more even distribution of libido. Initially the child may pay scant attention to non-sexual relationships.'

Developed self-awareness

All carers felt that they needed to have a highly developed awareness of self and their own sexuality to avoid becoming involved in situations which may recreate the dynamics of abuse with the young person. Several residential carers linked the issue of secure personal boundaries to the sexuality of the carer and a clear location of the carer's sexuality outside the workplace in order to avoid what one carer aptly described as young people and carers getting into a 'Greek Tragedy' scenario together. This interviewee felt this could be especially complex if the carer had themselves been abused and had not yet been able to resolve their feelings about this. The carer may become over-identified with the young person and seek to resolve their feelings through the young person to the detriment of the young person, or the young person may inadvertently bring up memories the grown-up had not dealt with themselves.

What helped carers

All carers agreed that supervision was of great importance to them in their work whether they were foster carers or residential carers. In supervision, carers felt that they had to be able to be very open and honest with their supervisor about how the work made them feel and that supervision should not simply be to monitor case management or to discuss child care.

Foster carers valued the opportunity to meet as a group and to share their feelings and concerns about the young people with whom they were involved, possibly because foster carers work in the 'isolation' of their own homes. In contrast, residential carers valued individual supervision, the reverse of working in a team.

Other supportive factors mentioned included the importance of good record-keeping, clarity of one's own role, access to training, the value of one's own experience of child-rearing and the availability of a supportive partner.

In addition to these findings, my research revealed a powerful anxiety on the part of carers about allegations which was initially expressed in the context of carers' responses to my questions. Gradually, this issue began to take on a life of its own and proved to be very significant in a number of ways. It bears some examination and discussion.

Allegations

In discussing the subject of allegations it is always important to recognise that children are not only abused by members of their family but that some children who are removed from abusive situations are subsequently abused by substitute carers, be they residential workers, foster carers or in some situations by therapists. The extent of this abuse is not known.

Interviewees were highly aware of the potential for allegations and in most cases this affected their work to varying degrees. For the most part, interviewees were wary of being with a young person who they knew had been abused, particularly if they were left alone with them. Some interviewees said they were reluctant to be in such a situation. All interviewees felt that the anxiety about allegations meant that they treated the young person differently.

Malicious allegations

Carers were aware of the possibility of children making malicious allegations and one foster carer said he felt that this would stop him making a close relationship with a young person. Carers did not feel a malicious allegation would only be made against a carer of the same sex as the person who had abused the child. They recognised that young people were capable of making malicious allegations which could be called *revenge allegations*. Of these Cairns (1993) writes 'We have all worked with children who hated us and wished to destroy us. It has never been easier for them to fulfil their wish than in the current climate in child protection.'

However, malicious allegations are rare and most often located within a particular constellation of factors: false allegations by children are usually opportunistic rather than pre-meditated; such children usually have an adult confederate; mothers with a psychotic illness are frequently involved in allegations that are later shown to be false, and false retractions are also common (Adshead 1994).

Non-malicious allegations

Allegations which *appear* to be malicious but are not are less easily understood. Many carers are working with children who are confused. This may be seen in the child struggling to separate fantasy from reality, or even being confused about where they are or who they are with at times. This sort of mental disarray should be considered as a feature of the aetiology of allegations. There are two aspects I wish to explore.

First, children have intense feelings of all sorts about people who have abused them and from time to time the child may transfer on to the current carer the feelings they have about the abuser. The likelihood of this happening may be increased by the current carer being a safer and more present object than the abuser themselves. Such allegations could be called a *transference allegation* and is a phenomenon written about by Cairns:

> ... there are potential allegations based on the child's experience of some of our best work. We are there to make reliable caring relationships with children. We are not therapists and our training (if we have any!) does not qualify us to make deep therapeutic interventions. Yet all our relationships with hurt children involve an element of transference. When children are able to accept the care we offer, and begin to trust us, they begin to discover safe space in which to explore and work

through the fear, rage and hatred which will otherwise devastate their lives. They are able to use us as safe and trustworthy substitutes for the adults who have caused them harm ... Out there are almost certainly people who from time to time find it difficult to distinguish between the adult who helped them and the adult who hurt them. (Cairns 1993)

Similar ideas are developed in an article by Ironside (1995) who considers in detail the potential for the unconscious dynamics of the abused child's inner world to be enacted in the professional group, in particular where a child has little capacity to communicate about their experiences (the experiences are as yet unthinkable) and consequently these experiences are acted out: 'Working with any child who has suffered multiple abuse places immense strain upon the therapist and the professional network. There is a constant pressure to re-enact with the patient his perverse internal object relationships' (Ironside 1995).

As already made clear in the earlier quote from Hoxter, children who have suffered emotional deprivation often have an impaired or underdeveloped capacity to think. In its place, acting-out is likely.

> In a recent playroom session with myself and J. [S.'s keyworker], S. constructed an elaborate role play with her as 'herself' and ourselves as parents. She described herself as surrounded by a crowd of boys who all fancied her. The reason for their interest was the clothes we had made her wear, against her wishes [e.g. a mini skirt], S. saying 'now look what has happened.' Within this was some awareness that she had been failed by her parents and that they were in some way to blame for her emotional struggles. In her playroom sessions S. expresses herself with sexual power and omnipotence. There was definitely pride within her descriptions of the various situations, as though she was convincing us that the world does agree with her inner world. (Residential carer)

Secondly, children's confusion may show in highly distorted ideas about child–grown-up relationships, and carers recognised that one of the effects of the experience of sexual abuse on the young person was that children expected such relationships to be or become sexual. Carers understandably felt that their actions or words would be misinterpreted by the young person resulting in an allegation being made:

> There are allegations based on mistakes. All care staff struggle with the conceptual gap between the world of the child and the world of the worker. Our best intentions can be misconstrued, while our unconsidered actions can seem positively threatening to a hurt child whose social constructs have been formed in the context of abuse and betrayal. (Cairns 1993)

It is important that these sorts of allegations are not simply taken at face value. They tell us something very important about the young person and have the capacity to inflict damage on the lives of those who are accused.

For foster carers, these anxieties extended to their family and friends. Many of them agonised over whether to warn other people or not about the possibility of being misunderstood and falling down the 'conceptual gap'. Carers tried to strike a balance between respecting the child's privacy and protecting others. In some cases, the fear of being misinterpreted resulted in what could appear to be quite extreme reactions to children. For example, one residential carer told me:

> One of the children who came to us, his foster carers were really worried about this issue [allegations] and they refused to touch him at all. He lived for a year without being touched except for a peck on the cheek at bedtime. The foster mother ... described him as coming home distressed from school one day, and she would not cuddle him even though he was in tears.

Another example given was of a foster family in which an unproven allegation had been made against the foster father and to protect him his wife would lock him in the bedroom every morning when she went to feed her horse!

This is a clear example of the anxiety created by the task resulting in defences developing which impaired task performance. It is worth noting that one of the effects of sexual abuse on young people is to equate sex with power. These sorts of responses to young people can only serve to reinforce such distorted messages.

Although carers had these anxieties, they were also very much aware of how deeply deprived the young people were and recognised that sexual abuse is part of a complex multi-faceted picture of neglect and abuse and should not be viewed in isolation. This was often articulated in carers' reflections about the importance of touch. Carers recognised the importance of close trusting relationships which could involve physical contact so that abused children would have tactile experience which was non-abusive. They also recognised that touch plays an important part in healthy child development. A graphic example of this was given by a female residential carer:

> Nothing had been proven that he had been sexually abused ... he'd come for a cuddle and rub his head against my breasts. When it was time for bed he would lie there arms akimbo and I am sure his legs akimbo as well ... and say 'kiss me, kiss me' and so I would kiss him on top of his head. So many times he would move his head in a way that he would be trying to get my lips ... he was very needy and he really needed an adult to look after him ... but at the same time as

looking after him there was a hidden agenda ... if you could look after him ... you had to let him rub your breasts and kiss you on the lips.

This is especially complex where children have had poor early tactile experience and are 'touch hungry' (see Chapter 15 for fuller discussion).

Anxieties about allegations exerted a powerful influence on carers' relationships with young people. There was an awareness on the part of all carers that the very nature of their work and the 'conceptual gap' between themselves and the young people made them vulnerable to allegations.

Carers needed opportunities to discuss anxieties about allegations and to explore the conceptual gap between them and the young people. It was important that this was coupled with an understanding of the external factors in the child's life as many children's experience of deprivation and abuse is compounded by multiple placements which actively mitigate against the development of the mental machinery needed to process experience.

Understanding the aetiology of allegations cannot be divorced from the nature and complexity of substitute care and the inherent vulnerability of carers.

Implications for practice

The importance of supervision and support

The availability of a close supportive relationship was important especially provided by partners with whom feelings could be addressed frankly. Carers recognised that they needed to be able to be honest about their feelings as there would be less likelihood of acting them out.

For supervision to be effective, it needed to be in an environment in which anxieties and feelings relating to sexuality and sexual abuse could be discussed openly. In one of the few pieces of writing about supporting carers of sexually abused young people, Ixer comments: 'I discovered that it was not techniques staff wanted, it was an opportunity to explore their own feelings towards this subject' (Ixer 1987).

Effective supervision has to take as its basis the concepts of projection and projective identification. Many young people struggle with scarcely thinkable memories and feelings about abuse and, until they become able to think about them, it is likely that it is the grown-ups who, parent-like, will be required to think about what has happened to the young person. Initially this may not be in coherent pieces. It may be a feeling experienced with the young person or a repetition in play. Alvarez expresses this in the following:

… maybe each single aspect of the abuse, the bits and pieces of the experience, particularly if it was chronic, may need to be digested one step at a time. My guess is that this is particularly true for the children who have been abused at a very young age and have also suffered mental and cognitive damage. Such shattered, blunted children may need the pieces of themselves to come together in order to have a sense of I, of YOU, of HE long before they can comprehend: 'He – someone – did that to me, and I felt he shouldn't have.' That statement itself requires an enormous degree of mental development. At the very least it requires the existence of mental equipment with which to think about experience. The treatment may have to start by facilitating the building up of this equipment. (Alvarez 1992)

To begin with 'holding the young person in mind' and becoming involved in caring for them is likely to involve containing and processing these unconscious memories for the young person. Alvarez comments:

I was also thinking of the children who … wish to push into someone else the shock and outrage they were not allowed to express, nor even to feel … the child may need that experience contained by someone else who can stand it better than he can. This may have to go on for some time, months or even years perhaps, until the experience is less overwhelming and less indigestible. (Alvarez 1992)

Moreover it has to be recognised that at times of stress, supervision is most likely to be pushed aside whilst other more 'pressing business' is dealt with. Paradoxically, these are times at which supervision is needed most as carers under pressure may be prone to becoming defensive (see Bullock 1990 above). Most of the carers interviewed had experienced unwanted sexual advances from young people and needed time and support to talk about how they felt.

Recognising vulnerability

It is important to recognise that the vulnerability so powerfully expressed by carers is inherently part of the job of substitute care; ways of dealing with it need to be developed rather than simply becoming defended and hardened against it. Supervision individually and in teams is part of this as is the creative use of consultancy and training.

The role of guidelines and codes of practice

These are crucial in providing carers with a framework in which to make decisions. However, it is important that guidelines and codes of practice are not riven with anxiety, perhaps leading to the prohibition of physical contact, but that guidelines encourage carers to think about the individual child rather than develop rigid institutional practices (see Ward 1990). Research reflected the possibility of anxieties about physical contact between carers and young people as an area in which carers could become so anxious about allegations being made that they avoided contact or else 'hid behind' the approved policy of their organisation. It was in this area that there was real potential for anxiety to impair primary task performance.

Sexual abuse as one part of many experiences of deprivation

It is important to recognise that sexual abuse is one part of a picture of emotional deprivation experienced by the young people, many of whom had poor primary experiences of holding and physical care which left them craving affection and contact (see Ward 1990 for further discussion).

Protecting children from revictimisation or becoming abusers themselves

There are implications for the supervision of young people who have been sexually abused to protect them from re-victimisation and to be wary of the potential for some young people to become abusive.

Whilst it is important not to assume that all children who have been sexually abused will become abusive, it is also important not to be naive. Therapists working with adult offenders have repeatedly documented the early onset of abusive patterns of behaviour. Issues such as this have implications for referrals to units. It has to be considered whether it is possible to work with children who have been abused and those who have been abused and have become perpetrators. What of the child who shows both sorts of behaviour?

Carers' role *vis-à-vis* the family

The implications for carers working with families were that carers needed a clear idea of their role in relation to the family and what was expected of them. Carers also needed support through consultancy and supervision to help them to focus on interactions between the child, themselves and family members.

Conclusions

Research into the feelings of carers involved in caring for sexually abused young people has revealed numerous areas worthy of future investigation and many implications for practice. The feelings aroused in carers are very influential and these feelings need to be addressed openly and honestly. The intimate nature of substitute care, whether in foster families or residential care, means that complex conscious and unconscious forces are at play. Understanding how these affect grown-ups dealing with sexually abused young people is crucial if carers are to develop the skills needed to respond rather than react to the young person. In responding rather than reacting, carers provide a model of a 'parent-like' figure who can think and feel (in relation to action). Such models help to develop the young person's potential to think and feel about their own experiences, a crucial part of coming to terms with abuse. In addition, therapists working with young people who have become perpetrators have documented the lack of empathic feeling perpetrators display towards potential victims, perpetrators' behaviour being governed by feeling and action. Thus the potential of the substitute carer as an empathic model for identification could be pivotal in dealing with young people who already display abusive tendencies.

Carers are often too caught up in anxiety to be able to think and feel their own feelings. They are then not able to spare these resources to the young people in their care. Defences become erected against powerful and primitive anxieties and the capacity of the carer to be open, honest and receptive to the young person will be impaired in such a way that the needs of the young person cannot be met. The area of physical contact between carers and sexually abused young people is one such problem area.

Further research into the needs of carers is vital. Meanwhile, using the current state of our knowledge, we must expand our provision of support, supervision and training for carers. A renewed commitment within agencies to greater sensitivity in the process of management or, in too many, a first-time commitment, would be enormously helpful.

Bibliography

I am indebted to Bobby Molloy for permission to quote examples of practice from his essay on working with sexually abused children.

Adshead, G. (1994) 'Looking for Clues: A Review of the Literature on False Allegations of Sexual Abuse in Childhood', in Sinason, V. (ed.) *Treating Survivors of Satanist Abuse*, Routledge.

Alvarez, A. (1992) *Live Company: Psychoanalytic Psychotherapy with Autistic, Borderline Deprived and Abused Children*, Routledge.

Archard, D. (1993) *Children: Rights and Childhood*, Routledge.

Bentovim, A. (1995) *Trauma Organised Systems: Physical and Sexusal Abuse in Families*, London: Kamac Books.

Bray, M. (1997) *Poppies on the Rubbish Heap*, 2nd edn., Cassell.

Cairns, K. (1993) *The Demands of Residential Child Care*, Exeter.

Finkelhor, D. (1986) *A sourcebook on child sexual abuse*, CA: Sage.

Ghate, D. and Spencer, L. (1995) *The Prevalence of Child Sexual Abuse in Britain*, HMSO.

Hoxter, S. (1990) 'Some Feelings Aroused in Working with Severely Deprived Children', in Boston, M. and Szur, R. (eds) *Psychotherapy with Severely Deprived Children*, Karnac Maresfield Library.

Hunter, M. (1995) *Child Survivors and Perpetrators of Sexual Abuse: Treatment Innovations*, (ed.) Mic Hunter, Sage Publications Ltd.

Ironside, L. (1995) 'Beyond the Boundaries: a patient, a therapist and an allegation of sexual abuse', *Journal of Child Psychotherapy*, 21(2): 183–205.

Ixer, G. (1994) 'Helping Staff who have painful memories', *Social Work Today*, 24 August.

Menzies-Lyth, I. (1988) *Containing Anxiety in Institutions. Selected Essays*, Volume 1, Free Association Books.

Utting, W. et al./Department of Health (1991) *Children in the Public Care. A Review of Residential Child Care*, HMSO.

Ward, A. (1990) 'The role of physical contact in child care', *Children and Society*, 4:4.

Warner, N. et al./Department of Health (1992) *Choosing With Care: The Report of the Committee of Enquiry into the Selection, Development and Management of Staff in Children's Homes*, HMSO.

Wheeler, R. (1993) 'What are the feelings aroused in substitute carers of sexually abused young people and the implications of these feelings for practice', Unpublished MA thesis University of Reading Library, Caldecott College Wingate Library.

Yates, A. (1982) 'Children Eroticised by Incest', *American Journal of Psychiatry*, 139(4): 482–485.

15 'Residential staff should not touch children': can we really look after children in this way?

Adrian Ward

Introduction

> For their development children need the respect and protection of adults who take them seriously, love them and honestly help them to become oriented in the world. (Alice Miller 1984)

Adrian Ward's chapter on touch hardly needs any introduction. The way we look after children is no longer a simple matter of following our instincts. Every aspect of care needs to be thought out in relation to the individual needs of each child or young person. Consistency of practice across a care team is vital and underlines the need for sound management and care plans. Therapeutic work with children and young people is now a very disciplined activity. Supervised practice based on clear plans and consistent leadership have to be the order of the day. Simple things such as touch become strategic and demand creative thinking. Adrian Ward's chapter offers a model of thinking about simple things which are now complex. The model can and should be applied in other areas, for example, provision of food.

15 'Residential staff should not touch children': can we really look after children in this way?

Adrian Ward

There is so much anxiety about physical contact between children and residential staff that it sometimes seems safer and simpler to prohibit such contact altogether. Indeed, in the wake of the many court cases and public inquiries in the UK during the 1980s and 1990s, some employers have attempted to introduce such prohibitions. There are understandable anxieties that *any* physical contact in a residential child care setting might lead either to staff abusing children, or conversely to children 'abusing' staff (in the sense of making false and malicious allegations). But we cannot go on like this: children need physical contact if they are to grow up healthily, and some amount of it is virtually inevitable in everyday life in residential care. The question is: how can it be made safe, appropriate and manageable?

Touch is a powerful medium of communication, and one which certainly needs a lot of thought and reflection if it is to be used appropriately. I will be arguing in this chapter that it is possible to allow and plan for physical contact between children and their carers, within limits and within a framework of open awareness. I will begin by outlining some of the anxieties which arise and by suggesting in general how these might be addressed. I shall then say something about the importance of physical contact in children's development, before making some more detailed suggestions about ways of approaching the problem. It will not be possible here to prescribe answers for every situation, of course, but I do want to show that physical contact can and should be acknowledged as an integral part of professional care for children.

Anxiety about contact

What is it that people are worried about and why? We need first to be clear as to who is worried about what. Employers, children and their families, and the staff themselves all have versions of these anxieties – but each with a different emphasis.

Employers rightly want residential care to be 'safe' for everyone, partly on moral grounds and from concern for the individuals involved, and partly because they do not want to be open to public condemnation or (especially) to be liable for prosecution. They are charged by Government with seeing that legal requirements are enforced and they are increasingly subject to external inspection as well as being required to maintain their own internal inspection and monitoring arrangements. These anxieties are experienced by senior managers and by their political seniors, governing bodies (or proprietors, in the case of commercial organisations), and in some cases it is anxieties such as these which have probably led directly to some of the highly restrictive policies indicated above.

The children themselves (and/or their parents) may have their own anxieties. Even though they may recognise their own needs for cuddles and other forms of appropriate physical care, they may be worried that something inappropriate, improper or even abusive might happen. In particular, the child him- or herself may have experienced physical or sexual abuse before entering the residential setting (whether at home, at school or in foster care) and may have learned to be very fearful of adults. Such experience of abuse may have left the child so highly anxious about physical contact that they may have developed excessive and unhealthy fears – that all adults are seeking ways to exploit and hurt children, and that any contact may quickly lead to abuse. An abused child may also have become prematurely and inappropriately sexualised, so that they appear actually to want and invite sexual contact with adults – and indeed there is some evidence of some adolescents in care being experienced in prostitution. In either case we need to think about the implications for the task of the residential team: should they aim to just become aware of the child's difficulties but no more, or should they become involved in trying to offer the child some form of constructive help with these difficulties?

Even those children who have not previously experienced sexual or physical abuse may be likely to be fearful about such abuse in the residential setting. The public image of such care has suffered disastrously and residential care is frequently portrayed in the media as potentially a place of danger rather than a place of safety. In these circumstances, it is hardly surprising that children and their families are anxious.

In this atmosphere of mistrust and suspicion, the residential staff, too, may become anxious, worried that any physical contact may be liable to be interpreted by the child or by others (at the time or some time afterwards) as a physical or sexual assault. They may feel that their hands are tied. Their practice is constantly monitored and inspected, and their motives are questioned, although they also tend to be among the least-trained and lowest paid members of the caring professions. Meanwhile, they are faced daily by the very real physical needs of the children in their care – we will discuss these in more detail in the next section – and they are therefore challenged continually with real-life dilemmas about how they should act.

The dilemmas of employers tend to be about what sort of rules to set, and anxiety naturally leads them into making tighter and tighter rules because then, as they imagine, they will have less cause to be worried. On the other hand, employers and law-makers do at least have the luxury of having time to sit together and consult with experts and polish the rules away from the urgent demands and awkward behaviour of individual children. The dilemmas of the care staff themselves, however, are far more immediate and concrete: how should I respond to this child who links her arm through mine as we walk down the street? What should I do when this child wants to sit on my lap or play a tickling game? Should I sit and talk to this child at bathtime? How should I judge such situations – should I rely on instinct or on my own common sense? Is there a specific rule I can follow, or should I constantly play as safe as possible?

What can staff do in these situations? The first thing that they need is awareness and understanding. They need to know about the importance of physical contact in children's emotional, psychological and physical development; about the different types of contact and their relative importance at different stages in childhood; about the effects on children of previous difficult experience in physical contact, and about how they can be helped to understand and overcome these effects. They also need to know about the law and about whatever practice guidance has been issued by their employers, and about specific 'custom and practice' in their own unit. They also need the skills to put all this knowledge into operation and the support and back-up to do so. There is therefore a great deal to be aware of, and I will only be able to address some of these issues in the rest of this chapter, which means that staff will also need to know how to find out more about the specifics of their own situation.

The role of physical contact in children's development

The main knowledge which staff need to be able to draw upon in this area of practice is knowledge about the role of physical contact in children's development. There is clear research evidence that good experience of physical contact is essential for the healthy development of children, right from the moment of birth (this research is summarised in an excellent book by Montagu 1977). Such contact arises naturally in infant care, of course, while the baby is being fed and cleaned, but most babies also experience a large amount of tender holding and stroking: what is sometimes known as 'gentling'. As babies develop on into toddlers, young children and eventually into adolescents, their needs for physical contact evolve and change, but these needs certainly do not go away. Research and clinical evidence (for example, Barnard and Brazelton 1990) point clearly to the potentially serious consequences on children of deprivation or gross distortion of physical contact in childhood, as well as to the lasting effects which these may produce in later life (for example, Hopkins 1987).

In one sense what becomes clearer as children grow up is that touch has many distinct functions. In contrast to the care of babies, where all the caring functions often seem to overlap in one overall task (what Winnicott called 'holding'), the care of toddlers, children and adolescents involves touch in several different ways. These can be broadly categorised as follows:

- *Nurturing touch* – in which the contact is a necessary part of the physical care of the child, in the activities of bathing or dressing, for instance.
- *Incidental touch* – where the physical contact is the by-product of another activity, such as teaching the child to read, or working together on a practical task such as cookery or woodwork, or where the contact occurs while playing sport, etc.
- *Communication through touch* – in which physical contact is used to express emotions such as tenderness, sympathy and encouragement. Here touch is very often used to emphasise other channels of communication, especially verbal contact – which suggests likewise that one way in which to lessen the risk of misinterpretation of physical contact is to always accompany it with verbal communication.
- *Controlling touch* – which ranges from holding the child's hand while giving a verbal admonishment through to physical punishment – which is now thankfully outlawed in UK care and state education

settings, but which still appears to have a firm place in much parental care of children. Some child care professionals may be reluctant to admit that they use touch to control the children in their care, although I would suggest that some element of it (if only via the use of physical proximity) is inevitable. This category is clearly an important one for those in the residential setting to consider, since the children with whom they work, especially those who have been physically or sexually abused, may have had very negative experiences of 'control touching' and may consequently experience any touch as controlling touch, and any overtly controlling touch as physical attack.

- *Sexual touch* – Even very young children may experience physical contact as sexual, and this is clearly a principal means by which they begin to learn about sexuality and about their personal boundaries. The literature on the range of children's sexual experience has been described by Bentovim and Vizard (1988), but there is little research on the topic of normal children's differentiation between sexual and non-sexual experience of touching. This is perhaps the area in which research is most urgently needed, so that parents and those working with children may have a clearer understanding of how children interpret their experience. Again, those children who have had abusive experience in this area may be especially likely to find physical contact with their carers problematic but that does not mean that all contact should be outlawed, otherwise how will they ever rediscover the difference between what is safe and appropriate and what is not?

- *Touch in play* – The role of play deserves special mention here, since it is such an important part of a child's life, and since so much of it involves physical contact with others. Some of this contact may overlap into the other categories, but it is nevertheless useful to focus on play as a primary arena for the development of the experience of physical contact. One especially important function of touching in play is that it provides many opportunities for children to rehearse and experiment in giving and receiving the other types of touching listed here. Conversely, my own experience working in child care suggests that it is often those children who have never learned to enjoy playing who turn out also to have difficulties in the area of physical contact.

- *Healing touch* – Here I am thinking of those times when the comfort of safe, warm, human contact is used to offer children relief from physical, emotional or spiritual distress, or to offer a partly-symbolic 'containment' of panic, etc. It seems helpful to distinguish this therapeutic use of touch from its simpler use as a medium or reinforcer of relatively simple communication. There is growing medical and psychiatric evidence of the healing power of some forms of physical contact, as well as about the spiritual dimension of touch (see Pratt and Mason 1981). This may be a more specialised use of touch, although it may also be just as basic and fundamental as the others listed here – the problem for residential carers will be one of knowing how and when to use such an approach.

These various categories of physical contact are intended to help practitioners think more clearly, not only about the different ways in which children need and experience physical contact, but also about what sort of contact (and when) can be appropriately offered by their residential carers. A first aim in practice might be to work as a team collecting together whatever evidence is available about each child's previous experience of physical contact, and then to observe daily life in the unit to identify their current patterns and needs. Once this information has been gathered, it may then be possible to make informed judgements about what a particular individual or group's needs may be. In the next section I shall outline a few examples of how this can be done.

Using touch in residential care practice

Having acknowledged the need for careful assessment and planning in the use of physical contact, I now want to offer a few examples of the issues as they arise in practice. These examples have all been adapted from actual situations which arose in practice settings, though all names and identifying details have of course been changed.

Example 1

R. was seven years old, and had been living in a children's home for several months following the sudden breakdown of his fostering placement. He appeared quite wild in his behaviour, and seemed beyond adult control for much of the time. Staff found him very difficult to manage, as he seemed completely unamenable to most forms of adult influence. However, there were times when he could sit quietly and look through a large pile of comics which he kept under his bed. R. was too troubled to manage in mainstream schooling, but he had 'home tuition' in the children's home. His teacher gradually realised that R. sometimes responded positively and calmly to very small amounts of physical contact, such as a hand on his shoulder for a moment when he was trying to concentrate on his work. From what could be gathered about R.'s earlier history at home in an extremely chaotic family environment, it appeared that he had had very little experience of positive physical contact. He certainly had the forlorn and dishevelled look of a child who had never felt physically cared for; although he had probably received some harsh physical punishment, he did not appear to have been sexually abused.

The staff team and the teacher reflected together on this pattern, and decided to try increasing the amount of 'incidental touching' offered to R. They were aware of the risk of moving too fast, and made a very cautious plan for one or two of the residential staff to simply make an effort to occasionally put a hand briefly on his shoulder or arm when talking with him. The response was instant and strong – R. warmed to the contact and appeared to visibly relax when offered even the slightest physical contact. The temptation was to increase the contact further, but the team retained their caution, and probably rightly so. Touch is an extremely powerful medium, and the team felt that they still did not know enough about R. Over the ensuing months, the amount of planned physical contact was gradually increased, especially within the context of his relationship with his keyworker, who began to talk with him about his feelings in relation to touching and being touched. He was also able to start enjoying games with other children which involved some contact. By the time R. was ready to move on into a new foster home, he was beginning to relate with people much more warmly, and it was hoped that he would be able to transfer this ability into his life with his new foster parents. The use of physical contact did appear to have made a contribution to this change in R., although it was of course only one element among many others.

In this first example, the planned work with the child will be seen to have been based on careful observation of his behaviour and assessment of his needs, followed by a period of discussion in the staff team. The outcome of this process was a relatively simple but effective plan, based on increasing the amount of 'incidental touching', and the boy's own increased use of 'touch in play'. In the second example, a similar process led to a very different plan, because the needs of the young person were seen as being so different.

Example 2

E. was 13 years old and had recently been admitted to a short-stay unit for adolescents in crisis. She had run away from home (where it was suspected that she had been sexually abused by her step-father and older half-brothers) and she was seen as being at considerable 'moral risk'. Her behaviour and language were highly sexualised, and she frequently made sexually provocative approaches to both male and female staff, stroking their hair and sidling up close to them after which she would suddenly accuse them of trying to indecently assault her. Staff became extremely anxious about their contact with E. and wanted to withdraw from contact with her altogether. A meeting was held between the staff and the social worker to discuss these anxieties, after which they also met with E. herself.

It was agreed that, for a period of a few days, staff would have no physical contact with E. They also took great care to record carefully any such contact which she attempted.

Nobody was happy with this arrangement, and it soon became clear that E. desperately needed physical contact, but also needed it to feel as safe as possible. In E.'s case, this meant arranging that as much as possible of her care should be provided by female staff, and that as far as possible physical contact should only happen when there were other staff and young people present. It was difficult to operate this arrangement, and it meant that 'care' felt rather artificial and un-spontaneous at times, but at least the anxiety on all sides began to subside, and people could feel more relaxed in E.'s company – and she in theirs. After a few weeks E. was found a place in a short-stay foster home, where a similar set of arrangements was then made, drawing on the experience in the residential unit.

The work with 'E.' took place in a short-stay unit for adolescents in crisis, in which it was not appropriate to undertake planned work with a longer perspective, and indeed it was best to just 'contain' the situation – and the anxiety – by agreeing on some ground rules. In our final example, which is set in a small therapeutic unit for children with emotional difficulties, it was possible to develop a whole-unit approach to the issue of ground rules for physical contact.

Example 3

In one unit for young adolescents the whole subject of physical contact became increasingly fraught, following an incident in which a twelve-year-old girl accused a ten-year-old boy of touching her inappropriately. There was a heated argument with accusations flying and tempers raised. The matter was investigated, and no assault was found to have taken place.

In the wake of this incident, the staff team felt that what was needed was a clear set of ground rules for all – and rules which could be owned and agreed to by the whole group rather than simply imposed on the young people by the staff. In this unit a system of regular weekly house meetings (attended by staff and young people alike) had been in operation for some time, and it was in this forum that the subject was debated. Over several weeks the subject was argued out including, of course, many arguments between individuals and subgroups outside the meetings themselves. At the end of this time, the whole group was able to agree on some basic rules of behaviour between each other, based on respect and need rather than on anxiety and reaction. These rules were agreed to by staff and young people alike, and they covered staff behaviour as well as children's behaviour towards each other. The rules were printed up on a large sheet of paper and pinned on the kitchen wall. The arguments did not stop; indeed for some time they increased as the young people became more and more aware of their physical needs and boundaries. As is the way with adolescents, some of the views expressed were extreme and needed much further reflection before they could be written down in a usable form.

In this third example, a well-established team was able to work together with the group of young people to agree upon a way of living together.

It has only been possible here to select a small number of examples to show how staff teams responded to various aspects of young people's needs for physical care. Beyond these specific examples there are many other aspects of physical care which can also evoke strong feelings in all parties, but which there will not be scope to explore in detail here. Among these will be feelings to do with issues of power and prejudice, and particularly in terms of gender, sexuality and sexual orientation. For example, what is acceptable in terms of the contact which male and female staff may have with boys and with girls respectively? Are women assumed to be 'safer' than men, and why? How acceptable is it for young people to experiment with gay and lesbian sexual identities by exploring physical contact with each other?

Meanwhile, another set of strong feelings will attach to the issue of race and ethnicity. It is well known that different national groupings evolve quite different assumptions about what sort of physical contact is acceptable and normal – think of the different approach to touch, just within 'white' Europe, between the typically reserved English and the highly expressive Italians. Religious beliefs may also contribute to these differences, and the British system of residential care contains such great diversity that, for example, a Rastafarian man may be employed to care for a Muslim young woman. Many of the white British people employed in residential care may themselves have grown up with little knowledge or understanding of the cultural norms in the different groupings, so there is clearly a great need for training in this field, and for knowledge which goes beyond stereotypes and other assumptions.

Conclusion: finding a way of working

I have tried to suggest ways of thinking about the use of physical contact in residential care, although I am well aware that putting such ideas into practice is not always simple. Residential care must involve close cooperative teamwork amongst a group of staff who respect, support and understand each other or it will fail (see Ward 1993 and Chapter 19). If children are to experience safe and appropriate physical contact, they will need to be in the care of a team of people who can talk to each other openly about this aspect of their work, including about their fears and anxieties, and who can offer each other support as well as challenge wherever appropriate. Such high-quality teamwork is not at all easy to achieve, and it depends in part upon clear and communicative leadership, decent working conditions, opportunities for staff training and development, and regular ongoing supervision and team meetings. Without all of this, it will be extremely difficult for people to provide good physical care.

This is why, if I am asked to work with a staff team on the issue of physical contact, I will usually start by inviting them to simply talk with each other about the issue in as open a way as they can manage, so that they can start to understand each other's assumptions and feelings about the whole issue. Physical contact, as we have seen, is a very personal business, and we all come to it with our own histories and assumptions. In a team we need to be able to talk with each other about these personal aspects if we are to be able to incorporate them into our professional work, and especially if we are to find a compromise between the different attitudes and experience we bring. I would also argue that, as in the third example above, the staff team as a whole should aim to meet regularly with the group of young people as a whole to talk about those aspects of living and working together which matter most, which will include the use of physical contact. This can be achieved – though again not without clear leadership and considerable investment in teamwork – in the form of a regular children's meeting or community meeting.

It will be seen that I have written in terms of general advice and the need for knowledge and understanding, rather than in terms of absolute rules about what should or should not be done. This is deliberate, as this is an area in which it is very difficult to make rules. In fact, despite the proliferation of rules and official guidance which flowed from the introduction in England and Wales of the Children Act 1989, there remains very little formal advice about the use of physical contact. In one sense this is helpful, just because it is an area which is so difficult to regulate but in another sense it is problematic, in that it leaves the rules and guidance to be drawn up by employers, managers and inspectors, with the inevitable results of enormous differences from one place to another.

It is in this context, then that I would offer the following broad comments summarising my conclusions about the use of physical contact:

1. Touch is a powerful medium, to which people attach very strong feelings. Those caring for children need to consider what these feelings may be for themselves, both individually and as a team, and they need to find out what the equivalent feelings of each of the children may be – partly by asking them and talking with them, and partly by observing their behaviour and assessing their needs. Children have the right to say 'No' to touch.

2. Staff should be aware of the risk of touch being misinterpreted, but this should not inhibit them from having safe and appropriate physical contact with the young people in their care. In order to lessen the risk of misunderstandings, it is often best to accompany such contact with verbal communication, and to ensure that the contact happens at a place and time where at least one other person is present. Staff also need their own support systems, in which they can talk about their feelings and anxieties.
3. Specific rules about aspects of contact (whether in terms of 'nurturing touch', 'incidental touch' or 'controlling touch') can often be helpfully discussed and negotiated with the young people in each unit, although ultimately the operation of such rules will remain the responsibility of the team of carers, under the guidance of the employers and within the framework of the law.

Physical contact, then, does not have to be so fraught with anxiety and uncertainty. It is just another medium of communication – albeit a powerful one – and many of the difficulties which people experience in this area can be managed positively and productively. The answer to anxiety is understanding and awareness. Some of this can be provided by factual knowledge, some can be provided by the security of practice guidance which fits well with the demands of practice, but some will always have to be provided in practice by frequent and regular opportunities for planning, reflection and review.

References

Barnard, K.E. and Brazelton, T.B. (eds) (1990) *Touch: The Foundation of Experience*, Madison, Connecticut: International Universities Press.

Bentovim, A. and Vizard, E. (1988) 'Sexual Abuse, Sexuality And Childhood', in Bentovim, A., Elton, E., Hildebrand, J., and Tranter, M. (eds) *Child Sexual Abuse within the Family Assessment and Treatment*, London: Wright.

Hopkins, J. (1987) 'Failure of the holding relationship: some effects of physical rejection in the child's attachment and in his inner experience', *Journal of Psychotherapy*, 13(1): 5–17.

Miller, A. (1984) *Thou Shalt Not Be Aware: Society's Betrayal of the Child*, London: Pluto.

Montagu, A. (1977) *Touching: The Human Significance Of The Skin*, New York: Harper & Row.

Pratt, J.W. and Mason, A. (1981) *The Caring Touch*, London: HM&M.

Ward, A. (1993) *Working In Group Care. Social Work In Residential And Day Care Settings*, Birmingham: Venture Press.

16 Adolescence and the struggle to feel real

Judith Woodhead

Adolescents can be seen to be struggling to start again as if they had nothing they could take from anyone ... Young people can be seen searching for a form of identification which does not let them down in their struggle, the struggle to feel real, the struggle to establish a personal identity, not to fit into an assigned role, but to go through whatever has to be gone through. They do not know what they are, and they are waiting because everything is in abeyance, they feel unreal and this leads them to do certain things which feel real to them, and which are only too real in the sense that society is affected. (Winnicott 1961)

16 Adolescence and the struggle to feel real

Judith Woodhead, with thanks to Philip Maggs for case material and shared thoughts

Introduction

Work with adolescents is a very complex, multi-faceted task which arouses great anxiety. Carers are faced daily, often nightly, with the stark reality of primitive expressions of sexuality and aggression. They have the demanding task of providing a milieu which offers supportive containment for rapidly changing identity. Adolescent processes render the task particularly challenging. In addition, twentieth-century adolescents have little role or recognition. The negative view of them as neither children nor adults deprives them of a status of their own: 'But while adolescence is a true in-between period it is not one of empty waiting. All too often it is a period during which all too much is happening, more so than in the more stable developmental stages' (Bettelheim 1950). To be adolescent and disadvantaged brings little social and economic hope or aim. To be black can be an additional complicating factor. The odds are stacked against effective therapeutic work facilitating healthy development. In all forms of care work, it is important to recognise and counter this pessimism. Adolescence needs to be viewed as a clearly defined transitional state with its own specific developmental path.

Activity 1

Think about the word 'adolescence'. Think very freely and write down every word that comes to mind that seems to be associated in your mind with 'adolescence'. Keep these in mind as you read the rest of the chapter.

- Think back to your own adolescence and recall experiences and feelings that stand out for you as you look back.
- Remember sexual thoughts, feelings and experiences.
- Reflect on times when you felt depressed, or separate, or alone, or unhappy, sad, excited, isolated, one of the crowd/outside of the crowd and the ways you found yourself dealing with those feelings.
- What kinds of secrets did you have?
- Do you feel now that you could have been helped in some way?

A young person easily evokes in us a stereotyped response – a feeling that we know the kind of young person they are, and the difficulty of the problems they present for themselves and society. Being black may reinforce this image we hold so that their adolescent identity is compounded by subtle racism.

Even the word 'adolescence' can have a stereotyped sound. Like their teachers we are likely to hope that they will go elsewhere and not be people we have to work with. But there are very many young people like M. and they require very skilful work that seeks to discern beneath the behaviours the feelings that are part of M.'s emotional and mental functioning.

The sense of 'I am'

M., aged 16, is an adolescent in trouble. He is referred to a psychologist for assessment for court as he has been involved in the robbery of a teenage boy. The assessment reveals that M. lived with his grandmother in the Caribbean until he was 13 when she became sick and could no longer look after him. Hence he came to England to live with his mother from whom he had separated at the age of six months. His mother was living in a very deprived inner-city area with his stepfather, who left the family soon after M. arrived.

In the Caribbean M. lived in a rural village, and his mother reported that he attended school regularly and there was no concern about a lack of ability. M. also said that he went to school without difficulty, but was often chastised for being late. He revealed that he had been beaten up badly by a relative.

On arrival in Britain, M. was met by his family, and encountered immediate antagonism in his stepfather. He was placed in a local secondary school but failed to settle. He found the work too difficult, could not understand what he should do, and became excluded on account of incidents of aggression. He was placed in a local tuition centre after being out of school for several months. He associated with older unemployed males and was soon drawn into delinquent activities.

The psychology assessment reveals that M.'s cognitive functioning is at a moderate learning difficulties level. He is illiterate, with little sense of number. As the assessment progresses, the psychologist becomes aware that M. feels extremely vulnerable, needy, immature, and is emotionally and educationally deprived. During the assessment he increasingly reveals his dependency needs.

M. is functioning at the level of a ten-year-old, while presenting as a cool, tough, teenager who needs to please older boys. His court appearance results in him being placed on a supervision order. He immediately becomes involved with two 19-year-old males in what is classified as armed robbery.

It is not at all difficult to make the connection between this boy's delinquent acts and his emotional history, his unmourned separations and losses, and the cultural disruption he has suffered: 'Adolescent troubles are relationship troubles' (Varma 1997). M.'s presentation to adults elicits the worst responses, especially where attempts have been made to provide him with appropriate education. Further feelings of humiliation, rejection and violence tend to be triggered. M.'s future is bleak because of the lack of appropriate compensatory emotional and educational and social resources, combined with his lack of marketable skills. He is likely to spend much of his life in the penal system.

Struggles in adolescence are struggles with a changing sense of self, with establishing new identity. To have a sense of 'I am', particularly in contemporary life, may mean expressing rebelliousness through violence, crime, sex and drugs, sufficient to dice with death. What is required is on the one hand understanding but Winnicott goes on to suggest the need also for 'confrontation ... Confrontation belongs to containment that is non-retaliatory, without vindictiveness, but having its own strength' (Winnicott 1961).

Reworking old issues

Psychodynamic theory suggests that adolescence is a time in which conflicts and anxieties that were experienced as a young child, at the end of the second year of life, can be worked through in a new way. He or she becomes preoccupied with the drives, impulses, wishes and fantasies from early life. In this sense adolescence is seen as a second chance.

For adolescents in the care system, this is especially important as it is likely they have experienced many past emotional difficulties. Past emotional traumas may surface during the physical and psychological upheaval of adolescence, so it is crucial that there is a climate in which these can be expressed, understood, and thus reworked. It is also a time for assessing what kind of psychological/emotional help and support may be needed, so that mental illness, masked by difficult behaviour, does not go undetected. It is perhaps too easy to dismiss adolescent behaviours as just being awkward, delinquent, anti-social or shy. Beneath these external symptoms there may be an emotional suffering for which help could be identified and offered. Jealousy, scapegoating, externally directed aggression or self-directed aggression in the form of self-harm and suicidal feelings, rebelliousness, delinquency, depression and sexual concerns can all be acute in adolescence.

Activity 2

Think of some work you do with a young person:

- Imagine you have to give a thumbnail sketch of him/her to another person. What would you include?
- What behaviours/situations do you find the most difficult?
- Identify what aspect it is about the young person and their way of responding/behaviour that you find challenging.
- Think about all their present relationships, and feelings evoked.
- Identify their feelings that may accompany difficult behaviour. Are there underlying messages?

Complex feelings

Adolescents in care are likely to have suffered serious impingements on their early psychological development and their adolescent anxieties and conflicts are likely to be much the greater. Many such children have been physically, sexually and emotionally abused and/or have experienced neglect, deprivation and trauma. Many are thus likely to have experienced in their lives overwhelming anxieties, associated with their bodies and bodily feelings. They may have feelings of:

- Deprivation/abandonment.
- Fears of annihilation, of violence, of being killed.
- Fears of their own retaliatory aggression and capacity to kill.
- Seduction, traumatic sexualisation, bewildering excitement/terror, invasion of boundaries.
- Intolerable betrayal, being let down, deceived, tricked, feeling there is no place of safety and no protecting adult, outrageous intrusion, enforced intimacy, being put down, stolen from.
- Incomprehension, confusion without regulation.
- Arousal, lack of control.
- Disapproval, stigmatisation, humiliation, exploitation, secrecy, a sense of disorder, of catastrophe, of family disintegration.
- Intolerable isolating guilt.
- Being very powerful yet very dependent.

Feelings, too unbearable to keep in conscious mind, become relegated to inner darkness and silence. But their effects are played out through the mechanism of projection everyday in relationships and in behaviour, in how the young people perceive their world. The task of the carer is not to fall into the roles young people wish to put them into. There is such a propensity to try and elicit from adults the same responses that they experienced from adults in their personal past. Even if this means attempting to get adults in the present to be abusive towards them.

One of the likely outcomes of having been subjected to abuse is the tendency to identify with the aggressor and enact aggression experienced in relationships with others. Unless this process can be therapeutically addressed, such identification and acting-out is likely during adolescence to be strong – often with devastating consequences for carer and young person alike. Abused adolescents may use many subtle means to get carers to be in some way abusive towards them, re-establishing a perverse pattern of relationship. Carers are in any case easily open to accusations and allegations of misconduct. Their anxiety about this needs to be addressed through expert supervision. Awareness of the dynamics in relationships is crucial so that the way adolescents may attempt to manipulate carers to play roles with which they are familiar. Channels of communication between staff are essential. Young people may well try to split the staff team, or divide a male and female staff member as they experienced family divisions (see Chapter 17).

Bodily feelings

Adolescent young people feel very anxious about their rapidly changing bodies, or repress the feeling if it is too strong. They feel out of control of profound physiological changes. A body that seems to have a new and different life of its own feels embarrassing and dangerous. Accompanying thoughts, fantasies and dreams preoccupy and emotionally overwhelm. To remain unaffected by such changes would suggest considerable blocking-off of feelings, denial of deep changes and associated anxieties. Anxiety can be so great that bodily feelings are split off altogether, a kind of anaesthesia. Adults can reinforce this splitting by ignoring what is happening before their eyes as a defence against their own feelings. It is very important for the young people that the changes going on within them and visible from the outside can be simply recognised by those who are caring for them. It is an especially valuable time to try and repair distorted bodily perceptions.

Activity 3

- Think particularly about your own experience of your own body changing during adolescence.
- Give yourself time to recall memories and impressions surrounding sexual feelings.
- Remember the feelings you had in a first sexual experience.
- Reflect on your feelings about the physical and sexual development of young people you work with.
- Be aware of the views you hold on heterosexuality and homosexuality.

Confusion about sexual facts is frequent and very simple explicit information is required to counteract the muddled messages. This needs to be part of normal life, part of care plans, communicated throughout staff teams, rather than put out to special sessions alone.

Clear guidance on what is appropriate and not appropriate behaviour needs to be given, through very simple statements that name what is happening or needs to happen. Both unabused and abused children may be confused about their different bodily orifices – their mental representation of their different bodily parts being all mixed up. What is inside and what is outside may not feel clearly demarcated. There may be no sense of human beings being separate people. Thus relationships with carers need to be on a clear basis in which negotiated boundaries are consistently, firmly, yet flexibly, set and implemented. The keeping of well-formulated boundaries needs to be communicated and enacted within the whole staff team. Adolescents need to be helped through a clearly defined external structure of space, time and relationship to feel the difference between themselves and others.

The task of the adult is to balance helping the adolescent know better their changing bodily feelings, help them towards socially acceptable expression, yet at the same time not give the message that their bodies are disgusting or shameful. It is extremely tricky work, too close for comfort to the usual taboo boundaries, and hidden conflicts and confusions of the carer.

Other related conflicts arise. Can a former child, now adolescent, still be hugged, sat on a knee, tucked up in bed at night? And can these things be done by either sex? If not, then there is a message to the adolescent that bodily changes are dangerous. Physical touch is another area that arouses anxiety as described in Chapter 15. Adolescents who have suffered early deprivation of parental care and/or sexual abuse may have difficulties with physical contact. The usual boundaries may not exist for them. They may cringe from being touched, or inappropriately touch others. How to provide for safe contained physical contact becomes all the more important.

Activity 4

- Think of children with whom you work/have worked and reflect on your feelings about any physical contact that you have with them.
- Are these feelings you can take to supervision? It not, why not?
- Think in particular about any feelings of conflict you have about in relation to this. Think also of any change in contact between yourself and a child *before* and *during* and *after* puberty.

Homosexual feelings

An adolescent does 'not yet know whether he or she will be homosexual, heterosexual, or simply narcissistic' (Winnicott 1965). Homosexual feelings in adolescence may bring feelings of embarrassment, shame, guilt and confusion. Strong feelings towards carers of the same sex are likely to cause more confusion and conflict than feelings towards those of the opposite sex. Confusion is rife, both for the young person and the carer, especially as such feelings may be very strong. Carers may be uncomfortable with same gender intimacy. They may themselves, if homosexual, feel unaccepted within their workplace and experience conflict about whether to keep their sexuality secret.

How to allow young people to express such feelings in words rather than act them out is difficult and requires enormous sensitivity. Awareness in the adult of what is occurring in the young person is a first stage, so that the adult can respond in a sensitive way rather than react in a careless, punitive way.

Shame and disgust about sexuality, the more so in adolescence, may be accompanied by deep anxiety about being humiliated. Shaming as a form of control must never be used. To shame a person whether alone or in front of others is very damaging to young people who already feel shamed enough. Yet some young people may try to elicit this. To counteract the dynamic is difficult.

Disability

Young people in care who have a disability have the additional trauma of their bodily dysfunction. They are likely to have had their body examined, operated on (invaded) and discussed frequently, and have many complex feelings about their handicap – feelings which may have been split off because they are too painful to have, and too hard for those who care for them to bear. Lack of communication skills does not mean they have fewer feelings. Lack of speech cannot be equated with lack of feeling and understanding. Too often adults assume that disabled young people and adults do not have the same sexual feelings as others. This misunderstanding has to be understood as adults defending themselves against feelings of pain, confusion and embarrassment. Adolescent young people with any kind of disability require that their feelings are fully understood and appreciated. They too need simple clear naming of what is happening to their pubescent bodies, and appropriate ways of behaving. They also require the experience of safe physical contact with others.

Practical tasks relating to bodily care need a sensitive approach. Workers need to know that the anxieties evoked in them by the personal care of the young people in their care are normal. This is especially so when working with sexually explicit adolescents, where bathroom routines are difficult. It is also an area of anxiety when working with adolescents who have a disability and who need much greater help with intimate tasks. How their bodies are approached is so important, as much the attitude and mood of the carer as the actual personal tasks carried out. A fourteen-year-old learning disabled young man who is sexually aroused while being cleaned during his so-called 'nappy' change, may disturb and embarrass. Emotionally damaged young women often find menstruation difficult to practically cope with, and again need sensitive help.

Feelings aroused in both male and female care workers by adolescent girls who will not use, or misuse, sanitary protection can be acutely discomforting and evoke a punitive response. Normal taboos are being violated resulting in anxiety and the wish to hide what is being explicitly revealed. Again the worker needs to find the creativity to be able to respond to the young person in a way that is neither punishing nor humiliating. The young person needs responses that show that their own confusion and difficulty with changing bodily processes are recognised, are normal, understandable, and can be simply named and explained. This makes it sound easy, but it is far from it. It touches on the most primitive, intimate personal experiences of carers.

Attachment and separation

Conflict exists in adolescence between the wish to be adult, and the wish to remain a child, like Peter Pan. This is reflected in the care process in the conflict between helping adolescents experience dependent vulnerable feelings and helping them develop age-appropriate independence. The care process itself can infantilise adolescents, or on the other hand allow too much freedom.

A central task for the adolescent is to separate out from parental figures and establish independent identity. This means the emergence of real psychological and sexual separation. Childhood wishes to have their parents have to be given up. Childhood ultimately, often painfully, has to be left behind. For those with unsatisfactory, bonding and attachment processes, for those who were sexually abused when little, this separation process is extremely problematic. Panic, destructiveness and breakdown are a likely response to pubertal inner pressures. Associated feelings, unless identified and sensitively and firmly addressed by understanding adults may predominate and overwhelm, leading to a future spent in the penal or mental health system.

Activity 5

- Do an overview of all you know about the young person's life experience.
- Now look at it again and focus on what you know of his/her earliest life history. Try and piece together a story, as you perceive, it of his/her early experience.
- What kind of a baby was s/he, and what was the nature of any attachments?
- Describe the way s/he experiences and deals with current separations.
- Do there seem to be any connections between past experience and current feelings/behaviours?

Early damaging experience may leave a longing for the ideal infancy that was wished for and not had. This wish has to be given up for development to proceed securely. This requires a grieving process. The leaving behind of childhood *per se* also requires mourning, with all the processes of anger and denial until sufficient acceptance can be gained for the developmental line to continue. We can help adolescents by being accepting and naming different feelings – providing an atmosphere of allowance for tears and anger, sorrow and depression. This is contrary to the tendency to want to make things better, to protect the young person from feeling pain, and not provide the safety for rawest emotions to emerge and be positively worked with. It is natural to want to make things better and reduce pain, but it is only through allowing feelings to be expressed and worked through that pain can be slowly transformed.

Separation processes in infancy are linked with the development of the capacity to symbolise. When separation processes have been traumatic, then the young person's ability to form and use symbols is likely to be damaged. The adult task is to be sensitive to the current attachment/separation processes to try and work with repairing this difficulty. In Chapter 2 Christine Bradley explores symbolic communication further. The task requires that provision is made for adolescent young people to play at a much earlier level, and play/art/craft materials should be available, including sand and also water. With imagination these need not seem babyish. And, if there are younger children around, the adolescent may have an excuse to play. Adolescents should never be humiliated for playing at an early developmental level; it may be just the recapitulation they need for inner processes to develop. Seeing adults play may help.

Being in the care system itself brings its own additional trauma. Such may be the pressure on adults to provide security and safety that adolescents may find themselves colonised, part of an institutionalised system which does not encourage the development of individual identity. This means that close attention must be given in all provisions for adolescents; being in care should not only be a trauma but be an opportunity for repair of damaged early developmental processes.

Creativity

Adolescents require adults who will proactively rather than reactively engage with them in the tasks of day-to-day living, with maximum participation in planning and decision making. This means that adults have to develop a capacity to engage in negotiation as a model for interaction, for relationships. Conscious demonstrated sharing of tasks in a non-gender-stereotypic way is also crucial.

All kinds of domestic and creative activities and relationships are required for the young person as the substance through which to develop individual identity. They need adults who themselves have some sense of personal fulfilment reflected in enthusiasms, interests and hobbies. In other words, they need to find something creative and hopeful with which to identify in adults. They can then sense that the adult has an inner world, expressed in interests and feelings, and separate from their own. And there needs to be maximum provision for physical, musical, social and artistic activities, and psychotherapy where appropriate. Engagement is the basis of relationship, and comes from heightened consciousness – to engage really fully with others we have to be conscious.

Activity 6

- Think of a young person and reflect on him/her in depth. Identify where it could be more possible for that person to feel able to take more of a role in responsibility. Perhaps s/he may have some kind of interest or capacity that is not being drawn upon or used. It may also be that the experience of a residential placement is not allowing enough for personal expression.
- In what areas of your work do you feel really able to express your own interests and draw on your own enthusiasms? Could changes be made that would enable you to use and develop more of your capacities?

Feelings evoked in carers

Fundamental to that work is sensitive understanding of the feelings we as adults have and try not to have in working with adolescents. Why is work with adolescents so difficult and often painful, yet also sometimes enjoyable and rewarding? We believe this is because of the inner processes within adult carers concerning our own experiences of adolescence. So we need to be very aware of our own personal adolescent feelings.

All these feelings from our own individual experience of growing through adolescence are reawakened when we work closely with adolescents. They are primitive feelings, and it may be we are drawn into such work because we have an unconscious need to go on working with those feelings. One aspect of care work is that we rework our own feelings through working with the adolescent and their feelings – a kind of indirect personal work. This is not bad – it happens all the time as a very human process. What is important is that we become aware of this process, so that we can separate out our own inner experience from that of the adolescent. Otherwise confusion can occur, and we may see the adolescent through our own lens rather than more directly as they seem to be. If the dynamic remains, unconscious muddle can result, with the carer and the young person caught up in a mesh of mutual projections. An example of this is when an adult merges and colludes with a young person. This can be detected when there is a feeling in both of something shared, secret, and exciting.

Young people need adults who are brave enough to become aware and own that the adolescent problems they are working with are their own problems repeated, externalised in the young people. If they cannot do this then the adult denial is likely to promote denial of difficulty in adolescents, leading to acting out rather than to psychological growth. There is a difficult delicate balance between giving adolescents emotional closeness and protecting both carers and young people from the intensity of their feelings. Carers need to be aware of the strength of their own ambivalent and negative feelings evoked in response to individual young people, and to become conscious of the link between their own current feeling responses to the young people and their own feelings and attitudes acquired during early childhood.

The difficulty of all this work is that just as adolescents themselves feel to be in a state of confusing change, so too feel all those who work with them. Carers and young people alike struggle with their volatile emotional and physical feelings. This volatility also appears in the dramatic swings between the adolescent's wish to be treated as a child, to be dependent, and the wish to be treated as an adult, as independent; between dependence and defiance.

All of these factors form a backcloth of painful awareness which carers may wish to block out just as the young people have attempted to do. We wish to argue that it is this very pain which has to be consciously worked with within the activities of everyday activity. We believe that this cannot be relegated to the work of a psychologist or psychotherapist which may be yet another defence against recognising and working with emotional difficulty. While such work may be invaluable there are few resources for it, and the emotional work must be central in all aspects of work with adolescents.

The sheer difficulty of working with these changing states means that we attempt often to duck out of the responsibility of really working with them. Moving a young person on through the care system is one often damaging solution. A soft sentimental do-what-you like is another defence against the difficulty of the work, tantamount to neglect. Somehow space has to be created in which adolescents in care can find real support in their development, can experience real active work and genuine concern. They need to experience carers who are alive to their own and the young peoples' inner worlds. This is very challenging precisely because it is so painful for all those working with them. The temptation to take refuge in administrative or domestic tasks is understandably very strong. The wish to be busy or to hide in the office is great. Even studying the rota can be better than relating directly with difficult young persons.

Activity 7

- What ways (defences) do you use to avoid dealing with painful issues in your work?
- What defences seem to be built into your work-place to protect carers from raw feelings?

Warning signs

It is difficult to know what is within a normal acceptable range of adolescent behaviour and what indicates emotional illness for which further professional help should be sought. The beginnings of mental illness can be overlooked, so that help is not offered. Questions need to be asked. Is the adolescent:

- Too dependent on adults, too conforming to what they will think. In other words has s/he got problems with separation and the development of independent identity?

- Wishing to remain a child, indulging in child-like behaviours to a marked degree, unable to take up adult challenges?
- Overly withdrawn and avoidant, unable to enjoy being with contemporaries, too often alone?
- Depressed and lethargic, wishing to remain in bed too much?
- Overly shy, anxious or suspicious – too dominated by paranoid feelings about how others will view them, seeing things as very black or white?
- Often tearful, and seeking to be alone, perhaps overwhelmed with anxious thoughts?
- Unable to express feelings and react in an appropriate manner to experiences/events?
- Very pessimistic, fearful, hopeless about the future?
- Experiencing dramatic mood swings?
- Experiencing difficulties about eating and a preoccupation with body image?

If there are affirmative answers to one or more of these warning signs then professional help should be sought to determine the level of danger and necessary intervention.

Conclusion

We have shown the complexity of work with adolescent young people. Specific skills are required which points to the necessity of effective regular supervision and consultancy. Without this, adult workers cannot be expected to process very complex feelings. Yet in many establishments supervision often has to be missed to 'give way' to other so-called more important activities.

Activity 8

- Do you feel your own training has prepared you for working with adolescents? Which area do you feel you struggle with in your work?
- Do you get supervision that is skilled and is rarely cancelled?
- Is there some kind of extra help or training you feel you need, and can you identify a way of finding something to give you additional resources/support?
- You may require further training to help understand dynamics of mental illness and adolescent breakdown.

Conflicts are many, and rewards may feel to be few. Every at-risk adolescent is likely to remain at risk throughout life. It is thus important that, as they grow into adulthood, and leave adolescent provision, they are put in touch with other forms of help should they ever wish to use it, and that there are professionals in adult work who know of the kind of difficulties which may subsequently be experienced. We saw at the beginning how M. is unlikely to gain the kind of help he may need. All who work with adolescents have a responsibility to work with them consciously, directly, and to the full, to put them in touch with further support as they move on, and to try and help them avoid the only future which seems open to M.

We end with Winnicott's words that emphasise the importance of the experience of adolescence:

> Immaturity is a precious part of the adolescent scene. In this is contained the most exciting features of creative thought, new and fresh feeling, ideas for new living. Society needs to be shaken by the aspirations of those who are not responsible. If the adults abdicate, the adolescent becomes prematurely, and by false process, adult. The point about adolescence is its immaturity and the fact of not being responsible. This, its most sacred element, lasts only a few years, and it is a property that must be lost to each individual as maturity is reached. (Winnicott 1961)

References

Bettelheim, B. (1950) *Love is Not Enough*, The Free Press/Macmillan.
Varma, V. (1997) *Violence in Children and Adolescents*, Jessica Kingsley.
Winnicott, D.W. (1961) 'Adolescence: Struggling through the Doldrums', in Winnicott, D.W. (1965) *The Family and Individual Development*, Tavistock.

There is a bibliography on adolescence at the end of Chapter 10.

17 The re-enactment of family dynamics in child care

Babs Seymour and David Reeves

Introduction

And last, the rending pain of re-enactment
Of all that you have done, and been; the shame
Of motives late revealed, and the awareness
Of things ill done and done to others' harm
Which once you took for exercise of virtue.

T.S. Eliot From *Four Quartets*, 'Little Gidding'

The task of this chapter is to look at some of the outcomes of unconscious processes, not only on individuals but also families, groups of children, residential staff and other professional groups. Our aim is to demonstrate some of the practical applications of psychoanalytic understandings in a family, systemic and group framework.

Many troubled children and young people have lived in a disturbing environment – their family – for years before they arrive on the doorstep of substitute care. By then they have been established in a role within the family mesh of distorted relationships and they have become accustomed to acting out this role in many years. They are 'comfortable' with it and it should not surprise us if they seek to make themselves similarly comfortable within the substitute care setting. Unconsciously, they draw in their carers to be a part of this comfortable world and together they re-enact the abusive dysfunctional relationships of their family life. Babs Seymour and David Reeves illuminate these processes and show how they can be worked with in the care situation.

17 The re-enactment of family dynamics in child care

Babs Seymour and David Reeves

Working with families or children in residential and day care, we are looking at a range of social groups. The staff and children are social beings with their own language and place in that social group: 'We are born into a group, develop intricate and close relationships with others in our basic group unit of family and clan, learn to speak the same language and these constant complex interactions become our mind' (Foulkes 1948).

Though we may regard the mind as the most precious and personal aspect of ourselves and hence attempt to guard it from change through interaction with others, mind is in essence a group matrix. When looking at the interaction, reaction and behaviour of children in care we cannot leave ourselves out of the equation – we are part of the matrix. The matrix is the common pool of meaning, the network of communication which may be understood by the individuals on different levels and it includes carers and children.

We first became interested in the idea that professionals may re-enact some of the complex dynamics that exist within family systems when we were managers of a family centre. The families could be described as dysfunctional and we provided an intensive therapeutic programme to help them make the changes necessary to continue parenting their children or to receive them back into the family after they had been removed because of risk. We were fascinated by the way the staff working with these families began to behave in ways that mirrored some of the behavioural family patterns. Although these ideas were not new and we both had some sense of them from our respective family therapy training, it was fascinating to us that we could see and experience these dynamics in such a powerful fashion.

Without making the connection immediately, we were also very aware that whenever we appeared to be stuck in our work with the families or

361

individuals and then looked at our own professional system, this almost always freed up the work with the family and we and they were able to move on. We seemed to find a parallel 'stuckness' in the professional relationships.

We gradually began to put these two processes together. Were the dynamics in the professional system mirroring the stuck or repetitive patterns in the family system, thus creating a homeostatic position? That is, if we were behaving and thinking in the same dysfunctional way as the family then we were in a 'no change' position. The family would feel comfortable even with the dysfunction around them because it was what they knew. We realised that unless we identified and understood these patterns and dynamics we would not be able to avoid re-enacting them.

Since we were working with families where there were young children, primarily under the age of five, we chose to divide the therapeutic task so that one therapist attended to the children's needs or sub-system while the other attended to the adults. This was all described by Emilia Dowling (1979) in her chapter on co-therapy, 'A Clinical Researcher's View'.

We observed amongst the staff team similar examples of mirroring as described by Ms Dowling. Co-workers exhibiting similar patterns of communication as the parental couple, for example, passive father, controlling mother or vice versa, were frequently evident. Grandparental roles were mirrored by the hierarchical structure of the staff team, with supervisors interfering or undermining the work of the co-workers in the same way the grandparents in the family were undermining the parental role.

In this way we hoped to highlight the conflict between the needs of the children and parents, to give these needs a voice and the chance of resolution. This worked reasonably well with a third person or the entire staff group supervising these conflicts. The biggest difficulty came when the workers could no longer hold the needs of the individual or sub-group they were required to attend to. We recall that it was far more frequent for the workers with the adults to take on the needs of the children and disagree with the child's workers on these needs. This highlighted certain family dynamics for us and we were able to observe a combination of several possibilities. This tended to happen in some families at a time when the parent(s) were looking to the children to parent them and care for their (the parents') anxieties. This often coincided with perceived or real pressure on the parent(s) from other relationships in the extended family, neighbours or the professional network. At times it was a reminder that the staff were under pressure, perhaps not being valued or properly supported, especially if the time was approaching when important decisions were needing to be made with the local authority and their legal representatives about the long-term care of a child. It was as though the worker with adults would like to abrogate the responsibility and become the child and/or help to share difficult decisions that parents would inevitably fight against. They appeared to want to split off that part of the parents' needs that they had been holding and working with.

We gave a focus to the family conflict within and, as it proved, without, between the family and extended family, neighbours and other professionals. We worked on the principle that in joining the system in order to influence it to change from within, we would inevitably take on some of the family's unconscious dynamics, in particular splitting or projective identification that goes on between family members and the family and the outside world. We chose this way of working in order to make conscious as much of the unconscious dynamic as possible.

The learning and understanding of this process has also been valuable in our individual experiences of residential work with children. As staff joined with families, it seemed to us that this process would be repeated with individuals and groups of children. Staff would join part of the individual child's internal family construct, together with those of other children and other staff members. The member of staff would bring about changes from within. In order to do this we ensure individual and group supervision and regular case discussions that focus on our process and stuckness within the whole range of dyadic and group relationships including those of the wider establishment – reviewed through meetings of senior management and consultants.

First, we start from the premise that what we would hope to provide for the children we work with is a healthy and functional adult team who are able to understand the psychological needs of a baby/young child for healthy development. Therefore, it is imperative that this team understands the inner-world needs of the child as well as the functional patterns of behaviour within a family to meet these needs. To understand how the relationships of mothers, fathers, grandparents, siblings, relatives and so on have an important affect on the child is as imperative as to understand child development. The child carries around in their head at all times a 'construct' of their family life. It is a construct that the child expects the whole world to be like and, of course, by the very nature of the family not having been able to function well enough for the child to remain within it, the construct will be dysfunctional. So we need to understand family systems: those that are healthy enough to sustain a child's healthy development and those that are not.

What patterns of behaviour, dynamics and attachments may inevitably lead to dysfunction? What is the healthy state of a family which would support, protect, teach and care for parents about to have their first child?

What are the myths and legends in a dysfunctional family that are passed on through generation after generation that affects (dictates) the family attitudes towards different members of the family? There may be clear, different expectations of men and women, boys and girls; differences between the responses of families to first-born children and last-born; expectations of how relationships are between parents/child, couples, siblings, etc. Every family has their own unique 'family life' and we need to understand this for every child.

Although we speak of this 'uniqueness', of course we also know that there are common themes in dysfunctional families that will inevitably lead to breakdown in some way. So we need to carry with us, as we say, a picture of a 'healthy, good enough' family that will promote healthy growth.

Datelines and genograms

In order to work with the whole child we need a great deal of information regarding the family system. We have developed a way of collating this information in order for us to begin to understand the construct the child has of 'family'.

In order to understand the child's psychological needs, we use the information about the first years of life. We also need a dateline. This has many other titles and is often called a chronology in reports we receive from social workers. However, what is included in this dateline is most likely to be more comprehensive or different from some of the information we receive. The basis of it is history: a sequential list of important events, both preceding and after the child's birth until entry to the residential community. What we include on the dateline, however, is any information that gives us clues to the family system. We want to know about all life-cycle events that may not seem directly related to the child but will inevitably have some impact, the meaning of which may be different each time or may reflect a family response to such events. So we want to know about birth and death in the family, separations, significant changes, relationship patterns and so on.

This requires the workers to go through the information with a fine-tooth comb. It also requires a great deal of discipline, structured thinking and time. Very often how these datelines are constructed also becomes part of our thinking about re-enactment. A chaotic disorganised family system may have already been re-enacted by the professional system before the child reaches us and information may be similarly chaotic and disorganised. Of course, the social worker may just be chaotic and disorganised. We are not too interested in 'one off' experiences – our focus needs to be on a behaviour or dynamic that appears to be repetitive.

We often see in information that is sent to us quite clear patterns of professional behaviour that are either repetitive, despite different personnel being involved, or behaviour that does not seem to fit into a normal response. One might see in the child's history decision a being made that seems to fly in the face of what one would have expected. An example recently seen was of extreme level of concerns, and justifiably so, about a child over and over again but the responses seemed extremely unprofessional. Given that from time to time any individual social worker or team may make a mistake, one would not react. When this way of responding seems to be forming a pattern, then we would begin to hypothesise that the professional system may be caught up in a re-enactment. In this case, the denial that kept appearing amongst the professionals appeared to us to be exactly the same level of denial of the mother who consistently asked for help and then denied she needed it.

The residential social workers, therefore, must not allow themselves also to become chaotic and disorganised as described. The dateline is one way of putting some order into the process. If the dateline is produced and is not ordered, then one would give the staff the benefit of the doubt that they may just be repeating a pattern. However, looking at re-enactment does mean that all adults will need to look at their own predisposition to dysfunctional behaviour. If chaos is to be re-enacted, then the adults with a predisposition to being chaotic will take this on.

An interesting observation about the actual construction of the dateline has occurred many times. One of the co-workers may have drawn up the dateline on their own and later, when looking at the genogram, one has seen that one side of the family has a lot of information about the family members and the other side very little, if any at all. How interesting, therefore, to see that the person who constructed the history through the dateline and genogram is of the same sex as the parent of the side of the family with lots of history. This may be interpreted as coincidence but may well demonstrate a mirroring being re-enacted already.

The other crucial information we need is a genogram. This 'therapeutic family tree' gives us (or not, as the case may be) information not only about who was married to whom and who were the children born to, etc., but also a pictorial view of the way this family is. We always ask for a genogram from the referring agency.

Genograms come in many shapes and sizes and we use our understanding of these shapes and sizes to give us more understanding of the family. Some times the genogram is completely incomprehensible. There may be no clear generational boundaries – the way it is laid out may be confusing and so on. This may be due to an inexperienced social worker drawing it up or, as we hypothesise, it may be a reflection of the family. One theme that has consistently recurred over the years is the genogram of sexually abusing families. We have been struck by how many of these genograms are actually drawn out so that generational boundaries are blurred. When we construct genograms we would hope that each generation is on a separate line from the other. Therefore, if we are looking at a three-generational family – grandparents, parents and children – we would expect to see something like this.

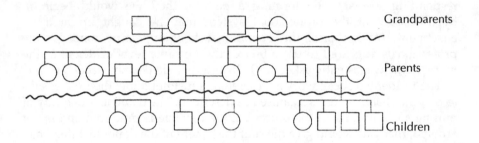

Figure 17.1 Genogram of a three-generational family.

It is without doubt too much of a coincidence that genograms of sexually abusing families are often received like this.

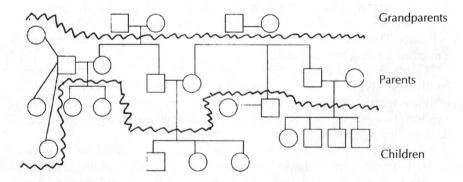

Figure 17.2 Genogram of sexually abusing three-generational family

Sometimes a genogram contains a great deal of information, sometimes not at all. We actually received a genogram that literally had a mother/father and two children. No grandparents were even represented, or other family members. What could this mean?

We can hypothesise on a genogram's meaning; each staff team does this when a child first arrives with us. Hypotheses can then be formulated by using the information and noting the response. For example, the already mentioned, sparsely detailed, genogram that looked like this:

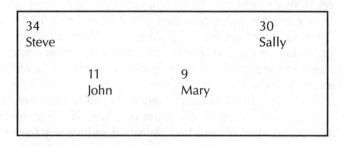

One hypothesis might be that history has not been seen as important to the person who constructed the genogram, probably the social worker. Are the family themselves disconnected from their history? This might imply issues of attachment. Is the history full of secrets because of dysfunctional behaviour amongst other family members which needs to be denied by the represented members? The way we can test out these hypotheses is to see if the social worker has in fact much more information than was supplied. If not, we would ask for more and, if there is expressed reluctance on the family's part to give more, we can continue our hypotheses. Sometimes we are simply given much more information on request and our hypotheses may be discounted.

Either prior to a child's arrival, or in the first few weeks, the co-workers will present the dateline and genogram to the staff team with any added information about the process to aid the hypothesis.

There are many examples of hypotheses one could make from the information in a genogram and it must be remembered that we are looking only for dysfunctional patterns that we hope not to re-enact. A criticism of the process often heard is that what we see may be coincidental or we may be interpreting too much. However, we need to be aware of the pitfalls to avoid and by identifying patterns of behaviour, family myths, individual identity and patterns of generational repetitive behaviour, we are not only able to understand the child better than just looking at their behaviour but also hopefully become aware of our behaviour in relation to the child. It will be helpful in understanding all that we have said by giving some examples.

A genogram and dateline was presented after the arrival of S. It was noted that in his grandparents' generation relationships between adults did not last very long and the man always left. However, from the dates in the dateline it appeared that the female engaged in a new relationship with a man before her partner left. This pattern of relationships was repeated in the parents' generation. There is much to hypothesise here. First, the nature of relationships which are not long term. We can hypothesise that S. has no expectation of parental relationships being sustained and would be anxious about the relationship between the co-workers. His expectation will be that not only will it end soon but someone else will come in to the system first, so he may be always looking for the replacement. His relationship with the male co-worker may be intense at some time as S. tries omnipotently to keep the father figure in the system but he may also reject him as he knows this is the inevitable outcome – his own rejection.

We also hypothesised that at the break-up of each of these relationships, the male was the 'bad object'. S. therefore has learned about males in his family with whatever labels have been attached to them by the mother, or others. 'Useless, violent, untrustworthy, stupid' and so on, are just a few examples of how we have heard previous partners described. We all know many more. So the expectation of males may be no greater than these epithets. The boys in the family, including S., would therefore not have a positive view of their own maleness.

The observation of the female always engaging in a new relationship prior to the current one being dissolved could indicate dysfunctional issues of separation. This was profound in both generations in terms of male–female relationships so we looked further. We looked at the way children separated from their parents. There was also a pattern here that confirmed our various hypotheses. There were many children in each family unit and there was clearly a pattern of a new baby being born and an older child being received into care. There were also two examples in the parental generation of a still-birth and an abortion with a baby being conceived very quickly.

This led us to another hypothesis which was that this family does not grieve. Relationships are broken or lost but they are immediately replaced.

From these last two hypotheses we thought about S. Presumably he would be forever anxious about a new child coming into the group. There would be an expectation that when a new child did arrive, S. may well be expecting to leave the unit fairly shortly. Secondly, transitions may be extremely difficult for S. or not, depending on how defensive he was about loss.

The staff team may re-enact any of these processes and the ways this might happen are recorded. When there is a pattern of dysfunctional relationships between a parental pair, there are various ways this may be mirrored in the whole professional system. It was interesting to note that when the genogram and dateline were presented to the staff team, the co-workers had already been allocated. Because of a shortage of staff and staff illness, a male co-worker had been identified to 'hold' the case until another one could be identified. The interesting point was that this male co-worker, P., was leaving in the next few months. So S.'s experience in the group would be exactly as in his family unless changes were made. The team did not feel it possible to reallocate to another co-working pair so it was decided that an alternative male co-worker would be chosen carefully and without haste. Indeed they felt it better for the female co-worker to work on her own with S. for a period of time whilst focusing on the loss of P. It was also necessary that S. should know about what would be happening and why. This was imperative at every transition or loss.

In another case with similar family dynamics, it was hypothesised that males do not stay for long in the family. A year into the work when the team were reassessing the hypothesis, it had clearly been re-enacted. In that one year the child had had one female co-worker and there was currently a fourth male co-worker joining the system. There were all sorts of rational and practical, unavoidable reasons given for this to be the case but when each of these was challenged we discovered that there had been an alternative course of action at the first two male departures that would have prevented it reaching four. If this team had looked at the hypothesis regularly, a re-enactment would not have occurred. It is thus imperative that the co-workers at least have all these major themes of re-enactment for the child firmly in their thinking.

S. as we have discussed, would have a view of maleness as represented by angry females. The female co-worker must be aware of not denigrating the male co-worker to S. In fact he needed a very positive male role model and a re-enactment could be that the male co-worker mirrored the male partners by fitting some of the epithets. The female might then be dismissive at times of her male co-worker. Indeed, in this particular case the female co-worker did have a predisposition to undermine men through projective identification and it was clear that she behaved in some way like the mother. Fortunately she was open to looking at her own behaviour and worked extremely hard at this particular dynamic. By doing so she was having a profound effect on S.'s image of maleness.

Another powerful re-enactment that occurs very frequently is that of the interfering and undermining grandparent. In the child's family, the grandparent may be over-involved with the family for many reasons. They may not be able to separate from their now-adult child. Their own partnership or lives may not be satisfying and their need to hold onto something perceived as satisfying to them may be greater. Or they may have real concerns about the parenting ability of the parents but not have the sort of relationship with them that is supportive but is rather undermining. Or they may have little confidence in their own previous parenting skills and want to prove themselves or have a second chance at parenting. Or they may be in a sibling-like rivalrous relationship with either of the parents.

Any of these can be re-enacted by the supervisor or someone who is in a hierarchical position similar to that of grandparent. We have seen all the above in our work with staff teams. The supervisor who insists on always liaising with social workers, or the one who writes all the reports, yet another who 'rescues' the co-workers whenever in difficulties with the child and takes over rather than supporting. The co-workers may be part of this pattern too and allow themselves to be undermined because of their own feelings of inadequacy. So the child experiences yet again a sense of 'parents do not parent, grandparents do'. This has serious implications for their own parenting abilities when adult, so the treatment we offer must include giving them the experience of 'parents can parent'. Again this demands an openness and honesty amongst the workers.

In the family where there are patterns of sexual abuse one must always hypothesise about secrets. So often we have seen information being withheld between co-workers or between team and school or amongst any of the professionals. An adult may get into a secretive relationship with the child, excluding others. Co-workers need to work extremely hard together at being open and honest with each other and all the other professionals.

K. was a child who, from the information in the dateline and genogram, had had very little primary care. When the staff team were hypothesising about re-enactment someone suggested she might not be nurtured by the co-workers or other staff. At this point one of the co-workers said, 'we have done it already.' It was K.'s third day in the Centre and she was being looked after by another group for the day whilst this team was in its staff meetings. Contrary to the nature of our work which would indicate that one of the co-workers should be caring for the new 'baby', they had passed her on to someone else. This team kept this hypothesis firmly in their sights from then on and challenged each other about any practice that was not nurturing. The child has grown in a very healthy way.

There are many other dynamics that can be re-enacted and our own practice indicates that there is an inevitability in intensive therapeutic work that this will happen. It is helpful to be proactive and prevent occurrence because of knowledge but more often the re-enactment has taken place before it is identified. Either way, identifying the patterns is imperative in the treatment of the child.

In our previous examples, we focused on the co-workers as being the potential adults who may re-enact the family dynamics but there are other symbolic couples in the professional system who may well become part of this process. Where education is on site there can be a symbolic partnership of school and care groups and exactly the same dysfunctional patterns can arise. It is imperative, therefore, that the understanding of this process is held by the whole of the establishment.

This may be more difficult with another symbolic partnership – between the establishment and external social work and education agencies. This sort of understanding may not be shared but identifying the problem and looking at ways that residential staff can change their part in the re-enactment is important. After all the thinking and hypothesising, it is so important that there is action to change if re-enactment occurs. Thus, when a dateline and genogram are presented, how re-enactment may occur must be recorded. This must then be shared with other professionals within the establishment and with other professionals if it is felt to be helpful.

Inter-agency re-enactment of dysfunction was described by Will and Baird (1984) as based on three main sets of factors:

> First, it should be recognised that the personal characteristics of individual professionals may contribute to the generation of interprofessional discord. Secondly, there are factors within particular sorts of families that are likely to precipitate such discord. Thirdly, there are real differences between different professions and different agencies which make some inter-professional relationships more vulnerable than others to trouble and conflict.

We have shown some of the ways we look at and use mirroring and re-enactment of what are often dysfunctional family systems and how the mirroring can inform us of the child's experience. Taking on, as we have described, the projected feelings and enacting them in ways that re-create similar family situations unconsciously for the child, it is important to remember that for projections to engage there has to be introjection. Someone to introject the projection because it fits and resonates with the familiar experiences of the introjector. When these are taken on by a worker or the staff team then initially the change needs to come from the adults. In our experience, all too often, professionals expect the child or family to make the changes that the professionals are not prepared to make, although it is the professionals that have the resources to change whilst the children and families may have limited resources.

Clearly, there needs to be a culture in a staff team that is trusting, open, insightful and confident. Adults need to be open to having their predispositional behaviour identified if it is the case. It is imperative that they understand that we are all potentially part of the dysfunctional behaviour and, therefore, all part of the problem and solution. We cannot see ourselves as being separate from the child and the family. We do recognise the importance of creating an environment where the carers can be open in dealing with the process of any or all of our relationships with individuals, groups and sub-groups made up of children, adults, families, the wider establishment and other professionals. It requires adequate time to look at our process which we do from various models. In trying to understand the attachments, loss, object relations, projections and projective identification, we use a range of models. From psychoanalysis we use transference and countertransference. From family therapy and systemic models we try to use these skills to understand the family system plus the therapist system in order to change from within the system. From group analysis according to Foulkes we try to look at the way the individual affects the group and the group affects the individual and to create a matrix that can contain and offer new experiences. If, as we believe, the child cannot change whilst feeling alienated, and to feel attached means they initially have to re-create with others a family familiarity pattern, then therapeutic work requires that we look at ourselves, our constructs, and consider how we can change and evolve having first allowed ourselves to join the child's family construct.

References

Byng-Hall, J. (1955) *Re-writing Family Scripts. Improvisation and Systems Change*, The Guildford Press.

Dowling, E. (1979) 'Co-therapy in a clinical researcher's view' (Walrond-Skinner, S. ed.) in *Family and marital psychotherapy: A critical approach*, 173–199. London: Routledge and Kegan Paul.

Foulkes, S.H. (1948) *Introduction to Group Analytic Psychotherapy*, London: Heinemann.

Thompson, J. 'From survival of the fittest/leaves on a tree', Paper presented but not published.

Turquet, P. (1975) 'Threats to identify in the large group', in Kreeger, L. (ed.) *The Large Group. Dynamics and Therapy*, Maresfield Reprints.

Will, D. and Baird, D. (1984) 'An integrated approach to dysfunction to interprofessional systems', *Journal of Family Therapy* 6: 275–290.

Bibliography

Britton, R. (1981) 'Re-enactment as an unwitting professional response to family dynamics, *Psychotherapy with Families*, London: Routledge and Kegan Paul.

Kennedy, R. (1986) 'Work of the Day: aspects of work with families at the Cassel Hospital', in Kennedy, R. Heymans, A. and Tischler, L. *The Family as In-Patient: Families and Adolescents at the Cassel Hospital*, Free Association Books.

Further reading

Ahmed, S. , Cheetham, J. and Small, J. (eds) (1990) *Social Work with Black Children and their Families*, Batsford/BAAF.

Bentovim, A. (1992) *Trauma Organised Systems: Physical and Sexual Abuse in Families*, Karnac Books.

Bettelheim, B. (1987) *A Good Enough Parent*, Thames and Hudson.

Bowlby, J. (1988) *A Secure Base*, Routledge.

Britton, R. (1990) 'Breakdown and Reconstitution of the Family Circle', in Boston, M. and Szur, R. (eds) *Psychotherapy with Severely Deprived Children*, Karnac.

Butler, S. and Willott, C. (1992) 'Untapped Power: Life Pattern Work as a Tool for Change in the Lives of Women Survivors of Childhood Sexual Abuse', in Fergusson, H., Gilligan, R., and Torode, R. (eds) *Surviving Childhood Adversity*, Social Studies Press, Dublin.

Copley, B. and Forryan, B. (1997) *Therapeutic Work with Children and Young People*, Cassell.

Davis, R. (1997) 'A violent child and his family', in Varma, V. (ed.) (1997) *Violence in Children and Adolescents*, Jessica Kingsley Publishers.

Department of Health (1995) *Child protection – Messages from Research*, HMSO.

Dockar-Drysdale B. (1993) 'Emotionally deprived parents' in *Therapy and Consultation in Child Care*, Free Association Books.

Farrelly, M., Butler, G., and O'Dalaigh, L. (1992) 'Working with Intra-familial child sexual abuse', in Fergusson, H., Gilligan, R., and Torode, R. (eds) *Surviving Childhood Adversity*, Social Studies Press, Dublin.

Foulkes, S.H. (1948) *Introduction to Group Analytic Psychotherapy*, London: Heinemann.

Graham, H. (1992) 'Caring for Children in poverty', in Fergusson, H., Gilligan, R., and Torode, R. (eds) *Surviving Childhood Adversity*, Social Studies Press, Dublin.

Hayley, J. (1980) 'A Family Orientation', in *Leaving Home*, McGraw Hill.

Hoghughi, M. (1992) 'Home and Family Problems', in *Assessing Child and Adolescent Disorders*, Sage.

Jewett, C. (1992) *Helping Children Cope with Separation and Loss*, Batsford.

Katz, I. (1996) *The Construction of Racial Identity in Children of Mixed Parentage: Mixed Metaphors*, Jessica Kingsley Publishers.

Kelsall, J. and McCullough, B. (1988) 'Initial Contact and Preliminary Work from Family Work', in *Residential Child Care*, Boys and Girls Welfare Society.

Kennedy, R., Heymans, A. and Tischler, L. (eds) (1987) *The Family as In-Patient: Families and Adolescents at the Cassel Hospital*, Free Association Books.

Klein, J. (1987) *Our Need for Others and Its Roots in Infancy*, Routledge.

Layzell, P. (1995) 'A Case Study of a Parental Involvement Scheme', *Therapeutic Care and Education*, 4(2).

Rutter, M. (1972) *Maternal Deprivation Re-assessed*, Penguin.

Rutter, M. (1975) *Helping Troubled Children*, Penguin.

Skinner, R. and Cleese, J. (1983) *Families and How to Survive Them*, Mandarin.

Trowell, J. and Bower, M. (1995) *The Emotional Needs of Young Children and their Families*, Routledge.

Winnicott, D.W. (1964) *The Child, the Family and the Outside World*, Penguin.

Winnicott, D.W. (1986) *Home is Where We Start From*, Penguin.

Winnicott, D.W. (1995) *The Family and Individual Development*, Routledge.

18 Working with unconscious dynamics in groups

David Challender

As long as the informal/submerged aspects remain largely uncharted and unrecognised the overall organisation is likely to remain at sub-optimal levels of effectiveness. (Plant 1984)

In this chapter David Challender considers some of the processes which occur in groups and which affect both children and grown-ups. For those working therapeutically with children it is essential to have some knowledge of these processes and to be able to work in such a way that they are not undermined by dysfunctional dynamics. There will be many occasions when workers are functioning within groups or teams, and when children and young people are in group situations in their living space or in school. Some residential agencies will be constructed on a social or group design as, for example, in the case of a therapeutic community or an adolescent unit. In such instances it is fundamental for the staff to have theoretical formulations about groups.

18 Working with unconscious dynamics in groups

David Challender

Children are generally reared in the context of a group, whether it is the family, or substitute family, or group living in residential care. Exceptions occur in extreme circumstances such as Victorian servant girls hiding their unwanted children in loft spaces or even children cast into the wild and suckled by wolves. Such unsocialised children have been studied by developmental psychologists (see Clarke and Clarke 1976) and have been the subjects of single case studies to explore developmental processes in children. The vast majority of children will experience close interaction with other human beings from the moment of birth and will be socialised through being exposed to groups of other people on a progression from family to friends and neighbours and on to playgroups and schools. Of course, this process continues through life except for occasional hermits and Trappist monks, and grown-ups working with children will carry within them their own process of socialisation which will to a great extent be re-enacted with the children in their care.

Groups: function and purpose

At its most basic, a group may be defined as two or more persons interacting with one another, who share a set of common goals and norms which direct their activities, and who develop a set of roles and a network of affective relations. This would not include a dozen or so individuals who find themselves by chance rubbing shoulders in a pub. However, they may become a group in the face of a common threat such as a fire breaking out whereby they have to form a collective identity and also find themselves with a common objective. Usually, distinctions are made regarding sizes of groups with a main separation of small and large groups. A small group can be defined as a collection of individuals who are interdependent with one another and who share some conception of being a unit distinguishable from other collections of individuals (Thomas 1967). Its size is generally thought of as between three and 14 persons. Large groups will commonly contain up to thirty members but above this, larger social entities such as collectives, crowds and mobs begin to emerge. The large group really deserves separate treatment and for the purposes of this chapter the focus will be on the small group. Thomas' definition contains within it notions of a defined membership, interdependence and boundary and, if we add to these three the issue of size, then we have the four key concepts by which to understand small groups. Most of us will experience basic groups such as the family, playgroup, school class and social club. We may also have some familiarity with groups based on a variety of production tasks, decision-making tasks or problem-solving tasks – such as work teams and committees. At a rough estimate, most of us will belong to five or six groups at one time, and the vast majority of all existing groups have only a small number of members.

Exercise 18.1: Myself and groups

- How many groups do I belong to?
- How do these groups differ from each other?
- What role do I play in these groups?
- How do I function in groups?
- What do I gain from groups?
- What do I find difficult in groups?

The study of small groups is mainly the province of social psychology, which has drawn attention to group dynamics as they occur in small groups. Systems theory has also added to the fund of knowledge and will tend to view a group as an open system with input, process and resulting output. One important area of understanding groups came from the work of Bales (1950) who was interested in looking at pattern and content in groups. He developed a category system to help observers to code behaviour with some reliability. This has now been further developed to code and score non-verbal behaviour, such as physical distance, body positions, facial postures and gaze (Argyle 1969).

People belong to groups for good reasons. The first group to consider is the family and the primary purpose for belonging to this is for survival and being introduced into society via a small unit which enables the individual to acquire a sense of personal identity while also learning to relate to others. In general terms, individuals use groups for the following purposes:

- To satisfy social or affiliation needs (to belong and share).
- To establish a self-concept (to define self in relation to others, and to have a role).
- To gain help and support to carry out an objective.
- To share and help in a common activity or purpose.

These features of group membership apply to the family which also has the function of providing each individual with a small social unit from which to make the transition into the larger group of the community or society. The following exercise helps to provoke some thoughts about the connection of the family group experience to other group experiences.

Exercise 18.2: My family group

- What size was my family group?
- What position did I occupy in the family?
- What did I learn about groups through my family experience?
- Do I repeat learned family patterns in groups I belong to?
- Do the interactions I had with family members influence the kinds of transaction I have with colleagues at work?
- What attitudes did I acquire regarding gender and race from my family?
- What other groups did my family introduce me to?

Alongside this we need to consider that organisations also use groups and their purpose are different. Some examples of these are:

- To distribute work.
- To manage and control work.
- To allow problem solving and decision making.
- To process information.

So here we have another dimension through which to study groups and that is the organisational one. Yet another is that which derives from psychology and, for the purposes of this book, psychoanalysis whereby there is a formulation of conscious activities in groups alongside unconscious activities. According to this approach there will be a distinction between what appears to be going on in groups and what may be happening at another level. It is this aspect of small groups and their dynamics which is the main focus of this chapter and which links with other psychodynamic formulations contained in this book. Indeed, psychodynamic theory is helpful in promoting increased understanding of how groups function and can be relevant to the construction of organisations that are effective in carrying out work and which also allow and encourage people to develop their full working potential (de Board 1978; Obholzer and Roberts 1994).

Psychodynamic ideas applied to groups

Some of the clearest thinking regarding the application of psychodynamic concepts to group situations has been developed through the Leicester Conference organised by the Tavistock Institute of Human Relations since 1957. Participants in these conferences, which are run as group events so that they promote learning about group processes, are enabled to discover the presence of irrational and unconscious processes in groups. These processes will get in the way of conscious attempts to manage oneself and the group and also management of the task and of roles.

The main inspiration behind such thinking about groups was the psychoanalyst Wilfred Bion, whose contribution will be expanded on in the next section of this chapter. What he and other analysts have contributed to theory about groups has arisen from a preoccupation with understanding the inner world of the individual and their behaviour in groups. This inner world is regarded as having dynamic processes – particularly fragmentation and integration. The individual is said to have defence mechanisms such as denial of internal and external reality, splitting, projection and idealisation and these mechanisms are very evident in group situations.

Object Relations Theory points us to these fundamental mental resources which serve to protect the self which experiences itself as under threat from an imminent destruction in the group. The group as an entity can be seen as representative of the mother as experienced by the individual who in the group context regresses to an infantile interaction with the group. Projective identification operates in the group and will contribute to this process of re-enactment of mother–infant interactions. As one object relations analyst describes it: 'As internal objects are projected onto other individuals in the group in an attempt to force them into assuming desired roles, they are also projected onto the group entity' (Ganzarain 1992).

A group may also in the nurturing sense become a surrogate of the mother's breast and individuals will experience strong attachment and dependency with the consequent anxieties of losing the loved object.

Winnicott's thinking could also be applied to viewing the group as a transitional object which assists in the process of separation/individuation. A 'transitional object' is defined as a representation to identify with in passing from the state of being merged with the mother to the state of being separate from the mother (Winnicott 1958). One of Winnicott's great insights was 'There is a direct development from transitional phenomena to playing, and from playing to cultural experiences.' This essential process for the individual is available through the cultural experience of the group. Such then can be the therapeutic potential of groups at a profound level and the ideas just alluded to are crucial for those working with therapeutic groups of children or adults. These main psychodynamic ideas are also of interest and relevance in understanding the way in which groups function in general and can be illuminating regarding working teams and regular meetings.

Group processes – Bion's model

Wilfred Bion (1897–1979) who was a psychoanalyst of the Kleinian school, made a profound contribution to the theory of groups and how they operate in psychological terms. In the Second World War, he served as a psychiatrist with the Army and eventually came to work in the training wing of the Northfield Hospital which was a military psychiatric hospital. While working there, Bion conducted the so-called Northfield Experiment (first published in 1943) with the soldiers in his care. This involved the men being organised into groups to assist the process of helping others make contact with reality and to form social relationships as well as being able to cooperate on a common task. From this pioneering work, Bion developed a set of axioms about groups which formed the core of his theory. These axioms are as follows:

- Individual psychology is essentially group psychology. One member's behaviour will influence (and be influenced by) all the other members of the group.
- The emotions of group members have a considerable effect on the rational working of the group and this fact has to be acknowledged and tackled if the full potential of the group is to be released.
- Problems that arise in the group around managerial and administrative issues are both personal and interpersonal problems which are finding expression in organisational terms.
- Group development will occur when there is learning by experience in gaining greater contact with reality (adapted from Bion 1961).

Building on this core theory Bion went on to develop what became known as his theory of basic assumptions. This arose from various experiences in groups where members seemed to behave as if an underlying assumption was true. For example, two people might engage in intense dialogue while the other members of the group maintain an attentive silence. Bion suggested that all the members of the group hold the underlying basic assumption that the relationship of the pair is in some way a sexual one. This would be an unspoken assumption and probably quite unrealistic but it might operate as an unconscious basis for the members' behaviour. When operating like this the group can be thought of as being in '*basic assumption group mode*' and this can be contrasted with the work group mode when the group is setting about its task.

Another way of coming to terms with these theoretical notions about groups is to consider two differing aspects of groups and of individuals. At one level, a group may be best understood as an agglomeration of individuals. However, at another level, the group may be seen or experienced as more than the sum of its individual members. Bion, in advancing his thinking about groups, developed the idea that the group consists of two different aspects of the individual. On the one hand, there are those aspects of the individual which are acknowledged and open to awareness. On the other hand, there are the unacknowledged aspects which Bion sees as being pooled in the so-called '*group mentality*'. This can be both powerful and primitive and are not easy to deal with when encountered in unstructured groups. When a group manages to stay with its task, rather than being in this group mentality, it is said by Bion to be in the '*work group mode*' and in this mode it might learn, get therapy, make decisions, or whatever its task may be. While in this mode, members of the group are likely to experience things happening in sequence over time, and of there being the possibility of growth and development. In contrast to this work group is the group which connects with the pool of unacknowledged aspects of the individual group members. Such a group enters into the group mentality whereby time and growth and task performance are lost. In this group mode, individuals are no longer distinct from each other and there is a rather strange group cohesion with no learning from experience or process of growth and development.

According to Bion, groups will succumb to basic assumptions which members of a group will hold in common. He identified three such basic assumptions which are as follows:

1) *Basic assumption dependency (baD)* – When this assumption mode dominates, the group functions as though its primary task is purely to provide for the satisfaction of the needs and wishes of its members.

2) *Basic assumption fight–flight (baF)* – In this assumption mode the group functions as though there is an enemy or a danger and this requires either attack or flight.

3) *Basic assumption pairing (baP)* – Once under the sway of this assumption mode, the group operates on an unconscious and collective belief that a future event will solve the problems and needs of the group. This is likely to revolve around the possibility of a pairing between two members or of the leader with someone outside the group.

Each of these basic assumptions have their leaders who tend to be 'elected' by a mysterious process arising out of the operation of primitive group processes. This process has been described by Isabel Menzies-Lyth (1989):

> In the basic assumption group the leader is often 'elected' by a process of splitting off the unacknowledged facets of other individuals, and projecting them into the leader or an idea, agreement being reached rapidly and collusively as to which member or idea it should be. If an individual is 'elected' he is likely to find the natural characteristics which suited him for the job vastly exaggerated by the involuntary acquisition of similar aspects of other members, until his own identity is almost obliterated – a most alarming experience.

An individual caught in this leadership role in a basic assumption group will usually need to be helped to move out of it by a facilitator or group consultant, if indeed one is available to the group

This theory about the psychological operation of groups as developed by Bion tends to be somewhat difficult to grasp in its abstract form and it may be helpful to consider some examples. When the group is under the sway of baD (dependency), there will be a pronounced tendency for dependence on the leader who will be assumed to provide all the nurture or all the answers. The members of the group will tend to behave as if they are immature and inadequate with little or nothing of their own to contribute. A leader is found who will solve all the difficulties. Alternatively, an idea may be raised to a lofty level as the ideal for the group. Eventually the leader or the idea will be rejected and a search will ensue for a replacement. This happened, for example, in a group of child care workers who met in a group to work at team development. The work group pursuing this task soon gave way to the group mentality of baD in which the team members looked for magic solutions to their difficulties. This centred on unrealistic expectations of their manager providing perfect supervision for all and in negotiating new contracts of pay and conditions.

An example of a group entering into baP (pairing) occurred when a team of residential social workers met to discuss the needs of a child in their care.

Two individual members emerged as dominating the discussion and were allowed by their colleagues to develop an idealised and unrealistic plan for the child which involved rapid fostering. A shared unconscious fantasy had been entered into whereby a pair of team members created an idea that appeared to offer a solution to an anxiety-provoking situation.

Examples of baF (fight–flight) are not difficult to find in any group. One example occurred within a hard-pressed team who worked with looked-after young people. The team had some difficulties in agreeing on their task but spent a lot of time in their staff meetings criticising bitterly their senior off-site managers as well as other members of the wider 'system'. Rather than face the painful internal difficulties among the team members, it was more comfortable for the team to engage in 'fight' and attack what was seen as the external enemy.

In his observations on groups, Bion stressed that a group will switch in and out of basic assumption groups, and in and out of the work group. The basic assumption groups are by nature unstable and changing all the time and will forever be subverting the task of the work group. They are, in effect, unreal magical attempts to solve problems or to achieve objectives and so, by definition, will not succeed but only end in frustration. Once under the sway of basic assumption activity, groups or teams get caught up in a process which is operating at an unconscious level and has a life of its own which seriously impedes the primary task activity for which the team is constituted. Entangled in this process the group will be prevented from adaptive mechanisms and growth, and will not work effectively, face reality or tolerate differences among members of the group. This has implications, of course, for the capacity of the group to address issues of race and gender. Bion's prediction is that a group of workers dominated by basic assumption activity will pursue continuance of the group as an end in itself and become preoccupied with their relationship to the group rather than with their work task. If this is true it points to the need for workers in child care agencies to have access to external consultancy to assist their teams in managing unconscious processes and the mechanisms which impede task performance.

Defensive processes in groups

Bion's contribution to our understanding of groups is clearly linked to other formulations of basic defence mechanisms which are seen in psychodynamic theory as operating in individuals and in groups. Splitting, projection, introjection, identification and idealisation are primitive defence mechanisms which have been identified by the Kleinian school of psychoanalysis. Although they relate to the defences employed by young infants and can be very helpful concepts in understanding troubled children, they are also applicable to ordinary group processes.

Splitting

In the face of demanding and difficult children, staff may defend themselves through this mechanism. The staff team becomes split around different approaches or attitudes to the point of becoming polarised. Workers are able then to feel justified in their positions even in the face of unpleasant and painful tasks. This allows them to feel that the responsibility for any unpleasantness is with the other side. Such a defensive process in a team is organised unconsciously by the group for the benefit of individuals. An example of this process occurred in a team of child care workers around those who were seen as 'intellectuals' and those who were seen as 'workers'. Similarly, another team who looked after nine children in residential care decided to organise themselves into two shifts, each with its own distinct sub-team which worked quite separately from the other sub-team. In difficult situations, these two sub-groups represented very different ways of working with the children and became hostile to each other.

Projection

This involves some kind of transfer of something from one group or a person to some other group or person. The latter group or person will then suffer a loss of its proper identity. So it is that a group experiencing something unpleasant that it needs to avoid will seek out another group which in a sense can be exploited by being the recipient of the unwanted experience. This mechanism is very common and operates powerfully and persistently, especially if left unattended.

It is important to appreciate that collective defence mechanisms develop in human groups and that these contribute towards a dysfunctional attempt at cohesion. This was stated very clearly by Jaques (1955) some forty years ago:

> Societies provide institutionalised roles whose occupants are sanctioned, or required, to take into themselves the projected objects or impulses of other members. The occupants of such roles may absorb the objects and impulses – take them into themselves and become either the good or bad object with corresponding impulses.

To understand this process more fully it is important to include the concepts of projective and introjective identification – these are defined and explained at length in Chapters 3 and 4 of this book. Once again Jaques (1955) gave us a clear statement of what goes on for the individual:

> Individuals may put their internal conflicts into persons in the external world, unconsciously follow the course of the conflict by means of projective identification, and re-internalise the course and outcome of the externally perceived conflict by means of introjective identification.

This process which sounds very technical and difficult to grasp is actually very recognisable to residential child care workers who will frequently find themselves in a perplexing field of difficult and stressful emotions. One of the occupational hazards of working with emotionally troubled children and young people is the way in which the painful feelings of the child can be lodged in the worker through the operation of projective processes. Often workers will feel bewildered about where these feelings are coming from and to whom they belong and they will depend on skilful supervision to enable them to process this material. Without this help, workers in a team enter into a minefield of charged emotions which will very likely result in group tensions and conflicts.

A common example that arises in residential agencies is connected to the painful effect of feelings of abandonment which give rise at an infantile level to rage and terror. When these feelings are operating with accompanying projections, authority figures in the agency may receive projected rage for their perceived unsupportiveness towards staff. Equally, the staff may receive similar projections from young people in their care and, in part, be passing these on to managers.

Introjection

This very crucial concept in object relations theory, which is central to the understanding of the infant relating to its objects in the first years of life, is also of importance in the realm of group processes. Not only is the group or team enabling the individual worker to undertake collaborative work with conscious support but also there is at a less conscious level an internal support to the worker's personal defence mechanisms through the process of introjection or taking inside the other members of the group. Usually in groups there will be a process of collectively identifying together and thereby the development of collective psychological defence mechanisms. This process has been carefully explained by Menzies (1960) in relation to the nursing service of a hospital where she observed 'forced introjection' through which nursing recruits became unconsciously inducted into the collective defences of the nursing service.

Idealisation

The purpose of defence mechanisms is to defend against anxiety and pain. This applies to both individuals and to groups. One of the ways in which groups of workers can defend themselves from the pain arising from their work and from their own personal experiences is through the process of idealisation. Many child care workers will enter their work through the need to idealise the provision of help and support for troubled children. What often develops in groups of workers is idealisation of the context in which they are working in so far as the outside world may be perceived as a dangerous and threatening place to be avoided by the children and young people in their care. There may also be a counter-component to this which centres on denigration so that workers fluctuate between idealising their child care and denigrating the establishment in which they work. These processes require considerable understanding if workers are to retain a sense of balance and perspective whereby they can find realistic ways of developing living environments for children which will connect with future living in the community.

So far we have considered here the application of classic defence mechanisms to group situations and the interplay of individual and collective psychological mechanisms. This is by no means the full story in that groups of workers involved in handling such potent emotional material as is generated in caring for children will also experience the recreation of family dynamics relating to their own family experience, their idealised concepts of the family (as well as their denigrating concepts) and to the family experiences of the children. These important processes are further explored in this book in Chapter 17.

Team work and group processes

Therapeutic work with children usually depends on adults working together collaboratively in teams. Even where sole foster parents are caring for a child, they are usually collaborating with a network of professionals and are probably working in partnership with others who also are concerned with the interests of a child. Teams are, of course, groups and they will be subject to the mechanisms and processes which have been referred to in this chapter. In a socially constructed environment, such as a therapeutic community for children or young people, it is possible to select staff according to their personality characteristics and disposition with a view to creating a good fit in teams. There are well-known methods for achieving this, such as Belbin's (1981) instrument for identifying types of workers who will occupy different roles in groups and perform different functions. Basing his ideas on considerable research, Belbin has looked for the optimum mix of characteristics in a team. His typology includes such categories as the 'Shaper', the 'Plant', the 'Resource-Investigator' and the 'Monitor-Evaluator'. Through designing a team using a method like Belbin's the aim is to achieve as much compatibility as possible in a particular group of workers. However, even with the best efforts to make these sorts of conscious and well-informed choices teams will still be subject to the operation of unconscious processes which will get in the way of task performance. Provision, therefore, needs to be made for team maintenance through the use of group consultants and through supervision. Another useful means of enhancing the functioning of a team is to arrange for team days where the team devotes a whole day to reviewing its functioning and reflecting on areas that require attention. This is likely to include a review of role definition and allocation – an area where there is frequently confusion and overlap. Readers are referred to Chapter 19 for detailed consideration of this vital area.

An important part of team maintenance is to pay due regard to transitions within the group. Particularly important are transitions involved in workers joining or leaving the team. A well-functioning group will support new workers and offer induction to a new situation, and they will honestly acknowledge the difficult and sad feelings that arise through the departures of team members. Such transitions contribute to the life-cycle of the team since, like a family, it is a dynamic system growing and developing through time. It is helpful to consider the way in which groups appear to pass through various phases as they develop. Groups can be observed to have a fairly clearly defined growth cycle. This is easily remembered through the use of rhyming words to describe each phase of the cycle and is described in simple form in Box 18.1.

Box 18.1 The growth cycle of groups

Forming: At this stage the group is still a set of individuals and there is preoccupation with the purpose of the group, its composition, leadership and life: each individual is establishing their own personal identity in the group.

Storming: This is a stage of conflict when the preliminary and perhaps false consensus about roles and purposes and norms of behaviour is reworked. There may well be interpersonal hostility and confrontation.

Norming: Now the group needs to decide how it will operate in terms of making decisions, and how and when it will work. Also what level of trust and openness will be agreed on. Individuals test out the group to determine the level of commitment that seems appropriate.

Performing: The group can if it has passed through the preceding stages move on to maturity and to the performance of its task.

Sometimes a further stage is added – that of *adjourning* when the group is ending and the focus is on separations and leavings.

These phases of group development do not necessarily take place in an orderly sequence of a series of meetings with neat demarcations. It could be that in just one meeting the group passes through all the phases to some extent, or it may be that the group becomes caught in one phase for a considerable time and has difficulty in moving to the next phase.

Groups, and teams, do become stuck at various points in their development and this can prove very costly in terms of performance of a task such as providing therapeutic care for children. It is not uncommon for two members of a team to become emotionally and physically involved with each other. This arises from obvious sources, such as straightforward mutual attraction. However, there are other factors at work in child care settings – not least the unconscious wish of the child to pair off two workers as symbolic mother and father. Another factor can be the close proximity of workers demanded by the nature of the work and the need for close communication and emotional support between workers. Such emotional and sexual entanglements that arise in this way can be very problematic for teams and, of course, for the two individuals concerned. Quite often the relationship will be kept clandestine, especially if it is known that there is a group taboo on such matters.

The group then becomes affected by a secret which is contained within its midst and which inevitably affects channels of communication and levels of trust. There is quite likely to be a feeling of the group being held back from progression and development and a sense of avoidance being present. There may also be a level of collusion between some members of the group who have some knowledge of what is going on but are not prepared to confront the issues in the whole group or team. Such issues are difficult to resolve within the team and frequently point to the need for an external facilitator. At stake in such situations are the crucial issues of the maintenance of appropriate boundaries in professional work and also the importance of role modelling and integrity when engaging in the highly responsible task of working therapeutically with children and young people.

One further feature of group processes that merits mention here is what is usually called *mirroring* and is also known as *parallel process*. These terms refer to the mechanism whereby what is happening in the group of children or young people appears to be also happening in some form in the staff group. Perhaps there is a lot of in-fighting amongst the children with rivalry and hostility predominating. The staff group may be very aware of this and be concerned about it and try to find ways in which to help the children with their behaviour. However, the staff may not bring to awareness the reality that similar dynamics are present amongst themselves and as it were mirroring what is happening with the children. One of the strengths of the psychodynamic approach is that it encourages workers to bring such mechanisms to awareness and to be open to the complexities of interactions between children and workers individually and in groups.

Group work with children and young people

It is beyond the scope of this chapter to go into detail about the practice of working with children in groups. There are excellent books available on the subject (for example, Dwivedi 1993) which deal comprehensively with the theory and practice of working therapeutically and using the psychodynamic model in group work. Such work is demanding and requires considerable skill and knowledge. It is a specific treatment approach and, therefore, requires training and ongoing professional supervision. However, besides groups where there is a specific therapeutic goal and method there are also other group contexts for children in residential care and schools where it is valuable for workers to be aware of group dynamic processes of the kind described in this chapter. Whether it is the daily house meeting, the classroom, or the case review, there will be group mechanisms operating which workers will need to acknowledge and understand in the interests of more effective work with the children in their care. Such knowledge and awareness can be immensely important in enabling staff to use the potential of the group situation positively and to stimulate maturation and socialisation in children who previously have had very unrewarding and damaging social experiences.

Conclusion

This chapter has looked at the kind of processes which are likely to be present in group situations where children are offered therapeutic programmes to help them with emotional and psychological disturbance. Attention has been paid to the operation of conscious and unconscious processes in groups and to the importance of workers being able to bring to awareness issues that will otherwise impede the satisfactory performance of the therapeutic task.

Bion's model is especially helpful in illuminating some of these processes. It is one of the better-known psychodynamic models as applied to groups and is an important contribution to the knowledge base which workers in the field of therapeutic child care need to acquire in undertaking the demanding, challenging and often frustrating work of helping to repair the damage sustained by children reared in adverse conditions. Group environments designed for helping children can be minefields of accumulations of projections and difficult feelings and are likely to be beset with the operation of individual and group defences which if not understood and worked with will only serve to make what is already stressful work almost unbearable and unworkable. In fact, groups have enormous potential for providing positive and growth-promoting experiences for children and adults and these can be enhanced through awareness and knowledge of group processes.

References

Argyle, M. (1969) *Social Interaction*, Methuen.
Bales, R (1950) *Interaction Process Analysis; a Method for the Study of Small Groups*, Addison-Wesley
Belbin, R. (1981) *Management Teams*, Heinemann.
Bion, W. (1961) *Experiences in Groups*, Basic Books.
Clarke, A. M. and Clarke, A.D.B. (1976) *Early Experience: Myth and Evidence*, Open Books.
De Board, R. (1978) *The Psychoanalysis of Organisations*, Tavistock.

Dwivedi, K. (1993) *Group Work with Children and Adolescents*, Jessica Kingsley.
Ganzarain, R. (1992) 'Introduction to Object Relations Group Therapy', *International Journal of Group Psychotherapy*, 42(2): 205–223.
Jaques, E. (1955) 'Social Systems as a Defence Against Persecutory and Depressive Anxiety', in Klein, M., Heimann, P. and Moneuy-Kyrle, R. (eds) *New Directions in Psychoanalysis*, Tavistock.
Menzies, I. (1970) *The Functioning of Social Systems as a Defence Against Anxiety*, Tavistock.
Menzies-Lyth, I. (1989) *The Dynamics of the Social*, Free Association Books.
Obholzer, A. and Roberts, V. (1994) *The Unconscious at Work*, Routledge.
Plant, R. (1984) *Managing Change and Making It Stick*, Fontana.
Thomas, E. (1967) 'Themes in Small Group Theory', in Thomas, E. (ed) *Behavioural Science for Social Workers*, The Free Press.
Winnicott, D. (1958) *Collected Papers: Through Paediatrics to Psycho-Analysis*, Tavistock.

Bibliography

Agazarian Y.M. (1994) 'The phases of group development and the systems centred group', in Schermer V.L. and Pines M. *Ring of Fire*, Routledge.
Copley B. (1993) 'Psychoanalytic group therapy with adolescents; a journey in psychic reality', in *The World of Adolescents*, Free Association Books.
Evans B. and Cook P. (1993) 'Group work in residential child care', in *Group Work with Children and Adolescents: A Handbook*, Jessica Kingsley Publishers.
Greenhalgh, P. (1994) 'Working with the group dimension', in 'Emotional Growth and Learning', Routledge.
McGrath, K. (1993) 'Historical Development of Group Psychotherapy', in *Group Work with Children and Adolescents: A Handbook*, Jessica Kingsley Publishers.
Rose M. (1990) 'A network of interrelating groups' and 'The treatment process of a total approach', in *Healing Hurt Minds*, Routledge.

Further reading

Bion W. R. (1984) *Learning from Experience*, Karnac Books.
Bion W.R. (1990) *Experiences in Groups*, Routledge.
Hinshelwood, R.D. (1987) *What happens in groups*, Free Association Books.
Kreeger, L. (ed.) (1994) *The Large Group: Dynamics and Therapy*, Karnac Books.
Menzies-Lyth, I. (1988) *Containing Anxiety in Institutions*, Free Association Books.
Miller, E. (1993) *From Dependency to Autonomy: Studies in Organisation and Change*, Free Association Books.
Nath Dwivedi, K. (1993) *Group Work with Children and Adolescents: A Handbook*, Jessica Kingsley Publishers.
Nitsun, M. (1991) 'The anti-group: destructive forces in the group and their therapeutic potential', in *Group Analysis*, Sage.
Obholzer, A. and Zagier Roberts, V. (1993) *The Unconscious at Work*, Routledge.
Preston Shoot, M. and Agass, D. (1990) 'Defining the theory: psychodynamics',

'Defining the theory: a systems approach', 'Psychodynamics and systems: towards a working synthesis for the person-in-situation', *Making Sense of Social Work*, Macmillan.

Stapley, L. (1996) *The Personality of the Organisation*, Free Association Books.

Yalom, I. (1995) *The Theory and Practice of Group Psychotherapy*, Basic Books.

19 Coping with anxiety and complexity: a model of management

Andrew Hardwick

Introduction

Superteams develop their own internal success criteria. They articulate their own standards, expectations and objectives. They have their own way of summarising what needs to happen for them to be successful and how they will measure success. Superteams spend time negotiating these success criteria within the team. For instance, how is the team going to accomplish its task, who will do what and to what standards, what are the time limits and how will the team conduct itself with its customers and sponsors?

The quality that underlies these standards is an intense feeling of responsibility and commitment to others. Superteam members say what they are doing and then do what they say. They are utterly dependable. You can count on them to deliver on time or to give you warning if they can't. They understand how other people are dependent on them and they try to see the situation from those people's point of view. (Extracts from Hastings et al. 1985)

We do not pretend that managing a children's facility or school is easy but we are concerned by the extent to which managers make life difficult for both themselves and their staff. Management theory and practice are often a soulless combination of 'cover your backside' thinking coupled with an irrelevant hierarchical structure, none related to the task of meeting the individual needs of the children we care for or teach.

Much time is spent discussing, for example, what we can do to control a child's chronic 'bad' behaviour without considering the structure and culture of the environment in which the misbehaviour occurs or what contribution could be made by roles other than that of the keyworker.

Anxiety and complexity are two concepts central to the management task.

395

There has to be a model for dealing with both; otherwise our young people will act out their feelings of insecurity and frustration.

This chapter also draws on the work of the Tavistock consultants, especially Miller (1993), Menzies-Lyth (1988) and the papers gathered together in *The Unconscious at Work* edited by Obholzer and Roberts (1994).

19 Coping with anxiety and complexity: a model of management

Andrew Hardwick

Introduction

The aim of this chapter is to provide sufficient material for practitioners to be able to design and implement a management structure that works for their team and facilitates their task. We want to answer the question – How do we achieve our aims and objectives once they have been agreed with both our supervisory and referring agencies? There is increasing pressure on us to deliver pieces of work and packages of care. There has to be a model. The alternative is just a muddle of reactions to pressure where mistakes and poor practice are the most likely outcome.

In this chapter I have maintained a largely practical focus but I would recommend that you read it in conjunction with Robin Shohet's chapter on projective identification (Chapter 3) and David Challender's two chapters on staff support and group dynamics (Chapters 5 and 18).

This chapter will work through the creation of a model which can be accepted *in toto* as a basis for adaptation, or rejected as wholly unsuitable providing an acceptable model is substituted. Recent case material will illuminate the model. It is not an option to operate without a clear, purpose-built structural model. Why this should be so will be considered in detail below.

The task

At the outset it must be acknowledged that in residential homes, day centres, or special schools, managing a group of people who in turn manage a group of troubled children or young people is both a complex and sophisticated task. For the lone foster carer looking after one or two children, life is no less taxing. There may be less pressure of numbers but the demands of a most intensive relationship are coupled with performing the necessary sub-tasks of substitute care. The teacher and classroom assistant also face similar demands usually complicated by issues of control and educational progress.

These professional activities are the source of enormous anxiety and stress. We are after all responsible for young lives and for the attempt to rehabilitate them after years of environmental failure and abuse. The mental and physical organisation of this task needs structuring so that practitioners are helped to cope with anxiety triggered by a task which is of enormous importance not only to the client and the care agency but also to the nation. Facing acting-out which at times can be frightening and life-threatening demands huge personal resources of understanding, insight and confidence which can wear thin after weeks of assault on body and mind. For a good example of this, follow the stomach-churning acting-out of Siobhan in Dartington's study *A Life Without Problems* (Little 1994), where hanging from a motorway bridge and swallowing glass were the two strongest contributors to a high level of staff anxiety. The case of C. below spotlights areas of huge anxiety for staff in trying to discharge their responsibility to keep him safe.

Case Study – C., supplied by Cass Faye

C. was a 13-year-old boy, accommodated by his Local Authority with the agreement of both parents who admitted they were unable to control his behaviour and keep him safe. In a recent psychiatric report he was described as having 'psychopathic tendencies but this outcome was not inevitable'. He had been resident at the Centre for just over a year and had a reputation for persistently going missing sometimes for two or three days at a time. He would encourage other young people to accompany him on his travels and these frequently involved incidents of inappropriate sexual activity, drug and alcohol abuse and other forms of delinquent behaviour such as stealing.

Much adult time was taken up chasing C. around the town although the staff had become familiar with some of his routes and haunts. I addressed C's behaviour in a staff meeting and wondered what measures were being taken to prevent him being a danger to himself and others, pointing out that we could not begin any therapeutic work with him or the others until we could keep them safe. Staff response to my enquiry was varied, from mild irritation to a seemingly uncaring resignation which I suspected was a defence against the high level of anxiety this boy's behaviour engendered in them. My suspicions were confirmed when I witnessed a much more animated, hostile response from some of the staff on his return to the group late one night after he had initiated a mini-riot on the garage roof along with three other young people. On their return, when they were safely tucked up in their rooms, I asked a male member of staff to provide a hot drink and toast for all of them. He looked at me as if I was mad, with an expectation that I should send them to bed without supper. He replied 'If you're telling me I have to, I will but I don't agree with it.' Begrudgingly he responded to my order and the young people seemed confused by this show of nurturing that was obviously not standard practice. A highly intelligent lad, C. was usually the instigator of these run-aways and they had become part of the culture of the group.

C. was well into his pubescent phase, standing 5'6" tall, of stocky build and a well-developed musculature. The frequently abusive nature of the incidents that happened during these run-aways, especially in relation to smaller or younger children who got involved, was worrying and this reminded me of Anna Freud's concept of identification with the aggressor whereby 'children who are beaten or abused take inside themselves the aggressor and then their vulnerability and smallness is reversed as they themselves become the aggressor in relation to smaller children' (from Trowell and Bower 1994).

C. seemed to hold a lot of power over others (adults and young people) in the group and despite his well-established pseudo-adult persona I wondered whether this was too much power for a 13-year-old boy. What was the meaning of such symbolic behaviour? Why did he run away? Was he running from or to? When I asked him about this his reply was one of the most consistent things about him, 'I don't know.'

C. presented a high risk to himself and others during his trips outside the group and the Centre and, given the danger inherent in his two most familiar statements, 'I don't know' and 'I don't care,' we decided that he must be stopped for his own safety and the safety of others. After seeking permission from his parents and social worker, and at risk of contravening the Children Act, I engineered the removal of his clothes and, in particular, his shoes from his room. We kept these in a locked room and decided to stop him from leaving the group without permission from an adult. We drew up a plan which included plenty of structured activities outside, with adult supervision at all times. On these occasions he was given his shoes on going out and was expected to hand them in on his return. He chose his day clothes in the morning and these were taken at night when he changed into his pyjamas. After being repeatedly excluded from school for putting himself outside adult authority and being such a disruptive influence on other young people in this context, a decision was made with the Education Department that he would receive individual tuition within the Centre's grounds but outside the group.

I explained this plan to him fully and his initial reaction to the proposal was rage. He was furious at losing so much control and it prompted another of his familiar statements: 'Can't make me.' I assured him that we could and we would and took care in pointing out that this was intended as a caring response to his dangerous behaviour, not a punitive one. He did not and could not believe me but none the less eventually responded well to the provision of such a structure; he began to show signs of being able to relax more in the company of adults and the other young people, who seemed relieved that at last C. was safely tucked in by the adults. He even appeared to 'regress' sometimes to a developmental stage much younger than his 13 years, and could be seen lying on the sofa with his head on an adult's lap, a most unfamiliar sight indeed. He never played with toys but at this time, when I lent him some of mine, he could sometimes be heard in his room playing with them, out of the others' view lest it should challenge the street cred he held so dear.

However, he did need to test the boundaries and this led to some quite physical encounters by the front door. We were often able to use humour to make the situation more palatable for everyone involved. C. had an excellent sense of humour which could be tapped when he had to be stopped at the door by us women who greeted him with open arms offering him 'Love Therapy'. It was actually pronounced 'Lurve Therapy', and involved a huge cuddle in which he was central, surrounded by two or three women at a time. It never failed to get everyone laughing and C. always succumbed after a short show of trying to get away. It was important for us to convey the message that he would be 'held' by men and women.

On just one occasion after returning to the Centre after a supervised outing, C. was heard to utter the familiar words 'I'm running away.' He was met at the door by staff and became distressed when he was not permitted to leave. He became very angry, verbally abusive and physically violent which resulted in his having to be physically restrained. He eventually broke down in tears and at this point, his anger was directed towards the adults who had allowed him to leave during his first year with us. 'Why did you wait so long before you stopped me?' he sobbed. As the conversation developed it emerged that inadvertently and quite unconsciously, by allowing him to run away we had been party to an unconscious re-enactment of his past history. When he was eight years old, his parents had decided to split up and his father left the family home. His mother was not able to control C. and became violent towards him as she became frustrated in her efforts to manage his behaviour. As a way of coping with this violence at home he would run away, whereupon he became a victim of a paedophile ring for the next four years, a fact unknown to his mother and father who either did not care what he was up to when he was out of their sight or were more absorbed by their own needs and interests to notice their son being manipulated in perverted ways by persons unknown.

In this stimulating case study, Cass Faye also looked at the thought processes she and the staff team used to understand C. and his behaviour and the learning that followed. The extract here highlights the complexity and anxiety inherent in the challenges facing leaders in this field. The task of working with troubled children and young people has four aspects:

- Anxiety created by difficult, often dangerous clients and external pressures.
- Coping with change.
- Delivering performance and outcomes.
- Lack of resources.

Our test of a structural model is whether it helps us to deal with these four aspects of the task.

It is important to acknowledge and to recommend the work of Isobel Menzies-Lyth, notably her book *Containing Anxiety in Institutions* (1988) and the late Richard Balbernie who drew on her work and provided valuable case material and practical examples. His book *Residential Work with Children* (1967) is no longer in print but a useful paper (Balbernie 1973) is available from the Wingate Library at Caldecott College and gives a strong flavour of his 'Tavistock-inspired' approach and is still wholly relevant and much ignored.

Creating a structure linked to the primary task

We are being challenged to create both benign conditions within children's facilities and positive, hopeful outcomes and transitions in a climate characterised by the four aspects listed above. In classrooms, day centre and residential and foster homes, objectives for development and growth are now agreed as part of the referral contract and more and more agencies are using the Department of Health's 'Looking After Children' assessment system to monitor progress and identify areas of concern. Unless we are able to rise to this challenge the supply of referrals will dwindle *but, for the sake of our clients our facility must first ensure its survival*. Menzies-Lyth (1988) and the Tavistock approach start with this uncomfortable consideration and they have given us the concept of the 'Primary Task'.

The Primary Task of an enterprise is that fundamental task which must be performed to ensure the survival of the enterprise. Similarly, the Warner Committee (1992) recommended that every children's home should devise and publish its statement of aims and purpose which should be both aspirational and practical. The Primary Task must be clearly described and agreed with those who have most influence on the survival of the enterprise and detailed attention must be given to its practical achievement. Survival is one thing, success is another. The first is often connected to the ability of the enterprise to balance its books while the second is usually judged by its ability to satisfy its referring agencies by meeting client need. This just underlines our view above – we are operating in an anxiety-filled zone.

For the sake of designing a helpful model, which can be used as a base and stimulus for thinking, here is a simple example of a statement of Primary Task for a children's home: 'The management and improvement of the emotional, cognitive, social and physical health of each child in such a way that progress can be measured against an agreed set of objectives.'

In the case of C. above, the objectives included stabilising his behaviour, addressing his educational needs and helping him to cope with the emotional aftermath of physical and sexual abuse. These would have to be broken down into manageable, achievable portions.

The Primary Task could be made more comprehensive and it will vary according to local conditions and agency ambition, but it gives us a sufficiently useful starting point – the question 'how is this task performed?' This is where the concept of structure is most useful as an instrument for the effective performance of the Primary Task. What is a structure? Three useful elements have been identified by the Dartington Social Research Unit (see Chapter 6):

1) The mechanisms by which an institution achieves its goals.
2) An orderly arrangement of social relationships.
3) A continuing arrangement of kinds of people governed by a concept of professional behaviour in their relationships with each other.

By identifying and sorting out the sub-tasks which contribute to the performance of the Primary Task and locating these sub-tasks with people, a working structure as defined above can be created.

Sub-task One – Overall management and leadership

Someone has to create and maintain a management structure in which each team member understands their function in it and in which responsibilities, with the authority to discharge them, are delegated to an effective level of competence. While it is the job of the manager to create the structure, it is vital that each team member clearly understands the framework and importance of their task within it, if the whole is to work effectively. The perception by each team member of their effectiveness hinges on their understanding of the working of the management structure.

The manager also gives a clear lead about the way in which the structure operates. There will be a clear set of theoretical principles from which practice and supervision are derived. There will be policies for recruitment, selection and induction, equal opportunities and anti-discriminatory practice, working with families, training and development, promotion, teamwork and leavings – how often do we have a good leaving?

Clear guidelines will be issued for working with referring and other outside agencies, for example, child protection, and for appropriate work with families. Explicit criteria must be published for deciding which young people are admitted and admissions' procedures have to be designed and adhered to. Control of 'inputs' across the boundary of the facility must be controlled by its management and no one else (see Balbernie 1973). We are not proposing a return to charismatic leadership whereby all activities are under central control and inspiration and the enterprise falls apart when the leader departs or, worse, dies. Good leaders articulate a vision with the utmost clarity and are good managers if they can implement it through a structure which is designed to promote the sharing of anxiety and individual and group effectiveness. The manager's work in relation to C. in our earlier case encompassed detailed negotiation with two external agencies and C.'s parents.

It is, however, most important to take into consideration the resources available at the time. *There are never enough resources,* Menzies-Lyth (1988) reminds us. It is necessary therefore to make the commitment to do the best we can with the resources available. Otherwise our anxiety could scarcely be contained. Our young people ask for nothing more than this – a committed positive attitude within obvious limitations. They will have become all too familiar with the concept of limited resources so that surviving creatively in this climate is one of the key jobs of the manager which is supported by the assistants. A key question for the team in trying to cope with C. during his running phase was how they could keep track of him while looking after the other eight young people in the group, some of whom were joining in. You can almost hear them say 'But we haven't got enough staff on the rota!'

Implementation and, sometimes, design of policy and the provision of effective anxiety-absorbing practical leadership – creating a therapeutic culture which holds both children and adults and survives when under attack – are crucial parts of the manager's job. We have also to create a climate of appreciation in which we are quick to praise and slow to criticise, a climate of open communication within the staff team, recognition of initiative, support for coping with painful feelings and willingness to share learning. Cass Faye – by raising the issue of the group's failure to keep C. safe, and challenging what was becoming a punitive or resigned response – was taking the lead and taking a risk. That the team responded was a feather in her cap and theirs.

In a sensitive multicultural society, responsibility lies with the manager for thinking about and reflecting on issues of difference in both staff and client groups: practical recognition of the importance of relevant aspects of, for example, culture, gender and sexuality and how these can be made a part of each team member's practice.

The responsibility for the daily translation of the manager's lead into practice usually falls to assistant managers and the rest of the team. This is best done by identifying further sub-tasks, some of which senior staff will be responsible for and some of which can be delegated in line with the principle of effectiveness – who has the skill and experience to handle the task?

From time to time, it will be the task of the Leader/Manager to consider whether the structure in place is working well enough. Signs of stress in the structure could be a job which should be shared by the whole team but is being done by just one person, or jobs are not being done which should be located with one person. If it is thought necessary to change then a team exercise, an away-day, sometimes using an external objective facilitator is a useful instrument. The notes from the day could look something like this:

Sub-task Two – The therapeutic task

The therapeutic task is a senior responsibility mostly located with an assistant manager or senior practitioner, who is responsible for and with authority to implement the key components of the therapeutic task:

(a) Keyworking: Is it working? In a monitoring and advisory role, it will be necessary to outline what is meant by keyworking and what are its objectives in relation to each child. This leads us to the next step – b.
(b) Need assessments, treatment objectives and plans, 24-hour or daytime management programmes: These have to be done and written up and checked, either with an appropriate consultant or senior experienced figure. This is an organising task, for example, seeing that need

assessments are done, but the writing up and documentation and consultation could be delegated (see Chapter 7 on assessing needs).

(c) Supervision: Is it happening? Are people happy with what they are getting? Offer advice and guidance to both supervisors and supervisees.

(d) Prepares for case reviews: Who is to do it? Check reports before they go out, plan strategy for review meeting.

(e) Monitors/plans family contact and meetings: This will involve close work with the keyworker.

(f) Monitors child protection work.

(g) Leads team thinking on transitions, preparation for fostering or leaving care at a macro level, arriving in school in good shape at the micro level – and other changes in the young person's life. In the past transitions have always been traumatic.

(h) Gives 'therapeutic' input into other areas of responsibility, for example, creativity in living, symbolic content of food, bedtimes and getting up. Is conscious of the emotional state of the children and their level of communication. Promotes playroom and use of.

(i) Receives consultant support to hold all this and for advice. It has not been common practice for children's units to be provided with regular consultant support, advice and oversight, but that must change in view of the potential for later mental illness in our client group.

The potential for mental illness in C. identified by the psychiatrist underlines the importance of the therapeutic sub-task. The influence of this task is seen in the thinking and planning that went into stabilising C. in the case above.

Sub-task Three – Daily management and organisation

The assistant manager takes responsibility and has authority to 'run the day' or manage the shift:

(a) 'Plugs into' children and grown-ups, and reminds team of crucial management points in relation to individuals (from the 24-hour management programmes) and the group, for example, meals, and transitions, such as school and household routines.

(b) Deploys grown-ups to allow for individual work and group activities and has a creative role in stimulating creative activity.

(c) Deputises for manager, writes up incident reports, and does the rota.

(d) Backs up colleague(s) in potentially deteriorating situations, as well as anticipating them. Special skill in seeming to be very much involved in doing things but can easily detach without things collapsing, such as domestic chores. Was at the door for C.'s worst crisis.

Sub-task Four – Environment/atmosphere

An experienced staff member must be assigned the task of environmental/atmospheric maintenance:

(a) One person must always be responsible for maintaining the fabric of the group's environment, a very creative role. They have the authority to improve things and ensure that routines are followed which enhance the atmosphere – lighting intensity, curtains, cushions.
(b) Has the freedom to be creative in relation to interior decor, that is, needs to consult but is expected to innovate. Must have read *Home for the Heart* by Bettelheim (1974).
(c) Reacts instantly to damage when culture comes under attack. Does not always have to do the job – persuades/engages/raises consciousness in others.
(d) This task can involve putting one's hand down the loo!
(e) Is responsible for other areas – playroom in conjunction with Therapeutic Sub-task; garden/flowers, etc.; equipment for making and doing, and homework, reading and cognitive areas.

Sub-task Five – Domestic organiser

The domestic organiser must also be an experienced staff member:

(a) Is committed on the one hand to the superb quality of basic child care as seen in beautifully clean clothes, bedrooms and bathrooms and the children themselves, while on the other enormously creative, conscious and fun round food and the kitchen.
(b) Has oversight of things medical.
(c) Is a great facilitator of cooking, and devising interesting menus: food for season and celebration, fun dishes, things to do with spent packaging. Also a role model in the creative use of limited resources, especially money, an important task for preparing young people for semi- or independent living.
(d) Liaises with Therapeutic Sub-task for symbolic meanings, with Environment Sub-task for clean windows and other aspects of atmosphere and with Daily Management and Organisation Sub-task for execution of tasks involving individuals and group as appropriate.
(e) Again, does not have to do it all. Has to ensure that it all happens through others. This is a very creative role with authority to act.

If we stop to think about C.'s personality, we quickly realise how little self-esteem he has – unable to contain his emotions without adult help, under-achieving, not coping at school and just starting to play. He needs an environment of physical and domestic quality which passes a strong message that we value you, C., you are sufficiently important for us to put a lot of energy into giving you some good feelings about yourself. Sub-tasks four and five are crucial if we are to achieve this for C.

Smaller sub-tasks

These are examples of vital jobs but should be rotated often because they can become routine; it is important that an experienced staff member makes the judgement about who should do them. Some jobs are at basic care assistant level:

- Mentor for the induction of a new member of staff. What would a new member of staff make of the care/treatment programme for C.?
- Coordinator for transport and travel.
- Coordinators for events such as birthdays and other special occasions (cultural, spiritual, seasonal), trips and visits, holidays. Annual and other cyclical events can have enormous impact on our young people, for example C.'s birthdays may well bring back memories of abuse.
- Petty cash.
- Record keeping and documentation – what would happen if your facility was inspected tomorrow? The planning and work done with C. must be recorded in detail for open discussion with his social worker, educational welfare officer, child protection office and his parents.
- Fire, health and safety.

What cannot be left to chance?

From a simple statement of the Primary Task we have derived a set of Sub-tasks which must be carried out and these essentially answer this big question. Once a Sub-task is assigned, as they take up the task, and then at regular intervals, the team member must ask 'What are we leaving to chance?' Practice becomes more sophisticated as Sub-tasks are

- Expanded and levels of coordination and communication improve.
- Shared out on becoming too large for one person.
- Held temporarily to cover illness, holidays and gaps in replacing staff.

Where large staff teams are deployed, the manager's abilities to delegate, coordinate and motivate are crucial, whereas the lone foster parent or special needs teacher often must undertake all Sub-tasks on their own or with minimal help. They are still under the authority of their Primary Task and so bound to audit their work on the basis of what cannot be left to chance if they are to succeed.

Benefits of the primary task/sub-task model

How does this model cope with the aspects of the task of working with troubled children listed earlier? – First, let us look at anxiety created by difficult, often dangerous clients and external pressures. What assistance is provided by the model outlined above? There is a shared focus within the team on the needs of the clients and how these are to be met. As in C.'s case this is provided and coordinated through the Therapeutic Sub-task where important responsibilities such as assessing need, supervision of keyworking and monitoring the emotional state of children and their level of communication are carried out. This reduces anxiety. The manager knows that a major contribution to the Primary Task has been effectively delegated. Each member of staff knows that their work with individual clients is being encouraged and supervised and that group meetings to assess needs provide support and guidance.

In conjunction with his team, the manager decides policy and coordinates relations with agencies and players in the external environment. Some aspects will be delegated, others the manager holds in his role of protecting his team from unnecessary impingement from the outside. For example, the manager might be under pressure to take in a new referral at a time when the team is particularly under pressure in other ways. Decisions as small as how much of this issue to share with the team can affect the level of anxiety, morale and overall effectiveness.

Already we are seeing the Sub-task structure taking the strain and allowing the team to operate without being overwhelmed by anxiety or stress. The manager needs to understand, however, that staff teams can and do act out their anxieties in unconscious forms. This was certainly going on within the staff group looking after C. (See below and Chapters 3 and 18 for further exploration of unconscious processes within staff teams.)

Does the model assist with Coping with change? Delivering performance and outcomes? Lack of resources? A carefully conceived structure of Sub-tasks is built on the delegation of responsibilities within Sub-tasks to those who are sufficiently well trained and motivated and who can be given the full authority to exercise those responsibilities.

This is a liberating and creative system. Individuals are able to take initiatives and stretch themselves within the supporting net of the team. Being proactive, being given authority, being encouraged to take on a challenge are aspects of a team-working culture which promotes the achievement of objectives and outcomes. Such a culture should be able to take into account the availability of resources and the need to respond to changing conditions or, better still, this culture can bring about change by its very supportive and proactive nature. C.'s case is a good example.

In this model what is crucial is the location of Sub-tasks and parts thereof with individuals, who are given both the responsibility and the authority to carry them out and who have the necessary training and enthusiasm. Further useful study here can be made of Meredith Belbin's concept of team roles (Belbin 1993). Belbin has proposed nine types of person who can make a contribution to effective teamwork but it is necessary to understand each team member's strengths and weaknesses and use this knowledge to make the best use of each individual.

It is clear that a carefully designed structure needs to take account of the objectives which have been set for the performance of the Primary Task. It should be possible to assess the competence of the team based on its ability to make use of resources, human, financial and environmental. There are always limitations, yet the needs of clients are so huge. A well-managed team will not try for unrealistic achievements with clients but will rather establish a reputation for meeting realistic, agreed objectives. This develops trust and confidence in referring agencies and stimulates 'repeat business'. The challenging equation of objectives, performance and resources is built into the structure of task and sub-task. Without such a structure, there is a high risk of individuals burning out as they strive for unrealistic rehabilitation targets, a high risk of disappointing referring agencies through failure to achieve and a high risk of unpopular, constant demands for more resources.

Task and process

This basic theory of teamwork and structure needs to be used in conjunction with an appreciation of what is loosely called 'Task and Process'. In the diagram of the Task and Process Bucket, the surface is what any casual observer might see if they were to walk into the room – a classroom, a meal in progress, a group meeting, bedtime. This is a manifestation of a piece of action from the Primary Task, all Sub-tasks coordinated in action – on the surface.

THE TASK BEING PERFORMED
PROCESS ISSUES WHICH CAN UNDERMINE THE TASK These should, as far as possible, be known and discussed openly in the team
UNCONSCIOUS PROCESSES These could be acted out by both individuals and the whole group; an understanding of the concept of projective identification and group dynamics is important – see Chapters 3 and 18.

Figure 19.1 The task and process bucket

On the surface is what is happening in front of us, the everyday task. However, underneath this surface are the personal issues and agendas of the team members which may have been talked about in the staff team. They may be being kept secret until an appropriate moment comes in supervision or another opportunity. They may be being held by just one or two people because they are by their very nature confidential. Often these concerns are linked to our emotions – we have feelings about them. This may have some impact on the performance of the task – it usually does – but it is mostly available to the team to be included in their professional consciousness. This layer in the bucket is known as 'process issues' as they could get in the way of the task if the feelings are not processed (communicated), thought about by the team and resolved in some way.

The Primary Task/Sub-task model and the structure we have derived from it is able to deal with process issues. Open communication is very much a feature of good teamwork and if the team is working well together, process issues should not get in the way.

More problematic is the bottom, unconscious processes, layer of the bucket where the team's unconscious collects. Here problems of projective identification as outlined in Chapter 3 and Bion's group processes described in Chapter 18 emerge, though not always in an accessible form. If we accept that we are not in touch with our own unconscious as much as we should be, then we are likely to come across instances in teams of things happening, or not happening, which we do not understand and which interrupt the performance of the task. Menzies-Lyth (1988) points out how, through anxiety, staff teams build institutional defences and individuals lose their capacity for taking personal responsibility. I would suggest that teachers and foster carers will also experience this.

This feature of the task is usually omitted from generic training for teachers and social workers, and from some specialist training too. We have to accept that the unconscious distorted and damaged mechanisms for relating which our young people now rely on will stir up in us anxieties and feelings, some buried, some open and raw – that is, our own unconscious is stirred and we may not be aware of it. An understanding of transference and our own capacity for countertransference is important. Cass Faye in her assessment of what was happening in the case of C. used this thinking to identify a way forward. C.'s unconscious dumping of his uncontained emotions, his running away and his panic, onto her team, gradually provoked a strong apparently uncaring reaction, a countertransference, rather than a recognition of the real meaning of his behaviour, which was his need to be kept safe.

In defence of the Primary Task/Sub-task model, we can say that at least it provides a forum for exploring this aspect of our work with troubled children and young people. It also makes the case for employing external, objective consultants to work with staff teams and to point out these phenomena when they occur, explain them and advise on the practical learning from them. It is quite likely that the team itself will not know what exactly is going wrong, although they will know something is not quite right. For further study, recommended reading is *The Unconscious at Work* (Obholzer and Roberts 1994) in which Tavistock Centre consultants describe their cases and the learning to be derived from them. Eric Miller's *From Dependence to Autonomy* (1993) has an excellent introduction on the subject of anxiety and some fascinating chapters.

Coping with change

There are no easy answers. Change is never easy and in the current political, social and economic environment, uncertainty is the one aspect of life that we can be certain about. Right now we are a very anxious society. Having, through human genius, created a complex, sophisticated, unequal and unsustainable world, we do not appear to have the wit to manage it.

In an ideal world, the leader/manager would articulate a vision which would enable the staff team both to cope with change and to set an agenda for change. Sadly our internal, mental 'objects', on which we rely to help us make decisions, react to situations and interact with our external objects, have been formed over many years through experience, training and absorption through the senses (introjection). We operate under patterns of learned behaviour and reinforced attitudes to defend against anxiety and a sometimes conscious desire for the quiet life of the status quo. The leader/manager will not always be able to depend on the team grasping the opportunity. They will often just see problems. Individuals can scupper a new initiative not because they are against it but because they cannot summon up sufficient energy to get actively behind it. From the murky depths of the Task and Process Bucket things can emerge to ensure that the new idea is stillborn. What can the manager/leader do?

Generally, the team whose morale is high is best at coping with change. Challenge is what they thrive on. New, leader-generated strategies or fresh responses to outside pressure have a good chance of success if team spirit is high. Can we measure this so that we may have some certainty that the moment is right for change? Individual supervision sessions should provide clues but sometimes we hide or delay talking about some issues. A culture of appreciation, where criticism is absent but praise is constant, is a real help.

However, if, for any reason, members of the team feel that they are not being as effective as they would like to be in the performance of their part of the Task, this could undermine the new strategy for change. Process issues could break through to the surface of the bucket and disrupt the Task. In an ideal world, an external consultant would be employed regularly to help staff teams deal with their problems. But many facilities for children and young people can only afford such help when there is a serious crisis – I have heard of facilities where even this service is denied.

Self-help, then, is the only alternative and it involves reading. In an excellent book on change, *Managing Change and Making it Stick*, Robert Plant (1985) presents the 'Role Effectiveness Profile' as a tool for diagnosing readiness for change in a staff team. He stipulates ten dimensions against which staff task effectiveness can be assessed and has devised a scoring system to give a percentage score of effectiveness and indicators of where this can be improved. He also suggests ways in which constraints on effectiveness can be tackled.

A high-scoring team will, he suggests, be ready to undertake new initiatives or cope with new demands. Where there are low scores, these need either to be addressed or taken into consideration before attempting change.

The Profile is a very useful guide to staff morale and their feelings of effectiveness and a handy component of the manager/leader's toolkit for coping with change. All staff teams should complete the Profile every six months.

Summary

The use of the Primary Task and Sub-task model offers a structure within which staff teams can not only provide individualised care and treatment programmes for young people but also can face and deal with some pretty difficult internal and external problems. These are:

- Intense anxiety caused by the nature of the young people and the often unrealistic expectations of favourable outcomes by society in the form of referring agencies.
- The limitation on resources felt by all practitioners in the caring professions, and the need to set realistic targets in the face of ambitious ideals.
- The emphasis on personal performance in settings where it is only by teamwork and interdependence that the job can be done well.
- Coping with change both from the dynamic world outside and in response to the needs of individual young people.

It is important that team members should be aware of the potential of psychodynamic thinking in individual work with young people and for analysing areas of group work where, strangely, things are not quite as they should be. Task and Process are crucial concepts and this chapter should be read in conjunction with Chapters 3 and 18.

References

Balbernie, R. (1973) Paper given to social workers in Reading, available from Wingate Library, Caldecott College. Please send £3.00 and a large SAE.
Balbernie, R. (1967) *Residential Work with Children*, Pergamon.
Belbin, M. (1993) *Team Roles at Work*, Butterworth Heinemann.
Bettelheim, B. (1974) *Home for the Heart*, Thames and Hudson.
Dockar-Drysdale, B. (1990) *The Provision of Primary Experience*, Free Association.
Hastings, C., Bixby, P. and Chaudry-Lawton, R. (1985) *'Superteams', A Blueprint for Organisational Success*, Fontana.
Hawkins, P. and Shohet, R. (1994) *Supervision in the Helping Professions*, Open University.
Faye, C. (1996) 'Case study in the use of psychodynamic concepts in practice and management', Unpublished paper, Caldecott College.
Little, M. (1994) *A Life Without Problems?*, Arena.
Menzies-Lyth, I. (1988) *Containing Anxiety in Institutions*, Free Association.
Miller, E. (1993) *From Dependence to Autonomy*, Free Association.
Obholzer, A. and Roberts, V. (eds) (1994) *The Unconscious at Work*, Free Association.
Plant, R. (1985) *Managing Change and Making it Stick*, Fontana.

Salzberger-Wittenberg, I. (1973) *Psychoanalytic Insight and Relationships*, Routledge.
Trowell, J. and Bower, M., (eds) (1994) *The Emotional Needs of Young Children and their Families*, Routledge.
Warner Commission (1992) *Choosing with Care*, HMSO.

Index

415